Subaltern Frontiers

In urban and peri-urban areas across the Global South, politicians, planners and developers are engaged in a voracious scramble to refashion land for global real estate investment, and transfer state power to private sector actors. Much of this development has taken place on the outskirts of the traditional metropoles, in the territorially flexible urban frontier. At the forefront of these processes in India is Gurgaon, a privately developed metropolis on the southwestern hinterlands of New Delhi, which has long been touted as India's flagship neoliberal city. *Subaltern Frontiers* tells the story of India's remarkable urban transformation by examining the politics of land and labour that have shaped the city of Gurgaon. The book examines how the country's flagship post-liberalisation urban project has been shaped and filtered through agrarian and subaltern histories, logics and subjects. In doing so, the book explores how the production of globalised property and labour in contemporary urban India is filtered through colonial instruments of land governance, living histories of uneven agrarian development, material geographies of labour migration and the worldly aspirations of peasant-agriculturalists.

Thomas Cowan teaches economic geography at the University of Nottingham. His research interests are urban geography, South Asian political economy, labour studies, and economic development and growth.

Subaltern Frontiers

Agrarian City-Making in Gurgaon

Thomas Cowan

CAMBRIDGE
UNIVERSITY PRESS

CAMBRIDGE
UNIVERSITY PRESS

University Printing House, Cambridge CB2 8BS, United Kingdom

One Liberty Plaza, 20th Floor, New York, NY 10006, USA

477 Williamstown Road, Port Melbourne, vic 3207, Australia

314 to 321, 3rd Floor, Plot No.3, Splendor Forum, Jasola District Centre, New Delhi 110025, India

103 Penang Road, #05–06/07, Visioncrest Commercial, Singapore 238467

Cambridge University Press is part of the University of Cambridge.

It furthers the University's mission by disseminating knowledge in the pursuit of education, learning and research at the highest international levels of excellence.

www.cambridge.org
Information on this title: www.cambridge.org/9781009100472

© Thomas Cowan 2022

This publication is in copyright. Subject to statutory exception and to the provisions of relevant collective licensing agreements, no reproduction of any part may take place without the written permission of Cambridge University Press.

First published 2022

Printed in India by Avantika Printers Pvt. Ltd.

A catalogue record for this publication is available from the British Library

ISBN 978-1-009-10047-2 Hardback

Cambridge University Press has no responsibility for the persistence or accuracy of URLs for external or third-party internet websites referred to in this publication, and does not guarantee that any content on such websites is, or will remain, accurate or appropriate.

For Jess and Rosa

Contents

List of Figures	ix
List of Abbreviations	xi
Preface	xiii
Acknowledgements	xix
Introduction: Antinomies of an Agrarian City	1
1. The Experiment	43
2. The Village	87
3. The Plot	133
4. The Bureaucrat and the Survey	178
5. The Tenement	215
6. The Camp	264
Conclusion: Urban Limits	292
Glossary	309
Index	311

Figures

I.1	Maruti Suzuki factory occupation, IMT Manesar, 2011	3
I.2	Location of Gurgaon district in Haryana	4
I.3	DLF Cyber City, Gurgaon	6
1.1	Pre-consolidation cadastral map of Chatia Aulia village, Sonepat, Haryana	73
1.2	Post-consolidation cadastral map of Chatia Aulia village, Sonepat, Haryana	73
2.1	Residential developments outside Kherki Daula village	91
3.1	Residential towers near Nawada Fatehpur village, Gurugram, India	137
4.1	Gurgaon Patwar Ghar	184
4.2	Land cadastral surveys in Gurgaon, 2018–19	200
4.3	Land cadastral surveys in Gurgaon, 2018–19	200
5.1	Early morning walk from Kapashera to Udyog Vihar	217
5.2	Tenement lanes and blocks in Kapashera Extension, Delhi–Gurgaon border	228
5.3	Tenement floor, Kapashera Extension	229
5.4	Workshop, Kapashera	237

Abbreviations

AMRUT	Atal Mission for Rejuvenation and Urban Transformation
APEC	Asia-Pacific Economic Cooperation
BJP	Bharatiya Janata Party
BKU	Bharatiya Kisan Union
BPO	business processing outsourcing
CEO	chief executive officer
DILRMP	Digital India Land Records Modernisation Programme
DLF	Delhi Land and Finance
FDI	foreign direct investment
FMS	Faridabad Mazdoor Samachar
FSRE	finance, services and real estate
GDP	gross domestic product
GKS	Gharelu Kamgar Sangathan
HARTRON	Haryana State Electronics Development Corporation
HDRUA	Haryana Urban Development and Regulation of Urban Areas Act, 1975
Holdings Act	East Punjab Holdings (Consolidation and Prevention of Fragmentation) Act, 1948
HSIIDC	Haryana State Industrial and Infrastructural Development Corporation
HSVP	Haryana Shahari Vikas Pradhikaran
HUDA	Haryana Urban Development Authority
IADP	Intensive Agricultural Development Programme
IMF	International Monetary Fund
IMT Manesar	Industrial Model Township, Manesar
INLD	Indian National Lok Dal

JNNURM	Jawaharlal Nehru National Urban Renewal Mission
LAA	Land Acquisition Act, 1884
MCG	Municipal Corporation of Gurugram
NCR	National Capital Region
NGO	non-governmental organisation
NGT	National Green Tribunal
NOC	no objection certificate
NRI	non-resident Indian
NSM	Nari Shakti Manch
OBCs	other backward classes
PSRCA	Punjab Scheduled Roads and Controlled Areas Act, 1963
PSU	public sector undertaking
RAY	Rajiv Awas Yojana
RIL	Reliance Industries Limited
RWA	resident welfare association
SEZ	special economic zone
WHO	World Health Organization

Preface

To get to Gurgaon from the villages that flank the National Highway 48 (NH48) in southeastern Haryana, you have to either take a crowded intercity bus or pile into a shared jeep. As a young researcher, I tended to travel by shared jeep. Accounts of Gurgaon's landscape usually move from New Delhi, southward on the Delhi Metro to HUDA City Centre station at the heart of New Gurgaon, narrating a landscape that transitions from a historic urban centre to its boisterous, nouveau riche neighbour, from urban capital's (post-)colonial being to its unwieldy neoliberal becoming. And yet, I have spent most of the past ten years in Gurgaon moving in a different direction. The jeeps are stacked with twelve other passengers, all of us clutching our small lunchboxes, in Tetris-style formation, silently grimacing as the worn-out suspension ploughs through an assault course of BMWs, SUVs and freight trucks. The NH48 that runs through the centre of Gurgaon forms part of the 1,700 miles of highway that runs from Chennai to New Delhi and is incorporated into the 1 lakh crore rupees Delhi–Mumbai economic corridor. These economic corridors that tear through rural spaces are viewed by politicians as key engines of post-agrarian economic growth vital to the transformation of Delhi's agrarian hinterland into productive, capitalised urban space. They are what Grappi and Dey have termed a 'neoliberal institution', one that instructs and joins up the extractive and financialised operations of post-colonial capitalist development.[1]

Riding on the NH48 from Gurgaon's southern periphery, we tear through an expanse of partially irrigated, gridded fields interspersed by clusters of small, whitewashed bungalows and roadside garages. At this point the road becomes increasingly populated by a deluge of billboards hyping the land on our flanks with land brokerage services selling 'hot land' and 'investment opportunities' in real estate projects yet to materialise. In the winter this part of rural Haryana is masked by a dense, low fog and the warmth of human proximity the jeep affords provides welcome respite from the cold. In 2018 the World Health Organization (WHO) declared Gurgaon the most polluted city in the world and the winter is when the smog is at its worst. The summers expose a flat, gridded landscape interrupted only by the steep forest ridges at Manesar in the south and Gwal Pahari on the Delhi border. In these months the jeeps become insufferably hot, and we become increasingly stuck onto one another. Each time the jeep pauses to drop off a passenger, we take a collective intake of breath as the heat sets in, only to let out an audible yelp of relief as we get moving again.

The highway winds through the brokerage signposts into the Gurgaon district before a series of large, austere warehouses appear on the horizon to our left sitting in amongst village residences of Binola. From these modern-day sweatshops, constructed on village *panchayat* lands (see Chapter 2), an army of workers at e-commerce corporations of Amazon and Flipkart shoot out thousands of packages onto the highway and into the city each day.

As we edge closer to Gurgaon we are confronted with the Industrial Model Township (IMT), Manesar, the 1,500-acre gridded industrial estate masterplanned by Japanese industrialists in 1994 – that among others houses two of India's largest automobile assembly plants: Honda and Maruti-Suzuki. Initially devised as a Japanese-managed industrial 'township', IMT Manesar was where *kaizen lean* manufacturing styles would be fully deployed into Indian manufacturing in the 2000s, and where decades of industrial struggle would go up in flames in 2012. If one arrives at IMT *chowk* before sunrise, you will witness tens of thousands of young workers wearily march en masse from their nearby tenement rooms, under the watchful eye of village landlords, to take their positions on the assembly line for the morning shift.

Moving on we pass through a landscape that shifts dramatically from cultivated fields and roadside villages to semi-constructed residential towers sat within compact villages, and fenced and cleared fields, monuments to the uncertainty, compromise and political contestation that besets real estate projects on Gurgaon's urbanising periphery. Some of these projects are held up by obstinate villagers looking for higher returns on their land, others were financed in the flurry that led up to the global financial crash; now sat in permanent anticipation of the next real estate boom. At this point, the speculative land brokerage signs that dominated rural Haryana have been replaced with large real estate billboards depicting upper-class families in warm embrace under the shadow of luxury residential space in the city's emerging neighbourhoods. Soon traffic slows in wait of the controversial toll station at Kherki Duala village, a toll station that has been subject to frequent violent attacks by commuters irate that their otherwise seamless journey is forced to come to a faltering stop. Compounding the traffic at Kherki Duala, the highway enjoins the eight-lane Dwarka Expressway – built to connect Gurgaon to southwest Delhi but held up over the past decade as landowners contest the forceful acquisition of their lands. Further back is the fenced and emptied land of Harsaru village, which once formed part of a 25,000-acre land bank that was acquired by the Haryana state and Reliance corporation – one of India's largest corporations – for the largest special economic zone (SEZ) in India. In 2011, amidst mass protests from landowners coinciding with a slump in the real estate sector, Reliance withdrew from the project, leaving an expanse of flattened, fenced land lying vacant in the centre of Gurgaon (see Chapter 2).

Moving on the highway slides up and down the flyovers bypassing the less desirable remnants of old Gurgaon – the industrial villages, the old town and district government offices – and enters New Gurgaon and the paradigmatic landscape of the post-colonial neoliberal city: towering residential enclaves, a deluge of shopping malls and a Metro line that winds mid-air in between the residential towers servicing the city's upper-class commuters. Eventually the highway reaches what is Gurgaon's showpiece neighbourhood, DLF CyberHub, a privately developed and managed SEZ that hosts the offices of global tech, real estate, finance and consultancy firms in glistening glass towers. Cyberhub is encircled by the DLF Rapid Metro, the world's first privately developed and managed metro system that transports the city's upper classes from their condos on DLF's Golf Course Road to their offices. At CyberHub, the professional classes disembark the metro and take queue behind the security gates that ambivalently guard the glistening office complex. Our jeep however turns left again towards an entirely different city; at a stone's throw from CyberHub sits Udyog Vihar, Gurgaon's first industrial estate, home to large garment-export factories and hundreds of thousands of migrant labourers living in dense tenements in the numerous urban villages that surround and intersperse the estate. The jeep winds its way through the industrial estate, iteratively dropping off workers at their respective factories before making a final stop at Kapashera Border, Gurgaon's largest and most populous migrant worker neighbourhood, located just across the border in New Delhi. Reach the area at 7 a.m. and the narrow roads that link Kapashera's sprawling tenements (see Chapter 5) to the estate are packed wall to wall with workers making the dreary-eyed march to the twelve-hour shift in the factory.

I narrate my movement along the highway passing through the heart of Gurgaon in part to provide glimpses of the geographies of complicity, contestation and uncertainty written into real estate and infrastructural development across the city. Gurgaon's highway, obliquely referred to as the city's 'line of control' by many residents, feeds off the hundreds of enclosed urban villages that scatter the interior of the millennium city, the highway knits together and offers glimpses of the agrarian spaces, institutions and labours – roadside brokerage offices, paused development projects and densely constructed villages – that continue to mediate land's transformation into real estate, and the migrant worker's disciplining into a hidden, flexible form of labour power. The highway also, as

I discuss in Chapter 3, acts as a key frontier device, guiding speculative land markets into the countryside. The geographies of the 'trinity formula' of capital–profit, land–ground rent, and labour–wages that sustain the social production of accumulation (Chapters 2 and 5), are ubiquitous if tentative features of the highway. If for some the highway itself operates as a neoliberal institution violently restructuring the rural landscape toward market rationality, here the highway also brings to life politics and processes of disturbance, subversion and compromise, led by quite other actors, movements and urban practices. Reading this immanent 'rival geography' of Gurgaon's highway accounts for the often-hidden socio-material actors and practices that keep the city's bombastic capitalist accumulation in motion.[2]

ROUTES

In urban and peri-urban areas across the Global South, politicians, planners and developers are engaged in a voracious scramble to refashion land for global real estate investment, transfer state power to private sector actors and transform urban residents into attendant neoliberal subjects. Much of this development has taken place on the outskirts of the traditional metropoles, in the administratively ambiguous and spatially flexible urban frontier. Over the past three decades, Indian cities and peri-urban hinterlands have witnessed rapid social and spatial transformation. The vanguard of India's spectacular 'urban awakening' is Gurgaon, a newly developed 'private city' on the southwestern hinterlands of New Delhi. Since the early 1990s, 40,000 acres of agricultural land in this once sleepy district have been transformed by private real estate actors into the largest private township in the country – home to a series of elite residential enclaves, commercial districts and India's first privately financed and managed transport system. Buoyed by the miracle of the 'Gurgaon model' of privatised urbanisation, property developers, politicians and global consultancy firms declared Gurgaon, India's 'millennium city', ground zero of a new global India where the agrarian economic past, compromise with the urban poor and inefficient state bureaucracy could be bypassed and washed away.

Subaltern Frontiers tells a quite different story of India's remarkable urban transformation. Examining how the country's flagship post-liberalisation urban project has been shaped and confounded by agrarian histories, logics and subjects. Far from expelling or bypassing pre-existing social and political life, the book shows how the production of property and labour markets that underpin the private city is dependent upon unruly agrarian bureaucrats, living histories of agrarian capitalism and the material geographies of labour migration. Far from being passive actors in a story of market domination, these subaltern actors play a vital role in forging the urban frontier: transforming commonly owned agricultural land into globally legible property; transforming peasant-farmers into obedient neoliberal subjects; and shaping cheap, exploitable migrant labour that the city depends upon. The city's dependence on spaces and actors it ostensibly seeks to disavow is a source of constant anxiety. For the city's hegemonic actors, the other coheres in the centre. It is on these material grounds that the agrarian city is ultimately secured, stalled and appropriated for other means.

Notes

1. Dey and Grappi, *Beyond Zoning*.
2. Said, *Culture and Imperialism*, 266.

Bibliography

Dey, Ishita, and Giorgio Grappi. 'Beyond Zoning: India's Corridors of "Development" and New Frontiers of Capital'. *South Atlantic Quarterly* 114, no. 1 (2015): 153–70.

Edward Said. *Culture and Imperialism*. London: Vintage Books, 1994.

Acknowledgements

This book is the result of eleven years of visits to Gurgaon. My research proper began with initial visits to Gurgaon in 2010 and extended to my most recent stay in the city in 2019. During that time, I have accumulated debts to many people without which this book would not have been possible. My interest in Gurgaon was initially sparked by friends in Delhi, Benny Kuruvilla and Susana Barria, who impressed in me the importance of exploring the politics of land hiding behind the tumultuous labour movement at the time. I owe the deepest of debts to comrades at Faridabad Mazdoor Samachar (FMS) in Faridabad and at Nari Shakti Manch in Gurgaon for welcoming me into their organisations and supporting me to reach interview respondents. It was Sher Singh's indefatigable commitment to political solidarity, to the granular vibrance of proletarian culture and his embrace of the eccentricity and hope of the tenements that shaped my early engagements with the politics of labour in the city. And it was through FMS, and Garmaji, that I found a tenement room in Kapashera and was able to explore the mundane aspects of working-class life in the city. While I conducted interviews with migrant workers across the city, I owe a particular debt to the residents of Kapashera for letting me into their lives, to share stories, gossip, life histories, food and for the material and social support they gave me on a day-to-day basis. It was these experiences that informed, but could not be fully encapsulated in, my approach in this book. Indeed, the book barely touches the surface of working-class life in Gurgaon's tenements, which like anywhere else – full of drama and monotony, predictability and originality – far exceeds the bounds of scholarly representation. In addition, I would like to thank the members of Nari Shakti Manch, in particular Elizabeth and Santosh who became my great friends throughout the past decade. Both directly enabled my research on labour politics in Gurgaon, pushing me to consider and reconsider my approach and thinking. Their political organising under the most precarious and unglamorous of circumstances are a constant inspiration. I must also thank the members of Gharelu Kamgar Sangathan and those at Rokaplex, Azadiplex and Maruti Suzuki involved in the 2012 and 2014 strikes in Industrial Model Township (IMT), Manesar for allowing me to ask incessant questions, share stories, hopes, losses and aspirations. They each were a constant inspiration, pushing my thinking to the limits, and deeply influencing the political commitments of this research project.

I owe a great deal of thanks to Sambhav Sharma, Arya Thomas, Parag Banerji, Nayan Jyoti, Meghana Arora, Gayas Eapen, Deepani and Aparna Agarwal for their work carrying out interviews and household survey research support between 2014 and 2015. I am especially indebted to Shivangi Jaiswal for her support, teaching and encouragement during interviews in 2015 when my Hindi was not yet up to scratch. Outside of interpretation work, Shivangi significantly influenced my research practice and fundamentally shaped the methodology that formed the basis of Chapters 2 and 6. A scholar of Dalit labour history, Shivangi would castigate me for not taking caste more centrally; on our way to and from field sites, she would give me quick-fire lessons on the articulations of caste and work, correcting my partial and awkward knowledge, enthusing me to go home, read more and revisit my research assumptions. Shivangi pushed me to allow my interlocutors to speak freely, go off on a tangent, criticise me, my questions, my presence as a researcher; Shivangi compelled me to give up the interview as much as possible to the field. For this, I am especially grateful. Elsewhere, I owe much thanks to comrades in Delhi – Senjuti Mukherjee, Utsa Mukherjee, Ana Norman Bermudez, Shupriyo Maitra and Adele for their support throughout the research process. I would especially like to thank Matthew Birkinshaw for giving up so much time to listen to my rambling thoughts while carrying out initial research in 2014. The research that forms the basis of Chapters 3 and 4 of this book was entirely facilitated by the willing support and patience of the *patwari*s, assistant *patwari*s, *kanungo*s and surveyors primarily based at Patwar Ghar in Gurgaon. I am eternally thankful to them for allowing me to situate myself and take part in the professional life of the office. They made me feel most welcome within the everyday life of the office for nine months between 2018 and 2019.

This project started out as a postgraduate dissertation project in the Geography and Environment Department at the London School of Economics and Political Science in 2011 where I was first immersed in the world of radical geography under the guidance of Hyun Bang Shin, Asher Ghertner and Claire Mercer. It was in Hyun's classes on East Asian cities in particular that I caught the scholarly bug and I am indebted to his encouragement that I take up postgraduate study. I continued this work embarking on a PhD in the Geography department at King's College, London, where I was fortunate enough to be guided by Alex Loftus and surrounded by a politically and intellectually inspiring group of scholars who have shaped my thinking inordinately, including James Angel, Hannah Schling, Archie Davies, Sol Gamsu and Fiorenza Picozza. In 2015 I was fortunate to take part in the 'Cities, Labour and Politics' conference organised at the Sambhaavna Institute by Naveen Chander and was associated with Janaki Nair at the Jawaharlal Nehru University, both of great support and benefit to my work. In 2015, while writing my PhD thesis, I undertook two visiting fellowships at Rutgers University and the University of Minnesota and was fortunate to present my research to a range of incredibly sharp and incisive scholars who helped me develop my disparate ideas: these include Asher Ghertner, Sangeeta Banerji, Ben Gerlofs, Harry Pettit, Vinay Gidwani, Michael Goldman, Kriti Budhiraja, Julia Corwin, Lalit Batra and Arif Hayat.

In 2018 I joined the 'Frontlines of Value: Class and Social Transformation in the 21st Century' research project at the University of Bergen, funded by the Bergen Foundation, as a postdoctoral scholar. There I was immersed in a community of inspiring labour anthropologists whose attention to the political purpose of scholarly work pressed me to fine-tune my thinking. I would especially like to thank Don Kalb, Oana Matescu, Stephen Campbell, Sharryn Kasmir, Patrick Neveling, Charlotte Bruckermann, Dan Hirslund, Katharina Bodirsky, Gavin Smith and Sarah Winkler-Reid.

For their engagements, contributions, critique and feedback to various components of this book I would also like to thank Claire Mercer, Austin Zeiderman, Shubhra Gururani, Tariq Jazeel, Ashok Kumar, Lisa Tilley, Rohit Negi, Pritpal Randhawa, Kavita Ramakrishnan, Jon Silver, Ayona Datta and Pratik Mishra. I benefitted greatly from the support of colleagues at the London School of Economics, the University of Bergen and University College, London, while writing the book. Over the past five years I have presented many of the arguments in this book and received valuable feedback from participants at University College London (Centre for the Study of South Asia and the Indian Ocean World), Ambedkar University, Delhi (School of Global Affairs), University of East Anglia (School of International Development), Rutgers University (Geography Department) and the University of Minnesota (Institute of Global Studies) as well at the annual conferences of the Royal Geographical Society-International British Geographers, Research Committee 21, the British Association of South Asian Studies and the American Association of Geographers. The research for the book has benefitted from the generous financial support of the Economic and Social Science Research Council, the Bergen Foundation and the Leverhulme Trust. Some of the findings of the book are published and have received anonymous feedback previously, including parts of Chapter 2 in Antipode, Chapter 4 in the *International Journal of Urban and Regional Research* and Chapter 6 in *Geoforum*.

The book has been made possible by the support of my extended family. I am deeply indebted to the inspiration and support of Tom Royds, Grace Warland, Joel White, Anna Woods, Amy MacLellan, Harry Clarke, Cecil Sagoe, Luke de Noronha, Alex Kelbert, Emma Cashman, Tom White and Tanzil Chowdhury who have each dragged me through the past few years. And to Joseph, James, Lydia, Rob, Renata, Natalia, Hero, Grace, Annie, Richard and Tracey. Finally, Jess and Rosa Costar have been a constant intellectual and political inspiration throughout; they have shaped me as a person and scholar and influenced the research project enormously.

Introduction
Antinomies of an Agrarian City

A TALE OF TWO CITIES

On the hot evening of 18 July 2012, the Maruti Suzuki automobile plant on the borders of Gurgaon,[1] Haryana, was on fire. Earlier that day a supervisor had verbally abused an assembly-line worker, fights broke out with security guards, and 2,000 workers stopped production and set the factory alight. The Maruti Suzuki plant in Gurgaon's Industrial Model Township (IMT), Manesar industrial estate, is the largest car factory in India; producing two-thirds of all the cars in the country, the factory was the centrepiece of India's modern manufacturing prowess.[2] By the morning of 19 July 2012, the factory was partially burnt out, hundreds of workers and management officials were in hospital and a supervisor was dead.

Maruti began life in the 1970s as a government-owned car manufacturer based in central Gurgaon, then a small agricultural town on Delhi's southern border. In 1983, with backing from Japan's Suzuki, Maruti produced India's first mass-consumer car (the Maruti 800 'people's car') – a moment that anticipated imminent market liberalisation in the 1990s and the coming decades of mass urbanisation. Suzuki took control of the company in 1992 following India's economic liberalisation and by 2002 the Japanese conglomerate had a majority share. During that period Suzuki aggressively expanded production and iteratively reoriented the company towards flexibilised, lean manufacturing systems characteristic of contemporary globalised production regimes. By the late 2000s, Maruti Suzuki shifted production to a state-of-the-art industrial township – IMT Manesar – on the edge of Gurgaon, setting up shop in the largest factory in the country; boosting production output and restructuring the workforce, the factory became the country's engine of the future, a showpiece of globalised production and high-tech industrial prowess feeding the state's insatiable desire for rapid urban and infrastructural development.[3] The fire marks a denouement in India's embrace of globalised flexible production.

The fire of course did not come out of nowhere. The factory had been embroiled in near-constant workplace struggles for over a decade. A year before the fire, in June 2011 both temporary and permanent workers at the IMT Manesar plant carried out strikes, tool-downs and occupied the factory on two occasions, costing the company over 200 million US dollars, dipping the company's market share while suffocating the complex supply chain that extends across the region. The workers were not asking for anything out of the ordinary: an independent trade union, permanent contracts for long-term temporary employees, an end to unfair dismissals and better working conditions.[4] It did not take long for news of the strikes to reach international news outlets and what started as a localised industrial dispute blew up into a national crisis, drawing the attention of central government, civil society and business groups to the burning hinterlands of New Delhi (Figure I.1). For the workers themselves, the ongoing struggles offered moments of collective respite from the drudgery of the factory:

> [At the occupation] there was no tension of work, there was no tension of coming to the factory and going back, there was no tension of catching the bus, there was no tension of cooking, there was no tension that food has to be eaten only at 7 o'clock or only at 9 o'clock, there was no tension as to what day or date [it] was.... We had never come so close to one another as we came in these seven days.[5]

In the end this was all too much for the company, and its political backers, to stomach and on 18 July 2012 the workers' demands went up in the fire. After the fire the management embarked on what the Maruti Suzuki chief executive termed 'class war', immediately dismissing 500 permanent and 2,500 temporary workers. One hundred and forty-seven workers were arrested and held in a prison in south Gurgaon for five years without charge. In March 2017, 13 workers were given life sentences for their alleged participation in the events of July 2012.

For a short window in 2012, India's industrial workforce stirred, new imaginations of urban India swirled around the working-class neighbourhoods, informal workshops and industrial estates of Gurgaon, and new demands to everyday life were given voice on national and international

Introduction | 3

Figure I.1   Maruti Suzuki factory occupation, IMT Manesar, 2011
Source: Sushil Narang, 'Manesar Plant Problem Is Political Issue: Maruti Suzuki', *The Hindu*, 18 August 2016, http://www.thehindu.com/business/companies/manesar-plant-problem-is-political-issue-maruti-suzuki/article2435244.ece (accessed 23 February 2021).

news outlets. Contemporary analyses of urbanisation in the Global South often emphasise the iterative marginalisation of material production from city centres and the rapid ascent of rent-seeking and immaterial economies.[6] In this context, the worker, their politics, imaginaries and practices rarely feature in accounts of the contemporary Indian city. This book seeks to recentre the geographies of labour, exploring how India's contemporary urban moment is entangled in state desires to spatially organise and discipline a flexible and hidden urban working class. Just 20 kilometres down the national highway in central Gurgaon an altogether different kind of urban imagination had long been set in motion.

THE MILLENNIUM CITY

Just down the road from the burning factory, as Haryana's agrarian–industrial landscape iteratively blends into glass high-rises and commercial complexes, an altogether different urban India is unfolding. In 1981, around the same time the first Maruti factory was opened, the Haryana Town and Country Planning department issued the first development licence to real estate developers seeking to construct, service and govern residential space in the then agricultural region on Delhi's southern edge (Figure I.2). Fleeing

4 | Subaltern Frontiers

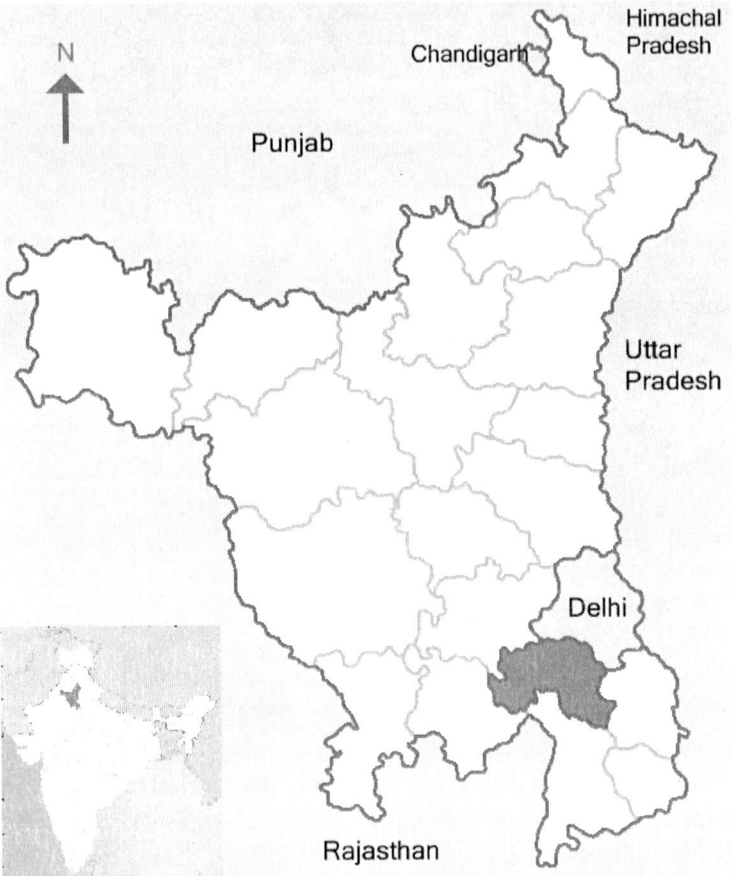

Figure I.2 Location of Gurgaon district in Haryana
Source: AbhijitSathe, 'Haryana Gurugram', https://commons.wikimedia.org/wiki/File:Haryana_Gurugram.png (accessed 23 February 2022); Joy1963, Creative Commons Attribution-ShareAlike 3.0 Unported.
Note: Map not to scale and does not represent authentic national boundaries.

tightening regulations in nearby New Delhi, developers flocked to Gurgaon in the late 1970s looking for space to capture and commodify for India's globalised, metropolitan upper classes. The Haryana government looked to capitalise on the moment, developing what became known as the 'Gurgaon model' of urban development. Put simply, the 'Gurgaon model' refers to a series of legislation enacted in the mid-1970s that liberalised planning and development regulations and introduced a licenced development system that allowed developers to purchase land directly from farmers, aggregate holdings and construct privately managed residential and commercial townships.

This private-sector-led approach to land acquisition and urban development contrasted with approaches in other parts of the country in which the state played a leading role in acquiring rural land through eminent domain on behalf of industrial capital. This latter model of development, which characterises what Mike Levien calls the 'land broker state', had in Gurgaon faced significant political opposition from well-organised and politically powerful landowners.[7] The Gurgaon model, a blueprint for the public–private partnerships that would become central to the urban development policy in the 2000s, has instead relied upon constructing direct coalitions between corporate capital and the agrarian world that I explore through the first half of this book.

From the early 2000s, as the Indian government iteratively liberalised the real estate sector, and developers and government officials aggressively marketed Gurgaon as 'the showpiece of a new urban India', the city experienced a frenzy of real estate construction, with licences issued for over 35,000 acres of development, transforming swathes of rural land into an archipelago of elite, privately governed residential and commercial complexes.

Working in partnership with state politicians who actively diluted development regulations and remapped land for capital investment (Chapters 3 and 4), real estate firms and city planners leveraged land to attract what neoliberal urban theorist Richard Florida calls the 'creative classes', the 'technology, talent and tolerance' that bring in capital investment.[8]

At the heart of this new private city is DLF City: once the largest private township in Asia, the 3,000-acre privately governed integrated township is composed of a mix of gated villas, towering apartment complexes and shopping malls catering to the new urban upper classes, and a series of commercial offices and IT parks hosting international business processing outsourcing (BPO), consultancies, banks and tech companies (Figure I.3). The city is serviced by an army of private security guards who stand at the gates of the malls and residential complexes, filtering out undesirable entrants, a network of privately sourced water, waste and energy infrastructure, and the world's first fully privately financed and managed metro system. Gurgaon's urbanisation is framed in the context of a new geography of post-liberalisation India, in which an overzealous state bureaucracy cedes control to the private sector, allowing for hegemonic coalitions of corporate capital and urban elites to produce sanitised, private urban space. As Gururchan Das writes:

> Modern India is in some ways Gurgaon writ large.... Middle-class Indians, who now constitute almost a third of the country, believe that their nation is doing well because the pre-1991 over-regulating state has gradually liberalized [and] ... [t]o them, the entrepreneur is at the centre of this success story.[9]

In opening the book with these two scripts of Gurgaon, I mean to emphasise the uncertain and unstable character of agrarian city-making on the urban frontier. Despite being heralded as a frontier of a new urban India, in Gurgaon material labours persist, agrarian property regimes and institutions infiltrate and punctuate development projects, and property markets depend on the speculative strategies of agrarian communities. These two scenes of Gurgaon, the violent showdown at India's industrial showpiece and the spectacular ascent of a post-industrial, neoliberal city, in many ways fall neatly into a narrative of India's urban transition. Both the riot at Maruti Suzuki and the development of DLF City offer a narrative of global urban India coming of age in the hinterlands of New Delhi. One cast through brutal violence of industrial struggle and the unbridled power of real estate capital. The riot at

Figure I.3   DLF Cyber City, Gurgaon

Source: Tarun4u, 'Cyber City View, Gurgaon', Creative Commons Attribution-Share Alike 4.0International, https://commons.wikimedia.org/wiki/File:Cyber_City_View.jpg (accessed 23 February 2022).

Maruti Suzuki, the subsequent crushing of a vibrant labour movement and the unbridled force of real estate and finance capital mark the high watermark of India's graduation to the top table of urban modernity.[10]

Theories of postmodern and post-industrial urbanisation emphasise the shift of city regions from incubating industrial manufacturing and planned state developmentalism to those driven by finance, 'creative capital' and real estate value creation.[11] This transition of course has a significant impact on the social fabric of the city: as the economic life of the city centres is hollowed out, erstwhile working-class communities are laid off from secure employment, turfed out to the peripheries by rising rents and replaced by real estate and a new class of immaterial workers.[12] Unlike older studies of 'agrarian transition' that traced linkages between increased agricultural surpluses and processes of industrialisation,[13] scholarly work on post-industrial urban economies assert the redundancy of labour and material production. This last step on the teleological ladder holds no developmentalist potential; workers the world over have been laid off, expunged and turned 'surplus' in the transition towards real estate and immaterial-based economic development.[14]

Despite drawing predominately from the experiences of cities in the North Atlantic, the implicit historicism of these accounts seeps into analyses on patterns of socio-spatial change in urban India. New urban India is commonly understood to be constituted by a great schism in the social and economic life of the country, productive of fractured landscapes of high-value immaterial modernity – IT hubs, elite real estate, shopping malls, financial centres – surrounded by a sea of backward, surplus inertia. To be sure, since the liberalisation of the economy in 1991, India's traditional metropoles *have* experienced post-industrial tendencies: manufacturing has been expunged from historic neighbourhoods, the 'knowledge' economy has come to dominate previous manufacturing centres, urban spaces have become targets of rent-seeking capital, and a territorial war has been waged on the spaces and livelihoods of the urban poor[15] – and indeed much of this is characteristic of Gurgaon. And yet such accounts only tell part of the story. By placing the millennium city in direct conversation with its agrarian and industrial geographies, this book challenges common teleological moves that ignore the complex class coalitions, which tangle both agrarian communities and migrant working classes into the making and unmaking of urban frontiers.

Frontier Scripts

The 'Gurgaon model' of privatised urbanisation showcased to the rest of the country the possibility of rapid land commodification, unadulterated 'world-class' lifestyles, globalised post-industrial economic development and landscapes cleared of the urban poor – a new urban frontier designed for the metropolitan elite. At the heart of this speculative narrative of Gurgaon's provenance is the projection of rural Gurgaon as a nowhere space, empty and underutilised. Gurgaon – an urban development project on the fringes of Delhi – has long figured as a frontier, what Anna Tsing has called 'a zone of not yet'.[16] More than simply a marker denoting the territorial boundaries of urban rule, the frontier is a crucial device for refiguring other social orders as in need of intervention, reform and development. The capitalist frontier is a site of intense desire, projection and predetermined expansion: to the capitalist, the projection of liberal property relations to an outside 'not yet' captured is always already 'soon to be' and 'couldn't have been anything else' all at once. The reimagination of Gurgaon as a hollowed-out place and people without history, where agrarian property relations are coded as 'inefficient' and act as a barrier to profitability, carries the imperative upon which land is urgently commodified and glass-and-steel structures erected to produce Delhi Land and Finance's (DLF's) millennium city. As the novelist Rana Dasgupta writes:[17]

> When Gurgaon opened its doors, proclaiming a 'new Singapore' of glass office blocks, gated communities, golf courses and shopping, it did not take long for the corporate classes to respond. Flush with boom cash, India's banks handed out loans to anyone who asked, and house prices were rising so fast that it made sense for everyone to put their savings into property. Microsoft and its ilk built their Indian headquarters in the *thrilling emptiness* of the Haryana countryside, and Gurgaon quickly became the largest private township in Asia, a dusty, booming expanse of hypertrophic apartment complexes, skyscrapers and malls. (Emphasis added)

This imaginary of a thrillingly empty Gurgaon, the remarkable transformation of a backward agricultural hinterland into a globally connected privatopolis, forms the central narrative of the city's very own origin story that saturates popular discourse on the city. 'Do you know the story of this city?' my interlocutors would frequently remark, before retelling the story of

K. P. Singh, the ambitious Delhi-based developer, exiled from the capital by an overzealous state to make his millions on the hinterlands of the city.

According to the story, Singh had a chance encounter with the future prime minister and Congress royalty Rajiv Gandhi at a roadside *chai* stand on the edges of Gurgaon, where Singh convinced Gandhi to provide the necessary clearances and deregulations for Singh's firm DLF to buy up 3,500 acres of agricultural land, transforming it into high value, residential and commercial space. In the origin story, the Gurgaon before the 1990s is a barren if bucolic landscape emptied of a social history, where impoverished village communities held back by antiquated government regulations awaited transformation by dynamic global markets. In Singh's autobiography he notes:[18]

> When the idea took hold of me that a world-class city could be built on the vast tracts of desolate land at the foot of the Aravalis [mountain range] in Haryana ... I just could not stop myself from driving down to the outskirts of Delhi and staring for long hours at the wide open spaces all around with nothing but miles and miles of rocky but austerely beautiful landscape. In my mind's eye I could see modern, tall buildings made of glass and steel, I could visualize wide, tree-lined avenues with smooth-moving traffic and people walking on them and children playing in the lush green parks.

Singh's mythical if much-cited account of Gurgaon's miraculous urbanisation is a story of the contemporary frontier and the settler; of the triumphant march of private enterprise and private property across the frontier and into the badlands of agrarian tradition. This is ascendant urban India, frequently viewed – even in critical accounts – as materially detached from the geographies of the agrarian and industrial city. It also, notably, serves as a reminder of the speculative character of frontier urbanisation. In order for K. P. Singh's urban imaginary to take hold, to be rendered sensible and urgent, rural Haryana must be shown to be open and desolate, set into a historical passage within which 'tall buildings made of glass and steel' are the only sensible remedy.

If these imaginaries press the political imperative for capitalist expansion, this leads a broader capitalist project to recapture and revalorise the remnants of uneven agrarian capitalist development. As Neil Smith writes, the 'new urban frontiers'[19] – of North America – invoked and reified social individualism, enterprise and free markets in order to reconquer under-capitalised inner cities that had been wasted in previous rounds of accumulation. In late twentieth-century North India, it is sites like Gurgaon, which as I discuss in Chapter 1 were scarred and rendered 'backward' by colonial extraction, that emerge as primary sites of reconquest and revalorisation. The histories of agrarian capitalism that have fundamentally shaped spaces like Gurgaon through the twentieth century are the protagonists in the repurposing and revalorisation of the peri-urban areas for new circuits of capital accumulation. The frontier relies on reifying and displacing history. Just as the global spinning of capital in and out of the built environment through processes of uneven and differentiated development drives processes of gentrification in Smith's account of the 'new urban frontier' capture of rent gaps, so too is peri-urban development in sites like Gurgaon shaped by the global movements of capitalist valorisation, devalorisation and revalorisation.

Nevertheless, just as Maruti Suzuki's desires for a lifeless, flexibilised workforce were met with some rejection by workers themselves, K. P. Singh's yearning for an empty *tabula rasa* on the outskirts of New Delhi was forced to encounter a stubborn social and material world. In practice this space of thrilling emptiness had to be *made empty*, ways of life had to be overcome, materials shifted, new kinds of labour mobilised, histories annulled, people had to be displaced, others accommodated, while the land had to be made recognisable and fungible as private property. Frontiers are *concrete abstractions* – fictions that are made constantly true through hegemonic discourses and practices of the state. The frontier requires work and the principal actors in this work are often those actors and histories new forces of accumulation seek to displace.

One of the key arguments of this book is that the expansion of property and labour markets across the urban–agrarian frontier is sustained and troubled by the work of agrarian landowning communities who are called upon to view themselves not as peasant farmers but rather as brokers, speculators and landlords. Labour and land markets on the frontier rely upon the enlistment of landowners into territorial partnerships with real estate firms, where they are called upon to repurpose agrarian property regimes and discipline the army of migrant workers that produce value in the city's economy. In this way, agricultural landowners are to some degree the point men of India's urban frontier, stitching together unwieldy and contradictory political economies of the contemporary Indian city and conducting the messy work of preparing land and labour for rapid commodification.

This set of alliances and compromises with the agrarian world has from the outset plagued the city's development with disruptions and uncertainties that relate to the conjunctural encounter of the fantastical myths of the city's provenance with their own internal limits. The first disruption is perhaps best demonstrated by the Maruti Suzuki struggle. Events at Maruti Suzuki in 2012 cannot be so easily subsumed into a script of merciless post-industrial transition. If neoliberal scripts place the city at the end of a fraught transition from agrarian and modernist society, the presence of industrial production side by side to monuments of late capitalist urbanity trouble the teleology of smooth transitions.

Subaltern Frontiers locates the provenance of the political struggles spilling out of the city's industrial estates in the aftermath of Maruti Suzuki as directly linked to conditions, spatial practices and spaces underpinning Gurgaon's spectacular real-estate-led growth, deeply embedded in a broader politics of agrarian capitalism, dispossession and rentiership unfolding in the surrounding city. Reverberations from the riot in 2012 struck across these working-class spaces of the city, sparking a series of urban and industrial struggles that this book explores. These struggles were not *only* born in the hermetic space of the factory but sprung from the labour tenements, worker lines and villages that scatter the interior of the millennium city. These subaltern neighbourhoods materially embody the hundreds of thousands of migrants who arrive in Gurgaon looking for work, sustaining the city's post-industrial landscape; and yet whose discourses, imaginaries and practices never figure in Singh's 'mind's eye' – they have no place in the discursive repertoire that has come to define the millennium city.

Importantly, these subaltern spaces are not only training grounds of working-class discipline and resistance but they also double up as spaces where agrarian landowners look to transfer agrarian surpluses into urban rentier power and transform themselves into key brokers for capital's unfolding into land markets across the region. The subaltern frontiers at the heart of the millennium city link the seemingly disjunctive political economies of new urban India.

If modernisation theories would presume that the workers at Maruti Suzuki would slip into work in the call centres and BPOs that characterise new immaterial economies, contemporary critical sociological debates would place the workers as part of a new army of 'surplus' populations, expelled from formal organised employment, never to return. No longer required for value production in the city, these populations become what anthropologist Jan Breman terms 'nowhere people drifting around in a nowhere landscape'.[20] *Subaltern Frontiers* tells a story of India's remarkable urban moment without effacing the practices, struggles, imaginaries of these so-called nowhere people. When we reject the historicism of transition-thinking and begin to consider the complex, dialectical interlacing of subaltern worlds within neoliberal value creation, we are opened to a millennium city of a totally different kind. This is the subaltern city in plain view, and yet it bears no resemblance to the *surplus wastelands* popular within accounts of urban poverty in India,[21] nor does it cleanly correspond to what Gyan Prakash terms the *unintended city*,[22] spaces never intended for the urban poor but nevertheless claimed as their own. Rather, the deep complicity of industrial and agrarian geographies in the making of neoliberal urban space in Gurgaon points to the radical contingency of capitalist urbanisation, where actors and practices effaced from the scripts of neoliberal modernity play a key role in both reproducing conditions of accumulation in the city and iteratively upending these logics and processes.

This shadow city in Gurgaon also points us to fractures in the story Gurgaon's boosterist elites tell about the city. As the dust settled on the boom decade from the mid-1990s, when at different times the city was touted to become the home of India's first Disneyland, the world's largest special economic zone (SEZ) and a futuristic driverless pod-transit system, the city became mired in a series of land scandals, protests from peasant farmers and beset with infrastructural breakdown. By the mid-2010s, the glitz of the Gurgaon model was losing its shine and new right-wing neo-populist politicians were urgently seeking to restabilise a shaky capitalist coalition.

The enduring figure in this urban malaise is the agrarian. Intercutting Gurgaon's landscape of elite condos and privately governed spaces, over a hundred urban villages are scattered through the interior of the millennium city – spatial reminders of the territorial compromises the real estate sector was forced to make in their quest for land. The agrarian landowner and village are frequent sources of anxiety for the city's boosterists and elite residents, spectres of an agrarian past that stubbornly endure in the present; the landowners' backward belief-systems and practices, the obstinate endurance of the village in the city, are attributed to the stalling of development projects, land scandals, crime, corruption, all of which restrain the promise of the millennium city.

This agrarian scare has filtered into popular representations of peri-urban development. *NH10*, a 2012 film set in Gurgaon, narrates the story of the violent agrarian underbelly lurking underneath the contemporary global city. When the film's protagonists, an elite couple living in a New Gurgaon high-rise, take a weekend trip to the city's bucolic periphery, they encounter casteist honour killing, corruption and gender-based violence. The film follows the couple's travails as they seek to escape the madness of the peripheral villages and make it back to the safety of the urban enclave. In a key scene in the film, a corrupted policeman tells the beleaguered couple, 'Where the last mall ends, this is where your constitution ends too.' In a mixture of Hobbes' *state of nature* and Chicago school urbanism, the film indexes the agrarian as brutish spaces of immorality, conservatism and chaos. This frontier imaginary that is present in orthodox urban theory and recounted in both Singh's fantastical origin story and the vengeful imprisonment of Maruti Suzuki workers falls into long histories of colonial encounter that cast 'monstrous geographical imaginaries of the unknown and unfamiliar'[23] in order to facilitate capture, control and revalorisation. The village and villagers that had figured as sources of national authenticity in Gandhian and Nehruvian discourses, in the contemporary urban moment represent figures of disruption that challenge the organic march of Indian society towards urban modernity.

In highlighting these tropes, I am not seeking to contribute to an already sizeable and suffocating literature on urban excess and dysfunction that dominates public and academic discourse on the Indian city, saturated with tropes of visceral inequality, spectacular greed, hapless government, febrile capital and an overflowing of surplus populations. On the one hand, descriptions of Gurgaon as an urban horror story fall neatly into these well-recited scripts, yet on the other hand the 'horrors' of Gurgaon are not viewed as in or of the city but are frequently figured as frontier points interrupting it.

This book explores these tensions, examining how Gurgaon's spectacular ascent as the supposed vanguard of new urban India is deeply dependent upon the very actors and spaces it seeks to disavow: the agrarian and the working classes. It is local agrarian bureaucrats who craft land into property through territorial devices of the title, survey and record book; it is the agrarian broker who translates complex landholdings into consolidated property; it is the village that mediates access of real estate capital to agrarian land; and the villager who disciplines migrant workforces, turning village rents into speculative investments in the city's land market. And it is of course millions of the working classes who construct and produce value for the city. The enemy coheres in the centre.

The production of neoliberal landscapes of accumulation in urban India are not simply realised by writ of capitalist desire, nor do they neatly unfold from the enactment of neoliberal territorial technologies – SEZs, masterplans, deregulated land-use policies – by the state. The production of the millennium city's expanses of high-value real estate has required work; the shifting of people, redrawing of maps, erasing of histories and the circulation of hegemonic neoliberal dreamworlds. It is the work of agrarian and working-class actors – objects of capitalist disavowal – that is explored in this book.

AGRARIAN CITY-MAKING

The central argument of the book is as follows. The expansion of capitalist land and labour markets that have underpinned Gurgaon's explosive urbanisation since the 1980s has relied squarely on a series of hegemonic territorial alliances (and compromises) with agrarian landowning classes. In order to capture rural land without direct state intervention, the state and real estate firms have brokered territorial alliances that have ceded certain territories and rents to agrarian landowners in exchange for market access to land (Chapters 2 and 5). In order to convert rural land into private property, the state and real estate firms have relied upon enlisting landowners to speculate on land, convert rural property regimes and aggregate large landholdings (Chapter 3). In order to secure property titles and author land boundaries, firms rely upon agrarian bureaucratic institutions (Chapter 4). Finally, the enlistment of the agrarian world into real estate and land markets depends upon the demand for and viability of low-wage tenement rental markets, which in turn underpin industrial manufacturing in the city hitched to industrial labour markets (Chapter 5). In this book I build on recent scholarly work on agrarian urbanisation in India[24] to understand processes of what I call agrarian city-making that predominate urbanisation in the contemporary moment. Amid the Indian government's forceful drive to reconfigure urban and peri-urban land for global real estate investment over the past two decades, agrarian city-making signifies the deep entanglement of the practice of carving out spaces for capitalist urban accumulation in decidedly agrarian spaces. In doing so, I wish to draw out the ongoing and active role agrarian histories, institutions, actors and spaces play in fashioning urban commodities from the rural world.

In the agrarian city, farmers, village councils, agrarian bureaucrats and the social structure of the village drive processes of urbanisation as much as they represent its antithesis and externality.

Gurgaon's landscape of real estate and industrial accumulation – of highways, IT hubs and luxury real estate – are articulated through histories of colonial–postcolonial improvement and uneven development hitched to promised inclusion of agrarian cultivating castes into real estate value and urban modernity. Agrarian city-making marks out the Frankenstein articulations of neoliberal urbanisation with its unlikely leading character, the agrarian.

In the *Grundrisse*, Marx notes that 'the modern age is the urbanisation of the countryside, not the ruralisation of the city as in antiquity'.[25] Dispossession, in these accounts, is the driving force authoring modernity, the basis of capital's pulverisation of non-privatised land tenures and translation of the rural world into commodity registers. The rural world, in this context, is commonly understood as spaces where dominant logics of capitalist primitive accumulation play out in the face of peasant and indigenous resistance and immiseration; sites in which capital's desire to steamroll space into abstract form is realised.

Proponents of planetary urbanisation theory have emphasised the increasingly dominant role urban processes (land-based agglomeration and extension of capital) play in hegemonic regimes of capitalist accumulation the world over. For planetary urbanisation theorists, India's dramatic turn toward urban-driven economic growth and the numerous real-estate-led expansions across the peri-urban frontier serve as prime examples of the 'extended urbanisation' that encompasses and operationalises agrarian spaces to the service of the continued agglomeration of capital. In a series of introductory papers on the topic, Neil Brenner sets out to produce a theory of urbanisation 'without an outside', that can get to grips with the 'complete urbanisation of the world'.[26]

For planetary urbanisation theorists there is no outside to urban processes; all other forms of world-making are subject to capitalist urbanisation's totalising death drive. This is of course a position most forcefully and eloquently put forward by Neil Brenner who, drawing on parts of the work of Henri Lefebvre, conceptualises capitalist urbanisation as a set of recursive processes of agglomeration, 'their changing role in regimes of capital accumulation, and their variegated expressions in diverse morphological forms and spatial configurations'. Importantly here, planetary urbanisation theorists conceive of the non-urban to be, if not entirely subsumed under urban processes than 'operationalised' through enclosure, zoning and design to service the needs of these processes.

In an otherwise illuminating attempt to stretch out the nominal epistemological boundaries of city and countryside that belie a processual reading of capital's creeping circulation, Brenner argues that urbanisation processes extend far beyond the boundary lines of the city to the faraway ski-resorts, mines and infrastructural corridors as capital's yearning to actualise surplus value sends it traipsing across the globe. These faraway sites in Brenner's work are considered 'operational landscapes' that play 'strategically essential roles' in supporting urbanisation processes in the centre. Following Marx's concept of original accumulation, Brenner also positions the non-urban as a key site of capital's presupposition, of certain dispossession and enclosure. This approach paints the non-urban, in all its complexities, as a watchful and immiserated bystander in the inexorable development of urban capitalism. Brenner notes urban landscapes as being

> comprehensively produced ... through a surge of infrastructural investments, enclosures and large-scale territorial planning strategies intended to support the accelerated growth and expansion of agglomerations around the world. Their developmental rhythms are thus being linked ever more directly to those of the major urban centers via worldwide spatial divisions of labor.[27]

Brenner's positioning of the rural as a series of constitutive outsides through which capitalist urbanisation is sustained and affirmed leans heavily on claustrophobic Hegelian dialectics, wherein the particularity serves and operates principally to establish totality. As Kasia Paprocki has argued, planetary urbanisation is 'a method of enframing urbanisation such that rural space is both marginal and central to its operational logics'.[28]

This mirrors older 'modes of production' debates that sought to grapple with the seeming coexistence of capitalist and non-capitalist production, particularly in the Global South. In classical approaches, so-called non-capitalist modes of production are understood to subsidise and articulate (in a monodirectional pattern) with urban capitalist modes of production.[29] Here, the relation between an agrarian non-capitalist and urban capitalist mode of production is purely instrumental, the 'pre-' and non-capitalist modes, while considered, are understood as either sites of capital's becoming (where the enclosures and dispossessions necessary for the creation of 'free wage labour' take place) or, like in planetary urbanisation accounts, as operational (where the vital resource and labour inputs are derived from and subsidised). In either case, capitalist modes of production retain a singular logic with a robust set of universal forms (for example, waged labour or agglomeration) from which all other forms of social and economic life are operationalised and extracted.

In a more heterodox development of the debates, Stuart Hall's examination of the conditions leading to apartheid in South Africa explores how racialisations are put to work to articulate agrarian and urban labour markets, structuring capitalist social formations in differential unity. For Hall, hegemonic capitalist projects rely upon the articulation (not equivalence) of a broad range of social, ideological and political-economic factors in differential unity, none of which are reducible to a totality called 'capitalism'.[30] Jairus Banaji's work equally draws out the heterogeneity in conjunctural capitalist social formations in ways that usefully confound the urban death drive. Capitalism, for Banaji, is complex and situated, accumulation depends upon in situ integration of diverse forms of exploitation and dispossession that incorporates localised systems of peasant agriculture with industrial and commercial capitalism.[31] Banaji's work forms part of a broader set of debates, discussed in Chapter 2, that focus on the differential articulation and composition of agrarian–urban capitalist social formations.

Drawing on this body of work, in this book agrarian city-making is understood as the set of articulated hegemonic relations of agrarian and urban social forces that piece together capitalist land and labour markets in differentiated unity. Agrarian city-making thus refers to the agrarian institutions, politic-economic conjunctures and practices required to churn land and people into severable private property and disciplined labour. These include the colonial projects to grid, enclose, valorise and devalorise the rural world in ways later grasped onto by real estate developers in the 1980s; the postcolonial technologies of agrarian modernisation that consolidated the wealth of landed elites and produced uneven development across the state; the agrarian institutions that continue to govern how land is formally converted into real estate; the agrarian territories that discipline and mobilise industrial labour markets; and the bleak post-agrarian futures that compel farmers to try their luck in the land market.

The profound urban transformations that India has witnessed over the past two decades has not simply taken place as planned by politicians, real estate firms, investment funds and planners. Rather, it has been led by differentiated yet 'dominant' agrarian caste communities, brokered by agrarian actors shaped by uneven agrarian development, filtered through technologies of the agrarian state and augmented by territorial compromises, trade-offs and partnerships. The millennium city is not preset by a singular history that has moved through unilinear development from the colonial to the postcolonial to the neoliberal. Rather, the city is selectively activated and activating of those histories. Urbanisation of the countryside is marked by, to borrow from Ann Stoler, the 'uneven, unsettled, contingent quality of histories that fold back on themselves and, in that refolding, reveal new surfaces, and new planes'.[32] This 'recursive' historical geography proceeds through the 'partial reinscription' and remediation of uneven colonial agrarian capitalism to forge new hegemonic coalitions driving capitalist accumulation.

Agrarian city-making is partly my attempt to read the spatially contingent articulations of agrarian and urban development that are producing the contemporary rural–urban spaces in the countryside. These agrarian urban geographies might be thought of, borrowing from Ananya Roy, as 'moments of fixture in otherwise volatile, ambiguous, and uncertain systems'[33] that are the result of hegemonic projects to enlist factions of the agrarian landowning classes into the interests and desires of corporate capital. Importantly, as I will argue, these projects are unstable, reliant as much upon the speculative promise of inclusion as its material realisation. Gurgaon's patchwork landscape of villages, blocked highways, labour tenements and skyscrapers is, I argue, anxiously upheld by characters and territories not completely subsumed to urban capitalist logics.

By pairing the incongruous agrarian and urban, I am interested in switching from transition narratives that attend to the single westward pointing arrow of Rostowian development, setting North Atlantic urban geographies in the Indian countryside, and in doing so, emptying space of its people, natures and histories. In order to understand the phenomenon of the countryside in the city, and the city in the countryside, we must look beyond the hegemonic narratives capitalists spin about themselves. The process of producing capitalist commodities, of achieving abstraction is the outcome of historically and geographically contingent practice, animated by social and cultural conditions that capital confronts and seeks to master but can never fully subsume. As a village real estate broker quipped in Praveen Donthi's long-form essay on Gurgaon's land market: 'We make the [developers] … we are his arms, feet, eyes and heart.'[34]

A Subaltern Frontier

The agrarian city-making that I develop across the book refers to an analytic for sketching out the *subaltern forces* that give expression to and constrain capitalist world-making – unveiling complex differentiated capitalist social relations geared toward commodification and exploitation for surplus value. The urban frontier in contemporary India is subaltern in the sense that capitalist urban expansion relies upon the work of actors, institutions and social formations subordinated but not fully subsumed under its rule. It is precisely the partial and provisional subsumption of agrarian life under urban domination that explain the disorderly and interrupted geographies of peri-urban development. While *subalternity* as a concept has been frequently deployed in contemporary scholarship to refer to an identity – an amorphous signifier of 'the working-class' or 'the exploited' – in examining *subaltern* frontiers, I return to subalternity as a processual *relation* of subordinated difference that simultaneously animates and disrupts hegemonic social formations. Subaltern frontiers reference those actors, institutions and logics under the command of urban capital but are never fully subsumed.

Writing on global 'commodity frontiers', Jason Moore explores the differentiated, historically specific patterns through which capital appropriates and commodifies nature on the frontiers. Frontiers for Moore are the 'bundles of uncapitalized work/energy that can be mobilized, with minimal capital outlay, in service to rising labor productivity in the commodity sphere'.[35] These frontiers form the germs of possibility for capital's appropriation of under- or un-capitalised resources, not geographically proscribed, and are found just as much on the 'geographical boundaries' as 'within the heartlands of commodification'.[36] Moore's analysis of 'commodity frontiers' is so useful because it not only affirms the role that the appropriation of 'uncommodified' resources plays in expanding capitalist social relations, but also the dialectical relation between such appropriation, uneven development and labour exploitation.

The frontiers of contemporary urban India are, as I discuss in Chapter 1, produced by the uneven development of colonial and postcolonial agrarian capitalism together with class projects that enlists certain agrarian populations to throw themselves into urban land and labour markets and repurpose their 'uncapitalised' land on behalf of real estate capital. This *subaltern* frontier relies upon histories of dispossession and exploitation enacted through agrarian capitalism, and the binding of all post-agrarian futures to real estate value.[37]

For the purposes of this present work, not only is the frontier a space which the ideological and material interplay to constitute hegemonic abstractions, but also importantly the appropriating, mapping and enclosing of the natures on the frontier is in practice deeply fraught and translational, involving a vast itinerary of compromise, internment, alchemy and disruption. Capital's confrontation with uncommodified natures – its attempt to appropriate – is never a transcoding of discrete, comparable forms from one space to another; it is rather translational, situated power-laden practices that always involve negotiation, compromise, mutation and that all-too-often-forgotten phenomenon, failure. The subaltern analytic affords the opportunity to denude the boisterous fantasies of capitalist urbanisation, displaying the compromises and contaminations that developers, industrialists, planners and politicians are forced to absorb and contend with, in order to establish provisional conditions for surplus accumulation. State and industrial capitalists' compromises with and absorptions of agrarian land systems are not simply subsumed into and flattened by a monolithic capitalist urban logic; heterogeneous agrarian worlds differently interlock with and articulate socio-spatial change in ways that can come to differently command the production of space and directly augment and challenge conjunctural capitalist projects of land-based accumulation and rent extraction.

Of course, the reliance of Gurgaon's capitalist classes on actors and logics outside of its own is a source of constant trepidation and uncertainty. Large-scale development projects are stalled and contorted by the provisional workings of local land brokers and bureaucrats, landowners earmarked for dispossession discretely resist displacement and, as we saw, the city's migrant workforce rise up, forcing the city to reckon with its own complex underpinnings. Like all hegemonic social forces, the idea of the millennium city has a material and social life outside its own, where the contours of what is possible are worked out, challenged and secured. In explaining how Gurgaon has come to form as the frontier of contemporary neoliberal urbanisation in India, in this book I am interested in exploring Gurgaon's own unruly frontiers – the disavowed and externalised social and material relations that are both vital and yet constant sources of anxiety and disruption to the city's development.

The title of the book is intended to gesture at the duplicitous character of contemporary neoliberal urbanisation in India. One not easily reconcilable to common narratives on Indian urbanisation of a monolithic rent-seeking capital hungry to expel populations and extract value from land, and an equally monolithically engaged 'dispossessed' resisting capital's brutal expulsions from the margins. Gurgaon's spectacular urbanisation has not simply worked through the brutal imposition of neoliberal economic principles onto a deferent agrarian world. *Subaltern Frontiers* signals how urbanisation operates through the stark encounter of accumulative logics – and their enactors, legal materials and powerful imaginaries – with their objects of desire: the heterogeneous subjects and spaces that must be refashioned and rationalised into attendant urban commodities. The outcomes of these encounters are unstable, shaped by the incoherence of state and capitalist interests (for example, the differing interests of state-level government officials and field-level officials); the necessary territorial and political compromises urban capital makes with its local accomplices; and the significant pushback it receives from working-class groups who carry out the material work of producing value for the city. It is at these frontier encounters in which the hubristic stories capital tells about itself confront their material limits and are appropriated by obstinate social actors, unruly land tenures and stubborn alternative imaginaries of the city.[38]

My use of the *subaltern* draws from both Gramsci's writings on hegemony and the subaltern, and the groundbreaking work of the Subaltern Studies Collective in the 1980s. Gramsci's writings were preoccupied with a study of uneven development in Italy. Gramsci was interested in why peasants in southern Italy had failed to express themselves as a unified class. Gramsci's study was focused on how subaltern positions took shape, how they were produced through class coalitions with southern intellectuals and rentier landlords in ways that stratified the peasantry, marginalising some while incorporating others into dominant social formations. In other words, at the core of Gramsci's understanding of subalternity is a rejection of a fixed, sociological identity position. Instead, subalternity for Gramsci refers to a set of situated class arrangements, a process wherein 'subordinated' and unorganised populations are differently produced, and enlisted in bourgeois capitalist projects. Importantly, subalternity is not a synonym for plain subordination, rather it locates a dynamic relationship of domination and dependence that make possible capitalist development.

Thus, hegemonic processes are central to a study of the subaltern. For Gramsci, state hegemony consists of a messy enjoining of the juridical–administrative components of the state (what is popularly understood as 'the state') and dominant class, social and cultural organisations and groupings. This social terrain, that includes the private sector is where subaltern classes are produced, others conscripted into dominant projects and bourgeois class interests naturalised. For Gramsci, hegemony rests upon the rhythmic harmony of both 'political' and 'civil' society such as bourgeois class interests are repeated everywhere in a common voice.

As a part of the Subaltern Studies Collective, Ranajit Guha set out to read histories of colonial India 'against the grain' in search of the effaced and disturbed histories within the colonial record.[39] Guha's project built on history-from-below approaches and principally aimed to dismantle the teleological historicisms of both colonial-liberal and Marxist historiography. In 'The Prose of Counter-Insurgency', Guha masterfully critiques colonial and liberal historiography for dismissing peasant rebellions under the British Raj as 'spontaneous' and un-political outbursts while accusing Marxist accounts of assimilating the peasant rebel into a figure of European history that 'excludes the rebel as the conscious subject of his own history and incorporates the latter as only a contingent element in another history with another subject'.[40] Rather, Guha and other contributors to the Subaltern project set out to prise open an analysis of politics and agencies of the 'people' undominated by western and colonial historicism. Just as with Gramsci, Guha understood subalternity in dialectical tension with domination. The hegemony of dominant groups is secured through the enlistment of subaltern groups, who in turn utilise their position to struggle against domination and for autonomy.

Gayatri Spivak's infamous intervention into the Subaltern Studies project acknowledges the collective's anti-teleological reading of history yet critiques the recovery of subaltern consciousness as a positivistic task that cannot but help to re-essentialise the subaltern as the subaltern – the undifferentiated other to the elite's will to recover. Spivak's much-discussed question 'Can the subaltern speak?' presses home the always irretrievable character of subaltern consciousness.[41] Rather than engaging in the paternalistic recovery of subaltern consciousness, Spivak pushes us to identify those limit points in which our will to recover is blocked or frustrated. The subaltern for Spivak 'is necessarily the absolute limit of the place where history is narratized into logic'. Spivak's intervention shaped the course of later subalternist analyses and sparked debates that have raged since the late 1980s.⁴²

Later subalternist debates concerned with the postcolonial character of capitalism have developed older subalternist concerns with the location of *difference* within regimes of domination. Postcolonial Marxist scholars have differently sought to identify this differential quality implicit to postcolonial capitalism. Perhaps most notably, Dipesh Chakrabarty, a central figure within the Subaltern Studies Collective, has sought to critique the pervasiveness of knowledge which sublates historical difference to the essentialising, all-encompassing logics of capital or the histories of European Enlightenment.⁴³ From *Rethinking Working Class History* (1989) to *Provincializing Europe* (2000), Chakrabarty's work follows that a critique of abstraction provided Marx with 'a way of explaining how the capitalist mode of production managed to extract from people and histories that were all different a homogenous and common unit for measuring human activity'.⁴⁴ Chakrabarty asserts that the heterogeneous social world remains 'living' despite its subsumption by capital, which both requires and must demolish the vitality of the social world, producing conditions for its own contradiction. Notoriously Chakrabarty marks this contradiction temporally, between the 'being' of capital and its apparent conquering of all differences (what he calls History 1s), and it is 'becoming', 'the historical process in and through which the logical presuppositions of capital's being are *realized* (History 2s)'. It is in the latter that Chakrabarty locates the disturbance of the former.

I find Chakrabarty's contribution incredibly instructive in thinking about the duplicitous role of the dominated within the social terrain of the dominant. Yet History 1s and History 2s resurrect an unfortunate historicism that sets a fairly uncomplicated and coherent being of capital arising from an unruly and peculiar terrain of becoming. The drivers of neoliberal land and labour markets underpinning Gurgaon's transformation have no unitary and coherent vision or practice. Gurgaon's coherent 'being' is not simply preceded by disturbing and peculiar becomings; the locus of disturbance comes from within the equally unstable and fraught settlement of the city's being. As David Featherstone notes in a reading of Chakrabarty's work on provincialising Europe: 'Subaltern activity coexists and engages with, rather than simply interrupts, capital can illuminate the alternative and competing universalities produced through subaltern politics ... [evoking] the multiple geographies through which subaltern activity is shaped.'⁴⁵

In the *Grundrisse*, Marx offers a 'two-sided' reading of capital: one as a totality that subsumes differences, 'stitching' together multiple forms of social life into the value form; and another as a possibility, of creative practices that remain un-subsumed into capital's abstractions.[46] Marx principally locates this possibility, through the slippery category of labour, that holds to both its being as 'abstract labour', an exchange value and commodity mobilised by capital *and* simultaneously 'living labour', a completely denuded set of subjective and creative practices that remain un-subsumed by capital. The conceptualisation of 'living labour' allows for a reading of labour as both a desired commodity–object of capital but equally one which – even when subsumed – holds disturbing, irretrievable characteristics that pose a threat to capital's existence. This, I argue, corresponds to a subaltern relation. The 'subaltern' being both those sites and subjects whose domination is vital for hegemonic relations of power and at the same time those un-subsumed remnants, what Lefebvre calls 'residues', that cohere in the centre of power.[47]

Subaltern Urbanism

Understandings of the politics of urban India have been prefigured and deeply influenced by debates within the Subaltern Studies Collective. A body of work that Ananya Roy has referred to as 'subaltern urbanism' has sought to trouble Eurocentric understandings of urban development and explore the diverse ways in which heterogeneous subaltern figures negotiate and mediate urbanisation projects.[48] As Shatkin has argued, subaltern urbanist approaches draw from the Subaltern Studies Collective, an understanding of a division within colonial and postcolonial society, between a subaltern or popular realm of politics and a state and elite realm of politics, attributing to Indian cities a distinct political, economic and social logic.[49] For Roy, as the work of the Subaltern Studies filters into approaches to understanding Indian cities, the former body of work's focus on retrieving subaltern consciousness is transposed into a quest for retrieving subaltern *spatialities*, wherein the 'slum' and 'slum-dweller' come to stand in as 'the subaltern'.

I read in subaltern urbanist literature an implicit synchronicity with Euro-American conceptualisations of the urban question, as they developed between the 1960s and 1970s. One of Lefebvre's key contributions in *The Urban Revolution* (2003) was to trace the switch of capital accumulation from the primary (industrial) to the secondary (urban) circuit of accumulation; the subordination of industry to real estate and financial modes of accumulation.

This 'switch' was equally vital for Harvey's formative work on spatial fixes. Despite their distinctions, the implicit assertion of both authors' work is that urbanisation processes are wrought through particular transformations in capital accumulation such that the primary sites of political struggle, agency and power are identifiable by their correlation to nominal urban forms associated primarily with the built environment. In other words, the contemporary site of a counter-hegemonic struggle is no longer the factory but the street, public-housing estate and field. In the postcolonial Indian context characterised by an absence of holistic state hegemony,[50] an absence of extensive levels of labour-intensive industrialisation and in the contemporary period an ascendance of real estate and finance actors' influence on the Indian political economy, it is perhaps not surprising that Euro-American urban epistemologies have found some, perhaps implicit, currency in studies of urbanisation in India. For Roy, while subaltern urbanist approaches usefully challenge Eurocentric tendencies within broader metropolitan studies (that tend to posit the Indian urban as a variant to European standards), there is an urgency to return to the subalternist focus on the 'demographic difference', which elides a foundational identity or territory. Roy argues: 'At best, subaltern politics can be seen as a heterogeneous, contradictory and performative realm of political struggle.'[51]

Similarly, in this book I am interested in pushing beyond notional urban forms that can delineate sensible urban development, following on Shatkin's call for 'reassessment of prevailing frameworks for analysing urban politics'[52] in light of dramatic transformations in the shape and form of social and political dynamics in contemporary urban India.

Subaltern Frontiers attempts to explore the 'heterogeneous, contradictory and performative realm of political struggle' that is so often internal to capital's world-making practices. To say that the frontier is subaltern is to point to the tentative alliances, trade-offs and dialectical struggles waged within the value relation that make and break totalising projects. The book centres on the integral role the practices and politics of the subaltern play in shaping hegemonic configurations of power. Yet, emphasising its fundamentally relational and dialectical character, the book identifies subalternity as those moments of discrete concealments and disruptions that puncture the stability of hegemonic forces.

The first half of this book examines how these hegemonic urban–agrarian social formations are secured and form the basis of land and labour markets that underpin Gurgaon's urbanisation. How the colonial, postcolonial and neoliberal state reproduced class-stratified social formations, incorporating cultivating caste communities into hegemonic capitalist social formations. As I show in Chapter 1, the production of dominant Jats and Ahirs, dispossession of lower-caste tenants and farm workers, shaped the incorporation of Punjab into global capitalist markets. These 'dominant' groups were later consolidated into a caste-based political coalition of 'peasants' that promoted the unity of the dominant peasant caste communities in ways that papered over latent class antagonisms and differentiations. The emergence of powerful real estate and industrial actors from the 1980s, whose fate was tied to accessing rural land, forged the imperative to partly wed accumulative projects in the trappings of agrarian social and economic structures. These projects structure the land–labour–agrarian class nexus that drives Gurgaon's urbanisation and, as I discuss in the book's conclusion, begin to unravel and crack towards the end of the 2010s.

That is to say, it would be preposterous to identify landowning Jats and Ahirs as *the* subaltern. Rather, the purpose of the first half of the book is to examine how the agrarian world became stratified, differently bound to property, and enlisted into hegemonic agrarian capitalism, only to later structure the shape of land and labour markets underwriting neoliberal urban India. This is, I suggest, a subaltern process, akin to Marx's theoretical critique of abstraction and Gramsci and others' commitment to a conjunctural analyses of capitalist hegemony that prioritises the disorderly settlement of class coalitions that satiate the desire for accumulation.

In this book, I foreground an understanding of subalternity as the vital and contaminating internal underpinnings of Gurgaon's remarkable urbanisation. As I have discussed, the city's development has depended heavily on the churning of two key commodities: land into property and people into labour. Both land and people feature as frontiers insofar as they are sites of state and capitalist *desire,* but as the book will detail, their 'actually existing' realisation is characterised by significant compromise and contestation. As such, borrowing from Vinay Gidwani's incisive analysis of agrarian capitalism, I conceptualise Gurgaon's urbanisation not as a singular, monolithic structure that has unfolded across its frontiers sublating all difference into the commodity form, but rather as holding to a 'molecular existence' a dominating structure that partially subsumes a variety of contingent social structures, but its existence is under constant threat by those subsumptions.[53]

As Gidwani affirms in his reading on Franz Fanon's non-sublative politics: 'The "master" may care not a whit for recognition from the "slave" but still needs her work to enable his life.'[54] So too might Gurgaon's pioneers, developers, industrialists and boosterists seek to vanquish agrarian and working-class pasts from the city's landscape but they still require their work to produce 'open fields' of accumulation. Thinking alongside both Gidwani and the earlier subalternist debates, subalternity signifies those internally cohering struggles through which subaltern actors denude the hubristic claims of urban modernity and stake a claim for quite other forms of urban life.

Drawing on the Subaltern Studies Collective's founding mission, *Subaltern Frontiers* reads the frontier and the city against the grain, identifying those elements that cohere within capitalist urban projects, that sustain its celebrated 'value creation' all while remaining a source of disturbance to hegemonic forces. Such an approach focuses on the everyday points of sustenance and disruption that destabilise universal epistemologies and materialities of the urban. In addition, a focus on subalternity assists in tracing the encounters of global neoliberal forces with the social world, not simply describing the inscription of global processes as people silently spectate from the sidelines of history or resist in triumphant disavowal. A focus on subalternity opens up seemingly predetermined worlds of dispossession, accumulation and immiseration to the political potential for quite other material outcomes. In this book, I argue that Gurgaon's expansion across Delhi's agricultural frontier is modulated precisely through these subaltern frontiers, telling the story of how histories of agrarian capitalism, bureaucratic instruments of territorial power, subaltern visions of urban futures and geographies of material labour work structure how (and for how long) capital makes urban life.

THE FRONTIERS

The book is structured around three 'subaltern frontiers': agrarian frontiers, property frontiers and working frontiers. These were not themes I had particularly set out to investigate. Having originally set out to conduct research on this celebrated private city I presumed the peril in the story would come in the form of some classic urban crisis, the territorial wars waged between competing groups over the use and meaning of urban space. What emerged throughout my fieldwork was that the 'enemy' was awkwardly integrated into hegemonic forces in the city – the low-level bureaucrat working the cadastral map and field survey to shape private property; the agrarian landowners who quietly broker land deals for international real estate firms; and the migrant worker whose collectivised claims for place trouble the foundations of the city's propertied citizens.[55] I explain these three themes here.

Agrarian Frontiers

The first two themes relate primarily to the quest for land, or the *land question* as it might more commonly be known. How exactly does the private sector go about consolidating swathes of agricultural land and transform customary agrarian land tenures into globally legible and fungible private property? Beyond the enactment of legal and institutional instruments, the upper-level statecraft that flexibly eases the passage of capital to land, private property at some point must be enacted, etched out onto the soil, written onto cadastral maps and land-record books, and finally claimed as property.

Capital's *quest for land* in contemporary India is notoriously troubled, informing a series of land wars that have stalled large-scale urban development projects,[56] prompted deadly guerrilla conflict still raging across the country after fifty years and recently led to the disposal of political dynasties of both state and central government.[57]

Subaltern Frontiers engages in debates on the land question from two perspectives. First, the findings of this book push back against dispossession-centred analyses of India's urban turn. Dispossession is something of a master concept within contemporary urban studies. From Marx's formulation of 'primitive accumulation' in his study of the English enclosures to the 'new enclosures' literatures,[58] David Harvey's influential expansion in 'accumulation by dispossession' and more recent literature on 'urban land grabs',[59] dispossession at capitalist frontiers – and the dispossession of non-capitalist forms of life in particular – is understood to be foundational to processes of urban and industrial development the world over. In accounts of Indian cities, each actor in the story of India's spectacular urbanisation takes part in a pitched battle over the purpose, use and value of urban land. Global capital seeks it out, the entrepreneurial state facilitates access to it, an emergent middle class demands control of it and subaltern actors are defined through their strategies to discretely hang on to it. Yet, to begin the story in 1980 misses the historic processes of agrarian development and dispossession that produced material conditions for urban expansion later down the line. Gurgaon's landowners of the 1980s and 1990s were not strictly dispossessed. Selling their land to developers, dominant agrarian classes unevenly form part of a new class of land rentiers, speculators and brokers who carry out the complex work of assembling the social and discursive materials to ready production.[60] It is through these practices and compromises that landowners attempt, with uneven success, to transform themselves from agrarian populations into propertied urban citizens. There is no neoliberal city, no 'urban' that does not carry with it the territorial scars of compromise, contest and discrete appropriation enacted by those that reside in it. Thus, Chapter 1, which draws exclusively from archival and secondary literature, explores the prehistory to the 'Gurgaon model', examining how the uneven development of agrarian capitalism, and regimes of agrarian 'improvement', set the stage for a series of experimental urban development policies in the 1970s that presaged the neoliberal moment. Chapter 2 draws from a household survey of just under 200 households across three clusters of villages in Gurgaon and Delhi[61] alongside fieldwork interviews with landowners and landlords across the city conducted between 2012 and 2018. The findings of Chapter 2 show how the 'urban village' and villager are far from external objects of the frontier, rather they are frontiering devices themselves: the enclosure and exemption of village lands across Gurgaon's interior enabled real estate developers to capture and transform the agricultural fields into urban property and set the stage for landowners' self-transformation into a nascent rentier class – charged with disciplining the city's incoming migrant workforce residing in their villages and enabled to reinvest accumulated rental capital into real estate and land in the city outside. Despite the Indian government's sharp entrepreneurial and real estate turn in the early 2000s, cities across the country are dominated by heterogeneous land tenures that remain not fully abstracted as private property. In Gurgaon's disavowed and dejected villages, I will contend, the 'trinity formula' of capitalist urbanisation – land, labour and capital[62] – crystallises in decidedly agrarian surroundings.

Property Frontiers

Attention given to dispossession and expulsion within urban scholarship also detracts from the far more ubiquitous if discrete alliances between the state, landowners and industrial capital that speculatively open up and convert land and secure private property on the frontier. Chapter 3 draws from field interviews with landowners, brokers and speculators called upon to speculatively invest in land, plot property and convert customary tenures in anticipation of rising land values and state authorisation. Research interlocutors were organised through a snowball methodological approach, most contacts of village landlords and political figures whom I had met while undertaking the household survey. The chapter examines how territorial ambiguity acts as a resource for aligning property claims with state developmental visions, and how state and real estate firms elicit the speculative territorial strategies of agrarian landowners by binding all post-agrarian futures to real estate development.

Chapter 4 draws from nine months of ethnographic observation within the central Gurgaon land revenue (*patwari*) office conducted between 2018 and 2019. My research engaged in the daily observation of bureaucrats, private land surveyors and office users (brokers, developers, lawyers, lay villagers) six days a week. The chapter explores how state bureaucrats and bureaucratic materials are deployed to secure private property. In both cases, agrarian property regimes and bureaucratic institutions afford degrees of uncertainty and pliability that can be captured by real estate actors looking to aggregate land and secure property. As a growing body of scholarship has observed, the stubbornness of Indian cities to European-style enclosures is a consequence of extensive bureaucratic negotiability and the deep entanglement of bureaucratic actors in the interests and agendas of localised social actors.[63] What Solomon Benjamin has called India's 'porous' bureaucracy[64] acts as a resource for different social and state actors to flexibly interpret and rework upper-level state mandates, stalling and augmenting state projects in the service of localised political and social pressures.[65] This book examines how the indeterminacy of agrarian bureaucracy acts as a resource for real estate actors embedded in the everyday life of the bureaucracy to flexibly navigate the various obstacles to land consolidation and transform commonly held landholdings into private property. *Subaltern Frontiers* explores how the everyday bureaucratic practices and the negotiations within the *patwari*'s office operate as key terrain where large-scale urban and infrastructural development projects are worked out, reshaped and sometimes stalled.

Both Chapters 3 and 4 thus examine the role state indeterminacy and ambiguity plays in shaping property markets. This builds on literature on the 'everyday' postcolonial state that examines how state authority is exercised not (only) by appeal to specification, rules or institutional norms but equally by appeal to ambiguity, negotiation and un-mapping. Rather than simply through showpiece legislation and policy announcements that form the focus of many scholarships on urban dispossessions, these negotiable territorial and bureaucratic practices come to profoundly underpin the ways in which globalised real estate capital 'grabs' urban and peri-urban land, accesses development licences, plans exemptions and transforms opaque and heterogeneous urban land into socially disembedded, fungible private property. *Subaltern Forntiers* hones in on the everyday temporal, territorial and bureaucratic workings of property formation, the logics and technics through which speculators claim customary lands, and bureaucrats discretely bend and contort land's contours into the shape of private property.

Working Frontiers

Chapters 5 and 6 explore migrant working-class geographies of Gurgaon. Drawing on ethnographic and interview-based fieldwork, Chapter 5 examines how Gurgaon's tenement villages articulate land rent, labour wages and capital in ways that reproduce conditions for industrial accumulation in the city. The chapter explores how everyday governance regimes within the tenements operate to discipline working-class tenants as a hyper-mobile, precarious form of labour, and how workers express their mobility in disruptive and rebellious ways.

Chapter 6, drawing on life-history interviews conducted with migrant working-class women in the labour tenements,[66] examines how conditions of migrant working-class life in and through the city produce and shape political agencies. The thousands of migrant workers that underpin the city's economy disrupt dispossession-centred scripts of contemporary urbanism. Urban dispossessions are after all undertaken primarily to access land, to establish new territories of capitalist rule. Far from contesting territory in the city, making claims on land, urban-service provision, access to the 'commons' – acts often attributed to a 'right to the city' politics – migrant workers, the 'nowhere people' whose everyday lives are explored in this book, make no specific claim to land in the city and have no particular interest in the territorial warfare between local subaltern actors and global capital. They have little to no land, reside in shared tenement rooms on rent, are frequently defined as *bahari* outsiders in the city and their futures are determined only by the certitudes of circular migration, precarious work and their temporary status in Gurgaon. Migrant working classes fundamental to immaterial economies of the contemporary Indian city operate outside the discursive and ideological terrains of dispossessive urbanism. *Subaltern Frontiers* instead explores the de-territorialised political claims and imaginaries of the city's migrant working classes, examining political identities forged through conditions of mobility, fraught social reproduction and precarious work that discretely disturb the certitudes of the neoliberal city.

As discussed, an emphasis within urban studies literature on the advent of post-Fordist, immaterial urban economies, has led to a relegation of questions of material labour from our conceptual frameworks of the contemporary city. Notwithstanding a small but vibrant body of work tracing the geographies of urban labour,[67] urban studies approaches tend to place material labours either as fully subsumed into informal service circuits – cleaning, transporting goods and hawking wares *in* the city – or else present workers as helpless bystanders to inexorable forces of dispossession and informalisation. Labour in the present conjuncture according to Samaddar is a 'floating commodity', expelled from land to make way for spectacular urban development only to be reincorporated as a reserve army and compelled into an unassailable current of migration that drags millions from one space of value extraction to the next.[68] For Breman, these systems of circular migration co-constitute labour's informalisation and represent a significant obstacle to labour's ability to collectively organise as a territorially defined class.[69]

The findings of the book in part challenge analyses that inscribe labour's redundancy as an outcome of their dispossession from land and spatial marginalisation in the city. I do so by focusing on the work that must be achieved in order to turn people into labour. In her work Leslie Salzinger chastised Marxist-feminist political economists for taking at face value women's 'preset docility' that arises uncomplicatedly from entrenched societal patriarchy.[70] In contrast, Salzinger develops an analytic of 'productive femininity' to describe the constant discursive (re)production of feminine tropes that both cheapen the value of working-class women's labour and operate as a terrain for workers' to appropriate and contest the terms of their cheapening. Salzinger's conceptualisation of labour feminisation strikingly reminds us of the dangers of re-producing hegemonic discourses of powerlessness and docility, which can only reconstitute powerlessness and docility as immutable, transhistorical characteristics.

As discussed at the outset of this book, the hundreds of thousands of migrant workers that circulate through the city each year to work on construction sites, factories, shopping malls and upper-class homes are far from powerless, nor is their marginality 'preset'. By delving into the everyday life of the workers' tenements across the city, Chapters 5 and 6 locate the making of cheap labour markets in Gurgaon's everyday disciplinary practices of landlords in the city's urban villages. This avenue of inquiry brings questions of *social reproduction* to the fore.

Social reproduction describes the broad array of social practices which underwrite and dialectically constitute conditions of capitalist production, inclusive of the daily and generational work to transform people and nature into commodity form. From the 1970s, feminist and feminist-Marxist scholars – predominately based in the North Atlantic – sought to highlight the (mostly) unwaged, gendered labours that are required to return commodities like labour to the factory, labours that in so doing underwrite the surplus value that labour produces for capital.[71] Crucially, it is the devaluation of women's reproductive labour, its deliberate location *outside* the space of production, and its disciplining by the family and household unit that allow for capitalist production to continue unabated. More recent social reproduction scholarship has sought to build on and remedy this earlier in important ways. First, scholarship has attended to the geographical essentialisms implicit within earlier works, for example, the fixation on the figure of the western housewife, presaging the contingent subjectivities wrought through social reproductive relations. Second, scholarship has emphasised the dialectical relation between production and social reproduction – that does not simply position social reproductive work as determined or structured solely by an economic relation but, as Katz remarks, 'embod[y] the whole jumble of cultural forms and practices that constitute everyday life and the meanings by which people understand themselves in the world'.[72] Finally, feminist scholars have emphasised social reproduction's deeply contingent territorial grounds, the boundary lines between the factory and home; production and social reproduction shift and contort as capitalists seek to keep up with the dynamic needs for surplus production. *Subaltern Frontiers* builds on these more recent developments in social reproduction theory. Drawing from the workers' tenements that densely occupy the city's urban villages, the book explores how social reproduction both frames migrant's disciplining as a cheap, disposable workforce for the city and also provides fertile terrain for migrants' decidedly de-territorial and collective political claims. Again, this draws questions of labour in direct confrontation with the question of land in India's blueprint private city. These migrant workers' social reproduction is intimately tied up in, and forms the economic base of, agrarian landlord's engagements in real estate across the city. Yet, it equally forms the basis of a set of struggles that looked to disrupt those rentier channels and stake a claim for an entirely different urban life.

The Conclusion, 'Urban Limits', narrates Gurgaon's fall from grace amidst a global property crash, cracks in the city's hegemonic alliance of farmers and corporate capital and the concurrent rise of both a Hindutva political agenda and subsequently counter-hegemonic agrarian political uprisings in 2020. Through the demise of the celebrated 'Gurgaon model', the chapter returns to the fundamental questions of the book set out in the introduction, highlighting the fragility and uncertainty of neoliberal urban landscapes, propped up as they are by logics, subjects and spaces with alternative and overlapping interests and determinations. In doing so, the book restates Gurgaon's various frontiers as terrains of possibility, sites that provide subaltern actors with the tools with which to reshape urban futures.

Notes

1. In 2016, Gurgaon was renamed Gurugram by the newly elected Bharatiya Janta Party (BJP) government in Haryana. In this book, I will use the name of the city used during my fieldwork. I discuss the significance of the switch from Gurgaon to Gurugram in the Conclusion.
2. The factory produced 550,000 cars per year.
3. Yadav, 'Maruti Strikes'. The consortium of Mitsubishi, Marubeni and Mitsui would later withdraw financial support after the Haryana government refused to prevent landowners from negotiating land prices.
4. See Barnes, Lal Das and Pratap, 'Labour Contractors and Global Production Networks'; Barnes, *Making Cars in the New India*; and Monaco, 'Bringing Operaismo to Gurgaon' for extended analysis of the politics of Maruti Suzuki workers in Delhi-NCR (National Capital Region).
5. GWN, *Gurgaon Workers News*.
6. Schindler et al., 'Deindustrialization in Cities'.
7. Levien, *Dispossession Without Development*.
8. Florida, 'Technology, Talent, and Tolerance'.
9. Das, *India Grows at Night*.
10. Scott and Storper, 'The Nature of Cities'; Scott, 'Emerging Cities'; Amin, 'Post-Fordism'.

11. See Florida, *Cities and the Creative Class*; Schindler et al., 'Deindustrialization in Cities'; Scott, 'Emerging Cities'.
12. This narrative is mostly used to describe processes of urban change in the North Atlantic but has been picked up to think about changing urban processes in India too.
13. Byres, 'The Agrarian Question and Differing Forms of Capitalist Agrarian Transition'.
14. Bhattacharya and Sanyal, 'Bypassing the Squalor'.
15. Sharan, 'In the City, Out of Place'; Baviskar, 'Between Violence and Desire'; Ghertner, *Rule by Aesthetics*; Goldman, 'With the Declining Significance of Labor'.
16. Tsing, *Friction*.
17. Dasgupta, *Capital*.
18. Singh, Menon and Swamy, *Whatever the Odds*.
19. Smith, *The New Urban Frontier*.
20. Breman, 'The Great Transformation in the Setting of Asia'.
21. Sanyal, *Rethinking Capitalist Development*.
22. Prakash, 'The Urban Turn'.
23. Noterman, 'Speculating on Vacancy', 4.
24. Balakrishnan and Gururani, 'New Terrains of Agrarian–Urban Studies'; Kalaiyarasan and Vijayabaskar, 'Why Does the "Provincial Propertied Class" Remain Provincial?'.
25. Marx, *Grundrisse*, 479.
26. Brenner, 'Urban Theory Without an Outside'.
27. Brenner, *Implosions*.
28. Paprocki, 'The Climate Change of Your Desires'.
29. Wolpe, 'Capitalism and Cheap Labour-Power in South Africa'.
30. Hall, 'Race, Articulation, and Societies Structured in Dominance'.
31. Banaji, *Theory as History*.
32. Stoler, *Duress*.
33. Roy, 'Why India Cannot Plan Its Cities'.
34. Donthi, 'How the Brokers of Land and Power Built the Millennium City'.
35. Moore, *Capitalism in the Web of Life*, 149.
36. Ibid.
37. This phenomenon has been traced elsewhere. In his work on the Brazilian Amazonia, for example, Jeremy Campbell, in *Conjuring Property*, tracks the ways class-differentiated colonists improvise property claims and produce land markets on the frontier.

38. While in part this approach resonates with James Scott's analysis in *Seeing like a State* of the troubles modernist states face in their attempts to 'make society legible', Gurgaon's urbanisation is not simply an outcome of state efforts to create a legible urban territory. Rather, much like contemporary urbanisation elsewhere in India, it has been facilitated by the territorial flexibility of state actors, their routinised imposition of ambiguity and illegibility, un-mapping of territories and mobilisation of pliable bureaucratic devices and materials. My approach to Gurgaon's flexible urbanisation draws from Ananya Roy's *City Requiem, Calcutta*, an influential work whose research in peripheral Kolkata explores how techniques of state un-mapping and the absence of state maps and records provided a flexible terrain for powerful market actors to make claims on land. In contemporary urban India, real estate capital's access to and transformation of heterogeneous land uses operates precisely through the unstable and negotiated workings of the bureaucracy.
39. Guha, 'The Prose of Counter-Insurgency'.
40. Ibid.
41. Spivak, ' Deconstructing Historiography'.
42. The many detractors of Spivak's intervention have decried the shift the collective took from seeking to amplify the unwritten role subaltern actors played in shaping the modern nation, towards an interrogation of how hegemonic European knowledge-power comes to delimitate a fixed, essential subaltern consciousness.
43. Chakrabarty, *Provincializing Europe*; Chakrabarty, *Rethinking Working-Class History*.
44. Chakrabarty, *Provincializing Europe*, 50.
45. Featherstone, 'Reading Subaltern Studies Politically'.
46. Marx, *Grundrisse*.
47. Lefebvre, *Critique of Everyday Life*.
48. Appadurai, 'Deep Democracy'; Benjamin, 'Occupancy Urbanism'; Bhan, *In the Public's Interest*; Dhareshwar and Srivatsan, '"Rowdy-Sheeters"'; Roy, *City Requiem, Calcutta*.
49. Shatkin, 'Contesting the Indian City', 2.
50. Kaviraj, 'On the Crisis of Political Institutions in India'.
51. Roy, 'Slumdog Cities', 11.
52. Shatkin, 'Contesting the Indian City', 5.
53. Gidwani, *Capital, Interrupted*.
54. Gidwani, 'The Subaltern Moment in Hegel's Dialectic'.
55. In this book I adopt a relational dialectical approach that seeks to draw attention to everyday, localised agencies, practices and discourses

deployed to forge property and labour markets, and yet recognises the role epistemological refraction and representation plays in articulating these processes in scholarly texts. In other words, the translation from the abstract to concrete and back again implicit in my reading of hegemony is also my translation. My study is partial, contingent and highly refracted through my own limited position as a foreign researcher. These debates were constantly on my mind as I carried out my fieldwork. I carried them around with me everywhere, thrusting them into the 'field' as my interlocutors thrust them back at me. My discussions, interviews and observations were refracted by my own position as a British, white, middle-class man in India.

56. Levien, 'The Politics of Dispossession Theorizing India's "Land Wars"'.
57. For example, the thirty-four-year rule of the Left Front (West Bengal) in West Bengal was brought to an end in 2011 following controversial land acquisition policies.
58. De Angelis, 'Marx and Primitive Accumulation'.
59. Harvey, *The New Imperialism*; Zoomers, 'Globalisation and the Foreignisation of Space'.
60. See Chapter 3.
61. The household survey was conducted alongside research assistants Shivangi Jaiswal, Meghana Arora, Arya Thomas, Parag Banarjee, Nayan Jyoti and Sambhav Sharma. The villages were selected and grouped into three clusters. Cluster 1 composed of Dundahera, Carterpuri and Kapashera (in Delhi), all villages located along the old Delhi–Gurgaon road. Cluster 2 comprising Nathupur, Jharsa and Badshahpur villages form part of New Gurgaon, to the south-east of the National Highway. Finally, Cluster 3, Rampura, Manesar and Kherki Duala are all villages in west Gurgaon which straddle the NH8. I chose these three separate clusters in an attempt to capture as diverse a range of experiences of urbanisation as possible.
62. Coronil, *The Magical State*.
63. Chatterjee, *The Politics of the Governed*; Gupta, *Red Tape*; Hull, *Government of Paper*; Anjaria, 'Ordinary States'.
64. Benjamin, 'Occupancy Urbanism'.
65. Gupta, *Red Tape*; Anjaria, 'Ordinary States'; Fuller and Benei, *The Everyday State and Society in Modern India*.
66. These life histories were designed and conducted with an interpreter, Dr Shivangi Jaiswal.
67. Chari and Gidwani, *Introduction*; Padmanabhan, 'Globalisation Lived Locally'.

68. Samaddar, 'Primitive Accumulation and Some Aspects of Work and Life in India'.
69. Breman, 'The Great Transformation in the Setting of Asia'.
70. Salzinger, *Genders in Production*.
71. Dalla Costa and James, *Women and the Subversion of the Community*; Federici, *Revolution at Point Zero*.
72. Katz, *Growing up Global*.

BIBLIOGRAPHY

Amin, Ash. 'Post-Fordism: Models, Fantasies and Phantoms of Transition'. *Post-Fordism: A Reader* 1 (January 1994): 1–7.
Anjaria, Jonathan Shapiro. 'Ordinary States: Everyday Corruption and the Politics of Space in Mumbai'. *American Ethnologist* 38, no. 1 (2011): 58–72.
Appadurai, Arjun. 'Deep Democracy: Urban Governmentality and the Horizon of Politics'. *Environment and Urbanization* 13, no. 2 (2001): 23–43.
Balakrishnan, Sai, and Shubhra Gururani. 'New Terrains of Agrarian–Urban Studies: Limits and Possibilities'. *Urbanisation* 6, no. 1 (2021): 7–15.
Banaji, Jairus. *Theory as History: Essays on Modes of Production and Exploitation*. Leiden, The Netherlands: Brill, 2010.
Barnes, Tom. *Making Cars in the New India: Industry, Precarity and Informality*. Cambridge: Cambridge University Press, 2018.
Barnes, Tom, Krishna Shekhar Lal Das and Surendra Pratap. 'Labour Contractors and Global Production Networks: The Case of India's Auto Supply Chain'. *Journal of Development Studies* 51, no. 4 (2015): 355–69.
Baviskar, Amita. 'Between Violence and Desire: Space, Power, and Identity in the Making of Metropolitan Delhi'. *International Social Science Journal* 55, no. 175 (2003): 89–98.
Benjamin, Solomon. 'Occupancy Urbanism: Radicalizing Politics and Economy beyond Policy and Programs'. *International Journal of Urban and Regional Research* 32, no. 3 (2008): 719–29.
Bhan, Gautam. *In the Public's Interest: Evictions, Citizenship, and Inequality in Contemporary Delhi*. Vol. 30. Athens: University of Georgia Press, 2016.
Bhattacharya, Rajesh, and Kalyan Sanyal. 'Bypassing the Squalor: New Towns, Immaterial Labour and Exclusion in Post-Colonial Urbanisation'. *Economic and Political Weekly* 46, no. 31 (2011): 41–48.
Breman, Jan. 'The Great Transformation in the Setting of Asia'. Public lecture to accept honorary doctorate, International Institute of Social Studies, The Hague, 2009. https://www.iss.nl/fileadmin/ASSETS/iss/typo3/about/history/honorary_fellows/Personen/Breman/breman_address_web.pdf. Accessed 15 April 2018.
Brenner, Neil, ed. *Implosions/Explosions: Towards a Study of Planetary Urbanization*. Berlin: Jovis, 2014.

———. 'Urban Theory Without an Outside'. In *Implosions/Explosions: Towards a Study of Planetary Urbanization*, edited by N. Brenner, 1–14. Berlin: Jovis, 2014.

Byres, Terence J. 'The Agrarian Question and Differing Forms of Capitalist Agrarian Transition: An Essay with Reference to Asia'. In *Rural Transformation in Asia*, edited by J. Breman and S. Mundle, 3–76. Delhi: Oxford University Press, 1991.

Campbell, Jeremy M. *Conjuring Property: Speculation and Environmental Futures in the Brazilian Amazon*. Seattle: University of Washington Press, 2015.

Chakrabarty, Dipesh. *Provincializing Europe: Postcolonial Thought and Historical Difference*. Princeton Studies in Culture/Power/History. Princeton, NJ: Princeton University Press, 2000.

———. *Rethinking Working-Class History: Bengal, 1890–1940*. Princeton, NJ: Princeton University Press, 1989.

Chari, Sharad, and Vinay Gidwani. *Introduction: Grounds for a Spatial Ethnography of Labor*. London; Thousand Oaks, CA; New Delhi: Sage Publications, 2005. http://journals.sagepub.com/doi/abs/10.1177/1466138105060758.

Chatterjee, Partha. *The Politics of the Governed: Reflections on Popular Politics in Most of the World*. New York: Columbia University Press, 2004.

Coronil, Fernando. *The Magical State: Nature, Money, and Modernity in Venezuela*. Chicago: Chicago University Press, 1997.

Dalla Costa, Mariarosa, and Selma James. *Women and the Subversion of the Community*. Bristol, UK: Falling Wall Press, 1972.

Das, G. *India Grows at Night*. UK: Penguin, 2013.

Dasgupta, Rana. *Capital: The Eruption of Delhi*. New York: Penguin, 2014.

De Angelis, Massimo. 'Marx and Primitive Accumulation: The Continuous Character of Capital's Enclosures'. *Commoner* 2, no. 1 (2001): 1–22.

Dhareshwar, Vivek, and R. Srivatsan. '"Rowdy-Sheeters": An Essay on Subalternity and Politics'. In *Subaltern Studies*, edited by S. Amin and D. Chakrabarty, 9:201–31. New Delhi: Oxford University Press, 1996.

Donthi, P. 'How the Brokers of Land and Power Built the Millennium City'. *The Caravan*, 1 January 2014. https://caravanmagazine.in/reportage/road-gurgaon. Accessed 01 June 2014.

Featherstone, David. 'Reading Subaltern Studies Politically'. In *Subaltern Geographies*, edited by T. Jazeel and S. Legg, 42:94–118. Athens: The University of Georgia Press, 2019.

Federici, Silvia. *Revolution at Point Zero: Housework, Reproduction, and Feminist Struggle*. Oakland, CA: PM Press, 2012.

Florida, Richard. *Cities and the Creative Class*. London: Routledge, 2005.

———. 'Technology, Talent, and Tolerance'. *Information Week* 13, no. 2002 (2000): 3–19.

Fuller, Christopher John, and Veronique Benei. *The Everyday State and Society in Modern India*. London: Hurst and Co., 2001.

Ghertner, D. Asher. *Rule by Aesthetics: World-Class City Making in Delhi.* Oxford: Oxford University Press, 2015.
Gidwani, Vinay K. *Capital, Interrupted: Agrarian Development and the Politics of Work in India.* Minneapolis: University of Minnesota Press, 2008.
———. 'The Subaltern Moment in Hegel's Dialectic'. *Environment and Planning A* 40, no. 11 (November 2008): 2578–87. https://doi.org/10.1068/a40271.
Goldman, Michael. 'With the Declining Significance of Labor, Who Is Producing Our Global Cities?' *International Labor and Working-Class History* 87 (Spring 2015): 137–64. https://doi.org/10.1017/S0147547915000034.
Guha, Ranajit. 'The Prose of Counter-Insurgency'. In *Subaltern Studies*, edited by Ranajit Guha and G. C. Spivak, 2:45–86. Oxford: Oxford University Press, 1983.
Gupta, Akhil. *Red Tape: Bureaucracy, Structural Violence, and Poverty in India.* Durham, NC: Duke University Press, 2012.
GWN. *Gurgaon Workers News.* Newsletter 48 (March 2012). http://libcom.org/book/export/html/56150. Accessed 2 June 2012.
Hall, Stuart. 'Race, Articulation, and Societies Structured in Dominance'. In *Sociological Theories: Race and Colonialism*, 305–45. Paris: UNESCO, 1980.
Harvey, David. *The New Imperialism.* USA: Oxford University Press, 2003.
Hull, Matthew S. *Government of Paper: The Materiality of Bureaucracy in Urban Pakistan.* Berkeley, California: University of California Press, 2012.
Kalaiyarasan, A., and M. Vijayabaskar. 'Why Does the "Provincial Propertied Class" Remain Provincial? Reading the Agrarian Question of Capital Through Caste'. *Urbanisation* 6, no. 1 (2021): 16–34.
Katz, Cindi. *Growing Up Global: Economic Restructuring and Children's Everyday Lives.* Minneapolis: University of Minnesota Press, 2004.
Kaviraj, Sudipta. 'On the Crisis of Political Institutions in India'. *Contributions to Indian Sociology* 18, no. 2 (1984): 223–43.
Lefebvre, Henri. *Critique of Everyday Life: Foundations for a Sociology of the Everyday.* Vol. 2. London: Verso, 1991.
Levien, Michael. *Dispossession Without Development: Land Grabs in Neoliberal India.* Oxford: Oxford University Press, 2018.
———. 'The Politics of Dispossession Theorizing India's "Land Wars"'. *Politics and Society* 41, no. 3 (2013): 351–94.
Marx, Karl. *Grundrisse.* UK: Penguin, 1993.
Monaco, Lorenza. 'Bringing Operaismo to Gurgaon: A Study of Labour Composition and Resistance Practices in the Indian Auto Industry'. PhD thesis, SOAS University of London, 2015.
Moore, Jason W. *Capitalism in the Web of Life: Ecology and the Accumulation of Capital.* London: Verso Books, 2015.
Noterman, Elsa. 'Speculating on Vacancy'. *Transactions of the Institute of British Geographers* 47, no. 1 (2021): 123–38.

Padmanabhan, Neethi. 'Globalisation Lived Locally: A Labour Geography Perspective on Control, Conflict and Response among Workers in Kerala'. *Antipode* 44, no. 3 (2012): 971–92.
Paprocki, Kasia. 'The Climate Change of Your Desires: Climate Migration and Imaginaries of Urban and Rural Climate Futures'. *Environment and Planning D: Society and Space* 38, no. 2 (2020): 248–66.
Prakash, Gyan. 'The Urban Turn'. *Sarai Reader* 2, no. 7 (2002): 2–7.
Roy, Ananya. *City Requiem, Calcutta: Gender and the Politics of Poverty*. Minneapolis: University of Minnesota Press, 2003.
———. 'Slumdog Cities: Rethinking Subaltern Urbanism'. *International Journal of Urban and Regional Research* 35, no. 2 (2011): 223–38.
———. 'Why India Cannot Plan Its Cities: Informality, Insurgence and the Idiom of Urbanization'. *Planning Theory* 8, no. 1 (2009): 76–87.
Salzinger, Leslie. *Genders in Production: Making Workers in Mexico's Global Factories*. Berkeley, California: University of California Press, 2003.
Samaddar, Ranabir. 'Primitive Accumulation and Some Aspects of Work and Life in India'. *Economic and Political Weekly* 44, no. 18 (2009): 33–42.
Sanyal, Kalyan. *Rethinking Capitalist Development: Primitive Accumulation, Governmentality and Post-Colonial Capitalism*. New Delhi: Routledge, 2007.
Schindler, Seth, Tom Gillespie, Nicola Banks, Mustafa Kemal Bayırbağ, Himanshu Burte, J. Miguel Kanai and Neha Sami. 'Deindustrialization in Cities of the Global South'. *Area Development and Policy* 5, no. 3 (2020): 283–304.
Scott, Allen J. 'Emerging Cities of the Third Wave'. *City* 15, nos. 3–4 (2011): 289–321.
Scott, Allen J., and Michael Storper. 'The Nature of Cities: The Scope and Limits of Urban Theory'. *International Journal of Urban and Regional Research* 39, no. 1 (2015): 1–15.
Sharan, Awadhendra. 'In the City, Out of Place: Environment and Modernity, Delhi 1860s to 1960s'. *Economic and Political Weekly* 41, no. 47 (2006): 4905–11.
Shatkin, G. 'Contesting the Indian City: Global Visions and the Politics of the Local'. *International Journal of Urban and Regional Research* 38, no. 1 (2014): 1–13.
Singh, Kushal Pal, Ramesh Menon and Raman Swamy. *Whatever the Odds: The Incredible Story behind DLF*. New Delhi, India: HarperCollins Publishers, a joint venture with the India Today Group, 2011.
Smith, N. *The New Urban Frontier: Gentrification and the Revanchist City*. London: Routledge, 2005.
Spivak, Gayatri Chakravorty. 'Deconstructing Historiography'. In *Selected Subaltern Studies*, edited by R. Guha and G. C. Spivak, 3–32. New York: Oxford University Press.
Stoler, Ann Laura. *Duress: Imperial Durabilities in Our Times*. Princeton: Duke University Press, 2016.

Tsing, Anna Lowenhaupt. *Friction: An Ethnography of Global Connection*. Princeton, NJ: Princeton University Press, 2011.

Wolpe, Harold. 'Capitalism and Cheap Labour-Power in South Africa: From Segregation to Apartheid'. *Economy and Society* 1, no. 4 (1972): 425–56.

Yadav, Anumeha. 'Maruti Strikes'. *Himal Southasian*, 27 March 2015. http://himalmag.com/maruti-suzuki-workers-strikes/. Accessed 1 June 2015.

Zoomers, Annelies. 'Globalisation and the Foreignisation of Space: Seven Processes Driving the Current Global Land Grab'. *Journal of Peasant Studies* 37, no. 2 (2010): 429–47.

1 | The Experiment

THE ROOTS OF THE GURGAON MODEL

This chapter explores the prehistory to Gurgaon's contemporary agrarian urbanisation, highlighting how neoliberalism on India's urban frontier is realised as an outcome of attempts to graft market-driven governance onto extant class, territorial and institutional settings. Studying a forebearer to neoliberal urban India reveals neoliberalism's earthbound mediations, an incoherent ideological project[1] compromised by the territorial and institutional alliances brokered to make space for capital on the edge of the national capital. Agrarian city-making in the twenty-first century has relied upon class projects that include the landowning peasantry into property and labour markets. But how were such class projects forged? How did certain rural populations become dominant? And why were they so easily conscripted to sell themselves and their lands into urban economy from the 1980s? In this chapter I explore how the articulation of capitalist uneven development, liberalism and caste came to structure social formations favourable to the Gurgaon model.

Gurgaon's urbanisation holds many of the characteristics of neoliberalism: financialised real-estate-led urbanisation; elite propertied citizenship; secessionary, privatised governance and infrastructural development; and a celebration of entrepreneurialism and liberal capitalism form the backbone of Gurgaon's story. And yet underwriting this façade is not only mass state-facilitated investment but also the yoking of land and labour markets to agrarian institutions and class compositions configured under colonial and post-colonial agrarian modernisation. The Gurgaon model, this chapter argues, is characteristic of what Brenner, Peck and Theodore call 'actually existing neoliberalism', the coming together of neoliberal actors and logics with local institutions and processes in ways that enable market-driven growth while giving space to quite other political-economic and spatial logics.

In this chapter I will move across three key moments that were foundational to the making of Gurgaon as a frontier for urban real estate capital. The chapter begins by outlining the infrastructure of the 'Gurgaon model' and discusses the model's early roots in pre-liberalisation Haryana. It was the repurposing of Nehruvian-era planning controls by pro-liberalisation politicians that gave the model its form and presages many of the neoliberal economic reforms of the 1990s and 2000s. I argue that the model's relative success has been dependent upon pre-existing social and economic conditions forged through colonial and post-colonial agrarian development.

The chapter then moves back to examine the ideological and material antecedents to Gurgaon's urbanisation located in colonial agrarian settlement and post-colonial modernisation. I do so to trace the continuities, spillovers and blockages in state engagements with the region that have come to ineluctably shape real estate capital's entrance into land markets in the city.

To understand how dominant agrarian landowners came to form a central component of contemporary Gurgaon's market-led urbanisation, and force compromises and disruptions to capital's free reign on land, requires exploring the particular conditions through which peasant proprietors were produced, private property consolidated and land devalued to the extent it could be recapitalised in the contemporary moment. The middle section of the chapter traces how nineteenth-century colonial land settlement programmes in Gurgaon instituted private property relations and integrated the state of Punjab into a global agrarian economy.

Delhi's barren frontier, prospected by developers and industrialists from the 1980s, was cultivated through the uneven geographical development of colonial and then post-colonial capitalism, laying the foundations for revaluation at the summit of India's post-agrarian turn.[2] Processes of underdevelopment in Gurgaon, the chapter shows, were rendered sensible via the recurring ideological deployment of liberalism. To the devastation wrought upon Gurgaon by the colonial encounter, British officers prescribed the myopic zeal of Victorian liberalism that pathologised and racialised the unevenness they had cultivated to the conduct and habits of Gurgaon's residents. These colonial ideologies of self-help and racialised improvidence which justified colonial rule and have come back full throttle in the entrepreneurial Gurgaon model. Finally, the chapter shifts to the immediate post-colonial period, where agrarian policy was being mobilised to industrialise agriculture and consolidate property on a mass scale across the state. It was during this period that Gurgaon's dominant peasant classes were transforming into agrarian capitalists consolidating their political and cultural power across the new-found state of Haryana, and it was at the end of this period in the late 1970s that real estate came to town looking for willing partners for a city-building project.

A Neoliberal Turn

In 1991 the Government of India embarked on a programme of economic liberalisation that would profoundly transform the political, social and spatial landscape of the country. Following a balance of payments crisis and an emergency loan of 2.26 billion US dollars from the International Monetary Fund (IMF), the government used the opportunity to accelerate the roll-out of radical economic reforms that began in the 1980s and would repeal decades of state protectionism and planned investment. The New Economic Policy sought to align India with a globally ascendant neoliberal mantra, integrating the economy into a burgeoning global market, and enticed global investments by relaxing state regulations on land development, banking, industry and financial sectors. The government allowed foreign investors to take majority stakes in domestic industries and offered various fiscal incentives including slashing capital gains tax on foreign investment projects from 60 per cent to 35 per cent. The reforms had an immediate impact: in 1991 India received 230 million US dollars in foreign direct investment (FDI); the following year, that figure rose to 1.4 billion US dollars as close to a thousand foreign investors – predominately non-resident Indians – began to invest in the 'emerging' Indian market. At the time, the international consultancy firm McKinsey released a report publicising the government's new economic agenda to the world propositioning India as a giant 'untapped market' for global capital. The report however also warned of lingering challenges to investment, urging further reform of the labour market to allow for unregulated retrenchment and 'flexible wages', deeper privatisation of public sector bodies and trade liberalisation.

India's neoliberal reforms were, and remain, anchored to a desire for urban modernisation. Under the New Economic Policy introduced by the newly elected Congress government in 1991 not only was there a centralisation and concentration of industry in ever tighter geographies, but also land itself – hyped by boosterist vision plans and place-making documents – became a central terrain and vehicle for economic growth. This has translated into a series of territorial experiments led by the private sector and facilitated by the local state: industrial corridors, greenfield urban developments, special economic zones, central business districts. The pursuit of global capital investment required the dismantling of the post-colonial developmental state and refiguring of the relationship between the state and capital. The seventy-fourth amendment to the Indian Constitution, passed in 1992, paved the way for devolution of powers from the national and state to municipal levels and aimed to transform Indian cities into entrepreneurial nodes of competition. In the post-liberalisation period, as competition for investment between states and city-regions heightened, 'under-maximized' land has become a key source of income for newly emboldened municipalities. The amendment includes provisioning for the state to cede territorial authority to private sector actors within specified *industrial townships*. These townships, originally envisaged as industrial sites, were later interpreted and expanded to include vast urban areas, typically on the rural edges of the traditional big cities.

In this regard, the liberalisation reforms set to establish what Harvey termed an 'urban entrepreneurialism'[3] where the mandates of (urban) government are reconfigured from the modernist managerialism of previous periods, to facilitate private, rent-seeking investments into and extraction from the built environment. The next three decades of fastening integration with global financial markets dramatically transformed the urban and peri-urban landscape of the country, sparking a boom in real estate development as planners, politicians and developers sought to refashion the country's cities, towns and villages to cater for incoming investment.

The local state's role in facilitating broad spatio-economic change is embodied in successive central government programmes (the RAY, JNNURM, AMRUT and Smart Cities programmes) that aimed to transform Indian cities into 'growth engines' by incentivising municipal governments to liberalise land development regulations and environmental protections, remove obstacles to land acquisition (such as the Urban Land Ceiling Act), encourage public–private partnerships, maximise rent-generating uses of public lands and privatise public infrastructure delivery. The Jawaharlal Nehru Urban Renewal Mission (JNNURM), for example, was a major provisioning of central government funding geared towards the reorientation of the socio-spatial fabric of Indian cities. Launched in 2005, the Mission required municipalities to privatise urban service provision; fund infrastructure projects through public–private partnerships; repeal land ownership ceilings and rental caps; introduce user fees for basic services; ease land conversion systems and development controls; and draw up urban development plans or 'vision documents'. These development plans looked to reconfigure and re-envision the space of the city, centralising development permissions and remapping land uses for commercial and residential purposes.[4]

The neoliberal urban moment in post-liberalisation India was however ostensibly *not* an event that unfolded easily from these legislative and regulatory reforms. The structural reforms to the Indian economy have required new forms of governance that combine the structural violence of rural land dispossessions and inner-city evictions with the promise of inclusion into property-powered development.[5] This is what Ananya Roy has referred to as *homegrown neoliberalism*: the practices and discourses 'through which a multitude of heterogeneous social forces in urban India actively produce and take up the norms of market rule'.[6] These discourses seek to secure a hegemonic order that assigns the troubles of the post-colonial settlement to political and cultural inefficiencies, to which free markets and urban-led growth mandates – commodification, commercialisation, entrepreneurialism – are a desirable and urgent solution.

In Gurgaon, these stories are not new. As we will trace later in this chapter, they draw upon older colonial logics of 'improvement' that sought to reconcile uneven development by yoking India's modernisation to colonial paternalism and projects of self-help, civility and property ownership. They are also refracted through post-Independence modernisation agendas in Haryana (and elsewhere) that sought to spark propertied agrarian–industrial modernisation while managing the social welfare of newly enfranchised and demographically powerful rural populations. Tracing the interplay of hegemonic discourses and practices of uneven development from the mid-nineteenth century to the present moment situates India's 'spectacular' urban turn within longer, albeit discontinuous projects to induce consent to the violent excesses of liberal development.

THE MODEL

Between 1981 and 2014, real estate developers purchased and developed over 35,000 acres of rural land into privately governed urban real estate largely catered toward India's emergent urban upper classes and a global finance, IT and service sector industry.

This rapid conversion of rural land into globalised real estate was processed predominately not through state-led dispossession – as discussed elsewhere[7] – but rather through direct sales of landholdings to the private sector. The 'Gurgaon model' of urban development is no one legislative programme, nor can it be reduced to a singular 'vision plan' or document. Rather, in practice, the 'Gurgaon model' refers to a series of modernist urban development reforms passed by the Haryana government in the 1970s and later augmented by an increasingly entrepreneurial state government in the 1980s.

We can locate the germs of the Gurgaon model in the Haryana Development and Regulation of Urban Areas Act (HDRUA) passed in 1975 that introduced a licence system of urban and commercial development across the state. The act, passed by Congress stalwart and chief minister of Haryana Bansi Lal, had been originally conceived to provide the state government with a legal framework to engage in urban residential development; the act states its aim to 'regulate the use of land in order to prevent ill-planned and haphazard urbanization in or around towns'. The HDRUA was followed two years later by the Haryana Urban Development Authority (HUDA) Act, 1977, which empowered the Haryana Urban Development Authority to engage in compulsory land acquisitions for urban and infrastructural development utilising licences provided under the HDRUA. The election of Bhajan Lal to the chief minister's office in 1979 would change the course of Gurgaon's urban development. From the 1980s, Bhajan Lal, a noted rival of Bansi Lal and later member of Rajiv Gandhi's pro-liberalisation cabinet, began to offer HDRUA licenses to private builders.[8]

Under the HDRUA, private 'colonisers' are required to assemble a minimum of 100 acres of contiguous land and are issued development licence from the Town and Country Planning Department for the development of residential and commercial townships inside 'controlled areas', designated under the Punjab Scheduled Roads and Controlled Areas Act, 1963 (PSRCA), across the state. Under what became known as the 'Gurgaon model', private real estate developers directly negotiate the purchase of land from farmers on market prices, while the state government establishes master-planned urban development areas within which development licences are issued for the private development of residential and commercial townships. The 'problem' of assembling and assetising India's fragmented rural smallholdings, and convincing farmers to part with their ancestral lands, is pre-emptively 'resolved' by offloading the responsibility to the private sector.

The HDRUA's transfer of land acquisition responsibilities to the private sector, which bought and consolidated land at market prices, while a precedent to neoliberal reforms that eased access to land from the 1990s, also reflects the particular constraints of land politics in Haryana. The ability for developers to buy up and transform rural land into urban real estate has been facilitated by decades of agrarian reforms that, however elastic and mutable, sought to reconfigure rural land as amenable to commodity registers, consolidated agrarian capital within the hands of large landowning communities and exempted village residential lands from private and state land acquisitions.

In doing so, the HDRUA inaugurated a system of privately financed infrastructure and uneven spatial connectivity across Haryana's urban areas. Under the act, licencees must provide internal infrastructure such as roads, electricity, water and sewerage connections within 100-acre townships and pay a one-off external charge for state-developed trunk infrastructure outside the boundaries of their colony. This dual system of infrastructure delivery that pitted privately financed colony infrastructure against publicly financed trunk infrastructure effectively produced archipelagos of disconnected urban territories.

This liberalised development model contrasted with emerging class dynamics and capital blockages in neighbouring Delhi. The 1962 Delhi masterplan produced a market for the development licences in Gurgaon. The masterplan seeking to put a check on untrammelled land prices by bestowing development controls over undeveloped land in the city to the Delhi Development Authority. This sparked a rush on land in neighbouring towns just at the moment that the Haryana government was legislating the liberalised development model that came to form the 'Gurgaon model'. Gurgaon was well placed to receive real estate investment. Not only was the land in Gurgaon cheap and property in principle consolidated but also the city's proximity to Delhi's international airport and pre-existing manufacturing allured commercial actors.

From the 1990s there was high demand for this kind of hyper-segregated, privately organised and managed suburban space. The 1990s and 2000s witnessed an emergence of what is sometimes referred to as India's 'middle-class': metropolitan, liberal, educated and fiercely segregationist. Liberalisation in the 1990s was in part an invitation for the urban upper classes to take a different role in the political life of Indian cities. Globalisation saw a greater connectivity of Indian urban elites and upper middle classes with global corporate culture and 'post-industrial' cities in the North Atlantic. Amidst a political-economic context in which India's developmental ills were increasingly blamed on the Nehruvian state, viewed to be in service to the urban poor, a new middle class began to fight back, utilising control of civic organisations, the judiciary and media, to secure the hegemony of their class interests – broadly the hegemony of liberal private property, individual self-reliance and entrepreneurial governance – and displace those of the urban poor.[9]

The very idea of a city in Gurgaon formulated by Haryanvi politicians in the 1970s and 1980s, and built by DLF, the developer who made their name building gated colonies for South Delhi's upper middle classes, presaged the rise of this middle-class politics. Gurgaon's model of privately organised, privately developed, privately managed urban life celebrated the demise of the post-colonial state and the emergence of an emboldened middle-class consumer Indian citizen upon whose back a new India might be built. As writer Gurcharan Das writes in an account typical of the political sentiment shaping those moving to the city in the 1990s:

> Gurgaon manages to flourish without public infrastructure because of its self-reliant, resilient citizens. They don't sit around and wait. They dig bore wells to get water when government pipes run dry. They put in diesel generators when power from the state electricity board fails. They use cell phones from private providers rather than landlines of the state company…. They use couriers rather than the post office. Many companies have even installed their own sewage treatment plants. Apartment complexes and companies employ tens of thousands of security guards rather than depend on the police. When teachers and doctors do not show up at government primary schools and health centres, people open up cheap private schools and clinics, even in the slums.[10]

In this regard, Gurgaon's urbanisation, while commonly triumphed as a cause célèbre for free marketeers has the ineluctable mark of regionally contingent shifts in state-capitalist coalitions from the 1970s. As land markets came under pressure from political coalitions in Delhi that willed the city first toward state-managed development, and later a middle-class-directed post-industrial economy, state development and planning infrastructures in Haryana sought out ways to capture and accommodate exiled capital. To this they would first need to resolve the problem of opening up land for capital.

Selling Up

Across the majority of the country, state governments have facilitated private capital investment in land by taking on the direct role of acquiring and assembling land through the Land Acquisition Act, 1884 (LAA). In the post-liberalisation period as state governments entered into increased competition for domestic and global capital investment, a state-brokered model of land development effectively provides a subsidy to capital as the state takes on the costs and political ire associated with mass land conversions required for industrial and urban development.[11]

And yet Haryana's politicians were cognisant of the social base from which they drew their political power. From the state's inception in 1966, Haryana has been governed almost exclusively by members of the landowning Jat community, historically elected from the Congress Party or the Indian National Lok Dal (INLD) and its subsequent offshoots, with the support of both the Bharatiya Kisan Union (Indian Farmers' Union), or BKU, and the village-level *khap panchayats*.[12]

In Haryana, the Jats as well as the landowning Ahirs (Yadavs) and Gujars form part of what Balagopal has referred elsewhere as the 'provincial propertied class',[13] a wealthy stratum of the peasantry who have benefitted from colonial agrarian policy and post-colonial agrarian capitalism. The provincial propertied classes, in Balagopal's account of rural Andhra Pradesh, are a vital engine of agrarian transition. By reinvesting their agrarian capital into provincial urban rentier business and the formal educations of sons they drive the movement of surpluses across rural and urban sectors. They also dominate politically, mobilising *kisan* (farmer) rural caste identity to gloss over latent inter-caste class frictions and secure power on the electoral stage.[14] In southern Haryana, as we shall see, this group of landowners have a slightly distinct story, one mutated by the particular affordances of colonial uneven development and rather constricted opportunities to reinvest agrarian surpluses. If in parts of south India we see wealthy landowners utilise agrarian political power and capital surpluses to 'transition' into industrialists and real estate developers, in Haryana the articulation of agrarian caste-class power is expressed through a quieter set of rural–urban coalitions – where landowners form equity partnerships, broker land and amass monopoly rents in service of industrial capital – that have each shaped what I call agrarian city-making.

In this context, any land development model entirely premised upon state-led acquisitions through *eminent domain* would be both politically toxic and highly litigious, effecting a significant barrier to capital investment. Not only is state politics dominated by a *kisan* politics that relies upon the reification of farmers' relationship to land, but also under the LAA compensation for land acquisition is offered at rates far lower than market prices. The private-sector-led model instituted by the HDRUA for residential and commercial development bypasses these obstacles and transfers the responsibility to negotiate land prices to private actors.

As such, the licence-led model in Gurgaon, which as I will discuss involved a series of partnerships and alliances between real estate firms and agrarian landowners, unsurprisingly received little substantive opposition. The model not only offers farmers the opportunity to profit from land of low agricultural value, but also offers the promise of inclusion into future-oriented propertied modernity which the city's real estate values represent. It did so, in part, by tightly integrating landowners into the real estate sector's ancillary industries of speculation, brokerage and land aggregation (see Chapter 3).

Planning Relaxations

The planning framework for the Gurgaon model is established in the PSRCA. The 1963 act was characteristic of what Mike Levien calls 'spatial Nehruvianism'[15] – focused on state-managed urban and industrial development; the act was passed during a period in which the young post-colonial Punjab state was undertaking the rehabilitation of Partition refugees from West Punjab, now Pakistan, to the state. The act intended to prevent 'ribbon' development along the state's arterial roads and curb the perceived threat of 'haphazard' constructions around existing urban settlements. Declaring as 'controlled areas' any land within an 8-kilometre distance of existing municipal town limits or 2 kilometres from any public institution, industrial estate and housing colony, the PSRCA effectively projected a future territorial image of rationalised, 'controlled' development on the existing landscape. In passing the act, the state instituted a developmental logic that is still present today.

As I discuss in Chapters 2 and 3, the PSRCA also instituted degrees of territorial porosity into Gurgaon's development plans. Indeed, both acts were creatively rewritten and repurposed from the 1980s to accommodate the territorial claims of real estate capital and agrarian elites, albeit in the name of 'public purpose' and inclusion. The control that PSRCA leverages chimes with what Ananya Roy has called 'state informality'; 'control' for Haryana's state planners plainly refers to the powers vested in senior state officials to selectively absorb and reject territorial claims regardless of their alignment with planning and development codes set out in legislation. Gurgaon's development plans ought to be thought of as living, nebulous creatures.

Importantly, while the HDRUA and PSRCA started out as post-colonial legislation characteristic of the developmentalist state, both were repurposed by pro-market politicians in the 1970s to open up land for private capital investment.[16] As development licences were opened up to the private sector between 1981 and 2014, the real estate sector acquired licences for the development of 17,000 acres of land in Gurgaon, over a third of these licences covering 6,500 acres, between 2000 and 2010 alone. Of all licences issued by the planning department, 68 per cent – 6,500 acres – were issued to just three developers, Delhi Land and Finance, Ansal Properties and Unitech, while ten developers own 53 per cent of all urban land in the city.

In this respect, despite holding to similar structural conditions, the 'Gurgaon model' is distinct from land-based capitalist development elsewhere in India. In Mike Levien's study of agrarian transformation and down the road from Gurgaon in Rajasthan, he notes that the 'conjuncture of increased demand for land driven by neoliberal policies, the lack of fully capitalist rural land markets and increasing inter-state competition for investment has given rise to a land broker state'. In Rajasthan the state plays a leading role in expropriating land and turning it over to capitalist rentiers. *Accumulation by dispossession*, Levien writes, is 'now one of the key features of the Indian states' relationship with domestic and international capital'.[17] In Gurgaon, like in Levien's study, there was a substantial demand for land beginning from the 1970s, there were also instruments that empowered the state to directly acquire land, and like Rajasthan, rural landholdings were fragmented, small and held under complex tenure forms. And yet in Gurgaon, and Haryana, in a pattern becoming ever more ubiquitous in urban development projects across the country,[18] the state's role has shifted back from dirigisme of direct land expropriation, towards the creative construction of flexible institutional frameworks that coordinate real estate capital investment, and *broker territorial arrangements* between corporate capital and local landowners that facilitate the conversion of rural land. What the state brokers in Gurgaon is not land itself, but rather economic and territorial alliances between capital and the agrarian elite.[19]

We return to the creative repurposing of the HDRUA and PSRCA in Chapters 2 and 3; in the remainder of this chapter, I am interested in how Gurgaon's landowners, property regimes and political institutions were readied for the urban turn by over a century of colonial engagements in agrarian capitalist development. If complex and opaque rural land markets have held back real estate development elsewhere in the country,[20] real estate capital arrived in Gurgaon in the 1970s confronted by an agriculturally depressed area, with gridded and consolidated property holdings owned by a political, cultural and economically dominant landowning caste-class. But how were these conditions produced? And how do their organising logics inform the urban politics and economic practices of the present?

SETTLING GURGAON

Gurgaon was formally annexed by the East India Company following the defeat of Daulat Rao Sindhia in December 1803. Initially leased out to local rulers, Gurgaon formed part of a buffer zone between British and western Sikh territories; in 1837, Gurgaon was formally 'settled' within the Delhi division and was later incorporated into the annexed state of Punjab in 1849. British colonial officers came to Gurgaon and Punjab, wary of their previous failures to secure a sustainable revenue base in the region and scarred by their experiences of the Permanent Settlement of Bengal. The much anticipated, if disputed, Permanent Settlement had transformed Bengal's medium-size farmers into a class of powerful but unproductive rentiers, who rather than leading an agricultural transition were parasitic of agrarian capitalist production. By the mid-nineteenth century colonial ideology, scarred by the uprisings, were wary of imprinting entirely 'foreign' systems of governance onto unruly populations. A new settlement system was required, one which remediated local 'custom', incentivised capitalist agrarian social relations and could be rendered legible and calculable to British rulers.[21]

The Mahalwari revenue settlement, originally devised by Holt Mackenzie in 1822, fit the mould. Deployed across Uttar Pradesh and Punjab through the first half of the nineteenth century, the Mahalwari system took British ideological constructions of the spatially bounded village and village proprietary body as its primary unit of revenue assessment. Rather than transferring power to a landlord class as in Bengal, or individual peasant proprietors as under Madras' *ryotwari* system, under the Mahalwari system in each village, or *thola* or *patti* (commonly held part of a village), a *lambardar* was assigned to collect taxes that were the joint responsibility of the village proprietary body *malikan deh*.

Under the Mahalwari settlement, British officers, armed with Ricardian theories of ground rent, devised a system through which the potential rental yields of the village would be routinely assessed every twenty years according to soil type, irrigation, access to manure and so on, and taxed accordingly. The routine enhancement of tax would, the British hoped, skim off surpluses that made for rentierism in Bengal and produce a class of competitive peasant cultivators jointly responsible for land revenue. The routine re-assessment of land's productivity also made necessary state calculative and inscription practices that bound and authored village life into record.[22] Mahalwari settlements required vast programmes of classification and codification, land was studiously mapped and boundaries set in, tenures were identified and rural life made sense of in anthropologies of caste. They did so not by stripping away existing social institutions and practices but rather by remediating them in colonial, Eurocentric terms. As Neeladri Bhattacharya has written, the village in Punjab, and its naturalness as a site of revenue assessment imbued with assumed local customs of joint liability, was constituted and made sensible by the bureaucratic practices of settlement.[23]

Legally substantiated in the Punjab Land Revenue Act, 1871, the Mahalwari system established mixed tenurial regimes of individual and joint property rights. The village residential area *abadi deh*, marked by the *lal dora* (red thread boundary), was bestowed as the joint property of the village landowners while agricultural fields (*khet*) outside the *lal dora* were the private property of joint-family units. As John Stuart Mill notes, under the Mahalwari system 'the peasant proprietors compound with the state for a fixed period. The proprietors [do] not engage themselves with the government but by villages.'[24]

Land settlement projects also dramatically transformed erstwhile communal land arrangements into privatised forms. As Chakravarty-Kaul notes, before British rule the collective ownership of these lands was 'central to a system of village management where the private and arable land was generally held in scattered strips, while the residential and pastoral land was arranged in compact holdings'.[25] Colonial land settlements bestowed ownership of pastoral and common lands to the village proprietary body, stripping landless and pastoral communities of their legal access to subsistence. While 'the commons' and grazing lands remained formal tenurial forms, and communal arrangements persisted, formally the 'commons' *shamilat deh* came to refer to the commonly held property of the village landowners owned by the village proprietary body, who in many cases enclosed and transferred the land for cultivating purposes. In effect, the Mahalwari system concretised private property relations cloaked in the form of jointness.

Colonial land settlement prompted quite dramatic differentiation among Gurgaon's peasantry. In a report to the Famine Commission, settlement officer B. T. Gibson writes that before the settlement of Gurgaon there was 'much less difference between the owner of the land, tenant with rights of occupancy, and tenants-at-will throughout the greater part of the district', rents were roughly equal to the level of assessment, and rights to common lands were shared with owners on equal terms.[26] The post-famine increase in the tax demand in 1877, Gibson notes, pushed up tenancy rents and made evictions more frequent. 'Since the operations of the present settlement began,' Gibson writes, 'the tendency to distinguish more sharply between these classes of agriculturists has been rapidly growing.... Property in land is becoming more valuable every day, and the rights of owners having been more clearly defined in the new settlement records.'[27]

The complex bureaucratic task of translating rural land into private property established a discrete category of landowner and tenant, as well as new calculative norms that rendered fixed rights and responsibilities, boundaries and exchanges sensible to the functioning of agrarian life. As Bhattacharya writes: 'Within the colonial legal regime, rights to land could be categorically fixed and made judiciable only if they could be clearly located within a defined space, and the boundaries of each field definitively marked.'[28] These calculative instruments of rural governance, as discussed in Chapter 4, would become central sites of urban property-making in the contemporary moment.

The binding and authoring practices of British colonialism sought to produce what James Scott calls the 'synoptic facts' that enable 'schematic knowledge, control and manipulation' of the rural world. The act of settlement *sought* to fix and settle rural life down into empirically knowable and separable objects. And yet the entanglement of socially dynamic local practices and institutions within colonial frameworks of codification meant that this desire to abstract the social world was only ever partially realised. Indeed, the *compromise* with 'local custom' of collectivity was such that numerous collectivised forms of land use – beyond the village body and not amenable to schematic knowledge – endured throughout the colonial period.

Take, for example, the practice of *panapalat*, a land ownership system wherein landowners organise land into scattered strips that were cultivated separately and periodically rotated in ways that enabled landowners to hedge their bets on the productivity of different land parcels. Collective members cannot sell or mortgage the *panapalat* land but can transfer their membership in the collective. *Panapalat* was particularly persistent in rain-dependent Gurgaon, where ownership of fragmented landholdings reflected the needs of landowners to take liability for poor lands and benefit from productive lands collectively. Much to the frustration of colonial officials, *panapalat* practices endured and even grew after the onset of commercial land markets in Gurgaon. In 1859, there were thirty-six villages across Gurgaon that practised *panapalat*; by 1877, there were seventy-three villages holding *panapalat* land. Importantly, it was these colonial practices of land settlement that formally institutionalised these non-normative property forms – both quasi-private forms of *abadi* and common lands or collectivised *panapalat* systems – into local property regimes. It was the instruments of 'schematic knowledge' that fixed opaque and amorphous tenures into state records. This mixture of privatised and non-privatised lands, an outcome of colonial anxiety over land settlement as we shall see in Chapter 2, would come to be vital to Gurgaon's urbanisation in the 1980s and 1990s.

Casting Property

The project of settlement was also keenly about producing an entrepreneurial property-owning class amenable to capitalist social relations. To this the British, influenced by the Ricardian political economy, spent a great deal of time attributing cultural traits and identities that could racially and socially differentiate colonised people's access to liberty, property and territorial power.

From the earliest settlements in Gurgaon, it is clear that the British had selected the cultivating Jats and Ahir (Yadavs) communities to be promoted as the natural members of this landed elite.[29] In Gurgaon, British settlement officers cultivated the image of the 'entrepreneurial Jats' and 'thrifty' Ahirs whose struggles with the tough soils, labour-intensive well irrigation and poor harvests made them perfect candidates as a landed elite.[30]

These landed communities were, importantly, not particularly resistant to the project of settlement nor enthusiastic participants in the 1857 uprisings and formed a larger contingent of the British colonial army.

To these communities, the British codified and integrated land tenure systems. The 'thrifty' Ahirs held property on *pattidari* tenures, wherein land is distributed among proprietors according to ancestral shares. *Pattidari* represented individual ownership organised through ancestral jointness of the village. Expressing both severalty and jointness, *pattidari* thus came to embody the integration of custom into colonial systems of private property that Ricardian liberalism strongly advocated. For the British, jointness of land lead to higher rates of cultivation and stayed the evils of subdivision that rather ironically market forces brought about. In Gurgaon, the Jats were positioned 'behind' the Ahirs, conjured up as equally industrious; but from the punitive standpoint of Victorian liberalism, their better soils provided a degree of comfort that led to improvidence and laziness. According to British eugenicist ideology that viewed the world through a prism of blood and soil, the Jats did not have to toil to work their lands and thus were slightly less worthy of the spoils of their labour.

In addition, the Jats held land through subdivided *bhaichara* tenures where land was held in relation to the physical possession of plots; under this system, poorly irrigated lands were usually left uncultivated or else given to tenants and pastoralists. *Bhaichara,* as Neeladri Bhattacharya writes, denoted subdivision, lower degrees of cultivation and parcellisation that rendered land opaque and difficult to govern.[31] In practice these tenure systems reflected the kinds of soil that different cultivators were working with, *pattidari* was undertaken best in areas of tough, scarcely irrigated soil allowing good and bad soils to be held collectively, and potential areas for cultivation extended. *Bhaichara,* on the other hand, dominated areas of well-irrigated soil where risk sharing was not necessary.

Finally, the Meos who live in modern-day Mewat were a particular obsession of colonial officials. Highly resistant to land settlement and enclosure[32] and the leading contingent in the 1857 anti-colonial resistance, the Meos stood in for the dangerous other to enclosure. Despite the devastation that settlement wrought upon southern Haryana, discussed ahead, British accounts of Meo resistance to enclosure frequently return to a favoured prism of blood and soil. The Meos in many cases owned productive lands, and it was these productive lands that bred ill-discipline and resistance. As Malcolm Darling argues, 'One explanation of these violent contrasts in character is that adversity either strengthens or weakens. The Ahir and the Jat are instances of the one, the Meo and the Rajput of the other.'

Of course, these stories of the pathologised hierarchies between cultivating castes were at the time just stories, yet ones that held instrumental value in codifying 'caste' in ways that justified the devastating impacts of British rule. Agricultural caste would become a central idiom through which property settlement and land revenue were constantly rationalised. As Gyan Prakash puts it, 'The British do not just misrecognise caste, but gave material shape to their misrecognition through their laws and administration.'[33] Agricultural castes in Punjab were always reified and overdetermined entities, expressions of colonial attempts to extract and accumulate. The idea of the 'Jat' and 'Ahir' in this sense was incidental to actual subject-identities at that time but rather acted as *resources* for colonial territorial rule and *pre-conditions* for agrarian accumulation. As Malcolm Darling, assistant commissioner of Punjab from 1904, would note, 'It may be said that in the whole of India there is no finer *raw material* than the Jat.'[34]

Needless to say, the actual economic productivity of land had nothing to do with concocted racial and caste-based categories. The famines and growing indebtedness across the nineteenth century hit the Jat and Ahir villages just as they did the Meos. What is more, settlement reports are inundated with British frustrations at the unwillingness of nearly all communities to settle their property, the intransigence of landowners to pay and of local bureaucrats to collect taxes, and the regular subversion of maps, boundary walls and wells that marked out colonial schematic knowledge.

Land revenue maps, caste codifications and tenure systems were a colonial speculation never anywhere as stable as suggested by colonial officers; most villages mixed aspects of ancestral shares and subdivision, while the confection of 'caste-attributes' served only as something to attribute the consequences of British calamitous infrastructure development and rapacious extraction that devastated the social and ecological life of the district.³⁵ This is not to say that caste prejudices and hierarchies did not exist in Punjab before, or autonomous of, colonial desires and practices. Nor was the inculcation of a casted peasant proprietary class the only intervention the British made with caste. Clearly the systematic dispossession and exploitation of Dalit communities, and their enrolling in casteist carceral and tenant *jajmani* labour systems across the state is indicative of extant inequality across the state that was built upon by British rule.³⁶

For the purposes of this book, it is important to highlight that the British keenly invented and augmented pathologies of cultivating castes in pursuit of the conditions of agrarian capitalism that would later lay the groundwork for agrarian city-making. In colonial Punjab, 'agricultural caste' was a lyrical verse of government, an explanation for the violence and incoherence of colonial rule, articulated through the conjunctural conditions of export-oriented production, British fantasies of racial supremacy and political expediency. While vital to the story of agrarian and later urban capital accumulation in Punjab, and later Gurgaon, the 'thrifty' Ahir and Jat only emerge as an immanently coherent empirical object within the British administrators' own accounts. These colonial ideations of caste that no doubt found willing support among the dominant landowners were abstractions but nevertheless came to be realised in practice – what some call 'concrete abstractions'³⁷ – by binding these categories into legal and institutional frameworks.

Wasting Gurgaon

The early land settlements in Gurgaon took place while the district remained a part of the Delhi division before 1837. These settlements set tax rates slightly lower than that of Sikh rulers in order to curry support for Company rule. Nevertheless, under these early revenue systems, for the very first time, rural people in Gurgaon would be paying taxes at a fixed rate in cash. In an agropastoralist region like Gurgaon dependent on flexibility across indifferent seasons, it is perhaps no surprise that colonial land settlements would put particular strain on rural life, and these early settlements routinely failed and villagers resisted collections.³⁸ The situation was worsened by drought and famine in the 1830s in the region, which brought landowners into significant debt.³⁹ Regarding the Palwal region south of Gurgaon in the 1830s George Barnes wrote that the previous settlement 'undoubtedly rated the resources of the district too highly ... [assessing] each estate at a much higher rate value than its cultivated areas could be brought to pay … [reducing the landowners to] extreme destitution.'[40]

These early calamities extended into the first full district-wise land settlement in 1837. Taking place during a period when the East India Company desperately needed to finance its expensive territorial wars, the first regular settlement in Gurgaon significantly extended the cultivatable area of the district – converting vast swathes of forest and grazing lands for cultivation – and excessively overestimated potential yields in a region that was sandy, arid and where cultivation was reliant upon rainfall. While other districts saw high revenue demands balance out with an expansion in cultivation and access to irrigation, Gurgaon's cultivatable area lay stagnant, canal irrigation broadly bypassed the region, and yet the revenue demand increased. During the 1857 uprisings against Company rule that swept through the country, revenue offices were attacked and set on fire across the Gurgaon district. The British were also coming under increasing pressure from industrialists back home to open up export channels from India in order to support their fledgling industrial production. In response, land revenue demands were lowered from 66 to 50 per cent across Punjab. After lowering tax rates, the British looked to fully integrate Punjab agriculture into the global economy.

The calamitous start to land settlement would be exacerbated by the integration of Punjab agriculture into global commodity markets in the mid-nineteenth century. The transfer of power from the East India Company to the British Crown in 1858 brought about a broader shift in gear within the political economy of colonial India, from the Company's focus on mercantilism to the territorial expansion of imperial production and consumption; India began to be viewed as a valve that could relieve pressures of overaccumulation at home. From the 1880s the British financed and constructed mass canal irrigation and land consolidation projects in the north and west of Punjab, creating the 'canal colonies' that drove wheat, cotton and sugarcane exports to Britain. As Manu Goswami argues, the key difference between the political economy of the Company and the subsequent British Crown was that while the former sought to control the extraction of commodities and raw materials from India, the latter 'sought to transform the geographical space of colonial India into a commodified, "second-order" space embedded within rather than merely tied to the broader imperial economy through external relations'.[41]

The opening up of Punjab to the transnational agrarian economic system exposed the state's agricultural production to the fluctuations of global wheat and cotton markets. As Mike Davies notes, Punjab's agriculture would become a 'shock absorber' for British and North American poor harvests.[42] This integration led to the acceleration of British policy to bring larger areas of grazing and fallow lands under cultivation and taxation. Between 1855 and 1891, 11 million acres of land were brought into cultivation across that state, of which Hamid estimates[43] 9 million acres came from the privatisation of grazing and forest lands.[44] The integration of Punjab into a global economic order in the latter half of the nineteenth century also brought to Punjab the instability of global wheat and cotton prices. Initially, high prices set against fixed revenue demands benefitted the rental yields across the region and incentivised landlordism over cultivation. The harvest failures in England in the 1870s brought with it a demand for export crops that enriched larger landowners but gutted the reserves of smallholders across Punjab.

Punjab's south-eastern districts (Hissar, Gurgaon, Rohtak) were particularly disadvantaged. The southern tracts were underdeveloped by design by British policy which incentivised cattle rearing and fodder cultivation that could supply cultivation in other parts of the state. Indeed, these three agriculturally 'backward' districts contributed 99 per cent of cattle to Punjab by the late 1930s.

The mass expansion in cultivation was facilitated by large-scale infrastructure building across Punjab. The construction of *bunds* (dams) and canals passing through Gurgaon raised British expectation of the land's net product, and thus justified the raising of higher revenue demands from larger parts of the district which exacerbated famine and impoverishment. Expanded channels of the Western Yamuna Canal and Agra Canal that fed into southern parts of the Gurgaon district from the late nineteenth century, as Whitcombe notes, brought malaria and cholera epidemics to the district. Revenue officers note that the West Yamuna Canal channel had 'in a few months' wiped out a sixth of the population of many neighbouring villages, 'scarcely a man is to be found who has not been greatly reduced in strength by repeated attacks'.[45]

The construction of the Agra Canal in the 1870s that passes through southern parts of the Gurgaon district, stimulated export crop cultivation (cotton, sugarcane) and expanded the cultivatable area of land, but did so at the expense of basic foodstuff cultivation, exacerbating a series of epidemics and famines. Ever-expanding cultivation required mass embankment and supplementary well-irrigation construction that in Gurgaon deepened disease and drought. As Clive Dewey argues, cultivation in Gurgaon had traditionally relied upon yearly flash floods and spillage from the Yamuna River on the eastern bank of the district that would replenish the district's *jhils* (lakes) in the wet springs and leave sodden soil during the dry season. The mass construction of dams to capture this spillage around the Yamuna effectively drained Gurgaon of its single access to irrigation. As Dewey writes, 'the complex system of embankments which once directed the flow of water over the fields became a vast earthen monument to Gurgaon's vanished prosperity'.[46] The various *jhils* became marshland pits of plague.

And yet in the face of economic and ecological devastation, a parsimonious Crown animated by the punitive ideology of liberal self-help responded by extending the area of cultivatable land and raising the tax demand by 16 per cent. Indeed, under the second standard revenue assessment in 1877, the impoverished and purposefully underdeveloped Gurgaon was given the highest tax demand in the state.

What followed in Gurgaon through the late 1870s were a series of floods, famines and epidemics that floored the district. Between 1877 and 1882, over a third (half a million) cattle died, and 400,000 acres of 'cultivatable' land entered into waste.[47] In a single year, between 1878 and 1879, some 14 per cent of Gurgaon's residents were killed by a combination of famine, drought and disease. According to F. C. Channing's 1882 report, some villages in Gurgaon lost 15 per cent of their population. Channing has described the impact of famine on Gurgaon as such:

> ... large tracts of land formerly cultivated [were] lying waste, villages half deserted and in ruins, and the ill-clad appearance, of the surviving inhabitants bore witness to the impoverishment of the peasantry.[48]

These processes only emboldened the rich landowners who could pick up land at cheap rates and moneylenders facing a boon from the entrenched indebtedness of Gurgaon's landowners.[49] As farmers in the irrigated tracts in northwest Punjab were enriched by high global wheat and cotton prices, those elsewhere in Punjab were squeezed, many facing drought and famine already indebted to moneylenders and yoked to the monetised economy could only sell up, emigrate north or deepen their self-exploitation on the land. By the turn of the century, Gurgaon's farmers were the most indebted in the state, with a total debt of 300 lakh rupees,[50] at some thirty times the land revenue assessment.⁵¹ The iterative indebtedness of landowners in Gurgaon caused mass dispossession and transfer of land to moneylenders and rentier landlords. Indeed, the total area of land cultivated by tenants increased from 10 per cent in 1860 to 49 per cent of land in 1937.

The abandonment and purposeful wasting of Gurgaon is an outcome of the district's integration into the uneven colonial capitalist economy. The formation of capitalist agrarian social relations in Punjab can be thought of as a differentiated totality wherein the abstraction and standardisation of social forms, commodities and relations were paired with the concomitant expansion of mass differentiation across the state. It is precisely this process of differentiation, and the wasting of southern Punjab, when paired with the consolidation of land within a class of large rentier landowners, that acts as a central resource for the later capitalisation of land. As Gidwani and Maringanti have argued:

> The conditions of possibility of capitalist value lie in bodies, places, and things that come to be designated at the front end and back end of capitalism as waste. Waste is a vital, heterogeneous entity that must be effaced, enrolled, exported, or expunged.⁵²

Casting Property

Such devastation did not go unnoticed by more senior British officials. It was clear that British rule had brought about significant impoverishment by design, particularly in districts like Gurgaon. The deputy commissioner of Gurgaon J. R. Maconachie was particularly perturbed by the export of depleted grain reserves to Europe during the 1880s, writing that

> in the early months of 1888 stock of grain in Gurgaon was almost nil ... such distress means greater susceptibility to disease and consequent greater loss of life.⁵³

In addition, there was anxiety that the universal laws of Ricardian rent theory expressed in the Mahalwari settlement were not necessarily producing growth in state revenue.⁵⁴ As Chakravarty-Kaul argues, famines were viewed as a pressing critique of colonial agrarian policy, especially toward 'wastelands' – those areas of grazing, forest and fallow lands that had previously formed the socio-ecological foundation of rural life. Nevertheless, in the face of growing financial pressures falling from the Second Anglo-Afghan War (1878–80), the official position as stated in the Famine Commission, 1880, was that the devastation of Gurgaon was nothing to do with the revenue settlement nor the vicissitudes of the global economy. Rather, responding to what was becoming a crisis of successive failures in Gurgaon, the local British doubled down, blaming the district's plight on 'bad days' exacerbated by an unruly and lazy peasantry.

The official response was to offer temporary reductions but formally keep rates at current levels. Officials like Lyall returned to the founding Ricardian tenets of their agricultural policy, one that viewed the land's productivity not solely as an outcome of the 'power of the soil' or enhancements on the land but also on the 'habits and character' of the farmer. 'As a general rule,' writes B. T. Gibson, 'whatever be the nature of the soil he cultivates or the incidence of the revenue he pays [it is the] the caste of the agriculturalist, which determine his habits and customs and natural disposition will determine his economic condition.'[55] Considering the potential merits of reducing the revenue assessment in 1882, the Gurgaon district commissioner J. D. Tremlett exemplified the moral paternalism of British approaches to their pauperisation of Gurgaon:

> Constant watchfulness on the part of the local authorities ... appears to me what a district so situated as Gurgaon requires rather than a light assessment. The population is largely composed of improvident races placed under circumstances [of a light assessment] might well discourage even more thrifty and prudent ones.[56]

By the late nineteenth century however there was a growing anxiety related to the widespread indebtedness of Punjab's peasantry, and the increasingly powerful role so-called 'outsider' moneylenders were having on the sanctity of the village economy.

The Punjab Alienation Act, 1903, sought to intervene in the growing power of the urban moneylender over rural life and codify long-concocted caste categories into law. While existing legislation provided purchase and pre-emption rights to *anyone* with possession claims within the village, the Alienation Act circumscribed property transfers to a set of designated agricultural 'castes'. In the Alienation Act, the British took their own stories about cultural differences and legally coded them, affirming the propertied superiority of the Jats and in Gurgaon, the Ahirs. As Mahmood Mamdani notes, 'The genius of the British was not in inventing differences to exploit but in politicizing real and acknowledged differences by turning them into legal boundaries deemed inviolable and predicating security and economic benefits on locals' respect for these boundaries.'[57]

The restrictions laid out in the Alienation act strengthened the power of these designated agriculturalist 'castes' in Gurgaon, and in the years that followed the Act and subsequent Preemption Acts that extended pre-emption rights over village shares to agriculturalists, the land share of the Jats and Ahirs increased dramatically at the expense, not of urban moneylenders, but rather pastoralists and smallholding tenants.[58]

The Alienation Act in this way sharply accelerated processes of class differentiation among Punjab's peasantry. In 1877, 24 per cent of land was cultivated by tenants-at-will; by 1909 that number had risen to 39 per cent. Indeed, while the express intention of the act was to limit the influence of 'outsider' moneylenders in agrarian affairs, the act actively supported and consolidated the strength of agriculturalist moneylenders who could expand their property base at the expense of so-called non-agriculturalist lenders. As Frank Brayne notes of Gurgaon in 1925, 'Agriculturalist moneylenders … being unhindered by the Alienation of Land act … are continually buying up the land of their poor neighbours, and the tendency of these big men is to increase their estates at the expense of the smaller.'[59] The Gurgaon district had a particularly high number of moneylenders; by 1928 there were 458 agricultural moneylenders, the second highest in the entire state of Punjab.[60] Indeed, despite grave concerns over indebtedness in Gurgaon that was driving dispossession of smallholding farmers and landless workers, colonial officers wrote of their relief that much of the mortgaged land was going to more 'prosperous' agriculturalists and not outsiders.

What was an iterative process of land expropriation by dominant agricultural proprietors – at the expense of small and medium farmers, tenants and pastoralists – at the advent of revenue settlement became concretised in a landed elite heavily protected by the British by the early to mid-1900s. By the end of British rule not only was there caste differentiation between 'agriculturalist castes' with a monopoly on land, and Dalit and landless communities who made up the agricultural workforce, but also a sharp class distinction *within* 'caste' communities, between those large landowners who had used the Alienation Act to expand their rentier- and credit-base, and those small and medium cultivators who, in Gurgaon in particular, were turning to waged labour.

And so, while ostensibly designed to target urban moneylenders, the Alienation Act's most significant legacy was to consolidate property and territorial power within the large landowners and effect the legal dispossession of so-called 'non-agricultural' castes, predominately Dalits.[61] In Gurgaon and southern Haryana, this benefitted the Jats and Ahirs. These caste constructions were of course deeply contested and undermined by off-the-books, *benami* transfers between statutory non-agricultural landholders.[62] Nevertheless, if at the start of British colonial rule Punjab was a state characterised by heterogeneous communities of small peasant proprietors, by the end of British rule it was one marked by stark differentiation between and within agrarian caste communities. It was this dramatic transformation of class relations, an attendant politics of caste identity that conscripted political support for agrarian capitalism among otherwise marginal farmers, and the attendant devastation of the district of Gurgaon that lay the foundations for the Gurgaon model at the end of the twentieth century.

The Gurgaon Experiment

Eighty years before the implementation of the 'Gurgaon model' of urbanisation, Gurgaon was the site of a different experiment in socio-economic development. In 1929, the *Times of India* wrote of an 'experiment' taking place in Gurgaon, a 'handicapped' district of southern Punjab. The experiment, the article writes, 'aims at nothing less than a complete remodelling of the social and economic life of village India';[63] the experiment was tasked with constructing what the *Times* called, with some prescience, 'the New India'. Why was Gurgaon chosen for such an experiment? The 'Gurgaon Experiment' was a programme of rural development led by zealous British administrator Francis Brayne who, faced with the devastation wrought on Gurgaon by over a century of extractive British rule, diagnosed a series of technological and moral fixes – from water wells, manure composting and land enclosures, to the training of 'better ideals of living' associated with rationality, austerity and hard work. Not dissimilar from contemporary neoliberal development programmes that remedy impoverishment with entrepreneurship, self-discipline and exploitation, the experiment wedded ideas about civic prosperity to individual discipline and market integration.

The devastation of Gurgaon by colonial settlement, much like the 'backwardness' of K. P. Singh's Gurgaon of the 1980s, disturbed British liberal sentiments and justification for rule. Liberalism was deployed, as a number of scholars have argued, in the early twentieth century in part to reconcile the violence of colonial enclosures and extractivism with supposedly 'universal' conditions of liberty and freedom. As Lisa Lowe writes, the liberal tradition authorised 'the differentiated power of government over "backward peoples"' by recuperating colonial despotism as the necessary force to train colonial subjects 'unfit for liberty' in the moral, social and economic conducts of western modernity.[64] The experiment chiefly seeks to reconcile extant devastation of colonial uneven development with an ongoing justification for British rule.[65] The Gurgaon experiment is a direct expression of this colonial anxiety to enjoin liberty with exploitation, as the *Times* article notes:

> The value of Gurgaon is that it [shows] a practical and acceptable way of helping to remodel the social and economic system of village India and prepare the villager for their part we intend him to play in the future administration of his country … either it is the duty or not of Great Britain, as the arbiter of India's destiny, to assist in the social regeneration of that country. If it is not then condemn Gurgaon and forget about it…. If India is to remain a happy and contented member of the British Commonwealth of nations village 'uplift' must be spread all over India.[66]

Of course, neither the ruinous land settlement programmes enacted upon Gurgaon by colonial rulers, mass indebtedness and dispossession nor the programmes of enclosure that centralised property within the hands of the large creditors featured in Brayne's writings on Gurgaon. Rather, Gurgaon's impoverishment was explained by racialised and caste-based improvidence and fecklessness of the 'Indian peasant'. In terms that are echoed some seventy years later by neoliberal writers like Gurcharan Das, a new India would be built upon an ethos of do-it-yourself self-reliance, austerity and enterprise.

Brayne notes upon his arrival in the district that the people of Gurgaon were 'desperately dirty and unhealthy, with no conscious desire for anything better'.[67] Bracketing an interrogation of the violence of British settlement, the experiment instead presents Gurgaon's poverty as a consequence of the moral and intellectual incapacity to self-govern written into the Indian peasants themselves. Brayne, in characteristic racism of liberal colonialists, claimed Gurgaon's fate was the outcome of 'improvident', lazy, 'desperately dirty' 'races'.

And so, rather than attend to the underdevelopment of Gurgaon,[68] Brayne sought to 'train' Gurgaon residents in a whole manner of self-help practices that largely eschewed, and at points directly exacerbated the structural conditions of their poverty. Brayne's 'uplift' programmes indeed often discouraged technological innovations that would breed 'laziness' and prosperity rather than toil and suffering. Take as one example Brayne's opposition to canal irrigation, so essential to the wealth of farmers and extractive agrarian economies in the north of the state. Brayne believed canal irrigation would enrich Gurgaon's residents and make them lazy. So instead he implemented a programme of costly well irrigation, that was hard work, easily exhausted and the costs of which essentially prohibited cultivation required for residents to sustain themselves. As Clive Dewey notes, nearly all of Brayne's moralised technological innovations exacerbated Gurgaon's poverty. He also, importantly like many of his contemporaries, implored the practice of land enclosure and the virtues of private property ownership. The subdivision of land would later be central to the erosion of the village commons, and awkward conversion of customary land tenures into private property. The mass dispossession and indebtedness that enclosure caused in Gurgaon does not meet the pages of Brayne's various pamphlets on village improvement.

In lieu of popular support for his madcap schemes, Brayne instead had to rely upon 'soft power' tactics. He set out on a rather eccentric programme of propaganda in an attempt to influence and inculcate the conduct of Gurgaon residents to the virtues of liberal capitalism. He employed sages to wander the village imploring residents to enclose their lands, bury dung cakes for manure and install windows in their houses through song and poetry; he published newsletters and pamphlets; he even produced a film, *A Tale of Gurgaon, or Heaven Helps Those Who Help Themselves*, that was screened across the village. At the heart of Brayne's programme was a commitment to an ideology of utilitarian political economy which argued that through toil, self-discipline and property alone the Indian villager could traverse adversity and become a fledging capitalist, inaugurated into modernity. As Brayne wrote:

> Development therefore means first and foremost uplift. Teaching the people how to spend their money, how to clean their homes and villages, how to make their homes healthy and comfortable, how to avoid ill health and epidemics, how to bring up their girls and boys in

health and cleanliness, how to educate them and how to lead happy, healthy and rational lives.[69]

Brayne's 'experiment' in Gurgaon had little support from a government that was happily squeezing Indian agriculture and drawing army recruits from populations looking for a way out. Malcolm Darling's later report on the experiment noted that most changes had been superficial, with understandably few villagers adopting his recommendations.[70] In 1929, the very same years as the celebratory article in the *Times of India*, M. K. Gandhi remarked that the experiment had been 'virtually a failure'.[71]

The experiment's failures aside, the methods and ideology deployed by Brayne would be incredibly influential and no doubt prescient of later agrarian development projects in this corner of north India. The experiment constructed particular ideas of the village as a platform for a new kind of rural society, one in which enterprising villagers work gridded, rationalised fields and live in fruitful harmony among village banks, hospitals and schools – the modern institutions that express the founding tenets of 'modern' civic life. As Brayne later claimed, the experiment was 'here to stay, not only in Gurgaon but in India at large'.[72] As we see in the following chapters, Gurgaon's villages would, around eighty years later, play host to different modes of civic modernity, one driven by similar principles of enterprise, rationality and liberal capitalism.

Programmes of 'village uplift' like those in Gurgaon should also be viewed within a context in which the British government was being increasingly forced to justify their ongoing despotism in India; 'uplift' gave force to the idea that if India was to progress along the civilisational march of history, it would need the expertise in the government of the British. Uplift arrives as a key saviour of British rule in India, a driving normative force that reconciled increasingly apparent failures of British colonial interventions to improve the lives of people with the impossibility of India's development in the absence of British expertise.

This central anxiety, expressed in the experiment, is that the 'content' of the Indian nation be tied to the ongoing presence and expert guidance of the British. The Gurgaon experiment is of course strikingly similar to the Gurgaon model. Not only do both act as a technological remedy to the underdevelopment of Gurgaon, but they also prescribe heavy doses of liberalism, individual resilience and market integration to such underdevelopment. As Brayne's 'experiment' demonstrates, the problem of capitalist development in this small corner of northern India has long been occupied by a twin movement of establishing conditions of uneven development while mobilising various ideological and normative projects that seek to enlist people into market rule.

Post-colonial Modernisation

The post-colonial period set questions of agricultural development under an entirely different footing. Nevertheless, the trappings of liberal modernisation that justified late colonial rule and sought in the name of 'development' to come to terms with the inevitable limits and contradictions to colonial capital accumulation were inherited by the post-colonial leadership after 1948.

Post-Independence rural Punjab was characterised by socially and territorially dominant communities of self-cultivating peasants – Jats and, in Gurgaon, Ahirs – who were nevertheless starkly class differentiated. According to Naved Hamid, by the end of British rule less than 4 per cent of the agricultural population owned more than half of the land in Punjab[73] – a divide that not only sharply cut between self-cultivating landowning castes, tenant farmers and landless caste communities but also one that produced stark class differences within supposedly unitary Jats and Ahirs. To this, the new *kisan* movements in north India, most keenly expressed in the politics of Jat leader and one-time prime minister Charan Singh, and the powerful BKU, which came to reify and mobilise the unity of cultivating Jats, Ahirs, Gujars and Rajputs[74] in ways that glossed over class divisions and promoted the class interests of the large landowners, and soon-to-be agrarian capitalists, under the veil of caste identity.[75]

The new political leaders of post-colonial Punjab oversaw two agrarian policies that would dramatically alter the fortunes of the newly partitioned state. First, the consolidation and gridding of landholdings across the state, and second, the introduction of the Intensive Agricultural Development Programme (IADP), otherwise known as the Green Revolution. Together these policies created the material conditions for Gurgaon's urbanisation from the 1980s.

The post-colonial period set questions of agricultural development under entirely different nationalist and democratic conditions. The partition of Punjab had left Indian 'East Punjab' worse off. West Punjab, now in Pakistan, had the canal colonies and 70 per cent of the canal-irrigated districts, while the violent upheaval and movement of people had left an imbalance in the amount of cultivatable land to population. The rehabilitation of Partition refugees would involve a mass project of land valuation, redistribution and standardisation across the state with far-reaching effects beyond the immediate scope of this chapter.[76] This programme gave immediate impetus to a project to standardise and grid land in east Punjab. The fragmented and scattered composition of landholdings in Punjab had long been viewed as an obstacle to agrarian modernisation by the British. The assistant commissioner of Punjab in the early 1990s Malcolm Darling campaigned for rural land enclosure, arguing that persistent customary landholding forms that produce a fragmented cartography of land ownership 'block the way [to development] … it cannot be too often repeated that, till landholdings are consolidated, no great advance can be made'.[77] Without large-scale land consolidation, bounding and enclosure, the British believed their mission to modernise the 'improvident' Indian peasant, consolidate territorial power and crucially, extract agricultural revenues would remain forever partial. The socio-economic logic of the fragment, one that allowed farmers to spread risks and hedge bets on unpredictable harvest ill-fitted the modernist and calculative logics of late colonial rule. Fragments formed what Bhattacharya notes as the 'the anchor around which peasant lives often moved'.[78] In this context, British *colonial* ambitions to remove the fragment and consolidate landholdings were never fulfilled. While the countryside was studiously mapped, bounded and recorded by colonial bureaucrats, the gridding and consolidation of fragmented land plots were largely limited to the 'canal colonies' in districts of central Punjab in modern-day Pakistan.

If colonial rule failed to fully consolidate land into rationalised parcels, post-Independence government of Punjab, facing pressures to resettle millions of refugees and compensate them in kind for land lost, took a more aggressive approach (Figures 1.1 and 1.2). With rhetoric that near mirrored the developmentalist ideology of their colonial predecessors, one of the first acts of the newly independent Punjab parliament, passed unanimously, bestowed powers upon a consolidation officer within the revenue department to undertake the compulsory gridding and consolidation of all land. While the total land consolidated under colonial projects surmounted to just 700,000 acres up to 1947, between 1948 and 1966, the post-Independence Punjab government had completed the consolidation of over 22 million acres of land, reorganising the vast majority of the Punjab countryside into

The Experiment | 73

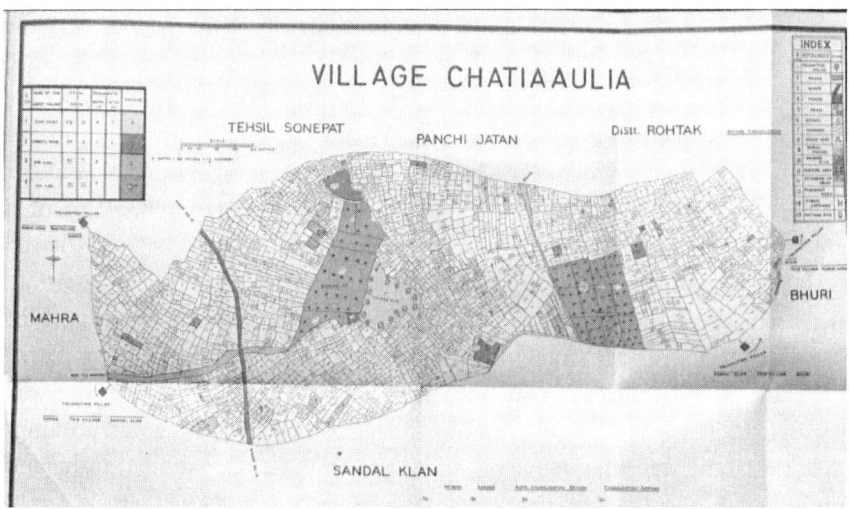

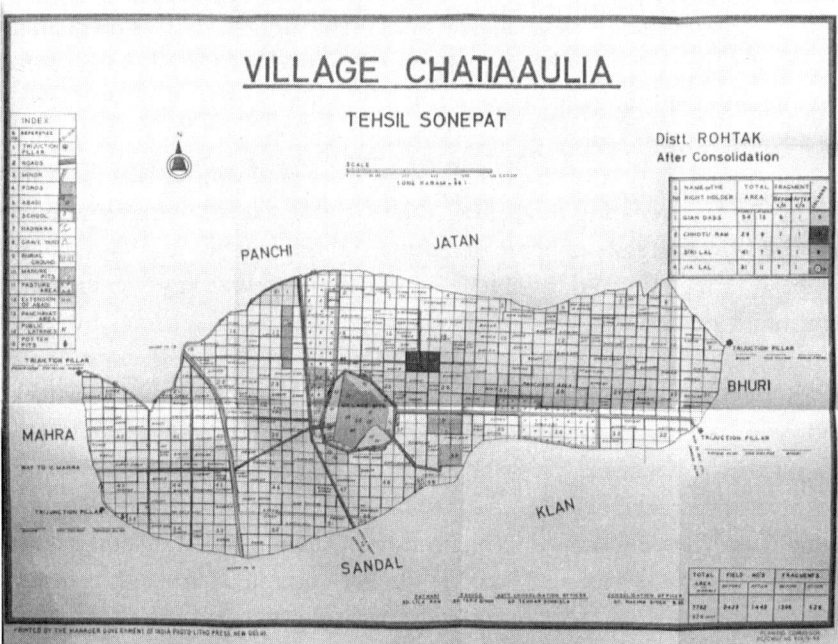

Figures 1.1 and 1.2   Pre- and post-consolidation cadastral map of Chatia Aulia village, Sonepat, Haryana

Source: Planning Commission, India, 'Consolidation of Holdings (Methods and Problems)' (New Delhi: Manager of Publications, 1957).

rectangular 27.5-acre village grids, each composed of twenty-five, 1.1-acre consolidated squares. This significant re-territorialization of Punjab (which in 1966 split into three separate states: Punjab, Himachal Pradesh and Haryana), worked to establish the modernist authority of private property, obscuring the historic uses and claims on land, and elevating the rectangle to an abstract, bureaucratic category able to be intervened in and disposed of in any number of ways.

Consolidation programmes, brought in under the East Punjab Holdings (Consolidation and Prevention of Fragmentation) Act, 1948 (hereafter, the Holdings Act), fundamentally altered the territorial and legal substance of property. It also radically transformed the landscape of the nascent state, involving fencing land, repositioning village residential lands and commons, digging trenches, manoeuvring hills and ponds. Consolidation was a project of mass abstraction and calculation, how to value and convert highly divergent lands (soil type, productivity, irrigation, improvements, location) and compensate landowners who lose out in the process. Consolidators were engaged in pricing trees, ponds, *bund*s and hills that could be exchanged in the process of rectangularising land. This process reposed land as a strictly financial asset, one that could accrue rents and command value. It was under these conditions that land was repackaged as a platform for real-estate-led urbanisation, preparing the land as calculable, knowable, visible and easily amenable to processes of homogenisation and fragmentation.

The burgeoning landed elite – Jats and Ahirs – were key benefactors of consolidation schemes. The majority of consolidation schemes extended villages' cultivatable areas substantially by reclassifying former forest, grazing and wasteland (previously included in the *shamlat*) as cultivatable. While most schemes did reserve non-alienable common lands (*shamlat deh*) to enable the extension of residential areas, the construction of roads and schools, other schemes replaced the traditional commons with new land uses altogether. These include lands reserved for revenue-generating purposes for village *panchayat*s and additional lands 'for common purposes' that were effectively leased to the *panchayat* from landowners. These processes of consolidation significantly extended the privatisation of the commons, but in doing so it also multiplied its tenurial forms. The commons, or what is known as *shamlat deh*, came to refer to a whole host of varied 'common' lands that, in the current conjuncture, have shaded certain lands with a degree of ambiguity in ways that present an opportunity to land prospectors and developers. As

I return to this in Chapter 3, these new layerings of property – of exclusion, authority and access[79] – have given ammunition to dominant actors to stake property claims on urban frontier and produce *de facto* property.

Needless to say, such a significant reorganisation of key land-based assets, essential to the social reproduction of the vast majority of the population, did not unfold neatly and without opposition: land consolidation and rectangularisation schemes were major village events and were intensely disputed and negotiated, leading many subversions and delay. Consolidation workers had to rely upon the trigonometrical survey markers laid during the colonial period, many of which had since been moved or destroyed in acts of rebellion to British calculation. Without these survey marks, land remeasurements and rectangularisation premised on existing holdings proved difficult and often swayed by existing social power dynamics of Haryanvi villages. In many cases, villagers objected to the land valuations, felling of trees and filling of bunds that rectangularisation demanded.[80] Densely plotted villages, undulating hills, filled ponds and desertified fields all proved difficult to consolidate, all proved difficult to consolidate, and many villages remain unconsolidated to this day. As I return to this in Chapter 4, perhaps the most significant compromise written into the consolidation process was the endurance of the share system in landholdings in which the vast majority of landowners own shares in rural property jointly. The presence of tens of thousands of unmapped shares hidden within state maps thus disrupts any notion of clear state sight that consolidation schemes sought to establish, and in the post-liberalisation era has come to shape forces of territorial flexibility so crucial to real estate markets.

Finally, the capacity for the private sector to acquire large land banks across Gurgaon in the 1970s and 1980s can be partly explained by the incomplete implementation of agrarian reforms in the aftermath of Independence. The Haryana Ceiling of Landholdings Act, 1972, was intended to prevent land monopolisation and redistribute surpluses to tenant farmers and landless communities. Not only was the act only partially implemented from the late 1970s, but also the Government of Haryana iteratively stripped back regulations that limited or put checks on large landownership, including elements of the Punjab Pre-emption Act, 1913, that gave pre-emption rights to family members. The partiality of post-colonial agrarian reforms is an essential component of real estate and labour markets discussed in the following chapters.

Green Revolution

Consolidation allowed for the extension of tube well irrigation and by converting so-called 'waste' lands substantially increased the cultivatable, thereby privately owned landholdings across the state. This lay the foundations for Green Revolution technologies in the mid-1960s. The Green Revolution, or IADP, involved the adoption of high-yield variety seeds, fertilizers and lift-irrigation technologies rolled out in north India with the view to increasing agricultural production. The Green Revolution transformed the uncertain agrarian fortunes of east Punjab, which was carved into three states – Punjab, Himachal Pradesh and Haryana in 1966. The combination of high-yield variety seeds, commercial credit options, and government subsidies on lift-irrigation infrastructure allowed medium and large landowners to significantly increase both overall landholding size and cultivation, and many began both taking back land previously leased out to tenants, and leasing and buying in land from smaller farmers. As Jodhka has argued, the influx of capital-intensive technologies transformed the tenure structure across Haryana, previously characterised by mixtures of owner- and tenant-cultivated land; the Green Revolution brought through a significant increase in the size of large privately owned landholdings. Indeed between 1976 and 2001, the amount of land held on joint tenures increased from 42 to 70 per cent. The territorial expansion of large landowners and increased demand for farm labour to keep up with high-yield seeds and multi-cropping practices, pushed small and tenant farmers off their lands and into debt tied labour contracts with larger landowners.[81] Among other things, the Green Revolution accelerated processes of dispossession and proletarianisation started under colonial agrarian policy[82] as marginal self-cultivators were pushed off their lands and turned into debt-bound wage labourers.[83] By integrating landowners into networks of commercial credit and agricultural surpluses, the Green Revolution took the cream of Haryana's 'thrifty' and 'prudent' Jats and Ahirs – established under colonial rule – and transformed them into capitalist farmers knitted to broader networks of credit, labour and production.

The Green Revolution is considered a success in Punjab and Haryana; today farmers across the two states have consolidated control over agrarian modernisation and produce 60 per cent of India's commercial foodgrains. The ideological and material work that went into cultivating the Jats and

Ahirs as a modern capitalist class of peasant proprietors in the colonial period is consolidated by the Green Revolution.

Amidst these dramatic changes in political-economic relations of property and production in Haryana, the consolidated territorial authority of the agrarian elites, predominately the Jats, but also the Ahirs in Gurgaon, equally translated to political and cultural hegemony. As early as the 1920s, Chhotu Ram's pro-British Unionist Party took advantage of the Alienation Act, to bring together the cultivating Jats, Ahirs, Gujars and Rajputs as a homogenous political constituency across Punjab and lobby their interests with the British. Due to the dominance of Jats and Ahirs in the political scene, Haryana became known as 'Jat-land', notorious for the political power of its conservative *khap panchayats*,[84] the state-elected chief ministers from the Jat community in nearly all state elections from Haryana's inception up until 2014.[85] The hegemonic coalition between the state and agrarian landowning communities in Haryana would come to play an important role from the 1970s.

Yet the impact of the Green Revolution, even among landowners, generally accreted onto already existing uneven development across the state. In an all too familiar pattern, the irrigated districts of Haryana (Karnal and Panipat) accessed the lion's share of Green Revolution technologies. Large landowning families were able to access agrarian capital inputs, consolidate territory and diversify surpluses into moneylending and other commercial activities. By comparison, Gurgaon remained one of the most impoverished and least irrigated districts in the state right up until the 1980s.[86] For what technological input did occur, much was allocated to the already existing large landowners who could access to initial credit and capital. Gurgaon's exclusion from the fruits of the Green Revolution distinguishes the case from the kinds of agrarian urbanisation that has been shown to layer onto Green Revolution capital elsewhere in the country. In Gurgaon it was precisely low land values that encouraged landowners to sell out from the 1980s. The district's exclusion also led to many landowning and landless farming communities diversifying out of agriculture, towards urban, industrial and pastoral employment linked to the Gurgaon and Delhi town economy. This shift of rural populations to urban centres, and the peripheries of New Delhi, prompted the urban planning legislation that came to form the Gurgaon model. 'Planning an orderly and balanced growth of urban centres in Haryana,' writes the *Times of India* in 1976 a year after the HDRUA is passed, is essential 'due to the fact that for some years villagers rendered idle by mechanisation of farming … have been migrating to industrial towns along the Delhi border in search of work'.[87] In early premonition of what was to come, the article reports that the Haryana government was planning a new sub-regional plan that would 'open up' Gurgaon to infrastructural development.

The devaluation of Gurgaon and its designation as a 'backward' region set the conditions for private capital to pick up cheap land and enlist propertied classes with few avenues to diversify into the logics of market-led growth. As Damodaran argues, the relative profitability of agriculture in Haryana and Punjab up until the 1990s, paired with the consolidation of commodity and money markets by other groups, left few avenues for the diversification of agrarian surpluses that have spurred agrarian city-building and industrialisation projects elsewhere.[88] The agrarian cooperatives in western Maharashtra, as Sai Balakrishnan writes, led a transition from sugar to real estate that drove the urbanisation of Magarpatta City. Of course, in Gurgaon, landowners neither had very profitable land nor surpluses to diversify, and agrarian cooperatives had not taken off in Haryana as they had done elsewhere across the country. What took place in Gurgaon then was a consolidation of property among the large landowners without the kinds of agricultural commercialisation, uptick in labour demand, nor incumbent rise in land prices that were seen in the north of the state. Gurgaon's land was rationalised and gridded, consolidated within socially dominant landowning communities, but remained cheap and as such landowners were amenable to parting with it at the right price. In the post-liberalisation era, as new forms of rentier and finance capital superseded agrarian capital, and the value of land itself became more valuable than the production that took place upon it, Gurgaon's neatly gridded, cheap fields became prime targets of urbanisation.

CONCLUSION

In this chapter, I have attempted to reoccupy the 'Gurgaon model' with the circuits of colonial uneven development, agrarian class formulation and liberal ideology that have animated neoliberal projects of urbanisation. Across each of the moments discussed in this chapter, from the neoliberal back to the colonial and post-colonial, Gurgaon has been subject to the vicissitudes of uneven agrarian capitalist development and various ideological and territorial strategies to assimilate local populations and institutions into the norms of market rule. The celebrated 'Gurgaon model' is not only a product of the longer uneven geographies of liberal capitalism that married political-economic waste with individual improvement but it also replicates its founding beliefs.

The partnerships discussed in this book between corporate capital and the agrarian world that characterise Gurgaon's emergence as the vanguard of a 'new urban India' have their foundations in the colonial settlement of Gurgaon's villages and pursuit of an agrarian landed elite, while the swift movement of corporate capital into rural land has been pre-empted by both the devalorisation and then gridding of rural property across colonial and post-colonial rule. In order to understand both the rapid private-sector-led urbanisation of Gurgaon and its deep vesting in the agrarian world requires attention to these longer histories of territorial intervention and experimentation. The next set of questions relate to how the property regimes and class formations forged through the colonial and post-colonial periods have been deployed in the present. How is it that the village and proprietary body come to mediate capital's largely unopposed capture and conversion of rural land into real estate, and how has this process transformed agrarian landowning classes? It is these questions that I turn to in the following chapter.

Notes

1. Shatkin and Vidyarthi, 'Introduction'.
2. In short, were Gurgaon a socially, economically, ecologically prosperous region, with a socio-economic structure akin to north Punjab, the myth of the frontier and the likelihood of acquisition would perhaps never have materialised. This brings the subject of the capitalist agrarian landowner to the fore.
3. Harvey, 'From Managerialism to Entrepreneurialism'.
4. Banerjee-Guha, 'Neoliberalising the "Urban"'.
5. Ghertner, *Rule by Aesthetics*; Balakrishnan, *Shareholder Cities*.
6. Roy, 'The Blockade of the World-Class City', 263.
7. Levien, 'The Politics of Dispossession'.
8. Bhajan Lal was initially elected from the Janata Party but defected in 1980 to the Indian National Congress following Indira Gandhi's rise to power and became a central figure in Congress's new economic reforms in the 1980s and 1990s. See Damodaran, *India's New Capitalists*; Namburu, *Moguls of Real Estate*.

9. See Chatterjee, *The Politics of the Governed*; Fernandes, 'The Politics of Forgetting'; Srivastava, *Entangled Urbanism*.
10. Das, *India Grows at Night*, 26.
11. Levien, *Dispossession without Development*.
12. A *khap panchayat* is a caste-based community organisation typically representing Jats. The *khap panchayat* oversees local inter-caste community issues and is notable for exerting social control and pressure within Jat-dominated villages. *Khap panchayats* have no relationship to village-level elected councils, *panchayats*.
13. Balagopal, 'An Ideology for the Provincial Propertied Class'.
14. This class of rich peasants, for Balagopal, are 'provincial' insofar as their movements of capital remain bound to rentier circuits of accumulation across certain regions.
15. Levien, *Dispossession without Development*.
16. And these two acts were not alone in shaping Gurgaon's modern trajectory. As Shubhra Gururani notes, the absence of an implementing agency for the urban land ceiling acts in Haryana, one of the final vestiges of post-colonial redistributive land policy, allowed the private sector to amass large land banks in Gurgaon amidst a political context in neighbouring Delhi entirely disposed to limiting land monopolisation. The 3,500-acre DLF City developed from the 1980s simply would not have been permitted elsewhere.
17. Levien, 'The Politics of Dispossession', 463.
18. Balakrishnan, *Shareholder Cities*; Kalaiyarasan and Vijayabaskar, 'Why Does the "Provincial Propertied Class" Remain Provincial?'.
19. Brenner, 'Implosions'.
20. Sankhe et al., *India's Urban Awakening*.
21. Bhattacharya, *The Great Agrarian Conquest*, 53.
22. Bhattacharya, *The Great Agrarian Conquest*.
23. Ibid, 53.
24. Gohit, *Social and Economic History of Modern India*, 138.
25. Chakravarty-Kaul, 'Two Centuries on the Commons', 11.
26. Channing and Wilson, *Land Revenue Settlement*, 44.
27. Ibid.
28. Bhattacharya, *The Great Agrarian Conquest*, 72.
29. The conditions of famine and drought across Gurgaon exacerbated the squeeze on smallholders' land and the ease at which larger landowners could eat up indebted land.
30. A position that aligns with John Locke's understanding of property. For Locke, an individual owns something only insofar as their labour vests value in it.

31. Bhattacharya, *The Great Agrarian Conquest*, 167.
32. Malcolm Darling in *The Punjab Peasant* writes that the 'restless life of the camp and the jungle has always appealed to them more than the settled life of the farm and the village'.
33. Prakash, 'The Colonial Genealogy', 86.
34. Darling, *The Punjab Peasant in Prosperity and Debt*; emphasis mine.
35. 'One explanation of these violent contrasts in character is that adversity either strengthens or weakens. The Ahir and the Jat are instances of the one, the Meo and the Rajput of the other.' See Darling, *The Punjab Peasant*, 94.
36. Commander, 'The Jajmani System'.
37. Ollman, *Dance of the Dialectic*.
38. Planning Commission, 'Consolidation of Holdings'.
39. The district was iteratively 'settled' between 1836 and 1841.
40. Channing and Wilson, *Land Revenue Settlement*, 96.
41. Goswami, *Producing India*.
42. Davis, *Late Victorian Holocausts*.
43. Hamid, 'Dispossession and Differentiation'.
44. Chakravarty-Kaul describes how by the 1860s the British consciously looked to enhance taxation on the village commons.
45. Whitcombe, *Agrarian Conditions*.
46. Dewey, *Anglo-Indian Attitudes*, 64.
47. Channing and Wilson, *Land Revenue Settlement*.
48. Ibid., 183.
49. As ground rents in many places tended to be higher than revenue assessments (that were tied to productivity), landowners began to draw income from leasing land, rather than cultivating it, and were incentivised to reinvest rental surpluses into extending their property base at the expense of smaller landowners. Despite the express intentions of settlement officers in Punjab, the revenue settlements produced a class of dominant rentier landlords.
50. Lakh is a unit following in the South Asian numbering system, where 1 lakh=100,000.
51. Dewey, *Anglo-Indian Attitudes*.
52. Gidwani and Maringanti, 'The Waste-Value Dialectic', 125.
53. Zurbrigg, 'Hunger and Epidemic', 2.
54. Chakravarty-Kaul, 'The Commons, Community and the Courts'.
55. Channing and Wilson, *Land Revenue Settlement*, 41.
56. Ibid., 88–89.
57. Mamdani, *Neither Settler nor Native*, 12–13.
58. Chowdhry, 'The Advantages of Backwardness'.

59. Brayne, Correspondence to Commissioner Ambala Division, 28th March 1925.
60. Chowdhry, 'The Advantages of Backwardness', 334.
61. Cassan, 'Law and Identity Manipulation', argues that British officers sought to restrict attempts of Dalits to gain status as agriculturalists.
62. Ibid.
63. Times of India, 'The Gurgaon Scheme', 8.
64. Lowe, The Intimacies of Four Continents, 112.
65. Gidwani, Capital, Interrupted.
66. Times of India, 'The Gurgaon Scheme'.
67. Brayne, 'Village Uplift in India'.
68. We would of course not expect a British colonial officer to attend to the violence of colonialism nor is it possible for colonisers to resolve the violence of colonialism short of reparations and self-abolition.
69. Notes on Gurgaon development, London, British Library, Brayne Papers, MSS Eur F152/29.
70. Darling, 'Rusticus Loquitur'.
71. Gandhi, The Village Reconstruction.
72. Brayne, The Remaking of Village India.
73. Hamid, 'Dispossession and Differentiation of the Peasantry'.
74. Jaffrelot and Kalaiyarasan, 'The Political Economy of the Jat Agitation', 30.
75. This coalition was of course never entirely coherent, particularly after the implementation of the Mandal Commission recommendations.
76. Kudaisya, 'The Demographic Upheaval'.
77. Darling, The Punjab Peasant, 185.
78. Bhattacharya, The Great Agrarian Conquest.
79. Hall, Hirsch and Li, 'Introduction to Powers'.
80. Planning Commission, Consolidation of Holdings.
81. Bhalla, 'Changes in Acreage, 1962–72'.
82. Jodhka, 'Caste and Power'; Bhalla, 'Liberalisation, Rural Labour Markets'.
83. Banaji, Theory as History.
84. Teltumbde, 'Haryana's Rapist Regime'.
85. With the exceptions of Bhajan Lal (1972, 1982, 1991) and Manohar Lal Khattar (2014).
86. Paul, 'Green Revolution and Poverty'.
87. Nath, 'Haryana's Part of Capital Region Development Plans', 6.
88. Damodaran, India's New Capitalists.

Bibliography

Balagopal, K. 'An Ideology for the Provincial Propertied Class'. *Economic and Political Weekly* 22, nos. 36–37 (September 1987): 1544–1546.

Balakrishnan, Sai. *Shareholder Cities: Land Transformations along Urban Corridors in India*. Philadelphia: University of Pennsylvania Press, 2019.

Banaji, Jairus. *Theory as History: Essays on Modes of Production and Exploitation*. Leiden: Brill, 2010.

Banerjee-Guha, Swapna. 'Neoliberalising the "Urban": New Geographies of Power and Injustice in Indian Cities'. *Economic and Political Weekly* 44, no. 22 (May–June 2009): 95–107.

Bhalla, Sheila. 'Changes in Acreage and Tenure Structure of Land Holdings in Haryana, 1962–72'. *Economic and Political Weekly* 12, no. 13 (1977): A2–A15.

———. 'Liberalisation, Rural Labour Markets and the Mobilisation of Farm Workers: The Haryana Story in an All-India Context'. *Journal of Peasant Studies* 26, no. 2–3 (1999): 25–70.

Bhattacharya, Neeladri. *The Great Agrarian Conquest: The Colonial Reshaping of a Rural World*. Albany: SUNY Press, 2019.

Brayne, F. L. F. L. Brayne, DC Gurgaon to Commissioner Ambala Division, No. 127, 28 March 1925. Punjab Home (Judicial) Department Proceedings, January 1927, 6, IOR P/11649, 1925.

Brayne, Frank Lugard. *The Remaking of Village India*. Vol. 2. Oxford: Oxford University Press, 1929.

———. *Village Uplift in India*. Allahabad: Pioneer Press, 1928.

Brenner, Neil. 'Implosions'. In *Explosions: Towards a Study of Planetary Urbanization*. Berlin: Jovis, 2013.

Cassan, Guilhem. 'Law and Identity Manipulation: Evidence from a Natural Experiment in Colonial Punjab'. Paper presented at the Lisbon meeting on Institutions and Political Economy, 8–9 September 2011, Institute of Social Sciences of the University of Lisbon and the Nova School of Business and Economics, Lisbon.

Chakravarty-Kaul, Minoti. 'The Commons, Community and the Courts of Colonial Punjab'. *Indian Economic and Social History Review* 29, no. 4 (1992): 393–436.

———. 'Two Centuries on the Commons: The Punjab'. n.d.

Channing, F. C., and J. Wilson. *Land Revenue Settlement of the Gurgaon District, 1882*. Lahore: Central Jail Press.

Chatterjee, Partha. *The Politics of the Governed: Reflections on Popular Politics in Most of the World*. New York: Columbia University Press, 2004.

Chowdhry, Prem. 'The Advantages of Backwardness: Colonial Policy and Agriculture in Haryana'. *Indian Economic and Social History Review* 23, no. 3 (1986): 263–88.

Commander, Simon. 'The Jajmani System in North India: An Examination of Its Logic and Status across Two Centuries'. *Modern Asian Studies* 17, no. 2 (1983): 283–311.

Damodaran, Harish. *India's New Capitalists: Caste, Business, and Industry in a Modern Nation*. Gurugram: Hachette India, 2018.

Darling, Malcolm Lyall. *The Punjab Peasant in Prosperity and Debt*. Oxford: H. Milford, Oxford University Press, 1925.

———. *Rusticus Loquitur, or the Old Light and the New in the Punjab Village*. Oxford: H. Milford, Oxford University Press, 1930.

Das, Gurcharan. *India Grows at Night*. New Delhi: Penguin, 2013.

Davis, Mike. *Late Victorian Holocausts: El Niño Famines and the Making of the Third World*. London: Verso Books, 2002.

Dewey, Clive. *Anglo-Indian Attitudes: Mind of the Indian Civil Service*. London: A&C Black, 1993.

Fernandes, Leela. 'The Politics of Forgetting: Class Politics, State Power and the Restructuring of Urban Space in India'. *Urban Studies* 41, no. 12 (November 2004): 2415–30. https://doi.org/10.1080/00420980412331297609.

Gandhi, Mahatma. *The Village Reconstruction*. Bombay: Bharatiya Vidya Bhavan, 1966.

Ghertner, D. Asher. *Rule by Aesthetics: World-Class City Making in Delhi*. New York: Oxford University Press, 2015.

Gidwani, Vinay K. *Capital, Interrupted: Agrarian Development and the Politics of Work in India*. Minneapolis: University of Minnesota Press, 2008.

Gidwani, Vinay, and Anant Maringanti. 'The Waste-Value Dialectic Lumpen Urbanization in Contemporary India'. *Comparative Studies of South Asia, Africa and the Middle East* 36, no. 1 (2016): 112–33.

Gohit, Rohit Kumar. *Social and Economic History of Modern India*. Meerut: Murari Lal & Son Publications, 2007.

Goswami, Manu. *Producing India*. Chicago; London: University of Chicago Press, 2004.

Hall, Derek, Philip Hirsch and Tania M. Li. *Powers of Exclusion: Land Dilemmas in Southeast Asia*. Honolulu: University of Hawaii Press, 2011.

Hamid, Naved. 'Dispossession and Differentiation of the Peasantry in the Punjab during Colonial Rule'. *Journal of Peasant Studies* 10, no. 1 (1982): 52–72.

Jaffrelot, C., and A. Kalaiyarasan. 'The Political Economy of the Jat Agitation for Other Backward Class Status'. *Economic and Political Weekly* 54, no. 7 (2019): 29–37.

Jodhka, Surinder S. 'Caste and Power in the Lands of Agri-Culture. Revisiting Rural North-West India'. Paper presented at the conference on 'Changes in Caste Hierarchies in Rural India and Their Political Implications', Indian Institute of Advanced Study, 2011.

Kalaiyarasan, A., and M. Vijayabaskar. 'Why Does the "Provincial Propertied Class" Remain Provincial? Reading the Agrarian Question of Capital Through Caste'. *Urbanisation* 6, no. 1 (2021): 16–34.

Kudaisya, Gyanesh. 'The Demographic Upheaval of Partition: Refugees and Agricultural Resettlement in India, 1947–67'. *South Asia: Journal of South Asian Studies* 18, no. 1 (1995): 73–94.

Levien, Michael. *Dispossession without Development: Land Grabs in Neoliberal India*. Oxford: Oxford University Press, 2018.

———. 'The Politics of Dispossession: Theorizing India's "Land Wars"'. *Politics and Society* 41, no. 3 (2013): 351–94.

Lowe, Lisa. *The Intimacies of Four Continents*. Durham; London: Duke University Press, 2015.

Mamdani, Mahmood. *Neither Settler nor Native*. Cambridge, Massachusetts: Belknap Press of Harvard University Press, 2020.

Namburu, Manoj. *Moguls of Real Estate*. New Delhi: Roli Books Private Limited, 2007.

Nath, Tribhuvan. 'Haryana's Part of Capital Region Development Plans'. *Times of India*, 24 April 1976.

Ollman, Bertell. *Dance of the Dialectic: Steps in Marx's Method*. Chicago: University of Illinois Press, 2003.

Paul, Satya. 'Green Revolution and Poverty among Farm Families in Haryana, 1969/70–1982/83'. *Economic and Political Weekly* 25, no. 39 (September 1990): A105–10.

Planning Commission, India. *Consolidation of Holdings (Methods and Problems)*. New Delhi: Manager of Publications, 1957.

Prakash, Gyan. 'The Colonial Genealogy of Society: Community and Political Modernity in India'. In *The Social in Question: New Bearings in History and the Social Sciences*, edited by P. Joyce, 81–96. London: Routledge, 2012.

Roy, Ananya. 'The Blockade of the World-Class City: Dialectical Images of Indian Urbanism'. In *Worlding Cities: Asian Experiments and the Art of Being Global*, edited by A. Roy and A. Ong, 259–78. Oxford: Blackwell, 2011.

Sankhe, Shirish, Ireena Vittal, Richard Dobbs, Ajit Mohan, Ankur Gulati, Jonathan Ablett, Shishir Gupta, Alex Kim, Sudipto Paul and Adirya Sanghvi. *India's Urban Awakening: Building Inclusive Cities, Sustaining Economic Growth*. Mumbai: McKinsey Global Institute, 2010.

Shatkin, Gavin, and Sanjeev Vidyarthi. 'Introduction: Contesting the Indian City; Global Visions and the Politics of the Local'. In *Contesting the Indian City: Global Visions and the Politics of the Local*, edited by G. Shatkin, 1–38. Chichester: John Wiley & Sons, 2014.

Srivastava, Sanjay. *Entangled Urbanism: Slum, Gated Community and Shopping Mall in Delhi and Gurgaon*. New Delhi: Oxford University Press, 2015.

Teltumbde, Anand. 'Haryana's Rapist Regime'. *Economic and Political Weekly* 47, no. 44 (2012): 10–11.

Times of India. 'The Gurgaon Scheme: Remodelling Rural India'. 19 April 1929.

Whitcombe, Elizabeth. *Agrarian Conditions in Northern India*. Berkeley, CA: University of California Press, 1972.

Zurbrigg, Sheila. 'Hunger and Epidemic Malaria in Punjab, 1868–1940'. *Economic and Political Weekly* 27, no. 4 (1992): PE2–26.

2 | The Village*

Vishan was walking me through his neighbourhood in Nathupur village, Gurgaon. The village sits on prime real estate in the city, enclosed on three sides by DLF Cyber City commercial hub and DLF Phase-3 residential complex, and encircled by the elevated Rapid Metro system that overshadows the neighbourhood. Nathupur sits on some of the most high-value real estate in India. Vishan was from an agriculturalist Gujjar family, his grandfather owned agricultural land long sold to DLF in the 1970s and 1980s and his father spent time in the Indian army. Today Vishan and his two brothers work 'in property'. From the balcony of his three-storey whitewashed villa on Nathupur's eastern flank, Vishan pointed towards the various buildings he owned along with his two brothers. The family business owned five buildings in Nathupur, two tall tenement buildings in the centre of the village that are rented out to 'labouring classes' and two 'apartment-style' tenement buildings that house middle-class call-centre and office workers. In a city with a dearth of public or low-rent housing, Vishan's village property business extracts rents from and facilitates the daily reproduction of Gurgaon's army of incoming workers. Vishan explained how he and his brothers, after coming into some cash from a property sale, had upgraded a tenement building into one- and two-bedroom set apartments for 'professionals' arriving from Delhi, Kolkata and Mumbai. Vishan's family had diversified their rental revenues across Gurgaon, investing in private schools, commercial and residential plots and a car lease business in the city. Standing on the balcony of Vishan's villa, overseeing the family's empire of densely packed tenements and apartment buildings surrounded by the glistening monuments of global real estate, the subaltern relationships between global real estate capital and

---

*A part of this chapter was originally published as 'The Urban Village, Agrarian Transformation and Rentier Capitalism in Gurgaon, India' in *Antipode* 50, no. 5 (2018): 1244–66. Reprinted with permission.

agrarian institutions, political actors and territories come to the fore. How were Vishan's family able to develop a mini-property empire amid some of the highest value real estate in India? Vishan, like all members of Nathupur's proprietary body, holds non-alienable, non-transferable property rights to land within Nathupur's *lal dora* boundaries. The liberalisation of Gurgaon's land market was facilitated by colonial-era property relations that vested monopoly property rights to agriculturalist caste communities within the village *abadi deh*. DLF City may present itself as a precocious substantiation of India's assent to urban modernity; at the same time, this assent is dependent upon actors like Vishan and spaces like Nathupur to buy consent, subsidise labour costs and drive speculative forms of investment. If during the colonial period the village was reified as the 'natural' site to establish agrarian property relations, then in new urban India 'the village' becomes the stage on which capital's access to rural land is brokered and agricultural communities unevenly enlisted into commodity logics that speculatively fuel land markets in the city. These enlistments are material, they involve preserving high-value land within the hands of agrarian actors, but they are also ideological and discursive, seeking to enjoin all possible agrarian futures to commercial land use.

These futures align with a capitalist conjuncture in which, as Sassen argues, land 'is more valuable to the global market than the people on it'.[1] This may be true of contemporary India but what about those people on it? Property in land is a sticky substance that rarely comes to market cleaned of its previous brushes with capitalist and colonial subjugation. Rural land is embedded in complex tenures, vested in local institutional arrangements protected and regulated by layers of legislation, and imbued with cultural and social meanings that are not so easy for the market forces to reckon with nor for the local government to strip away. The following three chapters of this book are dedicated to both understanding how this complex and lumpy object – land – is rendered open and amenable to real estate capture, and how complexity and lumpiness can as much aid as prohibit processes of land commodification. In this chapter, I am interested in how the state and private capital brokered political access to Gurgaon's land.

The exemption of the village *abadi* (residential area) from land acquisition and development and planning rules, and the monopoly rights of landowners over village property form the basis of Vishan's business. Like most village rentiers, I explore in this chapter how Vishan financed the construction of tenements iteratively, initially through the sale of family land to private developers; he then drew income by leasing out and mortgaging rural land banks, before constructing property on his *abadi* land. Nathupur today is an urban working-class neighbourhood in the shell of a village.

On Delhi's edge the character of colonial rule that struck bargains with agricultural elites and produced mixed-property regimes characterised by jointness and enclosure has given rise to unmapped, non-alienable territories deep in the heart of emerging cities. DLF City and Nathupur village in this way do not represent two distinct historical moments in Gurgaon's urbanisation, of a shift from village to city, nor two autonomous geographies that express the enduring inequity and disorder of India's supposed schizophrenic post-colonial condition. In Gurgaon, despite the precocious declarations of politicians and developers, the city has not consumed the countryside. Nor are Vishan's business practices substantively distinct from official processes of urbanisation in the city.[2] As we will discuss across the next chapters, a wide range of territorial claims across Gurgaon are selectively absorbed into official development plans often despite their incongruence to formal planning codes and rules. The Haryana government has proven fantastically adept at adapting to the 'frictions' posed by real estate and industrial capital's permeation of the countryside.[3] The village in Gurgaon territorialises a hegemonic class project at the heart of the region's urbanisation; a declaration of a grand territorial alliance waged between real estate capital and the agrarian world.

THE VILLAGE IN THE CITY

Contemporary accounts of capitalist development have tended to focus on the increasingly salient role land plays in expanded accumulation. Much of the discussion on 'primitive accumulation', 'new enclosures' and 'accumulation by dispossession' to a varying degree share a belief that capital – now primarily a rentier actor – no longer seeks to create new classes of wage-labourers, but rather seeks simply to access land. And yet in nominal liberal democracies as in India, with enduring legal protections for rural landowners as well as strong cultural, social and institutional embeddedness of rural land, how does private capital convince landowners to sell? How do global markets broker access to fragmented, rural landholdings? How is this task made politically and materially possible? And why, despite such a powerful impulse to collapse land into capitalist forms, do rural and peri-urban landscapes in the Global South continue to be marked by patchwork configurations of privatised and non-privatised lands?

The village, village property and the customary tenures through which villagers hold land, all open up new frontiers of real estate and industrial accumulation in the city. In order to overcome significant barriers to land-based accumulation, barriers that have significantly stunted real-estate-led urbanisation elsewhere in the country, developers and state authorities have engaged in a series of territorial alliances and compromises with Gurgaon's agrarian landowning classes. Meanwhile, landowners have looked to exploit tentative property claims on land in and around their villages to extend their territorial base and ready themselves for the city.

In this chapter, I argue that the maintenance of some customary land rights in Gurgaon have acted as a territorial fix for real-estate-based accumulation, a fix that opens up agricultural fields to be transformed into a financial asset in exchange for preserving fiefdoms of landowners' monopoly power and unevenly integrating landowners into the speculative promise of property-led modernity.

Haryana's customary system of land shares not only structures the capture of local land markets by real estate developers but also mediates consent to rapid agrarian churn. The construction of extensive unregulated tenement housing in the city's villages provides the city – which has a total absence of public housing – with cheap, off-the-map housing and disciplined living conditions that process the hundreds of thousands of migrant workers that arrive in Gurgaon each year to labour on construction sites, factories, shopping malls and upper-class homes. As I examine in Chapter 5, the construction of labour tenements is in this regard not only the material base through which many landowners collectively accumulate but also the lifeblood of the city's labour-intensive industries.

The village articulates the seemingly contradictory political economies of land and labour in the contemporary city. The necessary integration of agrarian landowners into urban land markets has however been partial. While many landowners have been able to transfer agrarian surpluses built up through the region's uneven agrarian development into urban rentier power, most landowners are restricted to the accumulating rents within the exempt space of the village and speculative investments in land outside the village boundary (Figure 2.1).

The Village | 91

Figure 2.1 Residential developments outside Kherki Daula village
Source: Photo by author.

The chapter begins by examining the production of differentiated forms of dispossession that have mediated the uneven transformation of Gurgaon's agrarian landowners into urban rentiers. The chapter demonstrates how private-sector-led land transfer operates alongside state-led dispossession to produce an uneven land market that produces different politics of resistance and consent among Gurgaon's landowners.

Second, the chapter shows how the exemption of the villages in Gurgaon from urbanisation acts to broker land for capital, expressing a key territorial compromise between politically dominant agrarian landowners and emergent forces of urban real estate that are essential to accumulation in the city. The exemption of the village comes to mediate key tensions within the city's political economy. Guaranteeing landowners a monopoly on land markets within village boundaries underpins both corporate real estate and landowner's rentier accumulation by first, allowing landowners to develop a mass property base *inside* the village, which in turn eases the passage of real estate capital to agricultural land *outside* the village; and second, building up a stock of cheap rental housing for the low-wage workforce essential to the city's economic reproduction.

The village, established as a coherent ideological and administrative object under colonial rule, today coordinates the distribution of rents, capital and wages that oil the cogs of the city's belligerent political economy. In this way the village, this chapter argues, comes to express and process what Marx calls capital's 'trinity formula': land–ground rent, labour–wages and capital–profits.[4] Reading Gurgaon's urbanisation as such allows us to trace practices of exploitation and transformation across the erstwhile borders of land, labour and capital, to a wider range of territorial and subjective forms.[5]

Finally, the chapter explores processes of territorial and class differentiation within Gurgaon's agrarian landowning communities. The village may provide *opportunities* for accumulation for some, but the boundary lines of the villages also act as a limit to landowners' capacity to accumulate; hemmed in on all sides by planned 'urban' development, landowner collectives look to reinvest revenues from land sales and significant rental incomes collectively into property markets outside the village boundaries. Those successful at the latter can, it is believed by many villagers, escape the jointness of the village and enjoin themselves to the 'future' historical march of liberal, individualist urban citizenship.

BEYOND DISPOSSESSION

Dispossession is something of a master narrative within contemporary urban studies. From Marx's formulation of 'primitive accumulation' in his study of English enclosures, to Harvey's influential expansion in 'accumulation by dispossession', to the 'new enclosures' literature, dispossessions have been understood as foundational to processes of the urban the world over.[6] Contemporary urbanisation under capitalism, understood through a Harveyian lens, is an outcome of the absorption of surplus capitals into the built environment through the violent process of 'creative destruction'. These processes dispossess and displace obsolescent land uses and users, replacing them with spaces and actors amenable to higher value creation. Dispossession is, Harvey writes, the 'mirror image of capital absorption through urban redevelopment'.[7]

In post-liberalisation India, dispossession is understood to be front and centre of the Indian state's attempts to facilitate capital's access to large swathes of rural land through eminent domain. Swapna Banerjee-Guha, in this context, argues that the drive to render Indian cities amenable to global circuits of finance capital from the 2000s has required

> displacement and dispossession of the poor and weaker sections ... aided by other methods of marginalisation, like closure of small scale manufacturing and retail units, anti-poor legal order, regulations

against informal workers, hawkers, waste pickers, privatisation of basic services like water, sanitation, housing, health, education and last but not the least, restricting access to open spaces for opening up more spaces for elitist consumption.⁸

Importantly, these spatial transformations have not enacted processes of proletarianisation like in older, European modes of 'primitive accumulation'. In the post-colonial context, dispossession is a process engaged in for land rather than against labour. Urban and rural dispossessions are not geared towards producing a class of proletarianised wage labourers for industry but rather intended to free up land for accumulation without the absorption of peasants into emerging spaces of production. According to Sanyal, post-colonial dispossession produces an army of surplus labour who shut out from formal capitalist markets are, instead, absorbed into an informal, 'needs economy' subsidised by the state.⁹

What sets Gurgaon apart from these narratives of dispossessive urbanisation is the leading role the private real estate sector has played in land acquisitions. In Gurgaon compulsory land acquisitions, enacted by the state, account for only around 15 per cent of land transfers in the city. The remaining 85 per cent of land in the urbanisable area of Gurgaon has been bought by developers on the real estate market. If 'so-called primitive accumulation' in the classical sense necessarily involves the use of 'extra-economic force' to separate land users from their lands and put them to work as wage-labourers, in Gurgaon we have to ask not only why extra-economic force was seldom needed but also how consent was forged for such dramatic transformation?

The urban question (for capital) in contemporary India – how to produce the conditions for the expanded absorption of capital into social and built environments – is tightly wound up in the land question: how to remove obstacles to land-based accumulation? Marx noted that while 'so-called primitive accumulation' at one level produced the monopoly power of landowners over apportioned parcels of the earth – by hurling peasants off from the commons and establishing the institution of private property – on the other it created a class of landowners whose own interests did not neatly align with the capitalist.

By claiming rents, for example, the landowner struggles against capital for portions of the surplus value, and the landowner's rights to increase rents may have little correspondence to the capacity of the capitalist to yield sufficiently higher levels of surplus value through production. In addition, in the absence of forces that compel landowners to throw rents back into productive outlets, the presence of the landowner – as a separately constituted material actor – can disrupt the free circulation of capital that the entire system relies upon.

This, Marx argues, puts the landowner in a conflictual relationship to the capitalist and labourer, each competing to keep a hold on bits of surplus value in ways that throw up tensions and struggles: while capitalists look to convert land into an 'open field' for exploitation, landowners seek to protect monopolies and enhance rents that underpin their social power. Capital's struggle against land has, in the North Atlantic and settler colony in particular, been successfully aided by the state who have willingly deployed all manner of violence to not only expunge land users from their land but to also constrain the social power of landed interests and force land to act like a value-bearing commodity.[10]

When treated as a 'pure financial asset', Harvey argues, ground rents play a crucial role in allocating and distributing capital flows in ways that support expanded accumulation. And in much of the world, especially the North Atlantic, the long history of these struggles has seen the social power of capital win out. One of the 'triumphs of capitalism', Harvey writes, has been to force landowners to subjugate their land for capital.

Yet, in the majority world, this struggle has been complicated by colonial and post-colonial development policy. Across history land has been differently enlisted for capitalist projects. In the colonial period in India, land was advanced purely for extractive purposes and utilised to secure territorial power of anxious colonial rulers. After Independence, land became an essential resource for the creation of a modernising post-colonial nation. A succession of five-year plans invested heavily in public-sector infrastructural and industrial development, organised under public sector undertakings (PSUs) that would be underwritten by large-scale agrarian industrialisation ushered in by the Green Revolution in Punjab and elsewhere. Post-colonial economic development relied upon the state's access to land in order to establish energy and industrial plants, dams, roads and new modernist cities.[11] Thus from the 1950s the central government utilised eminent domain powers bestowed under the LAA to forcibly capture land and dispossess rural communities. Such dispossession was, as I discussed in the previous chapter, accompanied by a string of agrarian reforms that capped and gridded landholdings, unevenly redistributed land from large landowners to tenant farmers and lower caste communities, and vested land in the *panchayat* government.[12] These reforms, while for the most part partially implemented,[13] when placed alongside state developmentalism, left behind a truncated landscape tenurial and institutional arrangements in rural property that from the 1990s began to interface with new demand for land from increasingly financialised private and public sector development actors.

These territorial hangovers are presented by international financial institutions and the central government as barriers to the expansion of fully functioning rural property markets.[14] Land in India is complex, composed in mass, fragmented smallholdings, held through mixed tenures, vested in an array of institutional arrangements and governed through dense, opaque bureaucratic networks. Amid the feverish intra-state competition to leverage land for global capital investment from the 1990s, the gargantuan task of bringing land to market has been taken on by state governments armed with the LAA. And yet, in Haryana the situation has played out differently. Land is rationalised, gridded, providing the image of legibility amenable to faraway investors and developers. What is more in Haryana, and Gurgaon particularly, the enduring presence of certain customary tenures has animated and brokered space for capital investment. The village in Gurgaon has opened up a path for private sector land acquisitions and urban development.

The extent to which agrarian property relations present a barrier to industrialisation is precisely the question that Marxist agrarian scholars have investigated over the past century. While the English experience of enclosures retains its standing as the 'model' of agrarian to industrial capitalist transition, agrarian scholars have looked to map out the divergent and nonlinear pathways through which agrarian social relations have been mobilised to spur industrial capitalism. Terence Byres' influential development of the agrarian question was concerned with the particular differential conditions within agriculture which contribute to primary accumulation for the purposes of industrialisation.

This, according to Byres, has not always required the development of capitalist property markets within the countryside, but rather for Byres the agrarian question can be effectively 'resolved' when agrarian landed property no longer presents significant inputs or obstacles to capitalist development elsewhere; this may be achieved through any number of means not limited to the English model of enclosures. Byres' analysis came out of experiences in

India that demonstrated a quite different experience of capitalist development from the European norm, one that rebukes the teleology of historical transition and undermines ontologies of sectoral 'development'.

As agrarian studies scholarship has highlighted, the development of capitalist industry and agriculture has been advanced through alliances of large landowners, industrial capital and state actors who have established islands of high-value capitalist production, cleaved from 'wastelands' of un-proletarianised peasants who are absorbed into informal economies and state welfare programmes. In this respect, the proletarianisation that capitalist landed property facilitated in Western Europe appears to have been bypassed in the Indian context. As D'Costa and Chakraborty note, rather than the 'classic' expansion of agrarian transitions, India has experienced a 'sharp but integrated dualism … generated between primitive accumulation and capitalism proper because of continuing dispossession on the one hand and the much higher growth in nonagricultural sectors'.[15] This dualist perspective is supported by evidence that since the 1980s agricultural production in India has not contributed significantly to non-agricultural capitalist development. Landed property's role in cultivating capitalist agriculture and, in turn, inputs toward industrial development appear 'bypassed' by large-scale investments from the state (in the post-colonial moment) and globalised private sector (from the 1980s onwards).

Contemporary agriculture, it appears, provides neither the social conditions (proletarianisation) nor the economy surpluses that spur non-agricultural sectors and drive forward the classical model of capitalist development. Since formal liberalisation of the Indian economy in the early 1990s, there has been a dramatic growth in the finance, services and real estate (FSRE) sectors and collapse in agriculture. In 1951 the services sector contributed a 30 per cent share of total gross domestic product (GDP), a figure that rose to 38 per cent in 1981 and 60 per cent in 2014. Within that same period, the contribution of agriculture declined from 52 per cent to 14 per cent while industry increased modestly from 16 per cent to 26 per cent.

This decline is reflected in a significant growth of rural households who draw incomes principally from non-agricultural employment. For some this is indicative of India's 'industry-less growth'.[16] While organised manufacturing accounted for 14 per cent of GDP and 13 per cent of the workforce in 2012, the FSRE sector accounted for 20 per cent and 2 per cent respectively. These changes in the sectoral composition of production, driven in part by a liberalising economic model have sidelined the socio-economic importance of agriculture to the Indian economy. The upshot for many commentators is that dispossessions, rather than indicative of primitive accumulation, form part of the ongoing expansion of the conditions of accumulation; land is today a full-fledged circulating commodity and struggles over dispossession are as such principally struggles over land's uses and purposing as a commodity.

These trends are mirrored in Haryana where the agricultural sector's contribution to national GDP has dropped from 30 per cent in 1990–91 to 14 per cent in 2014–15, while average landholdings have decreased from 7.6 acres in 1983 to 1.9 acres in 2011–12.[17] In much of the state this has had a detrimental impact on the Jats, and to some extent the Ahirs, whose economic and social power hinges on control of agricultural production and exploitation of Dalit farm workers who are now able to reject rural subordination for urban employment.[18]

In this context, Henry Bernstein's work has challenged the enduring relevance of the agrarian question.[19] For Bernstein, agrarian land reforms that integrated the peasantry into various forms of commodity production had effectively eliminated 'non-capitalist' agrarian relations, while the 'developmental' agrarian question – how to compel landed property to invest productively in agriculture and spur agricultural-industrial linkages – has been bypassed by the wide availability of global capital through which to furnish contained industrial and urban markets. The opening up of global markets in the late twentieth century and rush of capital into 'emerging markets' have diluted the imperative to develop domestic agricultural linkages to spur industrial development; the agrarian question of capital, according to Bernstein, was resolved by globalisation.

In Haryana agrarian decline, both produced and resolved by urban development, has been complicated by the Jats' exclusion from public sector job reservations afforded to the other backward classes (OBCs) under the Mandal Commission recommendations implemented in 1992.[20] An exclusion that blocks the Jats' access to formal urban employment together with broader agricultural decline has sparked political agitation calling for Jats' reclassification as OBCs.[21] As Kalaiyarasan and Jaffrelot argue, the 'dual process of Market and Mandal have partly dislodged Jats from their earlier economic and political position'.[22] In short, liberalisation had begun to tear apart the coherence of the already highly differentiated 'provincial propertied classes'[23] like the Jats in Haryana, opening them up for recomposition with emerging factions of urban capital.

These dynamics played differently in Gurgaon. First, land ownership in Gurgaon is dominated not only by Jats but also by Ahirs, Gujars, Meos, Rajputs, and so the fortunes of the propertied classes is not so easily tied into one caste-coalition; indeed, the vast majority of New Gurgaon was built upon Ahir villages. Ahirs while just as susceptible to agrarian decline, and just as internally differentiated, had access to Mandal reservations with which – in principle – they could access public jobs in the formal urban economy. Second, land in Gurgaon was never incredibly profitable, and many landowners, while holding onto land up to the 1990s, already had sons engaged in petty rentiership or urban ancillary economies in order to piece together the household income. Their surpluses, if not their cultural affinity, had already begun to spin out of agriculture. Third, while dominant landowning communities like the Jats and Ahirs have unquestionably suffered from agricultural decline, the extent to which coherent caste identities cleanly corresponded to agrarian class positions is perhaps overstated. Or not all suffered the same way. Finally, most importantly however, despite declining agricultural and Mandal exclusions of the Jats, these groups sat on land and controlled the political and social institutions that had to be remediated in a land-hungry post-liberalisation economy.

Indeed while 'agrarian bypass' narratives of India's post-liberalisation economy are well founded, they do not indicate an elimination of the social institutions of landed property nor importance of the concentration of agrarian surpluses for the transformation of the countryside over the past decades. The consensus that purports a 'resolution' to the agrarian question ignores the numerous ways heterogeneous agrarian property regimes and institution continue to riddle the functioning of post-liberalisation capital highly dependent upon access to land, and thus underestimate the crucial ways in which historically and geographically specific agrarian determinates continue to be deeply implicated in the making of contemporary peri-urbanising cities, of bringing land to the market.

In short, while the role of agrarian production in urban capital accumulation may be relatively minimal, the persistence of the 'agrarian' as a set of contingent property regimes, institutions and cultural-political categories endures. These institutions mark out both uneven capitalist transformations of agrarian society across the nineteenth and twentieth centuries, and the heterogeneous, incomplete ways that capital has come to 'settle' in the rural world in the present conjuncture. While the economic productivity and class relations of Gurgaon's agricultural sector has no doubt declining significance for expanded accumulation, agrarian property regimes and institutions – that include prevailing forms of customary landed property – have proved vital to the shape of both industrial and urban accumulation processes in the city.

This entangled composition of agrarian and urban, privatised and non-privatised land, that forms the bedrock of Gurgaon's urbanisation, is not unique to the city; indeed, there is a wealth of evidence of the ongoing dialectical entanglement of agrarian institutions in urban development. Gillian Hart's work, for example, examines the relationships between global industrial capital and rural institutions and territories in South Africa, exploring the integral role these institutions play in carving out a problem-free space for globally integrated industrial production in rural spaces.[24] Sharad Chari's work shows how Tirupur's flexibilised textile industry was captured by an agrarian caste community of 'worker-capitalists' who mobilised agrarian institutions and logics to discipline flexibilised industrial production.[25] Meanwhile, Gavin Capps' work in South Africa has highlighted the importance of institutions of 'tribal landed property' to the development of capitalist commodity production.[26] The agrarian, far from a bypassed or operationalised set of social relations, frequently holds sway over the course of urban development projects across the majority world.

Navigating Dispossession

Land conversions in Gurgaon are shaped by the entanglement of state dispossessions and private sales. The majority of urbanisable land within the city of Gurgaon has been bought up and developed by the private sector; that is, the majority of land in Gurgaon *has not* been subject to dispossession but rather has been traded on the market. In the 1980s HUDA acquired land and developed residential and commercial plots in and around old Gurgaon. However as early as the 1990s HUDA was struggling to compete with market prices, and as landowners came to realise the value of their land, state acquisitions were tied up in lengthy court proceedings that often led to enhanced levels of compensation. As such by the end of the 1990s HUDA ceased operations as a development agency and consigned itself to managing its existing sectors and providing infrastructural development for private colonies.

The other significant state landlord in Gurgaon is the Haryana State Industrial and Infrastructural Development Corporation (HSIIDC). Since the 1980s the HSIIDC has organised the acquisition and assembly of over 12,000 acres, around 14 per cent of the total acquired land in the city for industrial estates and SEZs. Indeed, state-facilitated foreign industrial investment was pioneered by the Government of Haryana from the early 1980s.

The HSIIDC provided subsidised land and infrastructural development to Gurgaon's key foreign industrial investors, Maruti Suzuki and Honda, to establish industrial facilities in the city. IMT Manesar started out as a joint venture between HSIIDC and a group of Japanese industrialists in the mid-1990s. The Manesar project was heavily promoted by the state government as one of the earliest public–private partnerships orchestrated between a regional government and international investors. It provided low-cost industrial land plots and streamlined infrastructure to Maruti Suzuki just as the company was looking to reorganise and flexibilise production and employment systems.[27]

The HSIIDC acquires land under eminent domain, using the LAA, and plots and then leases the land to industrialists under varying terms. Importantly, under the LAA the state sets land prices at 'circle rates'. The difference between circle rates and market rates are not only a consequence of the widespread use of cash in property transactions, but also an outcome of a desire to keep the acquisitions costs for state development projects low; circle rates are reviewed but kept low. The meteoric rise in the value of Gurgaon's land from the mid-2000s as the state government expanded the city's boundaries, and the central government liberalised FDI in the real estate and finance sectors, produced large differentials between state-designated circle rates and prices given on the market. These distinct forces of land capture – that value land differently – incentivise higher return land sales over state acquisitions.

According to my field survey,[28] (see Table 2.1) landowners[29] who sold their land to developers between 1981 and 2014 received prices on average eight times higher (per acre) than those whose land was forcibly acquired by state agencies.

The significant difference in price between state-acquired and private-sector-purchased land has mapped an uneven landscape of land value across

Table 2.1   Median land price per acre

Landholding (acres)	Price (in rupees)
3 and less	650,000.00
3.1 to 9.9	562,500.00
More than 10	1,034,000.00
Year	
1960–89	100,000.00
1990–2000	650,000.00
2001–14	18,750,000.00
Type of acquisition	
Government	325,000.00
Private	2,675,000.00
Caste community	
Gujjar	196,000.00
Jat	260,520.00
Brahmin	784,000.00
Yadav	1,100,000.00

Source: Data collected by author.

the city. Those whose land was bought up have been able to mobilise higher returns to diversify their economic activity, while those whose land has been acquired receive far less revenue per acre and tend to be consigned to petty rentiership within the village and agrarian economy.

Take, for example, land transactions in Carterpuri village in central Gurgaon. Land in Carterpuri was predominately bought and acquired by both a private developer and HUDA in the early 1980s for two separate residential projects. Landowners whose land was notified for state acquisition for HUDA's development received the circle rate of 50,000 rupees per acre, while landowners whose land fell under the developer's project received the market price of 200,000 rupees per acre.

This stark difference in land price has sparked a series of territorial strategies among real estate actors and landowners that look to position land for alienation. Brokers and aggregators on the hunt for rural land will visit villagers with news that their lands are earmarked for state re-zoning and development projects. The threat of dispossession, however fictitious, forces landowners to part with their land at cut rates.

The politics of dispossession also incorporates strategies of delay, negotiation and exemption. Well-connected villagers whose land is notified for state acquisition seek to utilise social and political connections to negotiate the release of their land and redraw the boundaries of the notified area to exclude their property. Other landowners see state acquisitions as an opportunity to litigate for incremental accruements in compensation.

Landowners may also look to exploit the lengthy bureaucratic process, what Sheth calls the 'urban time lapse' in his article 'Historical Transformations in Boundary and Land Use in New Delhi's Urban Villages', between the notification of land for acquisition and the physical possession of the land, to quickly sell land on the market. This benefits property dealers able to pick up notified land on the cheap albeit above circle rate prices. In 2009, 1,400 acres of land in south Gurgaon were notified for state acquisition; during the period allocated for appeal, 1,315 acres of the notified land was sold to developers at rates lower than market prices but higher than the circle rate. By 2014, the state released all of the land from notification, effectively passing the land onto developers on the cheap. In this way, while accounting for a small proportion of land transactions, the presence and sometimes enactment of state acquisitions play a direct role in compelling landowners to sell land to developers. The entwining of state dispossessions with private alienations has also conditioned a peculiar form of land struggles across the city ostensibly *for* alienation. For others, the forces at play in state acquisitions outweigh their local capacity to subvert or prevent state plans.

THE RELIANCE SEZ

Here they took all the land. Everything. It was a scam and everyone – the government, the opposition – they were all involved.[30]

Vivek Chauhan sat playing cards with friends underneath some shade offered by an abandoned lettings office in Harsaru village, a rapidly developing area of Gurgaon. The office overlooked an 1,800-acre expanse of fenced-off land.

In 2005 Vivek's 3 acres were compulsory acquired by the HSIIDC and turned over to Reliance Industries Limited (RIL), one of India's largest multinational conglomerates, for the development of what was touted to be the largest SEZ in India.

The Reliance SEZ covered 25,000 acres of land, was projected to receive 1.4 trillion rupees in private investment and provide half a million jobs. The SEZ was planned as a multi-sector development that included luxury residential and commercial real estate, manufacturing, e-commerce warehousing and a cargo airport. Under the Special Economic Zones Act, 2005, the SEZ was exempt from various export taxes and duties, while as a designated 'public facility' labour laws in the prospective zone would be significantly relaxed. The 2007 Gurgaon Development Plan was drafted to incorporate the SEZ into the city's boundaries alongside surrounding villages and agricultural lands that experienced a frenzy of real estate investment in response to news of the SEZ development. The SEZ was to be developed on the land of two Gurgaon villages, Harsaru and Garhi. Cheaper land in Garhi, a village a mile north of Harsaru, would be bought up directly by Reliance at market prices, while higher value land in Harsaru close to the National Highway was notified for compulsory acquisition under the LAA.

The SEZ model, a development of the economic processing zones of the 1970s, was the preferred model of new town development by the then Congress-led central government (2004–14) and was given legal weight through a series of SEZ policies at the central and state level through the 2000s. Haryana was one of the first state governments to introduce a Special Economic Zone policy in 2005. The policy was promoted as a way of unlocking potential real estate value in land otherwise bogged down in complex patronage relations, property rights and ownership titles, lowering the cost of labour prices by exempting the zones from the oversight of labour legislation and de-politicising points of accumulation by privatising the governance of industrial spaces. The SEZ was conceived as a unique juridical, disciplinary space that distils neoliberal techno-scientific managerialism cleaved from local sovereignties, contexts and constraints. The Reliance SEZ was to operate as an inland port in a landlocked state, directly tethered to global markets. Of course, in Gurgaon many of these conditions are already preset in the government's urban land acquisition and development model. But as an industrial 25,000-acre development, and one located at the heart of Gurgaon's rocketing land market in the 2000s, it is perhaps no surprise that the state government would take on some responsibility for land acquisitions. Under the Haryana SEZ act, the state government masterplan and notify areas within existing development plans as SEZs, and thereby exempt developers from applying for licences and land-use changes under the HDRUA.

By the end of the 2000s however the SEZ policy at the national scale was politically toxic. Plans for a 10,000-acre SEZ in Nandigram, West Bengal, were withdrawn in 2007 after violent clashes between the state and peasant farmers. The high-profile violence directed at the peasant protestors ultimately led to the downfall of the thirty-three-year rule of the Communist Party of India (Marxist-Leninist) in West Bengal. Building on this anti-SEZ current, in 2006 landowners in Harsaru and surrounding villages began to protest the acquisition of their land. In June 2008, as the Haryana government was due to take formal possession of the land in Harsaru, landowners blocked roads, held rallies, fought with the police and set fire to buildings. For six weeks amid the height of the protest, the villagers held camp on the land and the village was placed under martial law; all access to and from the village was shut down. For a moment in the summer of 2008, it seemed as if the movement was destined to become Haryana's Nandigram. Vivek notes:

> The police came and lathi [baton] charged us – there were ten thousand police here. They closed off the village for fifteen days no one could come in or out. We tried to organise a protest but we were crushed by the police.

The Harsaru landowners' protest was not against dispossession per se; rather many of the landowners were simply opposing the level of compensation they had received for their land. Across the road from Vivek's group was the grocery shop of Ashok Mehra, a key figure in the village's scheduled caste community. Ashok took a different position on the SEZ:

> As Harijans we never owned any land around here, [before] we always worked the land [but] these days we work in business, for companies, in the city and so on. [The landowners] only began to protest the land acquisition after they had been handed compensation ... a meeting of the Panchayat was called and we were asked to join their protest, but why should we? It's not our land, why should we kill ourselves for them ... it's wrong to take the compensation and then to protest. [Since the land was acquired] nothing has changed, only for the landowners – for everyone else no change.

The differing experiences of Vivek and Ashok speak to the uneven impacts of land transformations on communities differently assembled as proprietors and non-proprietors over the previous century. In my household survey I found that, expectedly, households from dominant agricultural classes (Jats and Ahirs) owned the most land and received the highest prices per acre for their lands, while scheduled caste households, seldom owners of agriculture land, received the lowest prices per acre. Ashok had received what he termed 'a strip' of land in the 1970s under land ceiling reforms. He explained, the land provided was 'cheap' and in poor condition without irrigation, and they had sold it a decade ago.

Yet despite formal acquisition of the land, the land we sat next to that day, six years since the protests, lay empty. Following the controversy of SEZs around the country and compounded by the global financial crisis, the Haryana government withdrew fiscal concessions connected to the project and called for an enhancement in land prices. Reliance subsequently withdrew from the project and returned the 1,400 acres of state-acquired land in Harsaru to the HSIIDC. The Reliance SEZ, projected to bring half a million jobs to this agricultural expanse on the western side of Gurgaon, and with it luxury, 'modern' standards of living, was over.

The failure of the Reliance SEZ is in part a consequence of a general downturn in the real estate sector after 2008, but also down to the relative similarity of the SEZ model and Haryana's already existing – and far less controversial – industrial and real estate development policy. There is little need for hermetic 'zones of exemption' when planning and development controls are already highly liberalised, and flexibly governed and deregulated across the state. In Haryana as a whole, of the twenty-nine SEZs notified under the Special Economic Zone Act, 2005, today only five are listed by the Haryana government as operational. Today, lying between the National Highway 8 and the Gurgaon–Pataudi road is a large expanse of flattened land interrupted on occasion by the villas of important local bureaucrats and businessmen who were able to force the release of their land during the initial state acquisition process. The villas, protruding from the horizon, are physical reminders of the uneven processes of dispossession that envelop India's post-liberalisation urbanisation.

And yet for many the failed Reliance project was incredibly profitable. The incorporation of the SEZ into the Gurgaon Development Plan also extended the boundaries of the city across vast swathes of rural land on

Gurgaon's western flank. While initially these sectors were zoned for SEZ and industrial purposes, after the failure and denotification of the SEZ, these sectors were re-zoned for residential purposes. Developers who had bought up land in these areas on cut rates prior to their re-zoning suddenly found themselves sitting on high-value real estate. The developer Ramprashtra Builders, for example, used a series of subsidiaries and affiliates to buy up 500 acres of land in Wazirpur and Garoli Kalan villages at around 1 crore per acre;[31] after the re-zoning of the area, land prices shot up to 40 crore rupees an acre, and increased even further once plotted and sold to property buyers.[32] The SEZ may have needlessly dispossessed hundreds of villages at Harsaru, and ultimately failed to deliver thousands of jobs to the city, but nevertheless, as an instrument of the state's pro-market industrial agenda, succeeded in stimulating land markets in Gurgaon's newly urbanised areas.

TERRITORIAL EXEMPTION

The exemption of village residential land from land alienation *and* dispossession, and preservation of village elites' monopoly power, however, is perhaps the single most important factor helping to explain how capital began to capture and circulate through rural land in Haryana without the direct coercion of state force. Landowners in Gurgaon had already consolidated their territorial power by the time DLF arrived in the 1970s; land was already gridded and rationalised in state maps and it had been subject to over a century of planned agrarian obsolescence. Landowners who sold their land to real estate developers from the 1970s were not selling *all* of their lands but preserved non-alienable rights to village residential property (*abadi deh*) that would soon be surrounded on all sides by high-value real estate. The entanglement of so-called 'customary', communal rights to land with modern, capitalistic land markets paved the way for Gurgaon's urbanisation. If elsewhere land-based capitals have required the state to step in and batten down barriers to rural land markets through coercive forces of dispossession, in Gurgaon the state exemption of village lands achieves a similar outcome while enlisting the village elites into logics of rentier accumulation.[33]

These territorial exemptions are a product of the PSRCA that, as discussed in the previous chapter, established the planning framework for urban development in Haryana. As we discuss in the following chapter, the PSRCA is a permeable instrument: Section 7A of the act provided the state government 'powers of relaxation' to exempt land uses from controlled area restrictions and shift the boundary lines of 'control' to selectively authorise corporate territorial claims. Here it is important to note that the act also exempts a variety of land uses and territories from controlled areas. Alongside temples, graveyards, the act exempts the *abadi deh* and land immediately surrounding the *abadi deh* (the *phirni* or *gora deh* utilised for husbandry and common village uses).

The act reflected the state government's aims to balance what it saw as the necessity of planned socio-economic industrialisation with the preservation of the much-idealised, and now demographically enfranchised, village. Industrial and urban development was to be encouraged but controlled, regulated and curtailed to designated zones.

In line with the central government's first three five-year plans (running from 1951 to 1966), the state government embarked upon land consolidation schemes and Green Revolution technologies that began to shift the territorial and socio-economic landscape in favour of Punjab's large landowners. Armed with theories of agrarian transition, both central and state government planners sought to mobilise agricultural surpluses to stimulate industrial development. The 1950s and 1960s saw the mass development of new towns and redevelopment of traditional metropoles that wrought significant changes to rural society, not only reconfiguring agrarian relations but also by pulling agrarian surplus capital and rural labour into the city.

While supportive of economic linkages between the village and the city, the cross-contamination of rural and urban cultural life perturbed Indian politicians, planners and sociologists. The imprint of the village lay heavy in the imagination of post-colonial modernisation, and politicians were wary to disrupt the sociological coherence of 'village community' during processes of industrialisation. As Ashis Nandy argues, mid-twentieth-century politics was informed by a 'journey from the village to the city', one that is influenced by the Chicago School of urban sociology,[34] aimed to preserve the bucolic simplicity of rural life while instrumentalising the village for urbanisation purposes. The PSRCA sits within this political context and mirrors the Delhi Development Authority's exemption of *abadi* areas from building bye-laws in 1963.

It is no surprise then that in Punjab, a state that as we have seen is politically and culturally dominated by dominant caste communities, whose power rests upon the control of village *panchayats*, the state would seek to mediate developmental ambitions with agrarian protections. The village – more precisely the village proprietary body – in Punjab, and later Haryana, forms the cultural, social and economic base of post-colonial capitalist hegemony.

By exempting village residential areas from land acquisition and alienation, the PSRCA effectively placates the land-based development strategy of the state by guaranteeing the non-alienable monopoly property rights to village landowners in exchange for the opening up of agricultural fields. As Vishan and so many others noted, the lack of opposition to land conversions in Gurgaon was due to a combination of unproductive agricultural land, prices well and above those offered by the state, and the preservation of landowners' monopoly power in the village. While scholarship on 'neoliberal exceptions' has tended to focus upon the legal and planning exemptions provided to real estate and industrial capitalists by an incipient neoliberal state, often overlooked are the territorial exemptions and politics of consent directed towards agrarian landowners.

When read alongside the HDRUA, the exemption of *abadi* (and their peripheral) territories produces a landscape of exempt *abadi*s governed by *panchayat* and, after 2008, the municipal government and privately financed and managed townships. Such exemptions feature in the planning legislation of numerous state governments across the 1960s, and yet the exemption of the *abadi* in Gurgaon and Delhi holds greater significance owing to the capacity for village landowners to exploit territorial exemptions amid high-value industrial and commercial real estate. The exemption provides to landowners' monopoly control of land at the heart of India's fastest growing and highest value markets.[35] Despite appearing as enclaved urban and rural territories that substantiate popular claims of India's unequal and exclusive urbanisation, the villages of Gurgaon are deeply enmeshed within, and support the ongoing existence of, industrial and commercial real estate outside their boundaries. As we discuss in Chapter 5, the villages provide cheap labour and commodity inputs necessary for industrial development outside their boundaries but they also mediate political and financial tensions and buy the compliance of local landowners by adjoining land sale revenues to the promise of absorption into highly speculative real estate markets. A promise that is materially substantiated in village property markets. These linkages are messy and shot through by splintering class tensions within the village boundaries marked by differentiated processes of dispossession.

In urban areas elsewhere, a politics of informal and formal, enclaved and dejected, authorised and unauthorised development characterises incipient forms of urbanism. In these spaces, a range of actors – from urban elites to the middle classes to the urban poor – incrementally occupy land, cut plots, build houses and produce documentation in order to substantiate territorial claims in the city. As we see in Chapter 3, this politics characterises the material practices of village rentier actors *outside* the village boundaries. Emerging from these spaces is a politics of occupancy that vests the 'informal neighbourhood' within a broad array of cultural, legal, institutional, aesthetic and political spaces in order to access state services and impress territorial claims into the city development plan.[36] As we have already seen, in the aftermath of the Reliance SEZ, many corporate actors appear to have done just that. There is a wealth of scholarship that explores these dynamics at length; the ubiquity of the 'informal' in contemporary cities, it is now well established, operates as a standing critique of planning ideals, so-called 'formality', and Eurocentric models of urbanisation. The urban village sits awkwardly with this literature.

While villages are exempt from land alienation, planning norms and building bye-laws, they are not *unauthorised*, *informal* or *illegal*. Villages are established administrative units, while village joint-owners and *lal dora* boundaries are codified and registered with the revenue department. The village forms part of a broader urban planning apparatus from which they are purposefully exempt. Gurgaon's urbanisation and the planning frameworks that produce it are porous and selectively answer to the territorial claims and demands of local elites, and in this case, landowning classes. But they are also unevenly deployed and discontiguous; written into the plan are a series of ambivalences, exemptions and compromises that etch 'urban' and 'rural' land uses into the soil.

What is more, while the impetus of much informal development, including elsewhere in Gurgaon (see Chapters 3 and 4), are motivated by future regularisation and inclusion into planning norms and codes, exemption is the lifeline of the landowner and rentier accumulation in the village. While Gurgaon's villages were integrated into the municipal government in 2008, the urbanisation of the villages – their integration into urban masterplans, rendering of legible property records and opening up of land markets – is fiercely resisted. Village landowners may lobby for the extension of *abadi* areas, as they successfully did in 2003, or the extension of municipal government infrastructures, as they frequently do, but they seldom call for inclusion into urban planning norms.[37]

Today there are over 100 villages that fall within Gurgaon's urbanisable area; they make up a small percentage of the total area of the city but house a considerable number of residents and play a vital role in the circulation of rents, wages and profits through the city.

Thus, landowners' uneven and altogether partial integration into Gurgaon's rampant real estate market is reflective of a broader mapping of real estate value onto agrarian spaces and subjects across Gurgaon. The ability of landowners, introduced at the outset of the chapter, to reinvest revenues from land sales into property construction inside the village boundaries is predicated on the village's classification as 'rural' and exemption from building bye-laws, urban development regulations, municipal jurisdiction and land acquisition by the PSRCA. The rentier economies that circulate through Gurgaon's villages are not incidental to capital accumulation in the surrounding city, the circulation of rents, profits and wages through the exempt villages make possible capital's unopposed access to land, cheapen labour costs essential for the functioning of the city and spark off networks of property investment among the former landowning classes.

Accumulating through the Village

In 2014, interested in how landowners were utilising revenue drawn from selling land, I conducted a household survey across 200 households in three village clusters in Gurgaon.[38] The landowners I spoke with invested revenues in a broad range of activities: they used revenues to pay off debts, send children to private schools, on weddings, house improvements and many invested in freight and transport businesses that fed demand for Gurgaon's insatiable construction boom throughout the 1990s and 2000s. Yet nearly every household surveyed invested part of their cash in urban property or rural land. That those who owned the largest landholdings, of 10 acres or more, invested in property and land is hardly surprising. Many of these landowners like Vishan, introduced earlier in the chapter, had long drawn incomes from landlordism, with investments in rural property markets and held positions within powerful local institutions, the village *panchayats*, local revenue bureaucracy and public sector offices. Around 98 per cent of these 'big' landowners invested land sale revenues in property and land.

More interestingly perhaps, 60 per cent of the smallest landowners, those households that owned 3 or less acres, also invested in land and property. These small and medium landowners are differentiated by a series of factors. While my data on caste background is not evenly representative of all groups, it does indicate that caste background has some role in shaping land prices: Ahir and Brahmin landowners received the highest prices per acre for their land – Ahirs receiving prices 82 per cent higher than, for example, Gujjars. Other factors are more incidental, for example, those villages incorporated into the development plan and acquired during the city's development boom from the early 2000s received prices 182 per cent higher than those in the prior period. This includes the land of highly differentiated groups including lower-caste communities who received strips of land after the Haryana Ceiling on Landholdings Act, 1974, former pastoral Gujjars and otherwise smallholding Jats and Ahirs, most of whom invested in property.

At the very least this demonstrates the prodigious if uneven practice of real estate investment among villagers from as early as the 1980s. While large landowners are likely to have the access to finance and political networks to invest in property within Gurgaon's plotted townships, for the small-to-medium landowners, who make up the majority of the landowning population, the exemption of the *abadi* territories opens up unregulated space to throw land compensation or revenue from sales into the construction of high-density rental housing. By providing landowners with unregulated land in the middle of the city, the PSRCA ensured that a certain 'middle' stratum of landowners was 'brought along' with and incorporated into the rentier interests of the state and real estate capital.

In principle there can be no individual private ownership of property inside the village boundaries or *lal dora*. The revenue department does not officially map the internal plots of the *abadi* area, and all village landowners are listed within land records together under one *khasra*, or survey number ('0').[39] The 'unmapping' of the village is an outcome of the Mahalwari settlements based on joint-village estates. The idea behind land settlement, as discussed in Chapter 1, was that they allowed colonial rulers to mobilise so-called 'customary' institutions that preserved social and political discipline while enabling the efficient extraction of revenue. Today, the jointness of the village estate provides a degree of illegibility that allows village landowners to accumulate rents through *abadi* property outside the formal view of the state while utilising political institutions and connections to the local state to extend and regularise their property base. In lieu of authorised records of property ownership, villagers' *ownership* of plots is substantiated by an array of improvised documentation proving possession and transfer of certain plots.[40]

ACCUMULATING IN THE VILLAGE

In early 2014 I sat on the stoop of an empty office room in Kapashera. Kapashera abuts the Delhi–Gurgaon border on the Delhi side, where tenement development has tripled the size of the village over the past three decades. While Kapashera is formally in Delhi, like Gurgaon's PSRCA the village *abadi* is exempt from acquisition, transfer and alienation under the Delhi Masterplan. Owing to Kapashera's relatively large size and proximity to Gurgaon's garment-export cluster in Udyog Vihar, the village has become the primary residence of Gurgaon's garment-export workforce since the 1990s. Landowners in Kapashera have plotted and developed a gridded matrix of four-storey tenement rental blocks that extend out from the original village towards the Gurgaon border.

Sat on plastic chairs hastily arranged following my arrival, Sanjay and three others smoked hookah in silence while observing a deluge of people passing up and down the village's central arterial lane. As discussed later in the book, the garment-export units in the adjacent Udyog Vihar industrial estate demand a cheap, hyper-flexibilised and hypermobile labourer, who can be propelled from contract to contract, workshop to factory, tenement to tenement, in seamless succession. Kapashera's dizzying matrix of cramped tenement housing provides the unregulated, disciplined environment intended to reproduce hypermobile, precarious workers the city's industries rely on.

Sanjay, alongside six other family members, owned nine properties and five tenements across Kapashera. Sanjay was a tall brooding man, who wore dark eyeliner and a white *kurta* that marked out the minority Yadav landlord population from the majority migrant residents in this part of the village. Sanjay was the middle brother of three sons, all living in Kapashera. Like many Yadavs, Sanjay's father was a retired soldier, while his brothers worked in lower middle-class employment in the police force and local bureaucracy. Most of Sanjay's family agricultural land was bought by private developers for luxury farmhouse development in the 1980s, leaving them with a small share in land on the outskirts of the village and two plots of property within the village.

Sanjay explained to me that it was not until some years after having sold his land that migrant workers began to come to the village and his fortunes dramatically transformed. Starting in the early 1990s, along with his brothers, the family began to develop a mixture of single-room rental lines and blocks for migrant workers on a small plot of land they owned in the western side of the village. Line housing predominately occupies land outside the *abadi* boundary, across the *gande nali* (dirty river) built on communal *phirni* land but now regularised and occupied by row upon row of line housing, informal garment workshops (or 'fabricators') and small clusters of tents occupied by migrant scheduled caste residents. Lines consist of four rows of ten brick rooms with an open area for washing at the rear. A line may not always stay a line but it represents the foundational structure of a 'block', the vertical development of the line incrementally built up over four or five floors.

From the mid-1990s, amid growing numbers of workers arriving in the village, the family began to reinvest rents from their original tenement into constructing more tenements across the village, starting with lines by the river which were later developed into larger four-storey blocks. Sanjay now has 200 rooms across five buildings on rent in the village, as well as a number of lines plotted informally on agricultural land. The latter informal tenements were successfully regularised and mapped by the Delhi government in the mid-2000s after lobbying from the Kapashera resident welfare association (RWA). Sanjay's family's net monthly income from rent alone is around 6 lakh rupees (9,000 US dollars). This is significantly higher than Gurgaon's median income. Originally drawing capital from selling land to developers, and now accumulating rents from property development within the village, Sanjay's family is an example of successful village rentiers.

The rentier interests of landlords like Sanjay are represented at a village level by the RWA. Just like those in municipalised areas of Gurgaon, and in neighbouring Delhi, RWAs play a central role in protecting the interests of property owners and promoting middle-class spatial priorities onto the city.[41] While this kind of RWA politics is prevalant within New Gurgaon's gated enclaves, in the urban villages in and around Gurgaon RWAs (and *panchayats* in areas not yet incorporated into the municipality) operate primarily as the political arm of landlord rentiers, working to formally extend the territorial reach of village boundaries and manage the internal infrastructural affairs of the village.

Over the course of thirty years, the Kapashera RWA, Gramin Uthan Avanj Kalyan Samiti (Rural Upliftment and Public Welfare Committee), have worked with the local revenue department and municipal councillor to extend the *abadi* boundaries and tentatively regularise tenements developed illegally on agricultural land. Manphool, an elderly landowner and member of the RWA, explained that the organisation was primarily formed to 'service our village issues', managing infrastructure development, community relations, events and employment for 'local boys'. As the village grew rapidly across the 1990s, it took on a greater role in managing what Manphool referred to as the 'chaos' of property development. The RWA, for example, appealed for the extension of the *lal dora* in the 1990s to encompass the vast neighbourhoods of tenement development known as Kapashera Extension. They have also sought to regularise 22 acres of brick tenement lanes, warehouses and industrial workshops on agricultural land, today referred to as Kapashera Border. Rentier accumulation and the incremental construction of property within *abadi* boundaries operates in step with these localised, and caste-oriented, village institutions. Much of their work to regularise property, as we discuss in the following chapter, is tentative. Property that extends out of the *abadi* and into agricultural land is often held under provisional regularisation certificates, which can be contested in court, particularly in instances where landowners have plotted on government land. Nevertheless, these documents have some political holding, substantiating a presence and facts on the ground that can be difficult to upend.[42]

The Committee

If the work of RWAs stabilise the political authority of rentier property, then smaller-scale investment committees drive rentier expansion. After finishing up the hookah, I sat in Sanjay's empty office, occupied by a small desk stacked with battered pieces of paper and two plastic chairs. Urban villages in and around Gurgaon have many of these empty office rooms, iteratively repurposed as makeshift tenement rooms, workshops or for small grocery shops. I had assumed Sanjay's room was much like the others and asked him what he sold from the room: 'This is no *dukaan*!' Sanjay extorted. 'This is for our committee.' Somewhat reluctantly, he pulled out an old ledger book, with a list of names of his tenants, rents, debts and total income of tens of buildings across the village. He explained that as landlords with large incomes, they needed somewhere 'safe' to put their money, and other landlords to invest it with. Sanjay's committee was essentially a collection of co-sharing landowners (registered in land-record books as *khata*s or *khewat*s) that have historically co-owned fragmented shares in agricultural land. The 'committee' is not a formally constituted organisation but a post-agrarian articulation of agricultural property regimes now put to work as an investment body.

Initially the six Yadav families in Sanjay's committee would collectively contribute a portion of rents each month to the committee pot. The committee then used the collective rents to provide loans to other villagers, finance large weddings and invest in tenement construction within the village boundaries.[43] I would often frequent Sanjay's dilapidated office, where committee members sat in the mornings and evenings playing cards, smoking hookah and overseeing migrant passers-by as if they were agricultural labourers on forgotten fields. The office, and hookah circle, was used to discuss potential investments, sewerage or water problems in the blocks, rival committee groups, plans for adding new floors to buildings and issues with migrant tenants. One morning I spent an hour sitting with Sanjay and his co-committee member Praveen while they heatedly discussed the expansion of a worker line into agricultural land through a series of sketches on the back of a piece of paper.[44] The expansion, Praveen explained, would start small with a network of single-storey lines that could be later developed vertically.[45] Sanjay's office doubled up as a space where problems would be worked out, day workers could be hired and committee meetings held.

Today Sanjay's committee was earning enough to invest in agricultural land in areas touted for urbanisation and plots in Gurgaon's developed colonies. He remarked with much pride: 'In the beginning we were dealing with just a few lakhs but these days we have crores, so our ambitions are higher ... we have bought plots here and invested in a mall in New Gurgaon.'

The prevalence of village property committees like Sanjay's across Gurgaon reflects the uneven way in which agrarian landowners have transformed themselves into rentier factions of urban capital. And yet it comes with the caveat that it is the monopoly power of local landowners within the *abadi* boundary and the non-alienable character of village property markets that has facilitated this transformation. And Sanjay's committee is by no means unique and I encountered village investment collectives all across Gurgaon's exempt villages; in Kasan, a village adjacent to IMT Manesar, around a quarter of Yadav landowning families participated in one single investment committee. The collective *form* in which village landowners amass and mobilise rents as property investments is directly drawn from the customary land shareholding practices that colonial and post-colonial revenue officials so obsessively sought to eradicate. As it turns out, there's more than one route to accumulation. Gurgaon's real estate sector – celebrated as an example of the potential of untrammelled supremacy of market logic – is sustained through non-alienable land and customary land tenures.

Aside from housing construction, landowners in the villages that surround Gurgaon's industrial estates also construct and lease out warehouse and workshop space that feed into local manufacturing supply chains. When conducting research in 2014, for example, there were around 300 workshops in Kapashera and Dundahera working with companies in the formal industrial areas of Gurgaon. These small-scale manufacturing facilities within the urban village provide a vital pressure valve for the city's organised garment-exports industry at times of high demand and seasonal labour scarcity. As such, the village workshops, while preferable to many landlords as they are only required to manage one tenant, are nevertheless responsive to the flitting demands of global garment production.

Landowners' monopoly control over villages allows landowners enriched by agricultural land sales to re-invest in rental properties within the village boundaries. The combination of high demand for agricultural land and exemption of *abadi* land allows village landowners to embark upon new avenues of urban rentier accumulation inside the village. Meanwhile, other networks of rentier capital that are spun out of the exempt villages, like those Sanjay was invested in, importantly mediate tensions between competing forms of capital in Gurgaon.

VILLAGE LIMITS

Material practices of village rentiers like Sanjay are entwined in multiple futures. Building tenements, tenement lanes, sewerage and power lines, managing tenants, running credit and leasing industrial workshops – each constitute the material base of the village rentier landowner and mediate tensions in the political economy. Yet they are also speculative in nature. When Sanjay invests in shopping malls and peri-urban land, he throws accumulated rents into the future in the hope that land will be captured and shopping malls developed; when building new tenements and lanes, Sanjay speculates upon the health of local manufacturing and ongoing demand for migrant labourers. These material practices are hedged on particular urban futures characterised by the certainty of ongoing commodification of land and labour in the city. Rent, after all, is merely an expression of value produced somewhere else. Former agriculturalists are now rentiers, planners, landlords and investors, engaged in anticipatory practices of urbanism premised on a seamless future of accumulation. And yet, of course, these futures are tentative and uncertain.

In 2015, when I completed my first batch of fieldwork, Sanjay had grand plans to extend his property base in the village, set up a small manufacturing business and shift his family to a residential colony in Gurgaon. When I returned to Gurgaon in 2018, a dip in Gurgaon's real estate market had scaled back Sanjay's plans. Sanjay still had his village tenements and credit running to tenants, but with development projects in the surrounding city, the committee shifted investments into village fabricators. With increased manufacturing demand coming from the industrial estate, the alleyways of Dundahera and Kapashera were again bustling with the humming of fabricator units that now occupied former grocery shops and tenement rooms. The fortunes of Gurgaon's village rentiers are uncertain, tied to the broader political economy of land, labour and capital in the city, and enabled and yet limited by the village.

The mixed success of villagers' attempts to expand *abadi* territories has put a check on the territorial reach of landowners' property base (albeit one the landowners creatively seek to bypass, as discussed in Chapter 3). For many village rentiers, the very boundary lines that enable them to amass propertied wealth *within* the village also painfully represent the limits to their class mobility and exclusion from the city proper. While the ongoing relevance of the villages to the city's economy point to the enduring importance of 'the people on the land' to capital accumulation, the production of a rentier class has been uneven and fractured, marked by the village itself.

This duplicitous experience of inclusion and exclusion is frequently retold in everyday conversation among landowning villagers. On chairing his investment committee, Sanjay noted that it was 'a great responsibility, for the development of our community, only a *bahubali* [strong man] can look after this money'. He drew great pride both from his modest property empire within the village and his responsibilities to the committee and carried himself with particular authority within the tight alleyways of the village. His everyday work involved supervising a network of building contractors, migrant tenants, tenant supervisors and rent collectors and liaising with committee members, local councillors, *panchayat* members and police officers.

Yet despite being a 'strong man' within the village, the infamy and proud manner in which Sanjay and many village rentiers across the city spoke of their property investments starkly contrasted with their physical emplacement within the village boundaries surrounded by 'modern' neighbourhoods of New Gurgaon, and their commonly expressed disquiet over their relative subordination within the millennium city.

This disquiet was expressed to me in two registers. In the first instance, Gurgaon's landowning Ahirs, Jats and Gujjars railed against the social mobility that Gurgaon's new service economies had provided for lower-caste members of the villages. One Yadav elder in Mullahera village opposite the Gurgaon Maruti plant remarked:

> These people who used to work our land, they now work in the companies in New Gurgaon and claim to have a rich ancestry. This is nonsense! The irony that we landowners have nothing and these people are rich.

Gurgaon's urban development brought with it new economic actors and interests that have not always aligned with the land-based territorial power of Jats and Ahirs in the twentieth century. The city's booming IT/ITES sector, for example, has provided many village residents without historic access to land, avenues toward social mobility. The landowner's complaint is not that only local Yadavs cannot get jobs in Gurgaon's IT sector, but rather that work is providing social mobility where under previous circumstances it was precisely the withdrawal of labour and one's caste-based ancestry through which social standing was derived.

Despite his claims to 'have nothing', his family had in fact invested in land in neighbouring Rewari and had developed rental accommodation in the village for industrial workers which he had used to send his grandson to an expensive private school and onto university in Australia. In this regard, the investment in land and property by Yadav village rentiers cannot be explained solely as a functional response to industrialists' desire for cheap social reproduction nor, despite the prodigious character of village rentiership, are all rentiers able to produce large surpluses from their investments in rental accommodation and land. For many the investment in land is fuelled by the desire to retain material and social standing amid rampant change in the social structure of villages that had bestowed power to agriculturalist castes. As he notes with some self-deprecation, 'The village has changed. Before we [Yadavs] were dominant, now whether you're Yadav or Chamar you can become big, now all are equal.'[46] While the claim that Yadavs and Chamars are 'equal' is certainly questionable – even my small household survey indicates the significant economic benefits the Yadavs have drawn from urbanisation, while caste and ethnoreligious violence remains a backdrop to Gurgaon's neoliberal urbanism (see Conclusion) – nevertheless this kind of remark gestures toward the anxieties felt within Yadav and other erstwhile landowning groups over their social and economic dominance within the villages.

Indeed, while there is much talk of changing relations between village communities, the most common point of disquiet was expressed over divisions that access to land markets has forged within Ahir and Jat communities. Almost every village landowner that remained living *inside* the villages in Gurgaon that I spoke with decried the 'breakdown' of village *bhaibandi* (brotherhood). Take, for example, the account of Raj Singh, a Yadav landowner in Rampura village that abuts the National Highway in western Gurgaon. His three-storey house inside the *abadi* was enclosed by 6-foot-high gates and surrounded by small, dilapidated bungalows of the other villagers. Sat drinking tea on his lawn, we were cast in the shadow of some residential towers being constructed on the agricultural land of the village. Raj Singh had sold fragments of land in the 2000s to a series of brokers and land agglomerators and reinvested the revenue in agricultural land in Sonepat district that he leases to a number of big farmers. Despite his transformation from a middling peasant-farmer to a capitalist rentier, Raj Singh was quick to deride the village brokers and middlemen that bought up his village land and sold it to developers at a profit. Gesturing over to the half-built towers hanging over us, he remarked:

> Here we were looted, we made a few crore but others [villagers] are making much, much more and here we're left with nothing ... a lot of people around here have been looted.

Technically villagers like Raj Singh were not 'looted' nor were they 'left with nothing'. To identify the 'losers' in a story of land-based class transformation, the 'looted' and dispossessed would require a close reading of those whose land was stripped of them in a century of enclosure and theft wrought through colonial and post-colonial agrarian reforms: the landless, lower-caste village residents who continue to be stripped of their rights to property.[47] While village rentiers locate their place in the contemporary city of Gurgaon by appeal to caste-belonging and through speculative investments in property, the containment of urban villages which in many cases provided the material terrain for the development of rentier capital equally represents the very boundary line of village rentiers' integration into the city. This is the double space of the urban village. Despite the village rentier's active role within real estate markets, the urban village for most village rentiers remains in a state of stasis, defined in immutable antiquity in relation to the glimmering high-rise apartments that jut up against it.

It is perhaps no surprise then that Yadav village rentiers openly derided men that had experienced social mobility for their greed, 'forgetting [their] culture' or for wasting away money on vices such as alcohol or material goods. Nevertheless, stories and anecdotes of the vast wealth and success of the village's *bade admi* disseminated the mystery of the transformative promise of property investment within everyday discourses and discussions of village rentiers. Amid these narratives and discourses, and despite village rentier's active role within real estate markets, the urban village for most village rentiers and indeed non-rentier 'villagers' remains in a state of stasis, defined in immutable antiquity in relation to the glimmering high-rise apartments that jut up against it. Devpal, the former *sarpanch* of Carterpuri village, so named after the legend that a former US president was born in the village, described this feeling of stasis to me as such:

> This village has not changed, look around! The old panchayat land is still used as a *goshala* [cow shed], it's been six or seven years since the panchayat ended, some of us have buildings there but it is not so profitable.... The village is captured on all four sides by sector people, they put up gates so we cannot pass through – we only have one entry and exit from the village. We have been captured on all four sides.

Gurgaon's real estate boom has been facilitated not by the blanket imposition of private property but by territorial instruments that preserve non-privatised and customary lands, and tentatively extend the territorial reach of agrarian landowners out from their villages. These have in turn 'brought in' small to medium landowners into factions of rentier capital. Yet while the village provides landowners with an opportunity to actively participate in village property and urban land markets, they equally represent village rentiers' exclusion from and limits to incorporation within broader urban political economy. 'Looting' discourse as such draws our attention to the complicated and contradictory position of the village rentier in the hegemonic space of the city: their participation in capitalist propertied lives constrained by the very boundary lines that enable them.

From the spaces of the village, from large village mansions and Sanjay's cramped, empty office, one can observe the inner workings of an emergent class identity in between two prevailing features of Gurgaon's rentier agrarian transition, experiences of social and material loss and the discursive often speculative hope, implicit in property ownership, of transition from mere village rentiers of migrant labourers to fully fledged members of Gurgaon's booming real estate economy.

Elite Rentiers

Unlike the majority landowners who draw their incomes from property construction within the village boundaries, Gurgaon's largest landowning families – some of whom collectively owned up to 60 acres of land up until the 1980s – have used significant revenues from land sales to position themselves as land aggregators, builders and middlemen brokering land for the corporate real estate sector. As we explore in the following chapter, while large landowners have been able to command the highest prices for their land, they also perform a vital function for corporate real estate firms: the aggregation of rural land. The capacity of developers like DLF to accumulate thousands of acres of fragmented land shares is dependent upon landowners doing the complex work of land's translation.

In late 2015 I attended the wedding of a Delhi politician who was originally from Dundahera, a Yadav village that borders Kapashera to the south. The groom's family owned a water park and a series of luxury resorts in and around the Delhi–Gurgaon border. Politicians took to the stage for photos with the bride, while drones circled the sky taking videos projected onto large screens behind the bride and groom. Informally dressed security guards with open-carry guns stood around the periphery of the tent watching events unfold. The wedding was lavish, alcohol was served, there were a number of international cuisines on offer and tables were populated by important Delhiites and real estate brokers and businessmen of Gurgaon's elite rentier networks. While a lavish wedding is perhaps not a rarity among the urban upper classes, the wedding contrasted with those of villagers that I had attended: typically modest affairs held in large tents in old Gurgaon, with brash disco music, *nimbu paani* (lemon juice) and vegetarian cuisine.

That day I was a guest of Vikram Yadav, a cousin of the bride who was also the president of one of Gurgaon's industrialist associations. Vikram was a middle-aged man from a family of Yadavs who moved out of Dundahera village to the neighbouring private colony, Surya Vihar, in the early 1990s. From the 1980s, Vikram's family had around 8 acres of land in Dundahera village acquired by the state to make way for the Udyog Vihar industrial estate and another 4 acres of their land in neighbouring Nathupur village bought by private developers. The family invested part of their revenues in land buying up property in a newly built residential colony and land on the outskirts of the city and the other part in a series of businesses that anticipated Gurgaon's coming real estate boom. Vikram's brother had invested early in the freight industry that supplied Gurgaon's developers with their insatiable demand for concrete, and today owned one of the largest transport contractors in the city. Meanwhile Vikram and his father set up a small construction contractor and won a series of contracts developing industrial estates across the city. Vikram's family were, he explained, unlike other local Yadav's who were 'connected to their lands', 'business-minded'. Not coincidentally, as relatively large landowners, the family also had a series of connections to officials in both the local Congress and Aam Admi Party. The wedding we attended that evening was his cousin's, a politician in the Delhi State Assembly.

Vikram's family, whose significant wealth came after their land was acquired by the government and sold to private developers in the early 1990s, typify the movement of factions of large landowning Yadavs in Gurgaon's villages into local positions of relative power, particularly tied to construction, real estate and industry. These families were not primarily reliant upon earnings from village property, despite leasing village property to migrant workers, and form part of an army of middle-class former landowners engaged in a variety of property businesses that underpin higher-scale real estate activity.

Today the family owns plots across Gurgaon's industrial estates that they lease to major industrialists and a share in a high-end commercial property in Gurgaon's Cyber City. Through Vikram I met former *panchayat* members who were leasing out commercial plots to multinational corporations and property brokers who agglomerate land across the city for real estate firms.

Vikram, and those he introduced me to, are an example of what I term 'elite rentiers'.

Many of Gurgaon's elite rentiers that I encountered drew incomes from leasing industrial plots to industrialists. Vikram explained the integration of villagers into industrial and commercial rentiership over the past twenty-five years:

> At first, here in Udyog Vihar [industrial estate], there were only automobile companies, then in the 1990s came garment-exports and after 2000 IT and e-commerce. Really it wasn't until the IT companies arrived that the estate had large demand that's when we began buying plots, today around 50% of plots are leased out here by ten or so families originally from Dundahera.

Vikram explained that villager investment in industrial plots back then was far less common as property did not seem a viable business for local people. Vikram's family, however, already had a series of property stakes and were involved in the construction business. They had connections with businesses so investment in property was seen as a 'natural' progression. He noted that by the time Gurgaon's other industrial estate IMT Manesar was built in the mid-2000s, local Yadav businessmen were well aware of the profitability of industrial real estate and invested en mass.

The HSIIDC, which develops and manages the state's industrial spaces, initially held relatively loose regulations on industrial plot ownership. Plot buyers were expected to produce on only 25 per cent of the plot and run operations for a minimum of one year before reselling, a stipulation which was later replaced with a one-time 25 per cent resale fee. The loose regulations on industrial plot ownership allowed local villagers a relatively risk-free avenue into speculating on industrial property. Vikram explained that in IMT Manesar

> only 30% of plot owners are industrialists, 70% are people from our villages who saw what happened in Udyog Vihar, had come into money and wanted to invest. There must be at least 200 families from our villages who own plots on lease to industrialists in Manesar ... these people have no real interest in manufacturing.

Increasingly these investments are held *against* industry, insofar as they are held speculatively with little interest in leasing to industrialists. Vikram notes that plot ownership, for most villagers is simply a quick way into property investment, the land is already assembled and 'cleared' by the state and there is little incentive to lease out the land. The Manesar Industrialist Welfare Association notes only 40 per cent of allotments in IMT Manesar are operational. A 2012 report put the figure as low as 25 per cent, contending that HSIIDC officers explicitly encouraged elite rentiers to draw value from land sales rather than engage in manufacturing.[48]

Vikram lived in a gated apartment complex that was encircled on all sides by, what he termed, 'encroaching' village land. As discussed in Chapter 5, village rentiers in the abutting villages of Dundahera and Kapashera had extended property constructions right up to the border with the residential colony, forcing the residents to build a 12-foot, electrified wall to distance the village from their 'urban' neighbourhood. I was interested in how he and his family felt toward his old neighbourhoods and their partial exclusion from the everyday life of the city. He remarked:

> The problem is both the government and the villagers. The government have no reason to extend services and provisions to the villages. The villagers are simple people, it is a question of rights, not service, they will demand water, electricity, pukka roads, but they're not willing to pay for it. This is why they are not developing.

This attitude towards the urban villages was common among the elite rentiers that I spent time with. Intriguingly, elite rentiers like Vikram drew no discernible identification with those agrarian pasts which had shaped their transitions into urban citizens, nor of their enduring relationship between their own positions and that of those who remained in the urban village. As the village rentiers would poignantly remark, Vikram had forgotten the village.

The accumulative strategies of elite rentiers are made possible by an activist state creating accumulative landscapes through agrarian and urban planning reforms, inserting both agricultural land and landowner subjectivity into logics of speculative property-based accumulation. Like village rentiers, it is within this articulation of an uneven agrarian social structure, state planning and the emerging urban imperatives that elite rentiers engage productively in the urbanisation process. Yet there remain key material and discursive fractures between the experiences and economic interests of the village and elite rentiers shaped precisely by their uneven positions within Gurgaon's political economy. Yadav rentierism, as an emergent intra-caste class project at the heart of Gurgaon's urban hegemonic alliance, might as such be understood as constitutive of a 'ruptural unity' that has both enabled capital accumulation and might also confound or provide its limits.[49]

THE VILLAGE FRONTIER

In Gurgaon the village, a form of monopolised land tenure held exclusively by the proprietary body,[50] oils the cogs of the city's political economy, freeing the exploitation of land and labour, while partially integrating landlord classes into networks of rentier capitalism. One of the 'triumphs of capitalism', writes David Harvey, has been to force landowners to 'use the capital they centralize in productive ways, rather than living off the fat of the land in conspicuous consumption'.[51] Such triumphant compulsion, wherein landlords mobilise land solely as a financial asset, Harvey writes, strips landed property of its autonomous and conflictual role vis-à-vis capital and transforms landowners 'into a faction of capital itself'. This compulsion in Gurgaon has partly operated through the maintenance of non-alienable, landed monopolies. Alongside the maintenance of customary landholdings, the village has proved vital for the settlement of real estate capital and transformation of peasant farmers into landlord rentiers. Landlord rentiers' capacity to accumulate, their ability to collectively throw rental surpluses back into circulation through the city's real estate market is not only predicated upon unregulated housing provision within the *abadi* but also mediated by the fitful wants of globalised garment exports. In leasing out space for informal commodity production within the village boundaries, the rentier activities of villagers knit together and process territorial conflicts between real estate (ground rents), migrant labour (wages) and manufacturing industry (profits) and shape class transformation within the village. The role of the village – jointly owned, non-alienable land tenure – in managing this tripartite jumble of social and spatial relations is characteristic of the uneven processes of accumulation and class transformation in peri-urban India.[52] The village pulls out the deeply relational quality of urban, agrarian and industrial forces unevenly producing capitalist value in contemporary Gurgaon.

This chapter has examined how the permanence of the village, a non-alienable land tenure in which village elites hold monopoly power, politically and socially authenticated the mass commoditisation and conversion of rural land into real estate capital. Amid a sea of luxury real estate, village property markets together with revenues swilling from land sales have allowed partial entry of village elites into the economic, cultural and ideological project of the millennium city. The partiality of this inclusion is marked in landowners' experiences of agrarian change. The spectres of colonial and post-colonial agrarian policy loom large over contemporary urban transformation on the frontier. The binding of identities and cultures to agricultural land, codified by colonial rule and mobilised by post-colonial government, is hard to shake off amid the slow post-agrarian transition; in subaltern fashion the peculiar non-alienable spaces at the heart of Gurgaon are both *enabling* and *disabling*, constitutive of the bizarrely composite socio-spatial relations of the city.

In doing so, the village as a particular property regime mediates and keeps in motion tensions within between labour, land and capital across the city. The village is a conjunctural social form of communal landed power that tentatively stitches together value relations on India's urban frontier. Gurgaon's uneven landscape of alienated real estate and exempted villages is an expression of the entanglement of the coming together of customary and so-called 'modern' modes of land use and authority. These entanglements, in essence, counterintuitively allow land to be 'treated as an open field for the circulation of interest-bearing capital'.[53]

In claiming the village to be a particular kind of 'frontier', I am drawing attention to the ways that 'the village' – spatial unit, customary land tenure and 'uncapitalised' terrain[54] – unlocks the conditions for land and labour-based accumulation in Gurgaon, allowing for the subsumption of agrarian land to capitalist rubrics and the conjuring of an altogether different kind of city. As Lund writes, the frontier can be thought of as an 'influx and presence of non-native private actors in pursuit of the newly discovered resources [and] offers a reconfiguration of the conditions of possibility'. As I discuss further in Chapter 3, frontiers are speculative spaces where the battle for urban and agrarian futures are contested and creatively secured.

When real estate capitalists came to Gurgaon from the 1980s looking to capture and commodify land into parcelised plots of real estate, they were forced into a series of compromises with landowning classes and territories and the translation of thousands of fragments of customary land. These compromises and translations have not smoothly led to the real estate sectors' clean totalisation of the land market, but rather they highlight the partial and mutated forms through which capitalist value is concretely settled. At the village frontier capital churns through land and labour for capital, but it does so at the price of a territorially restricted land market, a politically empowered class of landed property and unruly and uncertain investment patterns of a nascent rentier class.

Finally, as we see in the following chapters, the village frontier is driven by speculation. The practice of opening up land and readying agrarian property regimes for capitalisation is a speculative affair, pitched to a promise of ascending real estate value and caste-layered authority of territorial claims. This process is equally material. The very practice of representation and standardisation that translate the world into commodifiable forms involves the slippery, materially contested task of laying down markers, draining out water bodies, flattening uneven topographies, shifting clods of soil and pitching walls. Standardisations are always contested approximations, that play on confusion, contortion and subterfuge. Subaltern frontiers provide a way of considering the situated material and cultural techne through which natures come to be appropriated and authorised (or not) of the slippages, miss translations and compromises that are involved in capital's realisation (or not) at the frontier.

In this regard, when I claim that the village is a frontier that makes possible the commoditisation of land and exploitation of labour-power, I do so with the caveat that the processing and translation of land and labour through the village is productive of spaces and agents of withholding, what Lefebvre referred to as the residues, that both disrupt and animate hegemonic configurations of capital. The enduring presence of non-privatised, customary lands across the so-called 'private city', and their deployment as incubators of ground rent, has facilitated the transformation of agrarian landowning classes and the expansion of real estate capital across India's millennium city.

Notes

1. Sassen, 'A Savage Sorting of Winners and Losers'.
2. In Theresa Caldeira's essay 'Peripheral Urbanization', she argues that 'peripheries are spaces that frequently unsettle official logics' through transversal engagements. The transversality of urban formations, for Caldeira, exhibit 'multiple formations of inequality' that are 'inherently unstable and contingent'. Caldeira's intervention is important in foregrounding the instabilities and contingencies of 'official' city-making.
3. Tsing, *Friction*.
4. Marx, 'The Trinity Formula', in *Capital*, vol. 3, ch. 48.
5. Coronil, *The Magical State*.

6. Sassen, *Expulsions*; Glassman, 'Primitive Accumulation'; De Angelis, 'Marx and Primitive Accumulation'.
7. Harvey, 'The Right to the City', 34.
8. Banerjee-Guha, 'Neoliberalising the "Urban"'.
9. Sanyal, *Rethinking Capitalist Development*.
10. Harvey, 'Theory on Rent', in *The Limits to Capital*.
11. Roy, 'Why India Cannot Plan Its Cities'.
12. In Punjab and Haryana, the East Punjab Holdings Act, 1948; the Punjab Ceiling on Landholdings Act; the Panchayat Act.
13. Gill, *Land Reforms in India*, vol. 6.
14. Sankhe et al., *India's Urban Awakening*.
15. D'Costa and Chakraborty, *The Land Question in India*.
16. Maurya and Vaishampayan, 'Growth and Structural Changes'.
17. Jaffrelot and Kalaiyarasan, 'The Political Economy of the Jat Agitation', 33.
18. Chowdhry, '"First Our Jobs then Our Girls"'.
19. Bernstein, 'Is There an Agrarian Question in the 21st Century?'
20. In Haryana, Ahirs are classified as OBC.
21. Jaffrelot and Kalaiyarasan, 'The Political Economy of the Jat Agitation'; Datta, 'Backward Caste Movement'.
22. Jaffrelot and Kalaiyarasan, 'The Political Economy of the Jat Agitation', 30.
23. Balagopal, 'An Ideology for the Provincial Propertied Class'.
24. Hart, 'The Agrarian Question and Industrial Dispersal in South Africa'.
25. Chari, *Fraternal Capital*.
26. Capps, 'Tribal-Landed Property'.
27. Barnes, *Making Cars in the New India*.
28. Between 2014 and 2015, I conducted ethnographic fieldwork with landowning families in three villages, Kapashera, Badshahpur and Manesar, supplemented by a household survey (n=198) across three village clusters (see Table 2.1): (*a*) Dundahera, Carterpuri and Kapashera, all villages located along the old Delhi–Gurgaon road, in which land was acquired in the 1980s by the state for industrial and residential purposes; (*b*) Nathupur, Jharsa and Badshahpur villages in central 'New' Gurgaon, in which land was acquired by the private sector from the 1990s; and (*c*) Rampura, Manesar and Kherki Duala in west Gurgaon in which land was acquired by both the private and public sector from the late 1990s following the expansion of the Gurgaon–Manesar masterplan.
29. As landowners predominately hold land plots and shares as a joint household, here 'landowner' refers more specifically to a single landowning family.

30. Any quotation not accompanied by a formal citation is taken from interviews conducted by the author.
31. 'Crore' is a unit followed in the South Asian numbering system, where 1 crore = 10,000,000.
32. Singh, 'Builder Profits Soar as Master Plans Proliferate in Gurgaon'.
33. As we see in Chapter 3, this logic of exemption extends beyond the administrative and ideological boundaries of 'the village' to incorporate and deploy the 'commons' in distinct ways.
34. Glover, 'The Troubled Passage from "Village Communities"'.
35. In 2003, amid a property boom in Gurgaon, the state government amended the act to extend land under exemption to 'areas adjacent to the *abadi deh*', substantially boosting villagers territorial and rentier base.
36. Benjamin, 'Occupancy Urbanism'.
37. In 2020 the Haryana government announced a scheme to remove *lal dora* boundaries and enclose and incorporate *abadi* areas into property markets.
38. These clusters were selected on the basis of differing periods of inclusion into the Gurgaon Development Plan, and exposure to different forms of land alienation. Cluster 1: Dundahera, Carterpuri and Kapashera were predominately subject to state acquisitions in the 1970s and 1980s; Cluster 2: Jharsa, Nathupur and Badshahpur have been urbanised in the 1996 and 2007 development plans and were subject to private acquisitions; Cluster 3: Rampura, Manesar and Khoh were integrated in the 2007 masterplan and have been subject to both state and private sector acquisitions.
39. A *khasra* is a survey number allocated to a particular plot of land by the revenue department.
40. Pati, 'The Productive Fuzziness'.
41. Ghertner, *Rule by Aesthetics*.
42. Bathla, 'Planned Illegality, Permanent Temporariness'.
43. It was not clear to me how these committees related to the village *panchayat* that despite municipalisation in the 1990s still informally operated and met.
44. I suspected that the new tenements were to be built on *gorah* or *phirni* land, designated for cattle and grazing for administrative purposes, and collectively owned by the village *panchayat* – although I could not confirm this.
45. On my subsequent visits to Sanjay in the following years, I would learn that the development remained on paper.
46. *Chamars* are a scheduled caste in Haryana.
47. Cowan, 'The Village as Urban Infrastructure'.
48. Khandelwal, 'Manesar IMT'.

49. Gidwani, *Capital, Interrupted*.
50. In practice, informal property transfers among non-resident landowners are prevalent particularly in villages with high demand. See Pati, 'The Productive Fuzziness of Land Documents'.
51. Harvey, *Limits to Capital*, 366.
52. Coronil, *The Magical State*.
53. Harvey, *Limits to Capital*, 371.
54. Moore, *Capitalism in the Web of Life*.

BIBLIOGRAPHY

Balagopal, K. 'An Ideology for the Provincial Propertied Class'. *Economic and Political Weekly* 22, nos. 36–37 (1987): 1544–46.

Banerjee-Guha, S. 'Neoliberalising the "Urban": New Geographies of Power and Injustice in Indian Cities'. *Economic and Political Weekly* 44, no. 22 (2009): 95–107.

Barnes, Tom. *Making Cars in the New India: Industry, Precarity and Informality*. Cambridge: Cambridge University Press, 2018.

Bathla, N. 'Planned Illegality, Permanent Temporariness, and Strategic Philanthropy: Tenement Towns under Extended Urbanisation of Postmetropolitan Delhi'. *Housing Studies* (November 2021): 1–21.

Benjamin, Solomon. 'Occupancy Urbanism: Radicalizing Politics and Economy beyond Policy and Programs'. *International Journal of Urban and Regional Research* 32, no. 3 (2008): 719–29.

Bernstein, Henry. 'Is There an Agrarian Question in the 21st Century?' *Canadian Journal of Development Studies/Revue Canadienne d'études Du Développement* 27, no. 4 (2006): 449–60.

Blomley, Nicholas. 'Enclosure, Common Right and the Property of the Poor'. *Social and Legal Studies* 17, no. 3 (2008): 311–31.

Caldeira, Teresa P. R. 'Peripheral Urbanization: Autoconstruction, Transversal Logics, and Politics in Cities of the Global South'. *Environment and Planning D: Society and Space* 35, no. 1 (2017): 3–20.

Capps, Gavin. 'Tribal-Landed Property: The Value of the Chieftaincy in Contemporary Africa'. *Journal of Agrarian Change* 16, no. 3 (2016): 452–77.

Chari, Sharad. *Fraternal Capital: Peasant-Workers, Self-Made Men, and Globalization in Provincial India*. Stanford: Stanford University Press, 2004.

Chowdhry, Prem. '"First Our Jobs Then Our Girls": The Dominant Caste Perceptions on the "Rising" Dalits'. *Modern Asian Studies* 43, no. 2 (2009): 437–79.

Coronil, Fernando. *The Magical State: Nature, Money, and Modernity in Venezuela*. Chicago: University of Chicago Press, 1997.
Cowan, Thomas. 'The Village as Urban Infrastructure: Social Reproduction, Agrarian Repair and Uneven Urbanisation'. *Environment and Planning E: Nature and Space* 4, no. 3 (2021): 736–55.
Datta, Nonica. 'Backward Caste Movement Gains Ground'. *Economic and Political Weekly* 11, no. 17 (1999): 2630–31.
D'Costa, A. P., and A. Chakraborty, eds. *The Land Question in India: State, Dispossession, and Capitalist Transition*. Oxford: Oxford University Press, 2017.
De Angelis, Massimo. 'Marx and Primitive Accumulation: The Continuous Character of Capital's Enclosures'. *Commoner* 2, no. 1 (2001): 1–22.
Gidwani, Vinay K. *Capital, Interrupted: Agrarian Development and the Politics of Work in India*. Minneapolis: University of Minnesota Press, 2008.
Gill, Sucha Singh. *Land Reforms in India*. Vol. 6, *Intervention for Agrarian Capitalist Transformation in Punjab and Haryana*. New Delhi: Sage Publications India Pvt. Ltd, 2001.
Glassman, Jim. 'Primitive Accumulation, Accumulation by Dispossession, Accumulation by "Extra-Economic" Means'. *Progress in Human Geography* 30, no. 5 (2006): 608–25.
Glover, William J. 'The Troubled Passage from "Village Communities" to Planned New Town Developments in Mid-Twentieth-Century South Asia'. *Urban History* 39, no. 1 (2012): 108–27.
Hart, Gillian. 'The Agrarian Question and Industrial Dispersal in South Africa: Agro-Industrial Linkages through Asian Lenses'. *Journal of Peasant Studies* 23, nos. 2–3 (1996): 245–77.
Harvey, David. *The Limits to Capital*. Oxford: Verso, 1982.
———. 'The Right to the City'. *New Left Review* 53 (September–October 2008): 23–40.
Jaffrelot, Christophe, and A. Kalaiyarasan. 'The Political Economy of the Jat Agitation for Other Backward Class Status'. *Economic and Political Weekly* 54, no. 7 (2019): 29–37.
Khandelwal, Akshat. 'Manesar IMT: A Township Dream Turns an Infrastructure Mess'. *Indian Express*, 21 August 2012. http://indianexpress.com/article/cities/delhi/manesar-imt-a-township-dream-turns-an-infrastructure-mess/. Accessed 1 January 2021.
Marx, K. *Capital*. Vol. 3. Translated by B. Fowkes. London: Penguin Books, 1990.
Maurya, Nagendra Kumar, and Jayant Vinayak Vaishampayan. 'Growth and Structural Changes in India's Industrial Sector'. *International Journal of Economics* 6, no. 2 (2012): 321–31.

Moore, Jason W. *Capitalism in the Web of Life: Ecology and the Accumulation of Capital.* London: Verso Books, 2015.

Pati, Sushmita. 'The Productive Fuzziness of Land Documents: The State and Processes of Accumulation in Urban Villages of Delhi'. *Contributions to Indian Sociology* 53, no. 2 (2019): 249–71.

Roy, Ananya. 'Why India Cannot Plan Its Cities: Informality, Insurgence and the Idiom of Urbanization'. *Planning Theory* 8, no. 1 (2009): 76–87.

Sankhe, Shirish, Ireena Vittal, Richard Dobbs, Ajit Mohan, Ankur Gulati, Jonathan Ablett, Shishir Gupta, Alex Kim, Sudipto Paul and Adirya Sanghvi. *India's Urban Awakening: Building Inclusive Cities, Sustaining Economic Growth.* Mumbai: McKinsey Global Institute, 2010.

Sanyal, Kalyan. *Rethinking Capitalist Development: Primitive Accumulation, Governmentality and Post-Colonial Capitalism.* London: Routledge, 2007.

Sassen, Saskia. 'A Savage Sorting of Winners and Losers: Contemporary Versions of Primitive Accumulation'. *Globalizations* 7, nos. 1–2 (2010): 23–50.

———. *Expulsions: Brutality and Complexity in the Global Economy.* Cambridge, MA: Harvard University Press, 2014.

Sheth, Sudev J. 'Historical Transformations in Boundary and Land Use in New Delhi's Urban Villages'. *Economic and Political Weekly* 52, no. 5 (2017): 41–49.

Singh, Shalini. 'Builder Profits Soar as Master Plans Proliferate in Gurgaon'. *The Hindu*, 27 May 2013. https://www.thehindu.com/news/national/builder-profits-soar-as-master-plans-proliferate-in-gurgaon/article4753735.ece. Accessed 1 January 2021.

Tsing, Anna Lowenhaupt. *Friction: An Ethnography of Global Connection.* New Jersey: Princeton University Press, 2011.

3 | The Plot

MALL DREAMS

I met Mukesh Yadav sitting on the side of the Gurgaon–Sohna road in Badshahpur village in late 2015. Mukesh and two other elderly men were playing cards under the late afternoon shade while two others shared a hookah pipe. Badshahpur village was incorporated into the Gurgaon–Manesar Urban Complex in 2007, precipitating a rush on the village land by a host of domestic and international real estate firms emboldened by the liberalisation of the real estate sector two years ago. The historic territory of eighteenth-century Mughal military ruler Begum Samru, today the village is split into two by the road that connects central Gurgaon to its southern neighbour Sohna, a much quieter town that had recently been brought under its own urban development plan. Between 2008 and 2014, 560 acres of land in Badshahpur was purchased by developers and licenced by the planning department for the construction of a series of gated residential towers and colonies at the intersection of the highly sought-after DLF Golf Course Road. The village, akin to so many in Gurgaon, is composed of low-rise, fading and densely constructed tenement buildings linked by a maze of narrow paved streets, hemmed in on all sides by the porous boundary walls of posh residential colonies. The roadside is alive with dusty activity throughout the late afternoon and into the evening, with lorries, jeeps and cars shooting down the main thoroughfare passing small grocery shops and *dhabas* rubbing shoulders with small brokerage and dealership offices.

Mukesh's family had owned 4 acres of land across Badshahpur and like all landowners his family's landholdings were split into smaller shares scattered across different plots in the village. In addition, Mukesh's family had a non-alienable claim to both *abadi* property and the village *shamilat* (common) lands. As the eldest son, he had spent much of his life overseeing the family's land and was the final authority when it came to selling up in the mid-2000s. Like many of the small to medium landowners in Gurgaon, Mukesh's family did not greatly benefit from access to Green Revolution technologies in the 1960s. 'Land was never profitable,' he explained. 'We grew some wheat and mustard but it's difficult to make a living from this land and now with the builders coming here, there's no future in farming for people here.' Mukesh's family had long ceased operating as farmer-cultivators and drawn incomes from leasing out tough lands to farmers and tenants. Like many landowners on Gurgaon's frontier villages, narratives of agrarian decline, toughness and aridity – materially shaped by colonial uneven development – precipitated the common-sense conversion of land and landowners' livelihoods for future, real estate uses.

In 2007 Badshahpur was incorporated into the Gurgaon–Manesar Urban Complex, 2021, the village's agricultural fields re-presented in the city development plan in blank yellow boxes indicating their prospective future 'residential' land uses. The subsequent arrival of real estate brokers and aggregators to the village sparked a series of strategies among landowners to ready their lands for sale. As I argued in Chapter 2, the arrival of real estate capital to Gurgaon has predominately been met with an eagerness among landowning communities that contrasts with more popular accounts of dispossessive urbanisation.

Soon after, Mukesh and his family sold most of their 4 acres of land to Unitech, one of Gurgaon's most prolific real estate developers, who had by 2013 amassed a land-bank of over 1,000 acres in the city. The family sold their scattered land shares for a relatively cheap total of 30 lakh rupees (39,000 US dollars) an acre, earning around 1.2 crore rupees (156,000 US dollars) from the sale. Today luxury residential towers and gated colonies on Mukesh's former land, looming over the village, sell for around 1,800 rupees (24 US dollars) a square foot, or 7.8 crore rupees (1 million US dollars) an acre.

As I asked about how landowners felt about selling their lands, a routine question in my interviews and discussions, Mukesh countered in a matter-of-fact tone. 'Brokers came here, offering a good price far higher than our expectations, why would we challenge this? [The land] is in the sectors now,' he explained, deploying the term used to describe the master-planned, privately developed 'urban' areas of the city while gesturing to a residential complex in the distance.

As discussed previously, the arrival of planners, then real estate capital to the village had thrown landowners – otherwise facing an agrarian economy in terminal decline – into tentative and highly speculative strategies to secure high returns for their land, and productively utilise revenues drawn from land sales. These strategies are numerous. Mukesh invested the revenue he received from the sale of his 4 acres to rebuild his family home in the village into a 'proper' house and pay for the private education of his sons. In addition, seeking to capitalise on rumours of Sohna's pending urbanisation, Mukesh worked with a local broker to buy shares in 8 acres of agricultural land in Sohna. He said, 'Let's see if we can sell it, soon the builders will be shifting to Sohna, there is good land there … land is the only way we can make money these days.'

Mukesh's property strategies are characteristic of what a recent body of scholarship has referred to as India's 'speculative' urban frontiers.[1] Speculation on Gurgaon's urban frontier takes place in the context of agrarian decline discussed in previous chapters and comes in two forms. As Mukesh's statement indicates, agrarian city-making involves a collective projection of a strictured post-agrarian future that is solely bound to the realisation of real estate value in land. Speculative state development projects elicit local landowning Jats, Gujars and Ahirs to lead city-making on the frontier, to enjoin themselves and their lands to promised urban economy and ascendant land values therein. Speculative projections look to solidify private property as an always already established social fact by evoking temporal and perceptive registers that can re-present contested agrarian property regimes as antiquated and in urgent need of reform. Borrowing from Katherine McNeilly's work on legal temporality, we might posit the urban frontier as an 'untimely' concept, one that deals with the unknowable present by seeking by any means necessary to take the reins of and certainise the future.[2] It is precisely this unknowability that inserts a relation of subalternity to India's new urban frontiers. Speculative strategies mobilise these 'untimely futures' to impress the imperative – or compulsion – for the expansion and naturalisation of real estate capital. Secondly, speculation on the frontier involves the creative and performative work of repurposing complex agrarian property relations as liberal private property. No longer tied to agricultural productivity and irrigation,[3] land values today are drawn from land's proximity to interstitial rent gaps produced by state development schemes (on the agrarian-urban border, on common lands, and so on) and also from land's proclivity to act as a fungible resource for capitalist circulation and rentier extraction. Locating one's investments and repurposing complex agrarian property are speculative endeavours that profit from uncertainty and risk. This is wholeheartedly a caste and class project, one in which the state reifies the territorial claims and strategies of Jat and Ahir landowning classes like Mukesh, just as it admonishes and marginalises those of scheduled caste communities.

Mukesh's investments were speculative insofar as they involve the belief that rural land's uncertain present would soon be resolved and converted into urban real estate, that rural land in neighbouring Sohna would one day turn the kinds of value witnessed on his own land. The planning department's expansion of urban development plans across the 2000s, coupled with alluring rent gaps on Gurgaon's urban–rural periphery, motivate landowners like Mukesh to throw their incomes into rural land. As we shall learn later in the chapter, this frequently relies upon getting creative and repurposing complex and ambiguous agrarian tenurial regimes in order to establish property claims and position themselves for real estate accumulation. In lieu of direct state support, developers rely upon the work of landowners and brokers who in anticipation of land sales piece together rural landholdings into legible plots with clear titles. By speculatively investing in peripheral lands, landowners like Mukesh aim to profit from readying the land for uncertain commercialisation.

What is striking about Mukesh's continued belief in rural land and property markets are his own various failures to obtain a return on investment. Alongside a group of his former co-sharers in the village, Mukesh had invested in a proposed shopping mall development in central Gurgaon. In the early 2000s Gurgaon was dubbed 'city of malls' after a flush of speculative investment developed over twenty-four shopping malls along MG Road to cater to the upper-class residents of nearby private colonies. A decade later and the speculative gamble had not paid off, with few businesses willing to pay expensive unit rates, leaving half-empty malls across the city. The hype and rush of speculative capital on New Gurgaon in the early 2000s spurred by state policy was unmatched by demand for mass high-end consumption. In this case the developer leading the project had drawn in 160 crore rupees of investment from around 350 small landholders like Mukesh across Gurgaon who each had an equity share in the development.

Figure 3.1 Residential towers near Nawada Fatehpur village, Gurgaon, India
Source: Photo by author.

Echoing the credit-financed land acquisition model pioneered by DLF, the mall development transposed the agrarian share-ownership system into the financing of urban real estate. Unfortunately for Mukesh, the developer had not acquired the required clearances nor licence for the development and three years after their initial investment the developer and shopping mall were nowhere to be seen. Mukesh loudly cursed the developer:

> We were scammed, looted. All of us here invested, each of us gave five lakh, ten lakh, twenty lakh ... we were promised a proper mall with foreign companies coming here ... [and] we were going to receive much more, we were promised a proper mall with foreign companies coming here.

Why then does Mukesh invest his income in – highly speculative – land and property markets? The answer partly has to do with a commonly held view of development that pits modernity, and incorporation into hegemonic property regimes, along a constricted temporality of real-estate-driven accumulation. As I began to ask about the benefits of Gurgaon's urbanisation for local landowners, Mukesh interjected: 'Listen, son, we are peasants, we are in a situation without future nor past. We should never have sold our land.'

*

At the heart of Gurgaon's remarkable urbanisation over the past thirty years has been the rapid conversion of agrarian property into urban real estate. As discussed in the previous chapter, this process has not been enacted solely by the state, but rather has depended upon agrarian populations throwing themselves, their incomes and their land into the market (Figure 3.1). Both the state and real estate firms rely not only on finding farmers willing to sell their land but also on their reinvestment of surpluses back into readying land for recapitalisation. Former landowners (hereafter simply 'landowners') are called upon to push forward the frontier, picking up contested rural land and doing the complex work of plotting out the land, converting it into legible, fungible private property. This is an entirely speculative endeavour, involving the projection of ascendant real estate value and liberal private property onto contested agrarian lands. Landowners must anticipate the direction of development plans, speculate on 'good investments' and plot creative strategies for re-presenting their historic agrarian property claims as liberal private property.[4]

As I will discuss in the following two chapters, the capture, conversion and authorisation of agrarian property on the frontier relies upon a host of property technologies that operate not through calculative precision and legibility but rather through the reification of uncertainty, speculation and agrarian social power.

When I set out to understand property-making on India's urban frontier, I had to do away with my preconceived notions of property – those echoed by the maps of planners and politicians in Gurgaon – as individuated, spatially fixed and juridically clear. Struck through the heart of property in Haryana is a jumble of spatially overlapping claims, configurations of commodifiable and non-commodifiable lands – that by highlighting a quite different relationship between landed property and land-based accumulation – complicate classical understandings of capitalist property regimes and call for quite different forms of governance.

In Chapter 4 I examine the role of the local state and state-property technologies play in translating property claims and boundaries into state records. Before doing so, in this chapter I am interested in the anticipatory and speculative strategies engaged in by landowners to position themselves and their lands for real estate futures. Why do landowners so enthusiastically engage in highly speculative land and property markets? How does the state elicit speculative territorial behaviour on the frontier? Through which logics and strategies do landowners and real estate actors stake territorial claims, seek out recognition and prepare rural land for promised urbanisation? Drawing on a wealth of literature on 'speculative urbanisation'[5] on the capitalist frontier,[6] in this chapter I am interested in the dynamic and negotiated class struggles to produce urban private property and proprietary subjects.

SPECULATION AND UNCERTAINTY

On Gurgaon's frontier, landowners find themselves in a contracted space, where past agrarian power held by propertied Jats and Ahirs is under question and future prosperity relies upon risky mobilisation of rural land and rents into speculative land markets. Landowners celebrate past social power and are desperate to proclaim the future partly because they are anxious about an uncertain present. There is, in other words, a rather truncated, unidirectional understanding of development driving landowners on the frontier to throw themselves and their lands into the market.

Agricultural pasts that legislatively and culturally bound caste communities to agrarian property ownership have in a post-agrarian world become central to landowners' future participation in the city, not least to broader forces of land conversion, aggregation and commodification. This future for both landowners like Mukesh and corporate capital depends upon both the financial returns on landowners' conjecture on land markets and their creative work to undo pre-existing property claims and repurpose rural land as private property. Such is the uncertainty that laminate post-agrarian fortunes among the agrarian classes in Gurgaon, even landowners like Mukesh – who are relatively well positioned to take advantage of land markets – are held in a kind of suspension, lying in wait for opportunities to join the chorus of rentier accumulation driving the city's urbanisation.

This frontier work is imaginative, involving the deployment of 'monstrous geographical imaginaries' of complex and contested rural lands, in order to justify their expeditious conversion into legible real estate.[7] It is also deeply material. In order to translate diverse tenure regimes, territorial claims and formal planning processes that restrict rural land development, landowners must strategically arrange finance, position investments, gather ersatz documentation and physically clear and bind land parcels – utilising agrarian institutions to align property with broader hegemonic patterns of property-led development. And finally, this property-making work is highly speculative, it involves deploying and profiting from degrees of uncertainty. Landowners take risks on the uncertainty of drawing value from rural land markets, and of having contested territorial claims recognised and legitimated as future oriented. As discussed in Chapter 1, today's agrarian–urban frontier has been reliant upon the material production of rural land as barren and uncultivatable, of tenure regimes that are complex, opaque and antiquated, and a cultural political economy in which class power is anchored to land ownership. At this juncture the state and private actors invite landowners to take a gamble on their future and see the potential value hidden in their lands. In attempting to re-present complex rural land parcels layered with multiple claims and meanings as private property, this project is speculative; it involves appealing to an expectation among planners and political elites that the complexities of rural land tenure will be overridden and private property rights established in the near future.

Of course, landowners like Mukesh are not speculating in the dark. As we shall see, speculating on the urban frontier is principally guided by state-planning technologies and empowered by agrarian caste-class hierarchies that validate certain territorial claims while admonishing others.

The speculative character of landowners' property-claiming strategies is a reflection of broader vernacular planning and development processes led by the Haryana government and the Planning Department. Gurgaon's master-planning practice not only guides landowners investments but also authorises and retrospectively incorporates contested territorial claims of actors able to align their lands with real estate uses. In doing so, state planning and property technologies elicit a broader practice of property-claiming among aspiring real estate actors who seek to enjoin themselves and their land to real estate futures. The speculative co-production of space on Gurgaon's frontier resembles what Laura Bear calls 'speculative planning', where the realisation of state plans relies not on state-directed private investment but rather on planning instruments that 'stimulate entrepreneurial speculation' and utilise vernacular forms of social power. At the heart of Gurgaon's real estate industry are a set of highly speculative and informalised strategies engaged in by local actors to informally ready themselves and agrarian property regimes for urban conversion.

Landowners across Gurgaon flush with cash from land sales and *abadi* rentals engage in a series of attempts to both assemble and connect their lands to broader real estate markets and benefit from expected rises in land values. To do so landowners pitch their investments to state highways and draft development plans, pick up plots of land in anticipation of expanding city boundaries, and arrange their investments appropriately for conversion and further sales. Complexity and uncertainty are keenly deployed at the frontier – just as emptiness and vacancy have been before[8] – in order to impress the urgency of hegemonic real estate accumulation and antiquity of other forms of land use. Mukesh's crestfallen acknowledgement of his failure to productively utilise capital speaks to the highly fraught and uncertain character of Gurgaon's real estate market. Land investment is one of the few economic activities that agricultural landowners are able to take part in, enjoining once-agricultural subjects to a decidedly urban future. And yet how these futures work out, and whether all agricultural communities will be brought along into rentier land markets, is an open question. The capitalist frontier is an entirely confected and speculative geography, one that depends upon rendering spaces as bizarre, unknown and irrational in order to stimulate the imperative for future liberal property and labour relations. Within settler colonial projects the state has performed this task with the help of notionally unorganised colonists armed with property-making technologies – maps, surveys, ethnographies – that demarcate and codify land and people into capitalist forms of property and labour. As a wealth of scholarship has shown,[9] these technologies inaugurate a certain temporality to 'development' which makes broad-brush distinctions between an antiquated past, complex present and urgent future. The route through this disjunctive historical pathway is made possible only by the inauguration of private property. On the urban frontier, the neoliberal state remains an ever-present feature in this process. If the post-colonial developmental state took to directing the future directly through state machinery, in contemporary urban India the state relies on technologies that give cues to private actors to take on and realise state schemes for land commoditisation.

Critical scholarship on frontiers has centred on how masterplans and cadastral maps inaugurate new kinds of authoritative knowledge that remap existing geographies into severable private property, and in so doing erase and dispossess those whose lives and land uses fall outside those prescribed by the map.[10] As Noterman argues, 'Past and present possessors and forms of possession that do not promise future accumulation are cartographically vacated ... to make space for the future accumulation of settled (white) property and proprietary subjects'.[11]

On the urban frontier, a similar set of outcomes are reached for by a more complex and opaque set of technologies. Here, where real estate faces complex agrarian property regimes, maps and plans are shaped by informal, creative property-claiming and converting practices. Landowners stuck between a decaying past and an uncertain future speculatively seek to enjoin themselves and their lands to state development frameworks by creatively investing in rural lands and refashioning agrarian property for commodity purposes. These strategies often rely less on the cast-iron legibility of liberal property – etched into formal maps, development regulations and masterplans – as they do on the power of uncertainty, opacity and speculation.

Indeed, to concentrate on the ways maps and plans render liberal property legible misses the ways speculative land conversions on the frontier are often about making perceptible (and common-sense) territorial claims that which would otherwise be tentative and transgress formal planning and development codes. In light of heavily contested and unmapped property claims, landowners on the frontier appeal to what Louise Amoore calls, in a different context, an 'aperture of observation' that brings into view and authorises 'partial' territorial claims premised on their alignment with state development visions.

This is to say that landowners engage in speculative strategies that wage their future on the uncertainty of land values, development projects, investment patterns and territorial claims. Risk-driven accumulation plays an important role in Gurgaon's story, insofar as the capture of peripheral rent gaps, and incorporation of landowning elites into real-estate-laden futures are central to the Gurgaon project but beset with uncertainties. In an attempt to join the future Gurgaon's former landowners must 'anticipate and seek to influence emerging state and market regimes'[12] and position themselves to benefit from the city's future-oriented development.

These strategies fall into two registers. First, landowners speculatively recycle revenues from land sales and village property into land and plots in and around the city boundaries. These investments involve anticipating which land will bring potential high returns, gambling on the direction of city expansion and the future whereabouts of large-scale real estate and infrastructural projects. These strategies are speculative in nature. They involve landowners taking risks and investing in a broader imaginary of the future in which land prices rise, customary claims are regularised and former farmers are inaugurated as rentier capitalists. Landowner-cum-investors gamble on what kinds of land to invest in, where and when to invest and on the material, aesthetic and bureaucratic forms of property that are investible.

Second, and relatedly, landowners must arrange or 'clear' rural land – in all its complex affordances and contested claims – as a legible resource for real estate investment. Both corporate real estate firms and aspiring local rentier capitalists are confronted with a landscape of complex, opaque property claims that must be cleared out, or if not, dressed up as severable private property. What has emerged across Gurgaon is a series of conflicts over control of rural customary lands that culminate in competing actors occupying land for accumulation. Solomon Benjamin's work on 'occupancy urbanism' describes how local people quietly occupy complex land tenures and state institutions and in doing so disrupt corporate urban development trajectories. In Gurgaon it is real estate actors – both corporate firms and aspiring landowners – who occupy complex lands for capital. By repurposing village common lands and opaque customary tenures, landowners speculatively mobilise tentative territorial claims in order to substantiate customary rural land as private property. They do so in the belief that the state's porous planning machinery, single-minded real estate vision for land and sensitivity to agriculturalist caste power will authorise otherwise irregular property claims and with it bring high returns on investment.

Turning Gurgaon over for global capital relies upon what Jamie Cross has called economies of anticipation, that involve 'diverse ways of knowing about, imagining, and living toward the future' engaged in by state planners and agrarian landowners alike. Of course, the futures being anticipated are different, struggles emerge over conflicting values prescribed to land, or more commonly over control of the value arising from land proffered to the future.

What explains landowners' active participation in Gurgaon's highly speculative land market? Why do alienated farmers so willingly throw themselves into the uncertain world of land speculation? As we shall see, despite Gurgaon's topsy-turvy land market, agrarian actors invest in land with a degree of faith in the Gurgaon model, one that depicts the city's rural land as a bountiful resource perpetually increasing in value and tells a story of the untrammelled real estate supremacy. These stories are discursive, they are written into state planning documents and consultancy reports in the form of upward-moving graph points depicting rising populations, land prices and GDP figures all attributed to real-estate-led urbanisation. They are also, for many of my interlocutors, material – Gurgaon's 'hot' land market is impressed into the everyday fabric surrounding them in large-scale infrastructural development and international capital investment that now sits on the agricultural fields.

Selling Gurgaon

Up until the mid-1990s Gurgaon was a relatively modest suburb of New Delhi with a more pronounced industrial geography owing to the Maruti plant on the Delhi–Gurgaon road. DLF and Ansal's residential colonies attracted retirees from Delhi eager to escape the city for large, plotted bungalows with gardens, community clubs and wide, open spaces. Indeed, DLF marketed plots in its first residential colony in Gurgaon as 'DLF Qutub Enclave', referencing the twelfth-century minaret located on Delhi's borders in order to give a sense of the colony's cultural and social intimacy to the upper-class neighbourhoods in South Delhi. Liberalisation of the economy in the early 1990s initially opened up domestic sources of housing finance and drew in demand from non-resident Indians (NRIs). Residential developments were designed in western architectural styles, imitating the gated colony culture of North America and were given Euro-American names like Beverly Park and Malibu Towne. They were also heavily marketed towards NRIs: Malibu Towne, for example, a residential complex developed by an NRI investor, actively promoted itself as a sponge for investors in Hong Kong and the Gulf during the 1990s. By the end of the 1990s, controls on domestic lending to real estate firms were loosened, and by the mid-2000s direct domestic and foreign investment in real estate development was opened up. DLF's programme of landowner-financed land aggregation through farmer credit was no longer necessary, the whole world had come to rural India looking for a good investment opportunity.[13]

The Haryana government, following a pro-business policy line cultivated from the 1980s under Bhajan Lal and encouraged by the devolution of fiscal powers in 1991, embarked upon an ambitious industrial policy that actively sought out international IT and services investment into Gurgaon's industrial estates. In absence of a municipal corporation, the Government of Haryana (organised through the state industrial development corporation [HSIDC] and state electronics development corporation [Haryana State Electronics Development Corporation, or HARTRON] both within the chief minister's office) directly negotiated with international investors in an attempt to establish Gurgaon as a centre for public–private partnership (PPP) and foreign–direct investment.[14]

The state government, for example, took out full-page advertisements in the *South China Morning Post* and *New York Times* in order to attract foreign investment in real estate, automobile and IT clusters. Summing up the state entrepreneurial mood of the early 1990s, P. K. Tripathi, general manager of HSIIDC, noted in 1994, 'A few states have been marketing themselves aggressively [for private investment] and Haryana is perhaps at the top in this ... [and] we do even more aggressive marketing for foreign direct investment.'[15] In the early 1990s, in a move unheard of at the time, Bhajan Lal, then chief minister, led a much-publicised state delegation to Italy, the USA, UK and Germany, actively seeking out investment in Gurgaon. The tour reportedly brought in 100 crore rupees in projected investment from General Electric, Lockheed Martin and Alcatel to the city from the mid-1990s.[16]

In 1996, the state government promoted a 2,000-crore-rupee Japanese Model Industrial Town west of Gurgaon in Manesar. The project was to be partly financed by the Oversees Economic Corporation Fund and was to be managed by a public–private management firm including Japanese conglomerates Mitsubishi, Marubeni and Mitsui, and the HSIDC. The partnership, which followed Suzuki's takeover of Gurgaon-based automobile manufacturer Maruti in 1991, was to establish Gurgaon as the primary industrial FDI site in the country, bringing in 2 billion dollars in Japanese investment and brokering India's place on the Asia-Pacific Economic Cooperation (APEC) forum. APEC membership would not materialise, and the Japanese conglomerates involved at Manesar would later withdraw from the project citing disapproval of the state government's compensation package for affected landowners. Nevertheless, the idea of the deal held greater significance – it signalled the Haryana government's willingness to leverage land to capture global investment and pioneer industrial PPP models.

By the time foreign investment in Indian real estate was liberalised in the 2000s, the Haryana government had established Gurgaon as a primary site of international industrial capital investment, a testing ground for new forms of neoliberal governance and a refuge for NRI and domestic real estate capital seeking out large-scale residential development. This was subsequently aided, as Llerena Searle's work has shown, by crises of overaccumulation in western markets, which were pushing capital in the US and Europe to seek out new avenues for investment, to which 'under-utilised' land in 'emerging markets' became the principal solution.[17] Investment funds and real estate firms were attracted to the potential for India's land to mop up over-accumulated capital and offer long-term margins on investment. With the help of government deregulation and aggressive entrepreneurialism of state governments, this capital found its way to peri-urban developments like Gurgaon.

Aggressive state development schemes and private sector real estate development set the stage for the IT boom from the late 1990s. The opening of a General Electric office in the city, purportedly facilitated by K. P. Singh, is generally considered to be instrumental in transforming Gurgaon's IT and real estate sector. Not long after American Express, IBM, Microsoft and a glut of business processing outsourcing (BPO) operations were established in the city, leasing out large commercial plots from both the HSIIDC and DLF. Between 2004 and 2012, Haryana's economy grew by 17 per cent, and the share of FSRE to state GDP grew by 21 per cent while FDI inflows between totalled some 1.2 billion US dollars.[18] By the 2000s Gurgaon's IT sector was – second to Bengaluru – the largest IT hub in the Asia-Pacific with 30 million square feet of commercial real estate, employing 300,000 IT workers, 5 per cent of the global BPO workforce, and Gurgaon would come to be known as the 'call centre capital of the world'. With real estate in existing metropoles like Delhi expensive, in short supply and composed of significantly smaller plots, 'satellite towns' like Gurgaon with expansive plots and privately managed infrastructure became key investment destinations where real estate investors could profit from surging demand for commercial and residential real estate.

Elastic Plans

The explosive growth of Haryana's tertiary sector was facilitated by a state planning apparatus that malleably worked around private developers' existing land banks to guide investments and encourage land speculation. Provisions in both the PSRCA and the HDRUA allow for significant negotiation of licence credentials, planning boundaries and rules. Section 7(a) of the PSRCA, for example, allows the Haryana government to relax land-use restrictions in the 'public interest' and provides planners with a series of 'discretionary powers' to reclassify rural land and remap the boundaries of controlled areas. These provisions have afforded the Haryana government significant room to remap land according to the development and land assembly plans of real estate developers. Gurgaon's first urban development plan in 1971, for example, was redrafted twice, in 1977 and 1982, to extend the boundaries of the controlled area and reclassify 9,000 acres of rural land as 'urbanisable', much of which had already been bought up by developers. The release of provisional masterplans to developers auditions future territorial boundaries in time for private actors to alter the scope and shape of 'planned' development in the city.

Between 2006 and 2012, concurrent to the liberalisation of FDI in real estate, Congress politician and chief minister of Haryana Bhupinder Singh Hooda opened up 56,000 acres of land in Gurgaon for residential, commercial and industrial development, across three urban development plans in quick succession. The 2006 development plan – the Gurgaon–Manesar Master Plan, 2021 – would become the blueprint for the state government's real-estate-led growth model of the following decade.[19]

The state's discretionary powers imbued Gurgaon's urban development plans with plasticity that draws its authority as a calculative governmental document from its capacity to incorporate tentative and incalculable territorial claims of real estate capital. Shubhra Gururani has as such argued that Gurgaon's planning system has been facilitated by state 'flexibility' which she describes as 'a range of political techniques through which exemptions are routinely made, plans redrawn, compromises made, and brute force executed'.[20] By the early 1990s, the Haryana planning department publicly conceded that their role was merely to 'plan and not enforce' the controlled areas of the city.[21] Haryana's planning framework has in other words long acted as a speculative property technology. The plan controls the future by anticipating and selectively authorising the past, eliciting certain kinds of territorial action (the creation of value-yielding property) while excluding others.

The mapping out of Gurgaon's expanding and elastic urban boundaries has, since the 1970s, allowed the Haryana government to nimbly integrate private sector development plans into official state urban development plans, authoring the city's 'planned' sectors in response to the land agglomeration patterns of the private sector. For example, in the early 1980s the Haryana Housing Board, responsible for housing development in the state, acquired plots of land surrounding DLF's flagship DLF City for low-income housing development. The land acquisition effectively blocked the expansion of DLF's land base and was interpreted as a check on the territorial authority of the developer. An aggrieved DLF successfully lobbied the state to de-notify the land and release it for the company's acquisition. The elasticity of Gurgaon's controlled area ensures that private capital can not only court authorisation of land banks, but also dictate the uses of land it does not even own.

While accounts of the modern neoliberal state have traced how calculative technologies such as masterplans, grids and zones seek to render a kind of social world that is legible, calculable and intervenable in ways that justify dispossession and capitalisation, Gurgaon's malleable development plans represent different ways of managing urban space, facilitating capital investment and alternative ways of seeing and animating private engagements in rural land. The overarching goal of the post-colonial neoliberal state is to dress the most flexible and contingent apparatuses of government in the clothes of scientific rationality. In Gurgaon state territorial authority is derived precisely from the ability to dispose of and interpret fissures in state knowledge produced by shifting and mutable technologies. In this regard, Gurgaon's malleable 'controlled' areas should not be thought of as indicative of state failure or disorder. Rather, their plasticity forms a novel kind of urban order reminiscent of Ananya Roy's work on 'informality'. One that I argue not only accommodates the land assembly portfolios of real estate firms, but also more broadly elicits chains of speculative property-making practices that encase and permeate the post-dispossession activities of agrarian actors.

By the turn of the millennium, real estate developers were buying up vast chunks of land across Gurgaon in attempts to profit from rising land and property prices. As one newspaper column wrote in 2004, 'The ramshackle outskirts are the new pots of real estate gold ... in the National Capital Region, flashy suburbia has outshone the lure of South Delhi.'[22] What is more, real estate firms like DLF and Ansal had already amassed significant land banks by the mid-1990s and had free reign on the design and layout of commercial spaces. Accordingly, over the course of this period, land prices rocketed. In 1980 land for DLF Phases I and II was bought from landowners for the equivalent of around 9 rupees a square yard and residential plots were selling for around 350 rupees a square yard in 1990; by 2006 the price had increased to some 60,000 rupees a square yard. To the landowners who sold their lands in the 1980s the mirage of value rising from the ground was all too clear and these rapidly rising land prices in the 2000s generated a broader expectation and common sense around land uses that lured agrarian classes into speculative land markets.

Gurgaon's land market, much like that of the country at large, rests upon the government's capacity to turn land and those who own it – discursively and materially – towards perpetually growing 'pots of gold' in rural and peri-urban land. Countless newspaper articles, magazine columns and industry reports by the mid-2000s reported on fantastical development projects and regaled Gurgaon as a 'futuristic city' with an explosive, ever-expanding land market. The *Economic Times* writes:

> Gurgaon's image as a city of the future is staked more on its potential than its performance ... one of the dreams associated with Gurgaon is that it wears the air of a modern urban centre, thanks to blocks after blocks of state-of-the-art corporate buildings. A visitor who looks up may see a skyline that one normally associates more with Manhattan than, say, Manesar.[23]

These 'spectacular' narrative forms of development rely on what Anna Tsing has called an 'economy of appearances' whereby confident images of property wealth, foreign investment and 'world-class' infrastructure drive buy-in to accumulation strategies often in lieu of their actual materialisation. This buy-in extends to local actors who are partly relied upon to throw themselves into speculative land markets, invest in rural lands and ready assets for commoditization. These actions are yoked to 'untimely futures', to 'potential' and the idea of worldly modernity that speculative real estate development yields. For many (former) landowners in Gurgaon, there is no other sensible or ethical outlet to utilise compensation revenues. As a landowner in Kherki Duala remarked, 'We invest in land because we have to. We cannot just keep the money; it would be spent by our children on alcohol and cars ... or else the government would take it. It is better to buy land.... We cannot anticipate the next boom, we can only hope to be involved.'

Landowners in Gurgaon understand too well the capitalist imperative to keep value, or in this case, value-extracting resources, in motion to throw revenues back into property and speculative 'hope' for the next boom. Speculation, the anticipation that the landowner can reap benefits from a touted 'next boom', provides a way for agrarian middle classes to better their livelihoods and retain their social position all while remedying potential hold-ups in capital's circulation through land.

Property Supply Chains

Essential to India's frontier urbanisation has been the aggressive extension of private property rights and property governance systems in the countryside. Drawing on Hernando de Soto's influential work on land titling, the Indian government have aggressively facilitated real estate firms' capture of rural land by clearing away distributive post-colonial agrarian policies, masterplanning areas for development and rolling out aggressive marketing campaigns that sell a vision of post-agrarian futures bound intimately to private property ownership, urban development and rentier accumulation.

Landowner's speculative investments in land aid both the state and capital's opening up of the urban frontier by readying complex agrarian property regimes for commoditisation. While early obstacles of financing development had been overcome by economic liberalisation, and the political obstacle of agrarian landowners bypassed by the PSRCA, there remained the tricky task of converting agrarian property regimes with liberal private property. Projects to revalorise Gurgaon's fields and connect them into global circuits of finance and real estate capital face a landscape already considerably marked by agrarian capitalism.

And yet, as I discussed in Chapter 1, land on India's urban frontier is no *terra nullius*; it has been subject to centuries of colonial, then post-colonial agrarian policy that has left complex layerings of property claims and jurisdictions. These territorial projects marked Gurgaon's land with a thickness of material, cultural and ideological affordances that are difficult to shake off. It is these complex legislative, institutional and material integuments of property in land that have to be dis-embedded and traversed for rural land to be converted into a homogeneous and fungible resource for capital investment.

State development rules require a developer to amass a minimum of 100 acres of contiguous landholdings to obtain a development licence for a residential colony, and 10 acres for 'group housing' or residential apartments. Aggregating such large, contiguous parcels of land in Haryana is a complex task. Rural land in Haryana, despite the efforts of mid-century consolidators, is highly fragmented. Across India, 86 per cent of landholdings are smaller than 5 acres, a figure only moderately lower (67 per cent) in Haryana, one of the most consolidated and agriculturally productive states in the country. Land in Haryana is not just small but predominately held in shares, layered with competing claims, uses and meanings, and vested across numerous political institutions. The sheer complexity and number of landholdings in Haryana, when met with rising land prices, have amplified court disputes over competing territorial claims which ominously threaten capitalist investment. The situation provides an imperative to a neoliberal state to animate landowners to open up their fields, and importantly convert their property for real estate purposes.

This advantageously positions landowners and agrarian institutions on the frontlines of rural land's cleaning and conversion for capital. Underpinning Gurgaon's real-estate-led urbanisation is the work of farmers-cum-brokers, aggregators, developers and bureaucrats (what I will call for short 'real estate actors') who do the complex work of clearing and inputting land for capital. This work forms part of a land supply chain that extends from corporate offices in central Delhi and Gurgaon's Cyber Hub to the remote villages on the peripheries of the city that, enveloping the economic activities of low-level brokers, shifts heterogeneous rural landholdings into standardised, contiguous plots awaiting commodification.

Real estate developers in Gurgaon sit at the top of the supply chain, above land aggregators, liaisoners and brokers who work to piece together the legal, material and representational artefacts required to substantiate property claims and implant territories into Gurgaon's elastic urban development plans. Beneath the developer is usually a local landholding or aggregation company that manages the process of buying and aggregating rural land. For example, Gurgaon's 'big three' developers, DLF, Ansal and Unitech, own 68 per cent of urbanisable licenced land in the city, yet the vast majority of their land deals take place through subsidiary landholding and aggregation companies. Unitech's 1,500-acre stretch of luxury residential space in Sectors 46 and 47 of Gurgaon, on Badshahpur village land, for example, is formally owned and licenced to a series of subsidiary landholding firms, including Neil Properties, Cape Builders, Havelock Estates, among many others. Some of these firms are formally constituted subsidiaries of Unitech, others are partnering firms owned by successful local aggregators. The detachment of the developer from the ownership of rural land allows developers to skirt land ceiling regulations and bypass rules that put restrictions on FDI into rural land. Large development firms rely upon low-level brokers to mobilise the familiarities of Haryanvi dialect, caste-community and rural cultural practices in order to purchase land at low prices. A roadside broker near Rampura village in western Gurgaon explained the important role local actors play in the supply chain: 'If a Punjabi comes to our villages will he sit with the elders and discuss village issues? Will he drink milk, take hookah and speak with warmth?... No, he'll leave with empty pockets!' The performances the broker discusses signal the kinds of cultural and social work – intimately tied to landowners' caste and class dominance of the villages – required to re-deploy agrarian property for urban real estate.

Beyond their immediate work within the supply chain, nearly all of these low-level village actors engage in 'private work'. Across the city, these same actors are picking up rural land on the edges of the development plan, alongside highways and industrial parks. The planning department's minimum land bank restrictions exclude most of these actors from engaging in formal planning and development processes. Instead, landowners seek out speculative investments in rural land, and in some cases industrial plots, and engage in alternative strategies for aligning their investments in the path of future real estate development.

As Tania Murray Li has argued, 'Assembling land as a resource available for some purposes to the exclusion of others requires a great deal of complex cultural work' and the deployment of all manner of property technologies. Gurgaon's urbanisation not only compels agrarian actors to partake in rentier economies in order to be incorporated into real estate economies, but real estate capital also relies upon these speculative and improvised territorial strategies in order to access land pre-assembled as an investible resource.

As I will argue, this involves mobilising a perception of territorial legitimacy tied to caste-community, land use and an alternative infrastructure of property-making towards a receptive neoliberal state. Indeed, landowners are central figures remodelling land and linking agrarian pasts to urban futures, but the state also plays an important role in eliciting, guiding and authorising speculative territorial actions. As Laura Bear writes, capitalism in contemporary India is characterised by 'speculative planning' wherein the state 'driven by new financial speculations of public deficit' seeks to 'stimulate entrepreneurial speculation' among local elites, and in our case, agrarian propertied classes. While the capitalist frontier is often marked – by capitalists – as a space where rationality and calculative norms are established as apart from some induced exterior, on India's urban frontier as elsewhere the production of private property is an outcome of dynamic, heavily informalised and class-powered strategies to creatively align agrarian property forms within the grammar of future-oriented commoditisation.

ANTICIPATING THE CITY

I first met Dilip Yadav in 2014 in a small garden nursery-cum-property brokerage office. I was passed Dilip's phone number by his close friend and business partner who was also the former *sarpanch* of Dundahera village. 'Everything about real estate, you will learn from Dilip,' the *sarpanch* hurriedly explained, avoiding my questions on the matter.

Dilip's nursery was located on a strip of land wedged on an island in the middle of the highway between DLF Cyber Hub and the HSIDC's Udyog Vihar industrial estate. To get to Dilip's splendorous island office one must traverse the flurry of lorries and cars racing down the National Highway that splits Gurgaon into two, connecting the city with Delhi to the north and Rajasthan to the south. As we sat down in his portacabin office, Dilip explains at his mid-highway island property, 'Please do not call me a *dalal* [broker], I am not a registered, we buy agricultural land together, and see if we can sell it on.' Dilip's family land was iteratively acquired by different state agencies across the 1990s, first by HSIIDC to make way for the Udyog Vihar industrial estate, then by HUDA who plotted residential colonies along the old Delhi–Gurgaon road in the early 1990s. The family funnelled compensation into a concrete and steel business, taking advantage of high demand for construction materials in the 1990s, invested in an industrial plot in Udyog Vihar Phase IV, currently leased to an international BPO firm. Dilip used revenues from his business to send his children to elite private schools in Delhi and had utilised connections with local state actors in the registration and planning offices, connections built through figures like the ex-*sarpanch* to move into property work. He explained bluntly of the central region of the city:

> We came by this plot through a debt ... [otherwise] there is no money to be made in this part of Gurgaon. The companies, DLF and so on, bought much of this land years ago, now we only buy industrial plots and agricultural land ... we buy and sell plots here and elsewhere in Haryana. These days everyone wants land in Haryana, we buy the land,

clear it and make the proper arrangements ... sometimes we are able to make a profit, sometimes we can't.

Dilip's hobby – engaged in alongside three friends from Dundahera village – involved picking up agricultural land yet to be converted for urban uses, often on roadsides and on the edges of the development plan, before arranging ownership paperwork and physical possession with the hope of selling it on at a profit. By dealing solely with agricultural land not only are actors like Dilip targeting cheaper land that can draw in a higher return once 'cleared' of its encumbrances, but they are also making use of local agrarian conditions and connections to local state offices that govern the ownership of agrarian land.

Dilip described the land we sat on that day, with lorries and buses passing us on either side, as an investment, it had been notified for acquisition by the National Highways Authority some years ago and Dilip had taken ownership of the notified plot as collateral for an unpaid debt of the original owner. 'We have settled in the courts for an enhancement [to the compensation], soon they [the government] will come take this land.' The strip of land was technically owned by the National Highways Agency, who once the compensation claim was cleared would take formal possession. Until then the nursery Dilip had cultivated effectively acted as a green front for what was an unregistered property business working on land notified for state dispossession. Rather than clinging onto land and opposing dispossessions, speculative investments like Dilip's anticipate and look to capitalise on incrementing compensation won through the courts. These strategies are widespread across Gurgaon and contribute to a landscape of globalised accumulation truncated by choke points and hold out wagered by agrarian speculators.

As I discussed previously, dispossession compensation which had been enhanced through reforms to the Land Acquisition Act in 2014 has been a key source of income often actively sought out, rather than resisted, by Gurgaon's landowners. While Dilip was clear that his investments were strictly in agricultural land, I was interested in how Dilip knew where to buy. How did he identify a good investment? Where were the state or private sector likely to pick up land? Did he have some inside information on real estate firms' development plans?

'No no, it's not like that, you have to find a good investment,' he said. Pushing him further, I asked how one knows what a good investment is? 'Well, for example, we look to the highways.' Referring to the myriad debt-financed highway projects embarked on by the Haryana government and National Highways Agency since the mid-2000s, he explained, 'There are lots of roads coming up now, the Dwarka Expressway (DWE), Kundli–Manesar Expressway and others … the land around these roads, outside the city in village areas, is a good investment, roads come first then the builders [real estate firms] follow.' An elderly man who was sitting with us added in contradiction to Dilip, 'They call these [highways] the lifeline of Gurgaon, but in reality they are destroying our culture.'

Like corporate real estate firms, Dilip uses state infrastructure planning as a guide as to where to invest. State plans and low-level land speculation operate in concert to discursively and materially shape the city. Just as corporate real estate firms and investment funds must 'foretell the future'[24] and speculate on future land prices when making investments in rural land in Gurgaon, so too are low-level farmers, brokers and aggregators – flush with cash from selling family lands and renting *abadi* properties – forced to speculate on where to invest, what prices to pay and how to future-proof their investments in land often in lieu of formal state recognition. Landowners are engaged in visualising themselves and their lands in the future, and in lieu of the economic and political capital held by corporate real estate firms and industrialists, rely upon a separate set of shadow social and political practices – mobilising agrarian property institutions and caste-class power – in order to establish property claims and obtain returns on investment.

The highway, Dilip noted, mapped out an incrementing geography of value for low-level speculators, 'Say I have an acre here in Gurgaon, I can pick up three acres down the road in Manesar, ten in Dharuhera, twenty in Rewari, soon these places will be developing too, it is the same with industrial plots.' These speculative practices, that invest in the pervasive march of real estate capital along the highway and into the Indian countryside, require a degree of belief that capital expands outwards following state cues.

And there is reason for this belief. For the state and private actors, highways act principally as what Eyal Weizman has called 'frontier architectures' enabling the high-frequency movement of commodities and people around the city. The highways mentioned by Dilip have been described by successive governments as the 'lifeline' of Haryana, connecting the state's network of industrial estates with commercial markets and the international airport in Delhi. The 2021 masterplan introduced a series of 150-metre-wide highways that encircle the city, opening access to rural land on the edges of the city. The official literature on the Kundli–Manesar–Palwal (KMP) Expressway, which runs north along the western periphery of Gurgaon connecting a series of industrial estates, for example, describes how the road aims to meet the 'needs and dreams of investors' and spark a chain of real estate opportunities in 'cluster cities' along its route. The unveiling of plans for a new highway connecting Gurgaon with Sohna to the south – through Badshahpur village introduced earlier on – was met with claims in local newspapers that land prices in the area were bound to appreciate by 20 per cent within a year. The unveiling of the DWE in 2007 was another key engine for land speculation. The much troubled 10,000-crore-rupee, eight-lane and 28-kilometre-long highway – developed as a PPP between the National Highways Authority and Delhi-based developer India Bulls – has long been viewed by state politicians as essential to unlocking choke-points in Gurgaon's expanding urban development. Conceived to join up the Indira Gandhi International Airport in southwest Delhi with western Gurgaon's industrial parks and new residential complexes, land on either side of the expressway has been subject to undulating pressures of landowners and brokers seeking to take advantage of a three-fold jump in land prices on the flanks of the road.

Gurgaon's circling highways not only quite literally tunnel and churn through agrarian space converting it into concrete, but in doing so they also speculatively projects the 'dreams of investors' into the countryside, signalling an expectation of rising real estate values across Gurgaon's outer boundaries. And yet as frontier technologies they are also confronted by complex land tenures embedded in localised political institutions and territorial claims. It is, perhaps, unsurprising that these highways are key points of dispute and struggle between agriculturalists and the state, not only for those wishing to amplify their land claims and access compensation for dispossession like Dilip, but also for those whose socio-economic reproduction remain anchored to agricultural production. In 2020 the KMP Expressway would become ground zero for the largest farmer protests witnessed in India's contemporary history (see Conclusion).

Speculating on land around highways involves navigating and indeed incorporating these localised affordances in pursuit of a return on investment. The 'operational landscape' that the highway inaugurates is not simply the outcome of executive plans and procedures (the desires of the powerful), but rather one diffused with a politics of perception, uncertainty and subversion. As Weizman argues, frontiers are 'deep, shifting, fragmented and elastic territories' and it is precisely this complexity of rural land on the frontier that ignites landowners' speculative territorial strategies.

CLEARING LAND

Anticipating *where* to invest was one thing, it was quite another to know *what* to invest in, and more pointedly how one repurposes complex agrarian property regimes – layered with multiple competing claims, into a form instantly recognisable and investible to real estate firms. In my conversations with land brokers across Gurgaon during my first period of fieldwork, 2014–15, nearly all emphasised that investing in land required a deeper knowledge of the land itself. As a land broker who traded in land in Sector 106, Daulatabad village, on the northern periphery of the city, remarked, 'There are all kinds of land, you must learn them all if you want to understand our business … not all land is a good investment, [that is why] landowners are successful in property.' I soon learned the complex layerings of agrarian property tenures – not just *abadi* (residential), but *kheti* (agricultural), *banjar* (fallow) and *gair mumkin* (uncultivatable) lands, and *shamilat* (common), *marusi* (tenant possession) and *khud kast* (self-cultivated) forms of property – each layer of tenure represents the complex and uneven development of the social and political relations of agrarian capitalism in the region. Each equally shapes access and exclusivity of agrarian property, its propensity to express value and be translated and cleared for investors. Crucially, in Gurgaon, the diversity of tenure can force land speculators to appeal to quite other metrics of authenticity and legitimacy in order to secure property claims.

Upon my return to Gurgaon in 2018 I attempted to drop into Dilip's nursery and it was gone, bordered off and cleared of its greenery. Dilip had moved on to the next speculative investment. After exchanging messages Dilip invited me to visit a new plot of land he had recently bought with three friends. The land parcel was 18 kilometres west along the highway, sandwiched into the corner of Kherki Daula village and the DWE. Dilip's new land was occupied by a small farmhouse, chickens and goats roamed the area as freight trucks hurtled away to the side of us. As I arrived, Dilip was waiting with a friend and another ex-*sarpanch*, this time of Kherki Duala village and a private land surveyor who had been hired to demarcate the boundaries of the land parcel into a digitised cadastral map (we return to cadastral surveys in the following chapter).

This particular land parcel in question was formally a rural landholding, that like all land in Haryana had been formerly held by a number of co-sharers. Dilip had bought up each share and mutated the ownership to his shareholding group. The edges of the land had been acquired by the Highways agency leaving just under half an acre of land. Dilip described it as a short-term investment:

> It's just a small piece of land, but it's in a very hot area, with the [Dwarka Expressway] many companies are building here so the rate will increase many times ... we will clear the land and maybe in one year or two when the road is complete we will sell.

'Clearing' the land, he explained, was essential to securing property in ways that maximise a future sale. By 'clearing' (*saaf karna*) Dilip referred not to a physical process of clearing away the existing structures on the land, but to a bureaucratic and prescriptive process of readying the property for real estate uses. 'Clearing' involved consolidating separate land shares under singular ownership, settling tenancy claims, arranging mutation of ownership and changing land use in order to establish the material and legal form of private property most amenable to incoming investors. This involved hiring private surveyors to mark out often uncodified boundary lines (see Chapter 4), pitching down fences and altering where possible rural ownership records in the land registry offices. Clearing was a crucial opening move that figuratively shifted land in the direction of real estate uses. 'In order to sell,' he noted, 'it's my responsibility to make sure everything is clear and professionally arranged ... our business is quick we buy land, plot and sell on, if we don't clear the land, get the *jamabandi* [record of rights] copy etc, the builders will negotiate and offer less.'

Corporate real estate firms looking for quick investment are reticent to conduct this tricky bureaucratic and material work of clearing agrarian property regimes. This was, Dilip explained, long and arduous work. But it would nevertheless pay dividends when real estate and aggregation firms came to buy up the land at a later date. Clearing not only readies rural land for real estate conversion but also positions former landowners like Dilip into emerging real estate and land aggregation economies.

Nevertheless, it would take further work to substantiate ownership and ready the land for selling on. Paperwork is only one aspect of clearing land. Alongside documentation, Dilip had organised to fence off his property claim and explained that he would be keeping the abandoned farmhouse in order to retain possession of the plot. 'This paperwork is important,' he explains, 'but possession [*kabza*] is also important ... any person, a brother or grandson [of the seller], could come here, have a fence made and claim this land as their own, and what can I do then?' What was troubling Dilip was that while one side of his plot had been clearly demarcated by the National Highways Agency, the other side overlapped with an informally plotted residential colony that could potentially derail his investment. Across the city's peripheries, practices of occupation and encroachment play an important part of claiming territory. Within the alternative property-making system that operates through agrarian institutions and village politics, it is not enough to be the registered owner of a parcel of land on paper; physical possession of the land is also crucial.

At first, I was a little confused: if Dilip owned the land and has paperwork to prove it, why not seek recourse with the local state or courts? Why not force the eviction of the residential colony that overlapped with his land parcel. Dilip took my confusion as an accusation of impropriety on his part, sharply responding, 'Many honest people face this issue, it's not just here ... the police, *sarpanch*, the municipality, no one will help you with these *goondas* [gangsters], and if you go to court it will take many years to resolve.'[25] This strategy of claiming land or defending property is common among low-level land speculators across Gurgaon, one that highlights the ways territorial claims are often legitimised not only by their embeddedness in political institutions[26] but also indirectly by the threats of lengthy judicial processes ill-fitting of investment cycles.

In most cases without support from the local state or courts, disputing parties must compromise, agree to buy each other out or agree to share ownership on the land. 'No one will risk a good investment in the court, these issues are settled between parties ... this is why it's important first to clear the land.' Getting a return on an investment in rural land is risky, involving costs, an alertness to counter-claims and relies as much on owning land on paper as it does settling its social and material possession on the ground. Rural property claims, as Nikita Sud's work in Gujarat notes, entwines the legal technologies of property-making with de facto regimes of access and exclusion fortified by local power structures.[27] Of course, possession is acutely speculative, dealing chiefly in the uncertainty of having one's ground-claims and *ersatz* documentation recognised by appealing to quite other methods of recognition, attribution and perception.

As we see in the following section, across the city a wide range of actors from international real estate firms to state agencies and low-level land brokers engage in a politics of land occupation in order to stake a claim to property. These claims are partially substantiated within the land registry wherein influential actors have covertly converted precarious tenure forms – *kabza* (possession), *gair marusi* (tenant-at-will) – to these forms of possession and indeed are sites where powerful actors are able to covertly change land tenures from possession to ownership. Akin to Solomon Benjamin's work on 'occupancy urbanism' on the agrarian–urban frontier, real estate actors mobilise agrarian institutions and tenure regimes in order to occupy land, speculatively capture anticipated land values and establish property claims. That is on the frontier we find real estate actors, the state and aspirational landowners, occupying *for* property, not against it.

SETTLING THE COMMONS

Dilip's speculative real estate strategies rely on investing in rural land in anticipation of urbanisation, exploiting state acquisitions and arranging an *ersatz* infrastructure of urban development. Much of this work involves exploiting former agricultural land, but as the Daulatabad broker reminded us, not all agricultural land is the same. Indeed, one of the biggest obstacles towards its clean conversion into urban real estate is the diverse and layered forms of land tenure that govern use, ownership and management. Picking apart these layers of tenure and impressing certain interpretations of property over others is another key speculative strategy engaged in by local brokers and state actors in order to secure property and shape real estate development.

Over the past two decades, over 4,000 acres of village common and forest land in Gurgaon have been controversially bought, plotted and developed by the local state, landowners and private developers. Just like the previous cases, the conversion of rural land into urban real estate is a joint effort, embarked upon by state planners and consolidators, private consultancies, local landowners and real estate firms, who each look to prospect the perception of rural land and rural futures in the singular pathway of urban rentier accumulation.

One spring weekend, after weeks of chasing landowners and brokers in the region, I was introduced to Ram Singh and visited his small farmhouse in Gwal Pahari, a hilly and forested village in south-eastern Gurgaon on the border with Delhi. The modest two-storey building was empty and clearly not lived in. Ram Singh brought some plastic chairs to the porch and instructed a young boy to go to the nearest road for tea. Ram Singh did not live here; his family home was inside the *abadi* on the other side of the village. The farmhouse he explained was family land that his grandfather had cultivated years ago. His grandfather had a small strip of land as an owner-cultivator, his father like many Yadav village elders had spent time in the military while Ram Singh and he and his brother worked in construction, leasing out construction machinery in high demand across Gurgaon. Like many other landowners I had spent time with in Gurgaon, Ram Singh's shift into the property business occurred in tandem with the arrival of city planners to the village in the decade building up to the introduction of the Gwal Pahari Development Plan.

In 2010 the village of Gwal Pahari was incorporated into an urban development plan by the planning department. Gwal Pahari's incorporation forms part of a broader state project to open up forest lands along Gurgaon's southern tracts for commercialisation. According to a report by former director general of consolidations in Haryana Ashok Khemka, in recent years the government has routinely engaged in processes of consolidation within forest, hill and common land areas in southern Gurgaon and in doing so has transferred hundreds of crores worth of land to private actors.[28] These include the de-notification of forest areas and the privatisation of different forms of village commons.

Just as in the 1960s and 1970s when the Haryana government were drawing up the first 'controlled areas' and development plans, real-estate-led urbanisation figures as both the problem and solution to Gwal Pahari's development. Opening up village land in a largely forested region to real estate markets, the development plan presses the urgent need for an 'institutional township' and SEZ in the region, stating:

> [The village has] remained unaffected from the onslaught of urbanisation upto the recent past.... But these areas cannot remain isolated more due to increasing urbanization, because there is a pressure of the southern areas of Delhi as well as of the adjoining areas of Haryana. This trend has further been accelerated with the improved road linkages and the construction of Gurgaon–Faridabad road through Haryana Territory. This road has exposed very beautiful valleys in the vicinity of Gual Pahari, Balola and Bandhwari generally known as Gual Pahari area.[29]

Perversely, the state seeks to protect the region from the 'onslaught of urbanisation' by rezoning the land for urbanisation. As ever, discourses of the rural preservation animate planning instruments that pave the way for rural land's turning for capital. The development plan reimagines 82 per cent of Gwal Pahari's land for SEZs, residential townships, commercial and infrastructural uses. All of this, of course, exists only in the imagination of planners, and yet once zoned for real estate purposes, Gwal Pahari's land is set on a trajectory in which real estate and liberal private property are the only sensible, natural land uses. The trick capitalists perform is to render the 'fictions' of property natural, mundane and common sense.[30]

In a classic frontier turn,[31] the projection of an area under threat from malign forces gives urgency and sense to the production of speculative imaginaries of SEZs and residential towers. The speculative planning and development regulations not only open the doorway to investors looking to capitalise on significant rent gaps on the agrarian–urban frontier, but they also invite those on the land to (urgently) realise the hidden value lying in their ancestral lands, calling upon them to enjoin their lands to future real estate uses. In doing so, the arrival of the Gwal Pahari Development Plan sparked a rush of contested property claims as competing territorial actors – state agencies, local landowners, real estate firms – each sought to capture value from land.

The development plan pre-empted the mass expansion of urban and infrastructural investment into the area, which includes a series of luxury residential complexes and a 100-million-US-dollar IT SEZ developed by New York investment firm J. P. Morgan and the Indian developer, ASF Group. The Gurgaon–Faridabad road that passes through the areas has been widened by the National Highways Authority to facilitate the fast movement of people and materials from Gurgaon to the mountains. Today Gurgaon's planning and local land registration offices are bustling with brokers and developers seeking to get their various claims to Gwal Pahari's land on paper, and access licences for residential and commercial development. The village roadside today is marked by materials of expectant urbanisation – pitched fences, proxy farmhouses and roadside brokerage offices.

Yet the reason I was keen to visit that day was that Ram Singh's land fell within over 400 acres of land in the village, valued at over 3,000 crore rupees (500 million US dollars) that has been embroiled in an ownership dispute between the municipal corporation of Gurgaon (MCG), landowners and a series of property owners and real estate firms. For the municipality the vast stretch of land that encompasses the central and western sections of the village forms part of the village common lands reserved for community uses. The land was previously owned and managed by the *panchayat* and transferred to the municipality in 2010. Municipalisation of Gurgaon's villages is hotly contested by villagers who lose the financial autonomy of the *panchayat* system and become subject to property taxes once under the jurisdiction of the MCG. Controversially, municipalisation equally transfers highly valued lands previously under the control of the village *panchayat*.

The land in question has a complicated history. Up until the 1950s the land was commonly held by village proprietors until it was quietly converted into *shamilat*, or common land, with landowners holding notional shares in the land. In the 1980s state officials gave permission for the land to be subdivided and traded by landowners and only in the late 2000s was the land reassigned as *panchayat*, then municipal land. And yet by then much of the land had been plotted and sold for farmhouses, residential complexes and even research institutes. Indeed, in the 1980s, part of the landholding was donated by HUDA to an environmental research organisation, the Energy and Resources Institute.

The Institute, which includes a nine-hole golf course,[32] ironically justifies its location in the otherwise protected, forest area through a frontier lens, boasting of turning a 'largely barren and desolate land ... into a sustainable habitat'. Complicating the matter further, the 2010 Gwal Pahari masterplan designates parts of the common land for SEZ purposes, a position that conflicts with the municipality's claim on the land as common land for community purposes. The complexity of land tenure, in other words, shaped by historic undulations in ownership and use, facilitate competing territorial narratives and property claims.

Ram Singh explained his ambitions for the land as we looked across a sparse landscape of scrubland overshadowed with residential towers and large villas:

> We had this house built on our land many years ago but others here sold land when the companies came maybe ten years ago, they are rich men now ... the land here is not for farming, you would need a lot of fertiliser to make use of it ... it just isn't profitable, but we are still farmers only, land is all that we people know.

Ram Singh was planning to sell the land, entering into an equity-sharing partnership with a Delhi-based property dealer that was still at the time under negotiation.

A Private Commons

The dispute over the land owes much to the complexity of tenure regimes during the post-colonial period. In north India 'village common lands', or *shamilat deh,* refer to a diverse collection of fallow (*banjar qadim*), grazing (*chargah*) and uncultivated (*gair mumkin*) lands differently owned and vested between landowners, non-landowning village residents, pastoralists and *panchayats* that are themselves expressions of conjunctural rural struggles over control of and rights and access to land.[33] The codification of a vast range of tenures was in part an outcome of colonial efforts to rationalise and maximise the agricultural output of rural land. These were principally drawn from pre-existing socio-ecological arrangements in the villages. As Shubhra Gururani notes, in Gurgaon's southern mountainous villages where pastoralists and agriculturalists rubbed shoulder to shoulder, common lands operated as a 'critical glue that maintained a vibrant system of mutuality, sharing, support and sustenance' in Gurgaon's villages.

Under the land settlements introduced across the nineteenth century, previously customary commons arrangements were mapped and codified, and the village propriety body was given formal ownership titles over the common lands. Village proprietors held the right to use, manage, possess and partition these 'common' lands, while non-proprietor villagers – tenant farmers, pastoralists, lower-caste residents – held grazing and usufruct rights to the land.[34]

The colonial intervention violently enforced geographical imaginaries and systems of rule that made sense of customary common arrangements within the vernacular of liberal property ownership. In doing so, land settlement not only formalised commons arrangements into codified systems of obligations and responsibilities but also eroded non-agrarian land uses and precipitated the conversion of common lands into private property at the expense of non-landowning pastoralists and tenants.[35]

And so, while this diverse collection of lands was formally referred to as *shamilat deh* (common lands), by the turn of the twentieth century village landowners held a definitive share in the commons and could sell, partition, cultivate that share as they saw fit. Rights to the commons had been set on the pathway towards private property.

Post-colonial agrarian reforms in Punjab sought to reorganise property relations across the state's villages, put barriers towards excessive monopolisation and included measures to re-common the commons. The Punjab Village Common Lands Act, 1953, transferred rights to the commons exclusively to village *panchayats*, established under the Punjab Gram Panchayat Act, 1952. The act represented a significant check on the territorial power of village landowners, who no longer had partition or alienation rights on the village commons, and to an extent empowered the rights of other caste communities. In response Haryana's landowners successfully forced successive amendments to the act from the 1960s that exempted from the *shamilat* any common land brought under cultivation before 1950 and provided landowners notional shares in the *shamilat* in proportion to their agricultural landholdings. The moment of reform was short-lived, the acts re-established a degree of private ownership over lands to be used for common purposes. They nevertheless furthered additional historic layers of rights to lands that enable the flurry of claims in the contemporary moment.

And yet the dispute on Ram Singh's land in Gwal Pahari hinges upon a distinct post-colonial agrarian intervention: land consolidation. The land consolidation schemes across Punjab and Haryana in the 1950 and 1960s, discussed in Chapter 1, also intervened in the commons. In the process of converting rural landholdings into grids, land rights were swapped and repositioned en masse, and the commons had to be created anew. Across consolidated villages novel kinds of common or community-based lands were created. New common lands were needed to enable the future extension of residential areas, others were required for the revenue-generating purposes of newly empowered village *panchayats*. This land had to come from somewhere, and in many villages landowners vested their own lands with the *panchayat* on a pro-rata basis for these purposes. This land became classified as *jumla mushtarka malkan* (hereafter *jumla* land).[36] This *jumla* land was included in the *shamilat deh* and vested with *panchayats* but was nevertheless the undivided private property of village landowners, much of which remained utilised for un-taxed cultivation. The current dispute rests upon whether this land is private property, bound to the common use of landowners, or common land bound to the common interest of the village and now city.

The commons has always been a contested tenure conferring differing ownership, use and possession rights and occupying different locations across time. The commons is at once private property and communal property, for private and public use, vested with the state and owned by landowners. These interventions in land have layered historic claims onto individual landholdings that, while having led to significant contestation, have imputed in land a 'powerful fluidity' utilised by competing actors to project particular interpretations of history and settle de facto territorial claims.[37] Academic literature on urban tenure has tended to focus upon how de facto tenure allows for subaltern investment and the iterative upgrading of urban poor neighbourhoods. On the urban frontier, the complexity of tenure, use and ownership provide the grounds upon which multiple actors can legitimise claims that align land uses with hegemonic real-estate-led development. Indeed, as Gurgaon's agricultural land was opened up to real estate investment and landowners looked to extend their territorial base, many across the city began to build on the perception of their individual rights to *jumla* lands, plotted farmhouses, filled ponds and more broadly integrated their land into real estate markets.

A Grazing Ground in the City

Ram Singh's bungalow sat, he claimed again fingering his paperwork, on *jumla* land, by which he meant the property of the village landowners. Pulling out a certified land registry document, Ram Singh fingered the column that displayed his grandfather's name and size of the family's share in the land. Stapled to the back was a hand-drawn sketch of the land parcel signed and stamped by a government official in the revenue department. Much like Dilip, Ram Singh's family had been busy arranging the bureaucratic and material evidence to substantiate their ownership, assembling uncertified demarcation maps, sales deeds, and land registry copies that form the alternative infrastructure to property claims on the frontier. Ram Singh had plotted, he claimed, on his family's share of *jumla* land that the family had cultivated and leased to pastoralists for grazing purposes for decades.

The Gwal Pahari dispute came to a head in 2012 when municipal officials persuaded the land revenue department to mutate the ownership of the land in the state registry in their favour. For the landowners, real estate firms and the owners of luxury farmhouses that sit on the land, the municipalisation of the commons is an act of aggression, a denial of their rightful position as private property-bearing citizens. As Ram Singh explained:

> Why are they coming here now? They are all coming here to steal from us no? There come here looking for money only ... this [land] has been in our family for generations, and now the government are claiming it is *shamilat*? This is nonsense, don't we have rights as citizens?

A property dealer I met that evening at a roadside bar popular with visitors from central Gurgaon and Delhi echoed Ram Singh's frustration: 'The government have seen the value of the land and corrupt officials have stolen the land [but] the locals have a right to property, this is in our constitution, [the government] cannot take this away.'

Both Ram Singh and the property dealer's evocation of their rights to property reinforces a particular caste-based entitlement to property ownership. By narrowing the land's uses only to private ownership and discounting the existing common uses assigned even to *jumla* land, landowners aim to evoke what Anne Bonds has called 'specifically racialized [or here caste-based] regimes of accumulation and property entitlement', where ownership claims bound to caste-community under colonial rule are not only legally privileged but projected into the future as the only sensible uses and meanings for rural land. Indeed, as both accounts rightly note, the municipality stands to gain significantly from the land's market value as real estate. For both parties the only possible future for rural land is commercialisation. Such is the hegemony of real-estate-led development; few are willing to accept that the commons might actually be held and used in common.

In response, the Gwal Pahari landowners in coalition with corporate real estate actors have leveraged significant political and financial clout to appeal the transfer in court on numerous occasions.[38] The case remains, at the time of writing, active in the courts with each successive ruling grappling to translate the meaning and purpose of the land. The latest ruling issued in September 2018 went both ways, declaring the land to be the exclusive undivided property of village landowners, but also ruled that the land could only be used for village purposes. This divests the rights of proprietors – including corporate real estate firms - who do not come from the village landowning body but reinforces the rights of landowners to be compensated for any property transferred to the municipality.

These legal tussles of village common land speak to the ways post-colonial agrarian property regimes continue to shape territorial claims and urbanisation processes today. It is precisely the opacity and uncertainty of land use and ownership that allows powerful actors to assert particular claims as legitimate and align land uses with real estate development visions in anticipation of the land's formal incorporation into real estate markets.

Indeed, for Ram Singh and others in Gwal Pahari, constructing farmhouses and integrating the commons with shadow property markets was not only about securing claims to the land but also signally improvement against antiquated common land uses and tenures. It was about readying the land, no matter its existing legal status, for future commodification. Wanting to understand more, I asked how and why real estate firms were investing in land that was notoriously disputed, were these not risky investments to make before a final legal judgment? Ram Singh's cousin, Prem, had joined us on the porch while taking numerous calls on a Bluetooth headpiece, interjected confidently: 'Nothing will happen ... you see, if landowners make a proper house and there is a proper road here, then the paperwork will follow ... with companies [developers] and sectors [residential complexes] coming here year after year, this development is good for everyone, the government won't destroy this.'

Landowners in Gwal Pahari constructed farmhouses and plotted roads on rural land in order to establish future territorial claims in anticipation of regularisation or incorporation into the development plan. And yet for Ram Singh and others, plotting common lands relies on arranging land uses that align with hegemonic real-estate-led visions and political economies of development, regardless of ownership. These speculative practices are justified and indeed reified by state institutions that signal common lands to be out of step with history, one which stretches and contorts masterplans around the territorial claims of landowners and real estate elites.

Indeed, Prem's confidence in tentative claims to the commons might appear conceited if not for numerous official statements from state institutions that near echo his position. In the 2018 case, the senior civil judge considering the dispute stated:

> Since the land has changed its agrarian character, after coming in the municipal limits, it is essential that all the stakeholders in the society ... realise that a 464.6 acres grazing ground is not required in the heart of the [National Capital Region] ... with an increasing population [and] unemployment ... what is required is housing societies, markets ... special economic zones and IT Parks.

The geographical imaginary of Gwal Pahari's common lands, put forward by the court, was one that justified urbanisation not only as inevitable but urgent, positioning non-commercial land uses as out of step with a modern city regardless of its actually existing tenure. Much like the Gwal Pahari development plan, the judge's account relies upon a tautological historicity, an agrarian past is foreclosed by forces of urbanisation, and now these forces must be remedied with deeper forces of urbanisation. A 400-acre grazing ground that substantiated the region's 'agrarian character' has little to no place in this historical trajectory. There is, in other words, one historical path that rural land moves along, one in which it is owned as exclusive property (by the state, developers or agrarian landowners) and used for industrial and real estate accumulation.

Importantly, landowners like Ram Singh and Prem understand that their property claims are substantiated not necessarily by actually existing property regimes but rather by a mobilisation of who they are and what they are claiming. Practices of occupying ambiguous territories and navigating bureaucratic spaces to secure property in this sense are animated by both colonial codifications of property and caste, and a contemporary hegemonic conjuncture within which rural land on the frontier is in urgent need of remedy and improvement. Ram Singh, the MCG and others are in other words engaged in a practice of erasing and wilfully ignoring the other claims and uses through which common lands are assigned and came about.

OUT OF PLACE

In April 2015 HUDA, the body responsible for providing trunk infrastructure in Gurgaon, demolished the Dokhar-ki-Dhani colony in Fatehpur Jharsa village in order to make way for an approach road servicing the elite residential development, Uniworld Gardens. Fatehpur Jharsa is a small settlement located on the historic common lands of neighbouring Jharsa. The land was vested with the Kashyap community, formally a 'backward' caste in Haryana, in 1877 and had been held in three sub-divisions. Following the municipalisation of Jharsa, all village common lands outside the urban village boundary passed to the MCG. The Fatehpur Jharsa neighbourhood was suddenly municipal property, and 250 homes were rendered encroachments by the planning office.

I visited the village in the aftermath of the demolition. A large area hemmed in on each side by residential towers had been near flattened with bricks, household belongings and debris piled up by the road leant on a billboard advertising luxury apartments in Uniworld Gardens. Taking shelter under a lone tea stand, Ashok Kashyap explained how his village had been vilified by the local authorities in concert with real estate firms:

> The builders have come here and destroyed the whole village, they want to remove the poor from here to build multi-storey apartments ... they notified us at 6 pm and came to destroy these homes at 8.30 am the next morning, they were charging us with *lathi*s and so we had had to flee ... the police were ruthless, they took cash, belongings, some had left breakfast and they had ate that too.

The HUDA administration had declared the neighbourhood in the 'illegal possession of the land mafia' and justified the demolition drive arguing that the '*jhuggi*s on this piece of land' were being 'rented out to outsiders, [the] majority of whom are Bangladeshis'. HUDA's appeal to racist sentiment ('Bangladeshis' is a popular, less-than-coded term deployed to infer the foreignness of Indian Muslims) was prescient of an emerging fascist political environment brought to the fore by the election of the BJP at state and national levels in 2014. These sentiments are being increasingly deployed to patch together a consensus for dispossession and neoliberal accumulation among the class of agrarian landowners that feature across this book (see Conclusion). Of course, that these tropes were being deployed against a landless caste community speaks to the way casteism and Islamophobia entwine within contemporary Hindutva politics to enforce the supremacy of propertied accumulation. For Ashok, the claims were 'bizarre'. His village, he stressed, was no *jhuggi* (slum) and he was not aware of any Bangladeshis living in the area:

> It was not a *jhuggi* [slum] we have spent some 20–30 lakh on our homes ... we have land records from the patwari, voter IDs, tax records ... do I sound Bengali to you? This is nonsense. This land has been in our families for generations, over a hundred years, and suddenly we are encroaching? This government have changed our history by force.

Pointing to worn photocopies, Ashok explained how the community attained possession records through the land registry office back in 2005 just before the land was taken on by HUDA. The village's status, Ashok claims, must have been altered by the state in coalition with developers and local leaders in neighbouring Jharsa. 'We are poor people, most people here are unemployed and now homeless too.'

The government had offered partial compensation to the landowners, Ashok explained: 'All twelve *bighas* [around 6 acres] in total should be offered compensation, but the government offered compensation for only three *bighas*, only one family received this, the rest of us are forgotten.' Intrigued to find out why only three *bighas* were compensated, I returned to asking about the legal status of the land: Who held the title to the land? Did HUDA recognise some claims and not others? 'No, it doesn't matter if the land is legal or illegal,' Ashok patiently explained. 'They [the government] want multi-storey apartments on this land, the rules change where the money is, with one visit to the municipal office, there are no rules here.' He added, 'The government always liked to say us poor people lived in *jhuggis*, that we live in temporary homes you know? Of course, next to these multi-storey apartments maybe they looked like *jhuggis*, but for us they were proper, luxurious homes that we have lived in for generations.'

For the Fatehpur Jharsa landowners, the eviction had little to do with records of rights and claims to the land, their homes so intimately held were simply not considered in line with the future, their luxurious homes were rendered 'temporary' and their history easily brushed away by the power of real estate firms.

In many ways this case is characteristic of demolitions and evictions carried out across Indian cities in the current conjuncture. And yet, the Fatehpur Jharsa demolition brings to light the fault lines of speculative real estate markets driving Gurgaon's urbanisation. In principle there is little difference in the cases of Fatehpur Jharsa and Gwal Pahari. In both cases, it is alleged that landowners are illegally occupying village common lands in the possession of the state government. And yet, while landowners in Gwal Pahari have been able to repurpose complex tenurial claims into fully fledged private property – mobilising their caste-power and political connections to project their de facto territorial claims as future oriented and legitimate – the landowners and claims in Fatehpur Jharsa have been rendered 'temporary', foreign and in urgent need of redress. In other words, the speculative property-claiming strategies which ready rural land for real estate abstraction and animate Gurgaon's land market is deeply caste structured. The creation of private property in land in Gurgaon relies, on one hand, on racist narratives of 'temporariness', foreignness and illegitimacy to open up land for real estate purposes, and on the other allows agrarian caste elites to repurpose their grazing grounds for real estate capture and enclosure. In other words, the differentiated incorporation of some agrarian property regimes, and disavowal and destruction of others, grounds the hegemony of what Brenna Bhandar calls 'racial regimes of ownership' in Gurgaon.

PERCEPTION AND PROPERTY

Traditional accounts of land enclosure and privatisation have tended to focus on the instruments that birth private property in land, rendering land an alienable, identifiable and partible object. The boundary wall, property title and state land registry all, in these accounts, inaugurate land as a fungible commodity-like resource. And yet, as we have seen in the previous chapters, land in contemporary north India is strongly marked by histories of compromise and contestation that have shaped an array of customary and privatised forms of use and ownership. These thicketed layerings of tenure, coverage and planning use – rather than presenting obstacles to clear observation of property relations – afford local actors an array of avenues through which to tentatively establish property claims and speculate on future uses.[39] Landowners-cum-investors across Gurgaon arrange for unauthorised paperwork, partition reports (see Chapter 4) and plot small-scale constructions on rural land in order to produce a series of de facto property claims that align class-caste and developmental sensibilities of the local state. Conversely, the capitalist state at the frontier is more than willing to align with sectors of the agrarian population and privilege their tentative territorial claims in the midst of tenurial complexity, while admonishing and dispossessing others. This differentiating logic that devalues and de-valorises some just as it values and valorises others sits at the heart of hegemonic real estate development on the frontier and drives speculative territorial activity.

Indeed, rather than establishing clarity of ownership or use, many landowners opt to appeal to particular perceptions of rightful or sensible land use and ownership, often in lieu of planning codes and procedures. The property-claiming strategies of Ram Singh and Dilip, as well as municipal government and city planners, are each attempts to not only author but also perform city-ness. That is, insofar as the city is a set of normative, material, political economic and aesthetic registers – abstractions rendered sensible through colonial histories of planning and development – speculative property-claiming on the frontier can be thought of as a disorderly attempt to imitate the norms of private property using decidedly agrarian tools. The two registers of land speculation: first, the speculative purchase and resale of rural land plots engaged in by Mukesh and Dilip; and second, the improvised arrangement of property claims and uses, by Ram Singh among others, work together to precipitate and shape Gurgaon's real estate market and enjoin an agrarian propertied class to urban real estate futures. As Jeremy Campbell writes, property-making on the frontier is 'anticipatory mimes of the right and proper institution of property that exists in the future and over there' connecting the 'improvised political economy of the frontier' to broader networks of capital accumulation.

Land speculation in Gurgaon in other words operates less through certainty and clarity than through registers of anticipation, perception and recognition. In order to establish property claims and returns on investment, landowners seek to anticipate the geographies of urban expansion, appeal to perceptions of rightful future uses regardless of its unauthorised forms, and in turn seek to elicit recognition of certain claims and land uses over others. Land conversions operate through what Amoore calls an 'aperture of observation' that authorises otherwise illegible, tentative property claims. The appeal to perception is one that rejects modernist 'god tricks' and calls upon partial modes of seeing and recognising territorial claims. As Bear, Birla and Puri note, 'Speculation fuels, and is fuelled by, a heightened state of anticipation in which routines of calculation are often suspended.' It is in other words speculative in so far as it calls upon tentative, incalculable forms of value channelling agrarian caste and class structures of power to establish the legitimacy of territorial claims.

Notes

1. Goldman, 'Speculating on the Next World City'.
2. McNeilly, 'Are Rights Out of Time?', 2–3. See also Chowdhury, *Time, Temporality and Legal Judgment*. McNeilly, drawing on Elizabeth Grosz's work, explores 'untimely futures' as radical rejections of capitalist teleology, that which hold the germs of radical legal and social change. On the frontier nonlinearity is an animating condition for capitalist expansion, temporal uncertainty drives the imperative for capitalist actors to secure and certainise the future.

3. Balakrishnan and Gururani argue that 'the main drivers of the new caste–class–land nexus is the shift in registers of land value from agricultural fertility … to location and proximity to economic corridors and urban enclaves'.
4. Here I draw analogies with Karaman et al.'s *Plotting Urbanism*, which the authors conceptualise as 'individualised strategies of urban development and intensification of land use, strong processes of commodification and often a marked socioeconomic differentiation between property owners and tenants'.
5. Goldman, 'Speculative Urbanism'; Upadhya, 'Assembling Amaravati'.
6. Tsing, *Friction*; Noterman, 'Speculating on Vacancy'; Campbell, *Conjuring Property*.
7. Noterman, 'Speculating on Vacancy'.
8. Ibid.; Smith, *The New Urban Frontier*.
9. Blomley, 'Law, Property, and the Geography of Violence'; Tsing, *Friction*.
10. Noterman, 'Speculating on Vacancy'; Blomley, 'Law, Property, and the Geography of Violence'.
11. Noterman, 'Speculating on Vacancy', 2.
12. Campbell, *Conjuring Property*.
13. Searle, *Landscapes of Accumulation*.
14. Barnes, *Making Cars in the New India*, 83.
15. Bassi, 'Come to My Parlour'.
16. *Times of India*, 'Multi-Crore Plans for Haryana'.
17. Searle, *Landscapes of Accumulation*.
18. IBEF, *Haryana: State Report 2013*.
19. The plan also introduced new rules that set minimum acreage perimeters for licenced developments, of 100 acres for 'plotted housing' or residential townships, and 10 acres for 'group housing' or apartments in Gurgaon.
20. The powers have also been utilised by the private sector to informally lobby for pre-emption rights on land adjoining their property in the city.
21. Wahdan, 'State Collective Action'.
22. Karkaria, 'And the Living Is Easy'.
23. *Economic Times*, 'Hassle-Free Ride'.
24. Searle, *Landscapes of Accumulation*.
25. Of course, such is the complexity of rural property claims, I may have been witnessing this very practice that day. The record for the land parcel, to this date, does not bear Dilip's name; he had privately arranged documentation to establish his property claim and had plans to occupy the plot, informally constructing boundary walls against outside encroachment.
26. Benjamin, 'Occupancy Urbanism'.

27. Sud, *The Making of Land*.
28. Khemka, 'Khemka Report'.
29. Town and Country Planning Department, 'Gwal Pahari Urban Development Plan'.
30. Ghertner and Lake, 'Introduction: Land Fictions'.
31. Tsing, *Friction*; Safransky, 'Greening the Urban Frontier'; Smith, *The New Urban Frontier*.
32. The institute's own literature describes the land as a 'largely barren and desolate land … transformed into a sustainable habitat' by the institute.
33. Chakravarty-Kaul, 'The Commons, Community and the Courts'; Gururani, '"When Land Becomes Gold"'.
34. Chakravarty-Kaul, 'Two Centuries on the Commons'.
35. This was a project that intimately wove caste difference into property, producing caste-based subjects of agrarian property. See Bhandar, *Colonial Lives of Property*.
36. The Urdu word 'jumla' here translates as 'aggregate'. *Jumla mushtarka malkan*, then, translates loosely as aggregate-joint ownership. Interestingly 'jumla' is also colloquially used to describe a 'false promise' often attributed to over-zealous politicians.
37. Benjamin, 'Touts, Pirates and Ghosts', 251.
38. Khatry, 'Haryana Panchayat to Get Back Its 464 Acre Gwal Pahari Land'.
39. Solomon Benjamin ('Touts, Pirates and Ghosts') argues that varied tenures provide land with a 'powerful fluidity' with which to establish de facto property claims.

BIBLIOGRAPHY

Balakrishnan, Sai, and Shubhra Gururani. 'New Terrains of Agrarian–Urban Studies: Limits and Possibilities'. *Urbanisation* 6, no. 1 (2021): 7–15.

Barnes, Tom. *Making Cars in the New India: Industry, Precarity and Informality*. Cambridge: Cambridge University Press, 2018.

Bassi, Seema. 'Come to My Parlour, Say States'. *Times of India*, 20 March 1994, 16.

Benjamin, Solomon. 'Occupancy Urbanism: Radicalizing Politics and Economy beyond Policy and Programs'. *International Journal of Urban and Regional Research* 32, no. 3 (2008): 719–29.

———. 'Touts, Pirates and Ghosts'. *Sarai Reader* 5, no. 1 (2005): 242–54.

Bhandar, Brenna. *Colonial Lives of Property: Law, Land, and Racial Regimes of Ownership*. Durham; London: Duke University Press, 2018.

Blomley, Nicholas. 'Law, Property and the Geography of Violence: The Frontier, the Survey, and the Grid'. *Annals of the Association of American Geographers* 93, no. 1 (2003): 121–41.

Campbell, Jeremy M. *Conjuring Property: Speculation and Environmental Futures in the Brazilian Amazon.* Seattle; London: University of Washington Press, 2015.

Chakravarty-Kaul, Minoti. 'The Commons, Community and the Courts of Colonial Punjab'. *Indian Economic and Social History Review* 29, no. 4 (1992): 393–436.

———. 'Two Centuries on the Commons: The Punjab'. Working paper, Indiana University, n.d.

Chowdhury, Tanzil. *Time, Temporality and Legal Judgment.* Oxford: Routledge, 2020.

Economic Times. 'Hassle-Free Ride on Delhi–Gurgaon Expressway to Boost Gurgaon's Image as City of Future'. 19 September 2012. https://economictimes.indiatimes.com/news/economy/infrastructure/hassle-free-ride-on-delhi-gurgaon-expressway-to-boost-gurgaons-image-as-city-of-future/articleshow/16446447.cms?from=mdr. Accessed 10 January 2021.

Ghertner, D. Asher, and Robert W. Lake. 'Introduction: Land Fictions and the Politics of Commodification in City and Country'. In *Land Fictions*, 1–25. Ithaca, NY: Cornell University Press, 2021.

Goldman, Michael. 'Speculating on the Next World City'. In *Worlding Cities*, edited by Ananya Roy and Aihwa Ong, 229–58. London: Wiley-Blackwell, 2011. https://doi.org/10.1002/9781444346800.ch9.

———. 'Speculative Urbanism and the Urban-Financial Conjuncture: Interrogating the Afterlives of the Financial Crisis'. *Environment and Planning A: Economy and Space* (2021).

Gururani, Shubhra. '"When Land Becomes Gold": Changing Political Ecology of the Commons in a Rural–Urban Frontier'. In *Land Rights, Biodiversity Conservation and Justice: Rethinking Parks and People*, edited by S. Mollett and T. Kepe, 107–25. Oxford; New York: Routledge, 2018.

IBEF. *Haryana: State Report 2013*. Indian Brand Equity Foundation, n.d.

Karaman, O., L. Sawyer, C. Schmid and K. P. Wong. 'Plot by Plot: Plotting Urbanism as an Ordinary Process of Urbanisation'. *Antipode* 52, no. 4 (2020): 1122–51.

Karkaria, Bachi. 'And the Living Is Easy'. *Times of India.* 18 September 2004. https://timesofindia.indiatimes.com/india/And-the-living-is-easy/articleshow/855706.cms. Accessed 1 January 2021.

Khatry, Rajendra. 'Haryana Panchayat to Get Back Its 464 Acre Gwal Pahari Land'. *Tehelka*, 30 September 2018.

Khemka, Ashok. 'Comments of Dr Ashok Khemka, IAS, Formerly Director General, Land Records and Consolidation of Land Holdings, Haryana and Inspector General of Registration, Haryana, on the Report of the Committee Constituted by the State Government Vide Order No. 1/121/2012-1SII Dated 19.10. 2012 to Inquire into the Issues Raised by Dr Ashok Khemka, IAS, the then DGLR-Cum-DGCH-Cum-IGR, Haryana'. 19 October 2012.

McNeilly, Kathryn. 'Are Rights Out of Time? International Human Rights Law, Temporality, and Radical Social Change'. *Social and Legal Studies* 28, no. 6 (2019): 817–38.

Noterman, Elsa. 'Speculating on Vacancy'. *Transactions of the Institute of British Geographers* 47, no. 1 (2022): 123–138.

Safransky, Sara. 'Greening the Urban Frontier: Race, Property, and Resettlement in Detroit'. *Geoforum* 56 (August 2014): 237–48.

Searle, Llerena Guiu. *Landscapes of Accumulation: Real Estate and the Neoliberal Imagination in Contemporary India.* Chicago: University of Chicago Press, 2016.

Smith, Neil. *The New Urban Frontier: Gentrification and the Revanchist City.* London; New York: Routledge, 2005.

Sud, Nikita. *The Making of Land and the Making of India.* Delhi: Oxford University Press, 2020.

Times of India. 'Multi-Crore Plans for Haryana'. 4 November 1992, 21.

Town and Country Planning Department. 'Gwal Pahari Urban Development Plan'. Government of Haryana, 2010.

Tsing, Anna Lowenhaupt. *Friction: An Ethnography of Global Connection.* Princeton; Oxford: Princeton University Press, 2011.

Upadhya, Carol. 'Assembling Amaravati: Speculative Accumulation in a New Indian City'. *Economy and Society* 49, no. 1 (2020): 141–69.

Wahdan, Dalia Essam. 'State Collective Action and Local Governance a Comparative Analysis of the Regimes of Inequitable Transportation in Gurgaon, India and 6 October Egypt'. Thesis, Savitribai Phule Pune University, Pune, 2007.

4 | The Bureaucrat and the Survey*

DRAFTING THE CITY

'That's the problem with these maps: this one was in such bad condition we couldn't read it.' Squinting to read the scrawled handwriting of the field book, Ajay sifted through photographs, hand-drawn plot sketches, land record copies and a cloth cadastral map depicting the parcel of land our jeep was parked on in the western periphery of Gurgaon. With a laptop precariously balanced on his knees, we were attempting to draft the contours of property in the land on the AutoCAD software in preparation for the day's boundary demarcation. Pushing his fingers across his temples, Ajay lamented the poor condition of the records that Virinder, the *kanungo* (a senior field-bureaucrat within the Haryana Revenue Department), had brought along: 'These records are unclear, this road could be anywhere … they had a new one made, of course we have the *mussavi* [original cadastral map] and the GPS survey image but we have to be certain with these things.' Ajay explained that our attempts to survey and correct a disputed boundary between the two parties' property was likely to be difficult. Not only are there frequent inconsistencies and points of ambivalence within the documents we were sifting through, but also the land had already been subjected to two cadastral surveys over the previous twelve months. With each survey, each conducted using different technologies and methods, new certified maps came into circulation that would come to obscure the veracity of the boundary. As we attempted to map out a copy of the record onto the software, Ajay pointed out some of these inconsistencies from the jeep window: 'Look here on the ground the [grid] is not accurate, this here road is not straight like this, it is coming at

---

*A part of this chapter was originally published as 'Uncertain Grounds: Cartographic Negotiation and Digitized Property on the Urban Frontier' in *International Journal of Urban and Regional Research* 45, no. 3 (2021): 442–57. Reprinted with permission from John Wiley and Sons.

an angle, see? These plots are not square – there will always be difference between the maps, the survey [image] and the land itself. On top of all of this, not all land claims are recorded in the map. Post-colonial land gridding and consolidation screened out messy non-geometric property from the revenue maps, leaving thousands of property shares hidden from state view. To find these unmapped shares we search through the textual data of the *jamabandi* (landholding register) and field book (original settlement notes) and a series of smaller hand-drawn sketches of land parcels that are yet to make it into the cadastral map.

Land boundary demarcations are formally social affairs; legally the AutoCAD template has to be drawn up on the spot, and the demarcation must take place in the presence of the village landowners. If a party disputes the boundary line of their property or wants a new boundary line emplaced in the record, as is often in the case of large land agglomeration projects, the revenue department must call on the village *lambardar*s (headmen) and all village landowners to bear witness to the amendment, creation or eradication of property. The process of map-making that forms part of the legal basis of Gurgaon's real estate sector is an exercise in negotiation mediated by extant social hierarchies and animated by the awkward imposition of static metrics of calculation onto slippery, lived territories.

As we sat in the back of Ajay's jeep in the corner of a field in the shadow of half-constructed skyscrapers, the group was slowly assembling around us, peering over Ajay's shoulders. The negotiation of the boundary line had already begun. 'You think it is peaceful now?' Ajay quietly cautioned. 'You wait until we announce the results, it is always nice and peaceful before the results, if they start being aggressive we must get the [GPS] receiver into the jeep, that cost us lakhs.' As soon as we settled on a template of the land record in the AutoCAD software, and embarked upon measuring out the land, one of the onlooking parties took issue with our methods. Pointing at the boundary wall we were using as a reference point, the middle-aged man exclaimed, 'This wall is wrong, this is not accurate, it was put up a few years back only by *bhumidar*s [landowners].' After some disagreement, the man agreed to taking the reference point, but after retrieving a tape measure and rope took to conducting his own measurements alongside those we were running through the GPS signal. We had only just begun and already the map was under negotiation. Joining us to take a break from hosting the party of land brokers and landowners assembled in the hot midday sun, Virinder noted in frustration, 'There is too much tension here. What can we do?' Highlighting the complexities of incongruous and incommensurable maps, boundary lines, and records, Virinder explained, 'If we impose the record, this whole city would have to shift! We have to find compromises somewhere.'

While carrying ethnographic fieldwork alongside land surveyors and revenue bureaucrats like Ajay and Virinder, I was struck by the regularity with which we would be confronted by overhangs and undercuts between the digital survey image, the state record and land's concrete uses. At nearly every digital land survey these uncertainties would be challenged by competing parties with a litany of conflicting methods of measurement and differing documentation and settled not by imposition of the record but through flexibility and quiet 'compromise'. The proliferation of territorial compromises reanimates uncertainties between the record and the ground, which in turn leads to further calls for bureaucratic correction. As I was quick to learn, state calculations would always beget state calculations. Despite the certainty that digitised state maps and records confer, land is tricky to calculate, rural property claims are difficult to pin down and our attempts to do so often magnified uncertainties that bureaucratic work is intended to remedy.

My early experiences conducting land boundary demarcations with Haryana's revenue department, and their private surveyors, introduced me to the ways that uncertainty and improvisation structure the capture and record of property in Gurgaon. I had set out to conduct research within Gurgaon's *patwari* (land revenue bureaucrat) office in order to better understand how the state aggregated and converted rural land into private property. If the previous chapter explored how landowners anticipate the state, I wanted to know more about the state's own role. The *patwari* is the lowest-rank bureaucrat within Haryana's revenue department. Sat in field offices across different neighbourhoods of the city, the *patwari* is responsible for registering and mapping rural property, assessing harvests and administrating village records. While *kanungos* like Virinder supervise this work and oversee boundary demarcations and measurements out in the fields, the purchase, transfer, division, aggregation and conversion of rural land into urban real estate must be certified and mapped through the *patwari* office, and so my initial interest was simply to understand how this process operated. Who owned what land? How did paper, and increasingly digital, documentation mediate the capture and transfer of rural land into real estate? My fieldwork sought to trace the movement of paperwork and property across the office and the field, and between public and private spaces and actors. This early experience of conducting land boundary demarcations introduced me to the ways that ambiguity is structured into Gurgaon's land governance and calls upon the improvisational work of revenue bureaucrats and land surveyors to find compromises and creatively assemble land into property.

The previous chapter examined how landowners anticipate urban development and speculatively impress territorial claims on the frontier. This chapter turns to examine the role of the local state, and its calculative instruments, in translating these diverse territorial claims into state records. Here I am interested in how bureaucratic and cartographic improvisation structures property claims and city-making practices in Gurgaon. Counter to claims, shared by neoliberal economists and critical scholars alike, that bureaucratic materials affect a degree of inscrutable, synoptic authority to state and capitalist practices, as we saw in the previous chapter, in Gurgaon real estate and landed actors – embedded within distinct political spaces – actively pursue uncertainty. It is the opacity of agrarian property that allows powerful actors to assert de facto claims and secure property in state records. Deciphering uncertainty in turn signifies the spatiality of the local state who earn a living off interpreting uncertainty and assembling property. The role that uncertainty plays in structuring Gurgaon's land market is explored through a series of ethnographic vignettes that follow.

The chapter begins by exploring the composition of the *patwari* office and land record books, examining both how disaggregated data is 'dug' and assembled by revenue officials, and how increasingly private actors entangle themselves in these everyday acts of interpretation. Second, the chapter examines how uncertainty is produced in the process of mapping out property boundaries in the fields. There is no dearth of maps in Gurgaon. Everything is mapped. From planning maps to cadastral maps, to survey maps, to the maps held by each government department, to those ordered by private actors. These maps do not correspond to neat units across the city, they overlap and deploy territory for distinct purposes. The sheer litany of mapping across the city – each deploying distinct methods of calculation and visions of territory – interdigitate to produce degrees of uncertainty in territorial claims. Maps and records, as we shall see, are not still-objects but 'exercises in negotiation',[1] constantly challenged, reworked and remediated in social and material struggles that often take place within the state bureaucracy.

As discussed in previous chapters, these negotiations are animated by the shifting hegemonic class alliances and formations – as various members of the agrarian classes – staring at a post-agrarian future – scrap over ground rents and speculate to open up land markets. In this chapter I focus on the calculative, bureaucratic instruments deployed to fix these speculations into state records. The map, the title, the plot are material expressions of the agrarian frontiers animating the reconfiguration of both land and society in Gurgaon. More than simply assemblages of bureaucratic materials and spaces, property-making practices in Gurgaon are shot through by conjunctural class struggles among a class clamouring for integration into a highly speculative post-agrarian economy. This chapter dwells on the ways that these maps and analogue and digital records interdigitate with these shifting class settlements, to mobilise the uncertainty and secure territorial claims.

UNCERTAINTY AND THE POLITICS OF LAND

Territorial technologies have long been deployed to both make and make sense of the world – maps, lists, registries are intended to be brought together to delineate certain territorial practices as sensible, and to thereby legitimate certain forms of territorial state action. The allure of mapping to colonial rulers was that it allowed for the delineation of the very terms under which land could be understood, used and owned. The 'unmapped' has always been integral to this process. Historically, the 'unmapped' has been a site of disquiet – that which marks the limits of control and certainty – that animates the frontier, as discussed in the previous chapter, the construal of emptiness calls for filling in, colonisation and conquest. And yet, as discussed in Chapter 1, the ambitions of colonial rulers to produce clean private property regimes were never fully attainable; colonial and post-colonial agrarian policy produced complex rural property regimes, characterised by a mixture of 'customary' and communal tenures, private property and tenancy rights. Today these property regimes can affect barriers to capital's capture and rationalisation of land. Small, unmapped rural land parcels – ensconced by joint holdings and pre-emption rights – can be difficult and time consuming to aggregate for real estate development. To these barriers, uncertainty comes in handy. The unmapped plots, incommensurate records and shifting surveys that are discussed in this chapter act as internal frontiers, openings for the potential capture and creative substantiation of property. Much of this creative work takes place in the *patwari* office.

Uncertainty saturates land and property markets on the urban frontier. This may be viewed as evidence of disorder and opacity that the modern state makes its driving mission to eradicate. The 'continually frustrated goal of the modern state,' James Scott writes, is to 'reduce the chaotic, disorderly, constantly changing social reality beneath it to something more closely resembling the administrative grid of its observations'.[2] Yet, as post-colonial scholarship has argued, it is precisely the absence of calculative technologies, enclosed lands and fixed grids that affords the government the kinds of control and order most amenable to the demands of both contested political institutions and fickle, mobile capital.[3] On the agrarian–urban frontier, political control and capitalist value creation are advanced through the logics of translation, decryption and assembly of distinct parts.

Uncertainty, after all, is the currency of bureaucratic expertise on the frontier. Uncertainty holds anticipatory force; it demands things be straightened out, fixed, rendered certain. It is the driving force behind frontier expansion. The illegible title must be made legible, the unmapped territory must be mapped, the disputed boundary line arbitrated. That the bureaucracy both produce and fix uncertainty only to produce more uncertainty feeds a feedback loop that renders their services in high demand.

Ananya Roy's pathbreaking work on Kolkata's peri-urban fringe showed how the absence of land records and maps created a 'new spatial vocabulary of control' – one that enabled the state government to flexibly distribute and weaponise land for different actors within distinct political conjunctures.[4] Critical scholarship on land often looks to the ways rationalising technologies – the title, the map – are utilised to denude land of its idiosyncrasies and flex and repurpose it for a whole manner of financial and political purposes.[5] A plot of irrigated land on Gurgaon's southern edge, can in this way, be repackaged and traded in financial instruments in faraway offices. Roy's work demonstrates how an absence of these technologies, the unmapped plot, can hold equal power to contort and flex property. Unmapped land, as Katherine Verdery explores in her work in Transylvania, can be stretched and contorted through competing cartographic, juridical and social claims on its location and borders.[6]

In the following, I first explore the bureaucratic office of the *patwari*, responsible for registering, mutating, partitioning and mapping rural property. Here I examine the ways revenue officials translate uncertainty and aggregate land records data within the bureaucratic office. I explore how

184 | Subaltern Frontiers

Figure 4.1 Gurgaon Patwar Ghar
Source: Photo by author.

silences within the record can be used to conjure property boundaries in the record. Here the 'cunning' bureaucrat emerges as a figure able to translate and navigate uncertainty. The second half of the chapter moves to the fields, examining the negotiability of the cadastral surveys introduced at the outset of the chapter.

Patwar Ghar

The *patwari* is the lowest-level official in the Haryana Revenue Department, responsible for registering and mapping landholdings, facilitating land transfers, assessing cultivation and administrating village records. Each *patwari* – supervised by an office *kanungo* and supported by various informally hired assistants – is responsible for overseeing the records of four to five villages. I undertook participant observation ethnography of Gurgaon's central *patwari* office, Patwar Ghar, between 2018 and 2019 to better understand how Gurgaon's land is governed (Figure 4.1). At the time, the Haryana government was digitising its land revenue system, digitising the land record books (*jamabandi*), mutation registers (*intkal*) and cloth cadastral maps that detail landholdings for each village and bringing many work processes (property and mutation registrations) online. The process at the time was incomplete, both the analogue and digital systems operating in parallel, each substantiating the authority of the other, and a wealth of processes – including land partitions, boundary measurements, dispute arbitration, inheritance claims and the administration of unconsolidated villages – still operated through the paper office. What is more, the *work* of processing property through the revenue department, bypassing legal and administrative barriers, translating and aggregating data and exploiting ambivalences, all remained the central jurisdiction of Gurgaon's *patwari* offices. Here the constraints placed on rural land's conversion into a fungible global commodity are creatively swerved, property boundaries conjured and territorial claims substantiated.

Patwar Ghar sits on the back side of the old Gurgaon Civil Lines. Distinct from the Mini Secretariat, adjacent to the highway that houses senior district and revenue officials and the district courts in a multi-storey office building, Patwar Ghar is relatively inconspicuous. Fixed onto the gates of the courtyard are a set of rules and regulating the conduct of the office. A far cry from the air-conditioned offices of corporate Gurgaon, and the official stature of the Mini Secretariat, at Patwar Ghar lawyers, brokers, consultants and liaisoners jostle alongside farmers and village residents in the open courtyard and tucked-away rooms of the office.

Manoj was an assistant *patwari*. As the main worker of the land record in the room, Manoj knew the record books and maps intimately well; indeed having seldom spent time in the field, he would joke that he knew the record far better than he knew the villages they represented. Manoj's room was responsible for a number of villages that lie across the central-western stretch of the National Highway running up to the hotly contested Dwarka Expressway.[7] The villages under Manoj's jurisdiction had a mixture of commercial, industrial and residential development interspersed with informally plotted neighbourhoods, government land and farmland. Like all of the rooms at Patwar Ghar, Manoj's office had a desk for the *patwari*, one plastic chair for pre-eminent guests, floor mats and bookstands for the assistant *patwari*s and a filing cabinet piled with land record books, mutation registers, field books and cloth cadastral maps corresponding to the villages under the room's jurisdiction. Devendra, the *patwari*, was responsible for certifying all the documentation – residency and income certifications, title transfers, landholding partitions – that ran through the office but rarely sat in the office itself. Rather, when present he sat out in the courtyard, discussing business with associates, while assistants ferried documents for him to sign throughout the day alongside more specialist requests. Devendra would come to his desk at least once a day to oversee more complex requests, scrutinise some paperwork and sign off the day's work. The vast bulk of the office work however was carried out by Manoj and two other assistants who were informally hired by Devendra and took their salaries from the stream of informal fees paid by visitors to the office.

Each day from 10 a.m. to 6 p.m. a wealth of different actors would pass through the doorway and occupy Manoj's office making an array of requests. These requests can be broadly categorised into two kinds. First, what Manoj called 'village work', the *patwari* office deals with all manner of everyday village administration from certifying income and residency documentation, facilitating documentation to state welfare schemes, to keeping records of births and deaths in the village, to overseeing and recording the biannual crop harvests. Most of these requests are handled by the most junior assistants in the office, whose incomes depended on a steady stream of work flowing into the office. The assistants were also gatekeepers to government services, experts in interpreting the severity of a request and the status of the requestor before its utterance. Confident landowners in bright white *kurta*s strode into the office, perhaps with some friend or relative of Manoj in tow, asking for assistance in certifying documentation or transferring a title, while others in plaid shirts and worn jeans would tentatively tiptoe into the corner and make deferent pleas for the work to be undertaken. As Akhil Gupta has noted elsewhere, negotiating the everyday workings of the *patwari* office requires a degree of cultural and social capital, knowing the unspoken cues that can operate to exclude the unconnected or uninitiated from government services.

Manoj's job was to deftly interpret these performances and organise the work in correspondence to the profile of the requestor.

Manoj was however quick to defend the office's dealings with village residents. I had frequently asked Manoj, and others in the office, how he costs and prioritises these routine requests, how bureaucratic work gets divided between the field office and the 'desk office', whether someone needs to bring along a friend or relative or pay extra to get their file prioritised. Initially, my questions on this topic were met with short thrift: work happens as it happens, there are no fees, no biases, no 'tension'. One morning, early on in my time shadowing Manoj, as I began to ask again he interrupted, explaining:

> See it's not like this. There's no such tension. We are the guardians [*sanrakshat*] of the village, whatever they need we are here to serve the villages only. They must pay the government fixed rate and not a *paisa* more.

Mocking my repeated use of the word *naukarshah*, or bureaucrat, to describe his work, he continued:

> *Naukarshah* [bureaucrats]? We are not *naukarshah*. The *naukarshah* works 9 to 5, and to be honest he will never complete his work. If we were *naukarshah* the villages would be helpless! You see us, here we work anytime, night or day, Monday to Friday, but also Saturday, also Sunday. We are not stuck behind desks, we go to the villages, to weddings, but also to the courts, to the companies, even to Delhi. This way, we can be more helpful and find solutions for the people. For common people, you can say we are *naukar* (servants) – as you are a friend, a brother, neighbour, from our village, it is my duty to serve you. This is the *bhaibandi* [brotherly comradeship] that surrounds this place, it's like an energy, a warmth between us. If we were just *naukarshah* nothing would get done!... For the companies? This is different, they need us. With the companies we are *shah* [kings] and with the village we are servants [*naukar*]. It's like this.

Manoj's patient elaboration helps explain the social and spatial geographies of the local state, property relations and 'bureaucratic' work. Through the untethered spatio-temporalities of the office – work moves across public and private sites and navigates legal and administrative barriers to find solutions. But Manoj's comments also subtly point to the kinds of cultural and social exclusion this stretched out work reproduces, Manoj may be a *servant* but only so far as he is also a *brother*, a neighbour, a member of cross-caste agrarian landowning classes. The *energy* of *bhaibandi* is a reference to subtle gendered, social and cultural relations that continue to animate the work office.

Over the course of the following months, shadowing Manoj and others, this became clear. Successful visitors to the office, those not turned away nor thwarted by some paperwork issue, brought with them a village headman (*lambardar*) or had some affiliation to Manoj's extended family, village or school.[8] These extant agrarian relations distinguished the formal bureaucrat sat at *desks*, stuck to *protocols* and time-bound to the working week, and the *patwari*, who hedged their trade on their place within extant agrarian hierarchies and deployed creativity and improvisation in order to *find solutions*. This is particularly the case with the other body of work that flows through Patwar Ghar, that which dominated discussions and *patwaris*' creative juices throughout the day – property work.

Property work ranges from the ordinary – the addition of a name to a landholding account, a single mutation in ownership, a change in inheritance – to the more complex – the partition and aggregation of land plots, the mass mutation of hundreds of land-shares and reassigning of land tenures. Running parallel is a subset of requests related to ensuring the veracity of this work – ensuring consistency across land record books, amending translations errors, taking copies of the record books and so on. The kind of work the office conducts is dependent upon the type of village the *patwari*'s room represents. In rooms responsible for villages on the peripheries of the city, with highly sought-after undeveloped lands, *patwaris* made the bulk of their income directly from property work of the office.[9] In others responsible for village lands which are already fully acquired, plotted and developed, much of a *patwari*'s work may be concerned with record upkeep and routine villager requests.

These *patwaris*, freed from the routine demands of office work, moonlight as revenue consultants, brokers and fixers for local developers and land aggregators. In the early evening and weekends when the office is formally closed to the public, these actors filter into the office to access information on strips of *saaf* (clear) land lying dormant amidst high-value real estate. For this kind of work, *patwaris* and their assistants were always more candid about the sums of money flowing through the office and up the bureaucratic chain. Sumitji, a *patwari*, explained that 'this is private business only, no? Yes, we are paid well for this work, but these are wealthy builders, they need us to find their land, fix their problems, their paperwork, that's why you see them here all day, every day.' This work, as I soon found out, required creativity and cunning on behalf of *patwaris* like Manoj, creativity that uncertainties and inconsistencies in bureaucratic materials facilitated.

DIGGING

One morning in December I arrived in Manoj's office as a stream of brokers and villagers made their way through the office to make their daily requests. Each day numerous men, and it is always men, enter the doorway clinging to paperwork. This paperwork comes in different forms, the liaisoners and revenue consultants come with plastic wallets and clipboards, while the broker, lay villager or confused urbanite arrives with scraps of paper with a series of speculative *khewat* (landholder account) and *khasra* (cadastral survey) numbers scrawled across them. The first man in, dressed in a blue Nehru jacket and suit trousers that stood out from the white-kurta-wearing village elders, had already assumed the most senior position in the room and sat in the plastic chair. The man was a local land aggregator. He bought up small parcels of land in areas around the limits of the Gurgaon masterplan, then conducted the drawn-out and expensive process of applying to mutate hundreds of shares into a single landowning account, before selling on to a developer later down the line. Aggregators were near-constant residents in Patwar Ghar and placed a great deal of importance on keeping good relations with the office.

The man knew the *patwari* Devendra through a family member, and for a change Devendra was sitting behind his desk, fingering a rectangle on the cloth cadastral map while the man scrutinised a hand-drawn copy of a plot partition. Manoj, who sat in his usual position on the floor, was reading through the account on the land from an older *jamabandi*.[10] The man had bought up land in Sector 72, Fazilpur Jharsa, in 2010 that had been recently acquired by HUDA to build a service road. But there was a problem. The plot had been partitioned years before into two unequal parcels, each allocated a separate survey number, one larger 0.8-acre parcel (Plot A), and another small 0.2-acre strip (Plot B). At some point in the past, the two field numbers were swapped. Plot A shrunk to 0.2 acres on paper, and Plot B grew to 0.8 acres. Subsequently, when HUDA acquired Plot A, they compensated the man for 0.2 acres recorded in the land records but took physical possession of 0.8 acres. The whole office was digging back through old record books and mutation registers in an attempt to find the moment Plot A had shrunk.

Much of the *patwari*'s work comes in navigating disjunctures between different forms of data, the record and the map. The *jamabandi* and maps, as officials like Manoj were quick to concede, are not definitive expressions of land and property rights. Unlike urban masterplans, the land revenue records do not claim to provide a synoptic perspective of property in land. Rather, a series of distinct registers – separately detailing individual landholdings, mutations, village genealogies, customary practices – each provides a partial, not immediately commensurable representation of land ownership within a village. What is more, not all property claims are mapped (many land partitions are not mapped, distinct tenancy forms are not mapped), and not everything that *is* mapped corresponds smoothly to a clear property claim. Even when divisions in land are enacted, they are first sketched and offshored on bits of tracing paper paper-clipped to a secondary mutation register (*intkal*) before they can be entered in future *jamabandi*s. Property-making in the office thus requires moving between various incommensurate bureaucratic records – the *jamabandi* and the mutation (*intkal*) register for 'pending' transactions waiting in purgatory before they enter the record books.

Finally, in India's *presumptive* titling system, land's past matters. As with any property transaction, one will need to search through the history of encumbrances on the land, digging through old copies of records and mutations, to verify or discount any historic claim.[11] Aggregating plots of land and converting them into singular alienable titles thus requires moving through time, navigating data strewn across various registers and piecing together pieces of a disaggregated puzzle into something that appears tentatively consistent and believable, and matches the plot on the ground. The *patwari*, and their assistants, make their living by deftly facilitating these navigations and interpreting the ambivalences, blockages and incoherences they throw up.

Typically, a prospective buyer will come to the office with their own sector plans drawn out on tracing paper. First, they take out the cloth cadastral map. The map shows each gridded field with an allocated field number. Laying their sector maps over the cadastral map, the buyer will extract the field numbers of the land they are seeking to purchase. This information has been computerised over the past five years and increasingly real estate actors come to the office already armed with these numbers. Next, with survey numbers in hand, the prospective buyer searches through the land record books and mutation registers in order to identify who owns the land, in what form and under what tenure. This will impact the process of conversion. Perhaps the land has, for example, multiple co-sharers who need to be each negotiated with or is assigned as uncultivated (*gair mumkin*), grazing (*banjar qadim*) or common land (*shamilat deh*) and requires formal land-use change or subtle reassignment. If the land is held without possession or has tenants in possession, this again complicates the process further. While a perusal at Haryana's cadastral maps gives the impression of clean, gridded landholdings as Manoj explains, 'This is our biggest problem, the land here is never clear [*saaf*] and takes a long time to fix.'

All this information comes out through a process of digging. Digging was, I had always thought, akin to the environment of a record shop, with numerous actors hunched over a pile of books, flicking through the pages and between different registers in an attempt to conjure up intelligible land and property titles. Once successfully dug out, multiple copies of the records are taken, and the prospective buyer can go search out the owners in the field. Once a price is negotiated, these actors will be back to register a mutation in ownership and alteration in the *jamabandi*. Digging can be proactive – as previously described – but as we see in the next section, can also be speculative; real estate actors often use the *patwari* office as a resource to seek out ambiguities in the record and plan out work of land aggregation.

After half an hour of digging for the man's shrinking land, we had a eureka moment and Manoj pulled out a mutation report and passed it over to Devendra as the whole room watched in anticipation. '*Accha*, it's the computer system,' Devendra proclaimed. Pointing at the mutation register, he explained that the field numbers must have been inputted incorrectly when the record was recently digitised and another layer of disaggregation added to the land record labyrinth.

'You see,' Devendra loudly proclaimed to the room, 'this computer system has so many problems. These operators don't understand our records, they are not trained, they create all these mistakes.' A chorus of agreement echoed across the office. The digital land record was not only riddled with mistakes owing to problems of translation but also fixing the digital record was much more complicated and less negotiable than it was under the analogue system. In the transfer and remediation of analogue to digital data, the *bhaibandi* that so often oiled bureaucratic work had been interfered with.

Subtly referencing a likely fee for remedying the mistake, Devendra loudly explained to the room, 'Normally I would amend this right away, but now it is more difficult, it is out of my hands, we will go to speak with the Tehsildar[12] and find agreement.'

Many of the work processes of the *patwari* in central Gurgaon had now been digitised. All property registrations, mutations and changes to the land records in principle now operate through an online portal and are approved by computer operator at the Mini Secretariat, Gurgaon's central bureaucratic office. And yet, during my fieldwork between 2018 and 2019, the digital infrastructure remained patchy and at the time ran parallel to the paper record – with both digital and paper records in operation. The digital process remains reliant upon the retrieval of paperwork copies and certifications from the analogue office. Where inconsistencies arise between the digital and paper records, the two offices contest the veracity of each other's methods. Indeed, the parallel operation of both analogue and digital systems is reflective of a territorial war raging within the revenue department between the newly inaugurated digital office managed by computer operators and the paper systems of the Patwar Ghar. Part of the reason the digitised system remains partial is down to the reluctance of the *patwari* to fully update and convert the *jamabandi*s into digital form.

The current situation, however, in which the digital and analogue systems run side by side calls upon the *patwari*'s skills in interpretation. The entanglement of the two copies of record, paper and digital, not only multiply documentation each with a claim to authentically represent the image of property holdings but also, as we see in this case, frequently produce glitches in the records that obscure a 'clean' vision of property holdings and provide opportunities for competing actors to advance opposing territorial claims. With each inconsistency, each divergence between the paper and digital record, a space is opened up for navigation and improvisation enacted within the Patwar Ghar. Manoj explained the frustration in the room:

> There is many problems with the computer system right now. Sometimes it is working, sometimes it is not. Plus they only have the most recent records [digitized], the [paper] record gives us the full picture, the computer is just a 'snapshot', this is why a patwari is always needed ... [we] correct the record.[13]

In this case it was a matter of translation that had led to the contracting size of the man's land; in the process of switching the cloth map into digital form, survey numbers were inputted incorrectly and the property shrunk in size. The dual digital–analogue system both prevented Devendra from immediately fixing the record with the stroke of a pen and opened up a space in which Devendra was brought in to mediate a resolution. These issues are not then *only* the outcome of mistakes by poorly trained operators. Interpretation is coded into the record and the form and spatiality of property governance. Mistakes are in part the product of the ambiguous and non-commensurable data that must be 'dug' out, repackaged and translated in order to substantiate property holdings across the city. Calculative bureaucratic materials such as the map or register, as Timothy Mitchell has argued, are not ostensibly designed to reflect some empirical truth relating to land, but are rather authoring technologies, under constant negotiation, and wielded to selectively render claims to property in land that align with the broader political economy. Within this context, it is easy to see how, even under digitised auspices, fields shift and move around the record. The slippages between the ground and the record can equally be played by actors seeking to bypass legal constraints and convert their rural land into real estate.

Working with Noise

One early winter morning, I sat in the Patwar Ghar's central courtyard while Amit, an assistant *patwari*, prepared a hookah pipe for the arriving *patwaris*. Suddenly an elderly man – who I later came to know as Sher Singh – strode through the gates to the courtyard demanding to speak with the *kanungo*. Interrupting the quiet morning routine of the courtyard – when assistants sweep the office floors and ready the offices for the day – Sher Singh paced into each office room, loudly demanding to know what had happened to his land. Banging on the door of the *kanungo*'s office with his walking stick, the man shouted, 'Where is my land? My land has been taken! Who took my land?' Virinder, the *kanungo*, would not arrive for some time and after five minutes the man was gently ushered out of the courtyard and towards the *chai* stand by the road by a sympathising assistant *patwari*. Noting my intrigue, Amit shuffled his chair toward mine as we watched Sher Singh being ushered out of the courtyard and whispered, 'Don't worry, he comes here every few weeks. He has lost his mind. His land wasn't taken, it was moved.'

Through some digging of my own, and with the help of *my own* connections in the office,[14] I traced how, five years before our encounter, Sher

Singh's sons had applied to sub-divide their family's land into a series of small plots.

Ordinarily the partition of a jointly held rectangle is an expensive and drawn-out process. It requires a revenue officer to notify affected parties, hear objections, assess the validity and feasibility of partition, carry out an on-the-spot boundary demarcation and pass any objections onto the revenue courts to arbitrate. In practice, if all parties agree to the conditions of partition, and with an appropriate fee paid, the matter can be dealt with 'on paper' without need for any site visits. Unbeknownst to Sher Singh, the land had been partitioned under mutual agreement, without any objections. Without any opposition to the partition, the sons had allocated themselves a series of prime roadside plots (that they later sold on to a shell company of a Gurgaon-based developer) while their father's share had been shifted to the backside of the land parcel. The man's share in the land, as Amit cautiously explained, had not been stolen, it had moved. Sher Singh was yet to file a petition in the revenue courts appealing the partition, and instead made regular morning visits to Patwar Ghar to protest the 'disappearance' of his land.

The movement of Sher Singh's land can be explained, in part, as a consequence of uncertainties coded into Haryana's land records. Consolidation schemes of the 1950s and 1960s, as discussed in Chapter 1, were designed to rid rural land of the tyranny and irrationality of fragmented land plots and produce standardised units of property – on paper and on the ground. Consolidation schemes involved a grand calculative process of substitution and standardisation of land. The rectangle provided an easy framework through which to simplify and translate landholdings across diverse regions while not disturbing the sanctity of joint holdings. Consolidation inaugurated a system of property governance, and landholding, defined by the boundaries of the rectangle. No matter how the land inside the rectangle is actually possessed and cultivated, the clean rectangle and the joint family they are intended to preserve were documented in new state cadastral maps. In doing so, land consolidation in Haryana produced what James Scott calls a 'synoptic' view of space. 'Certain forms of knowledge and control require a narrowing of vision,' Scott notes, that 'bring into focus certain limited aspects of an otherwise far more complex and unwieldy reality'.[15] This 'tunnel vision', Scott argues, enables an 'aggregate, synoptic view of a selective reality' that makes state control and manipulation possible.[16] Haryana's land revenue system does just this – substituting messy land shares, undulating landscapes and incommensurable village boundaries with clean grids.

And yet, despite the inauguration of the grid in state representations of land, practices of holding numerous small landholdings spread across differently productive soils have endured and continue to form the predominate mode of rural property ownership across Haryana. This is expressed in modern land records in the 'share' system. The *jamabandi* lists groups of landowners and their individual 'shares' within a rectangle. One farmer may own shares in land spread out across the village, these shares run from one or two to up to twenty for certain parcels. The *jamabandi* lists a landowners' property rights over these discontiguous shares, but unless a formal partition in the property has been enacted, their physical location, shape and contours are not depicted in revenue cadastral maps. Here the map codes uncertainty into state records.

As Manoj patiently explained to me during my first few weeks at Patwar Ghar:

> Here we had *chakbandi* [land rectangularisation] that has made the land clear, we don't need to see the whole *gadbad* [jumble] of shares … it would create too much noise this way. Sometimes the *bhumidar*s [landowners] will have an oral agreement – I own this, you own that – sometimes three brothers will split the land equally … this will all be written in the record but not the map.

Hidden in each of Haryana's cleanly gridded cadastral maps is a *gadbad* of noise, unmapped ownership and possessions claims that are frequently sources of improvisation for those seeking to capture land. And so frequently bureaucratic uncertainty – of what is and is not written down in maps and record books – is struggled over by developers, landowners and revenue officials in their quest to consolidate territorial claims. The disjuncture between the land record, the cadastral map and the ground provide competing actors space to move land around the rectangle and conjure up property claims.

The mobilisation of uncertainty coded into bureaucratic materials was frequently described as 'cunning' (*chaloo*) work by those at Patwar Ghar. Laughing at my intrigue in the case, Amit explained:

> Don't worry he is not a poor man, his land is still worth some forty crore! He is just fine.... There is a lot of cunning work here. If somebody

wants some land they will use whatever they can – money, muscle power, connections, paperwork – to get what they want.... Of course, for this they also need a *cunning* patwari [in the office] to help them.

THE CUNNING STATE

The term *chaloo* was used frequently in jest by residents at Patwar Ghar to nod to the ethical dilemmas a *patwari*'s work required and was embroiled in. As Laura Bear has argued, neoliberal state development schemes that are heavily driven by private sector investment place local bureaucrats in awkward and 'parallel' relationships with the private sector through which local state actors broker political and economic space. In Gurgaon, I would argue that this bureaucratic awkwardness is made sense of by local state actors through a practice of 'cunning'. A *chaloo* was 'corrupt' in a mainstream sense, they will take payments to bypass or fast-track ordinary procedures, payments which are now near-mandatory for all bureaucratic work to be processed, and for this the term was used to lightly mock the necessary ethical transgressions of the office. As the majority of those working at Patwar Ghar are not salaried but rather earn solely through these payments, being cunning is an essential requirement for earning a living. This may mean that the *chaloo* bureaucrat is as likely to be hunched over mutation scripts and processing mundane paperwork as they are to be mixing with local politicians and elites. The *chaloo* is resourceful and innovative: they can navigate the system, find solutions to any manner of problem and remedy mistakes. As the previous case of the swapped land plots demonstrates, cunning and craft not only indicates a compulsion to engage in underhand tactics but also the necessity to fix the ambiguities and uncertainties that bureaucratic materials constantly throw up.

Parveen was an assistant *patwari* at Patwar Ghar highly renowned and sought after for such *chaloo* work. Parveen was originally from a village in south Gurgaon, a region that – as discussed in Chapter 3 – has been subject to significant real estate investment since its incorporation into the Gurgaon–Manesar urban development plan in 2007. Parveen was from an upper-caste Brahmin family and had utilised his social networks and connections to not only access a public sector job but also generate substantial work through the office. Parveen had an office but seldom used it. Where other offices were characterised by a dizzying coming and going of requests for mutations, partitions, income certifications and so on that were deftly prioritised and navigated by the assistant *patwari*s, Parveen's office was far quieter. The *patwari* for the office, involved in party politics in Rohtak, was a sometimes-present feature in the office, and the junior assistant sat in the corner of the room attending to the slow drip of 'village work' that every so often came in. Parveen on the other hand could be found in and around Patwar Ghar, often sat in the midday sun surrounded by a host of village headmen (*lambardar*s), brokers and lawyers. They came to access Parveen's services in navigating the revenue department. Some came requesting what Parveen called 'big jobs', hiring Parveen to work as a private consultant in the office, while others – corporate developers or upper-class Delhiites unaccustomed to Haryanvi rural life – hired Parveen to translate the system, access signatures or bypass certain prerequisites to property title mutation and registration. Parveen would, for example, work on contracts for local businessmen and property dealers, and frequently carried out work for a local *sarpanch*. The *sarpanch* of a village in north Gurgaon worked as a loan shark, taking land on as security and had built up a property empire from the business. Where creditors were unable to pay, the *sarpanch* would take on the land and hire Parveen to dig out the land from the record and organise the mutation in title.

Parveen was also well known for fixing clients with *lambardar*s. *Lambardar*s are village-level and sub-village level 'headmen' that are employed by the state to collect taxes, assess local cultivation and certify village documentation. The lowest position in the revenue department hierarchy, the *lambardar* is the final point of contact between the village and the state bureaucracy. The thumbprint or signature of a *lambardar* gives the impression of local connection to the village often necessary to certify notifications and property partitions and mutations. Just like everyone else at Patwar Ghar, the *lambardar*'s tentative connections to both the state bureaucracy and the real estate industry has provided many with opportunities to dodge dispossession orders, regularise their territorial claims and build modest property businesses. Parveen was an expert in sourcing *lambardar*s for faraway developers, equipping grand multinational property deals with a sense of localness that they required to pass through the bureaucratic office.

Chaloo work is frequently involved in sanctioning property transactions within Gurgaon's 'unauthorised' colonies discussed in the previous chapter. Formally under the HDRUA, all property transactions on land below 1 acre require a 'no objection certificate' (NOC) from the Department of Planning in order to regulate the development of unsanctioned, non-licenced neighbourhoods. But for small-time villagers cutting plots on their agricultural land like those in the previous chapter, the land aggregation requirements and costs of the HDRUA's licence system are such that many seek to quietly register property transactions without the NOC. Gurgaon's planning apparatus may be constituted through the selective incorporation of corporate layout plans and aggregation programmes, but it is not entirely disposed for small-time colonisers. For an NOC, one needs a *patwari*.[17]

Parveen's mid-day moonlighting is characteristic of those who occupy the 'shadow', informal spaces of public office.[18] Parveen is a private actor – informally hired as an 'assistant' – deeply embedded in the everyday running of public office. The splintering geography of the state bureaucracy is of course the subject of much scholarly work. In her writing on 'informality' in South Asia, Barbara Harriss-White notes that the rise of so-called informal economies in Karachi brought with them 'informal' manifestations of the state. The rapid transformation of Karachi from a 'pleasant' colonial port to a bustling megalopolis in the post-colonial period, Harriss-White asserts, has been facilitated by a 'shadow state' apparatus lodged with intermediaries of varying social background that informally legitimate and link illegal settlements with state services. These intermediaries – engineers, construction contractors, local party bosses and of course bureaucrats – tentatively stitch together the sovereign fragments of a 'non-hegemonic' state[19], representing the bleeding boundaries of code and practice that structure state power in post-colonial South Asia. As the respective works of Solomon Benjamin and Partha Chatterjee have shown, the 'messiness' of the bureaucratic structure opens up spaces for the urban poor to vest themselves and regularise tentative claims on urban spaces.[20]

And yet, while Parveen and others at Patwar Ghar are involved in regulating the improvised territorial settlements of marginal village actors, of doing 'village work', they are also at the same time utilising the office to service the interests of corporate real estate actors. At Patwar Ghar, corporate real estate is as much a beneficiary of the double-headed bureaucrat and their ambivalent records and maps – straddling both public and private, code and practice – as the urban poor. Indeed in agrarian cities like Gurgaon, which have only recently enveloped the rural world, where working-class migrants are locked into housing systems *within* village tenements (and not 'squatting' land as described in other cities) the low-level bureaucratic spaces are primarily spaces that link up global real estate with the aspirational agrarian world – where the tentative and shifting class alliances underpinning the Gurgaon model are assembled and bureaucratically smoothed over. With land and labour so tightly controlled in the first instance by agrarian Jat and Yadav landowners forged out of the colonial–post-colonial agrarian settlements, it is perhaps no surprise that the governance of land and labour is saturated by the 'casted' class interests of those same groups.

LIAISONING GAPS

Such is the importance of this revenue work to corporate developers in Gurgaon, there are other actors at Patwar Ghar. Alongside the *patwaris*, *kanungos* and their assistants, there is a host of private actors, billed as 'liaisoners', 'company *patwaris*' or 'revenue consultants' who sit resident in the courtyard and offices. These liaisoners are hired by corporate developers to dig for land, move paperwork through and between the various revenue offices, and facilitate the payments and persuasions to move files up the chain of clearances.[21] At first it was incredibly difficult for me to discern who was a liaisoner and who was a *patwari*. Many liaisoners are themselves former *patwaris* and are deeply involved in the everyday functions of the office. When not conducting their own work, they help assistants write out and make copies of paperwork, make amendments in the record, signpost visitors and contribute to office discussions over the best solution to a visitor's requests. The liaisoner's work is not simply to negotiate with *patwaris* – they are required to deeply embed themselves in the social life of the office and record. If *patwaris* like Devendra and assistant *patwaris* like Parveen are ostensibly of the state, stepping out, then *liaisoners* are outside actors *stepping in* to state spaces. State space, structured ineluctably by unstable hegemonic class alliances, is here composed like an unbordered lattice of public faces and private interests stretched across the city. Of course, as developers may have projects all over the city, liaisoners are more mobile than *patwaris*, they ferry paperwork and signatured notes pertaining to revenue work across scattered offices of the revenue department and between their employers' swanky offices in New Gurgaon and the planning department in the HUDA-developed district of the city.[22] While Patwar Ghar remains a central resting place, where the *kanungos* who oversee complex revenue work sit, the mobility of liaisoners and *patwaris* across competing public–private spaces of the city signify the vibrational space of the agrarian state in the city:

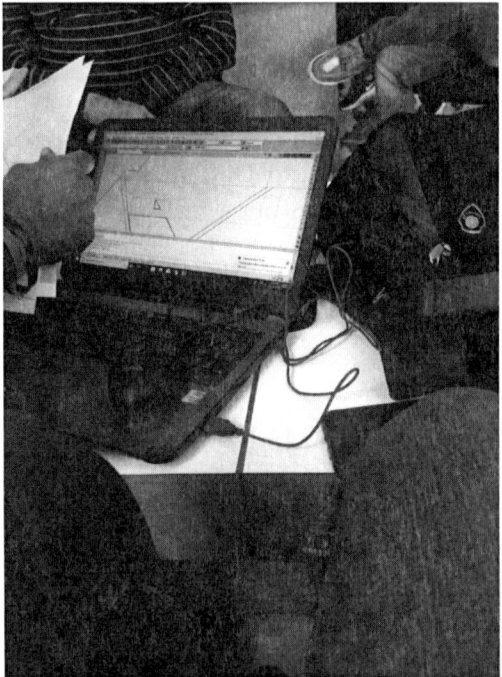

Figures 4.2 and 4.3   Land cadastral surveys in Gurgaon, 2018–19
Source: Photos by author.

occupied by shifting actors and servicing multiple interests within and across spaces each in competition for territory.

Neeraj Yadav was a liaisoner who, when not ferrying paperwork between his employers' offices in New Gurgaon and the distant offices of the revenue and planning departments strewn across the city, could be found sitting in the courtyard of Patwar Ghar, socialising and reading the newspaper.[23] One afternoon, in response to my intrigue in liaisoning, he explained to me that a good liaisoner does not simply process paperwork through the office, they must also be vigilantly aware of changes to bureaucratic actors and procedures, court rulings and changes to the urbanisable area of the city. 'We have to be seeing the masterplans before the landowners do, before the brokers and *goondas*, before even these *patwaris* see them!' A liaisoner's capacity to stay one step ahead of the game is facilitated by a tight emplacement and intimacy with the *bhaibandi* of the *patwari* office. Such is their entanglement in the everyday sociality of the office that any conception of 'the state' as a formally coherent, bounded and impersonal body seems ridiculous in Patwar Ghar.

As a senior planner at DLF who employed fifteen liaisoners to sit in *patwari* offices across Gurgaon relayed to me:

> We need these people as they have a wealth of connections with the revenue system, we professionals don't have this, they are [the *patwari*'s] family members, village members, they know them very well and have a very deep understanding of the community ... so we have them there to carry out all the appropriate work ... without them, we wouldn't be so successful.

And yet, the liaisoner does not simply *anticipate* changes to formal urbanisation plans of the state, they actively produce them. Neeraj was employed as a liaisoner for one of the largest real estate firms in Delhi-NCR, M3M. The firm had amassed over 2,000 acres of land in Gurgaon since it began operations in 2007, developing a range of high-end residential and commercial developments across the city, including the 600-foot under-construction Trump Towers. Known for its slogan 'Men, Materials and Money', the firm has been at the centre of a range of scandals over the past decades, including a series of tax-evasion scandals, allegations of illegally clearing forest lands for development and utilising political connections to fast-track property registration and development projects.

Neeraj's primary job was to mobilise, seek out and capture land from the office. At our first meeting he wore a smart plaid shirt tucked into his jeans with three pens clipped to his top pocket and was sitting in the courtyard discussing some mutation work – involving eight plots of land in Kadipur in western Gurgaon – with Virinder, the *kanungo*. Neeraj had worked eight years as an assistant to the Badshahpur *patwari* in south Gurgaon before taking up the position with the developer. As an assistant, Neeraj's income would have depended on the fees for work that run through the office; the liaisoner's job offered a salary, stability and the chance to escape the hectic life of the office.

'I hear you are interested in shares?' he said as we first met, having cottoned onto my incessant questioning about the share system. 'I'm an expert in shares, you can ask me anything. First,' he noted, 'we have to find the land.' The central tasks of liaisoners in the office, Neeraj explained, is to negotiate the share system and find unmapped property hidden away in the records. As each rectangle of property may be owned by numerous co-sharers, whose shares in possession are commonly unmapped, a liaisoner must either buy up all the shares in the rectangle or carefully navigate bureaucratic materials to decipher who owns what land and where. This is where class power is often visibly expressed as liaisoners like Neeraj put pressure on stubborn tenants and landlords to sell on, with the help of their connections to local agrarian institutions and state offices. This may take place over tens of hundreds of shares in order to accumulate the necessary contiguous plot of land needed for large-scale real estate development.

In this manner, the rectangle's opaqueness works for capital. On the one hand, the rectangle affords developers' the opportunity to buy up all the shares in an already consolidated rectangle of property, and on the other, provides the space of manoeuvre for actors to take possession of desirable shares and alienate them through processes of partition. The unmapped rectangle thus represents a canvas within which Neeraj can craft desirable property parcels. This work, Neeraj explains as we wait for the *kanungo* to return from the revenue courts, is a speculative project requiring an element of imagination:

> Most of time if we are buying shares at first, then we don't know the precise location of the share, perhaps the landowners have an oral agreement of possession – 'this is my area, that is yours' and so on – perhaps also the shares we want are not together but fragmented [across different rectangles or different villages], this is difficult, we don't know what we are buying!... But it doesn't matter, we know the boundaries of the rectangle, it's my job to read the records, visit the land, find agreement with the landowners and take possession of the plot.

If for Roy[24] this state of unmapping allows state officials to redistribute land, the absence of a map of land shares in Gurgaon allows private real estate developers sat resident in state offices to quite literally craft boundaries from the field and record book, and capitalise land. These material, imaginative and bureaucratic labours that unmoor land from its seeming fixity form the basis of large-scale land aggregation schemes that substantiate real estate formation on the agrarian–urban frontier. The liaisoner's search for land parcels demonstrates how the everyday workings of the bureaucratic office provide precisely that space where property itself is imagined and enacted out of silences. Silences in cadastral maps provide stronger parties space to manoeuvre the record through bureaucratic channels, to conjure up property's boundaries and substantiate property's 'fiction' in the record.

SURVEYING UNCERTAINTY

The ambiguities in the state records and duplicity of state spaces equally affect the performance of cadastral land surveys intended to shore up property boundaries across the state (Figures 4.2 and 4.3). In late November 2018, I travelled with Ajay and Virinder – the surveyor and senior *patwari* introduced in the opening of the chapter – to conduct a survey concerning a land-boundary dispute on the northern edge of Gurgaon. The survey had been ordered by the revenue courts in order to establish the location of a road that passed between two rectangles of land, one owned by a landowning family and the other by a group of small-time brokers.

As we wound our way through village alleyways and up to the disputed piece of land, our jeep took a decided zigzag around a construction site at the corner of the land. 'Here is our encroachment!' Ajay, the surveyor, remarked wryly as we neared the awaiting party. At the backside of the land towering over the land sat a recently constructed ten-storey private residential complex I will call Gurgaon Heights, developed by a middle-eastern real estate firm. One of the brokers was cousins with Virinder and greeted us with snacks and *chai* as we set up the laptop in the back of the jeep and began sketching up the template cadastral map on the surveying software. The broker explained how Gurgaon Heights had sent land prices rocketing and the group was lucky to pick up the land before bigger players got involved. Commonly, groups of brokers will buy up land on the outskirts of the city, conducting the complex work of negotiating prices with landlords and piecing together land shares into a contiguous plot of land, before selling on to larger developers a year or two down the line.

After drawing out a copy of the cadastral map onto the software, Ajay's assistant set up the GPS receiver on the roof of a nearby abandoned building and Ajay, his assistant and I set out in the jeep on a search for survey stones (*mustil patthar*). These entirely inconspicuous survey stones were initially laid by colonial surveyors during land settlement in the early twentieth century and were updated during land consolidation in the 1950s and 1960s; today they act to anchor the GPS survey image and digitised map to the ground. The location and authenticity of the stones are heavily disputed: some are marked on cadastral maps while others noted in the *patwari*'s field book. Yet the vast majority of Gurgaon's stones have either been destroyed by real estate developers and land brokers over the course of rapid real estate development over the past twenty years or shifted around by landowners, brokers and bureaucrats in an attempt to subvert or disrupt land surveying processes. The survey stones are constant reminders of the vulnerability of the cadastral map to the material and social world.

Today not only do surveyors like Ajay have to contend with an absence of reference stones, but they must also equally work with and against thousands of acres of real estate development constructed in reference to counterfeit or shifted stones. The territorially flexible manner in which real estate actors captured and consolidated land through the 1990s and 2000s set in stone vast swathes of real estate development that remains incongruous to state records.

As Ajay's assistant noted as we searched in earnest for survey stones, trawling through bushes, trudging through ditches and into construction sites, 'In many parts of the city, we don't take the [survey stones] … it's difficult, no one wants this, it causes too much litigation, too much of a headache from the landowners and developers….' He listed off some of the most well-known real estate developments across the city that have been constructed without strict reference to state records: 'In these areas, we have to mark boundary walls [of existing developments], we look for areas that match the record and work out a compromise to keep everyone happy.'

For Matthew Hull,[25] the pliability of survey stones acts as a key resource of protest and subversion for residents touted for dispossession, enabling them to 'affect the legal discourse of their houses by controlling the artefacts necessary for their production'. In contemporary Gurgaon the pliability of survey stones is not solely a resource for those earmarked for dispossession. Rather shifting, destroying and casting doubt on survey stones is equally a resource used by local real estate actors to consolidate land and secure property claims in the digital register. Property's uncertainty can also be a resource for capital.

After recording the location of a number of survey stones and boundary walls, Ajay, his assistant and I returned to the disputed boundary. After inputting the location of the stones and fixing the survey image onto the digital cadastral map, Ajay confirmed his earlier premonition: there was a slight boundary discrepancy of around 1,500 square metres. Walking the disputed boundary, we conduct the 'truthing' as one of the broker's assistants marks out the 'correct' boundary by pitching stakes into the ground. The onlooking party were immediately up in arms. Surrounding us, they called into question the authenticity of the stones taken and appealed for new points to be found and recorded. The brokers, dressed in smart *kurtas* that marked them out from the casual wear of the assembled villagers, took Virinder aside to discuss a suitable fee to extend the day's work. Virinder soon relented and appealed for us to get back in the van and record more 'accurate' survey stones. After another two hours of searching, the discrepancy remained. A rather frustrated Virinder, who was now taking refuge from the party in the back of the jeep, remarked, 'They are the problem,' pointing over to Gurgaon Heights. 'They have not used correct points, they are also encroaching on these people's land, just a metre of land is worth lakhs here ... what can we do? If we correct the encroachment, this whole village will need to shift!' The luxury development had secured itself on the ground utilising similar practices of bureaucratic manipulation that we were trialling all day. After a heated discussion between Virinder and the two parties that extended long into the early hours of the evening, the parties agreed that Virinder should not write up his report – rather, he should recommend a new survey be ordered to take into consideration a broader sample of the village. As I sat with Ajay watching the heated debate, he noted a new survey would only complicate matters, each survey produces slightly distinct results, not to mention reams of conflicting materials that can be mobilised to frustrate and delay a final arbitration of the dispute. Indeed, a constant source of frustration to state record is the survey itself – nearly every survey I conducted in Gurgaon, each purporting to use more precise GPS technology, had to contend with pre-existing surveys and the multiple authoritative materials that proliferated from them.

This mobilisation of uncertainty is not simply a cynical act of bureaucratic corruption, but rather like *chaloo* work, speaks to the challenges of imposing the abstract, geometric order of property records within contexts wherein territorial claims are predominately settled through practices of interpretation and improvisation. Calculating territory has always involved interpretation. This is particularly the case at the village edge. Post-colonial land consolidation schemes were conducted on a village-by-village basis, with one revenue official responsible for the two to three villages. Each official had their own techniques and arbitrated on ambiguities in differing ways. The smallest unit of measurement used at the time was a *karam*, then equal to 5.5 feet. A square-acre rectangle had a dimension of 40 x 36 *karams*. But officials rounded the *karam* differently; in some villages, officials in the first instance rounded the *karam* up to 6 feet, while in others the acre was rounded up to 40 x 40 *karams*. Where some officials took care to map out the precise curvature of a village boundary cutting through the rectangle, others rectangularised the boundary, cutting out portions of land. This produced village boundaries that overlapped and village property-holdings that sat in grey zones between villages. At one boundary-demarcation we undertook in Zakopur village, half of the farmer's land sat in a cartographic gap between the borders of two villages. To mitigate for spaces of interpretation, many corporate developers acquire land at a surplus, producing rings of un-unused land surrounding their developments. Just as Lewis Fry Richardson's 'coastline paradox' showed calculative projects are beset with uncertainties, boundary lines can stretch and contract in size depending upon the interpretation of territory, political struggles on either side, and the unit and method of measurement.[26] Projects of territorial calculation that incubate degrees of uncertainty demand interpretation and what Virinder called 'compromise', and it is precisely here that many private sector actors seek to infiltrate.

In the Gurgaon Heights case, both parties were aware of what they were up against, the government was unlikely to order the demolition of an existing, operational residential development, not least a luxury development like Gurgaon Heights, nor would it be possible for such a large number of landowners – nearly half the village running up to Gurgaon Heights – to shift and contract their land by 15 metres each. Both parties were eager to find a compromise on the ground.

Out in Gurgaon's partly urbanised fields, bureaucratic calculation invites in land a certain 'elasticity'.[27] By shifting, destroying and casting doubt on survey stones, international and more local real estate actors can contort the land's size and location and push whole areas out of kilter. These material practices constitute struggles to the author and lay claim to property in land. These struggles in turn compromise the authority of state records, maintain inconsistencies and reconsolidate territorial authority in local bureaucratic actors and spaces. While, in this case, we see how the de facto property claims of Gurgaon Heights shifted land across the village, the landowners' successful attempts to secure a delay in the decision over the boundary line demonstrates the ways smaller actors can equally play with property's earthbound vulnerabilities.

An understanding of the ways different territorial actors manipulate bureaucratic materials, reinterpret state mandates and manipulate silences and gaps in the state records, at times stubbornly imposing the letter of the law, while at others producing uncertainty and delay, matters for how we understand the uncertain formation of property that forms the basis of real-estate-led urbanisation and reveals how the bureaucracy's flexible authority in peri-urban areas is constituted precisely through competing claims on property.

FIXING THE MAP

The cadastral survey is thus a terrain in which powerful actors are keen to deploy the authority of digital technologies, mobilise uncertainty and remap land. While Ananya Roy's work powerfully demonstrates the ways 'unmapping' is utilised to redistribute land,[28] here control of digital surveying technology and practice allows bureaucrats and developers the opportunity to re-draw the map and conjure up seemingly fixed and universal property claims. During my months spent sitting in Patwar Ghar, a case in Gwal Pahari, a village in the hilly southern borders of the city, discussed in Chapter 3, would be sporadically discussed between the various actors sitting resident in the office. The case was of a forty-storey luxury residential complex constructed on the site of one of Gurgaon's few stormwater drains. The developer had been taken to the National Green Tribunal (NGT) by an environmental civil society group over the development, who had ordered a global positioning system (GSP) resurveying of the land to ascertain the extent of any encroachment.

One Saturday morning, sitting in the Gurgaon *patwari* office, I went with Suresh, the most senior *kanungo* in the district, to conduct the court-ordered survey. In the hilly villages like Gwal Pahari, in the south-eastern corner of Gurgaon where the development is located – state record maps are covered in shaded spots where mid-twentieth century patwaris were unable to consolidate the uneven topography of the landscape into the geometric grid. Where the cadastral maps denote marshlands and bodies of water today sit stretches of cultivated fields and housing developments. Here, land's materiality and the shifting geomorphic landscape are stubborn to the demands of state calculation. Such is the sketchy consolidation of the area, interrupted with blanks in the paper and digital maps, there are very few legitimate reference stones and boundary walls for surveyors to rely on.

The disputed residential complex we were sent to survey had already been subject to five land surveys conducted on the site by different private contractors for different state departments, each showing slightly distinct results – thickening land representations and adding to the ambiguity over the development's actual position. We went that day not with Ajay, who tended to work strictly with Virinder and was wary to engage in such a high-profile project, but with Suresh's nephew who had recently trained up in land surveying software and established his own company. There are numerous land surveying contractors operating across Gurgaon, each offering more flexible services to their clients as well as more 'exact' survey representations. Surveyors are highly sought after. Not only does the presence of multiple surveyors facilitate the constant surveying and resurveying of land but surveyors also themselves have perhaps the most up-to-date digitised maps of the city; their offices, just like Patwar Ghar, are constantly occupied by brokers, developers and farmers seeking out information on the latest movements in property and land.

As we drove up to the development, it was clear that the development had been constructed on a water body, the drain flows up to the site and then takes a sharp curve around the development, where builders had dug new banks, before taking its natural path at the backside of the site. With evident embarrassment as we stood in the middle of the construction site, Suresh's assistant shook his head and loudly cursed the terrible corruption that shrouded real estate development in the city. Seeking to redress any intimation of his department's wrongdoing, Suresh explained that the previous surveys were corrupted by politicians in the pocket of different interest groups; we were there that day – he assured us – to remedy the issue: we would he remarked 'find the correct references and fix the survey'. Over the course of the following three hours, I drove around with Suresh, his assistant, his nephew, a jeep full of officials from different government departments and a representative of the developer who plied us with salted snacks, fried bread and chai. Through much disagreement, Suresh led the group in experimenting with different combinations of survey stones and reference points. We would find a landmark, input its location into the GPS signal, return to the computer, the group would look exasperated and return to the jeep in search of more valid stones. Finally, the group settled on a survey that showed a slight ten-metre encroachment. The newly found encroachment altered the boundary wall of the development slightly but not so much as to require extensive demolition nor shift the development from the water body. At the end of the day, Suresh stood triumphant, hands on hips on the infringing boundary wall as two labourers conducted the 'truthing', pitching the newly authenticated boundary line into the mud.

While the previous survey showed how attempts to calculate and survey land boundaries were frustrated by the flexible settlement of property claims elsewhere, here we view the other side of the coin: digital technologies and their pliable foundations being put to work by powerful developers and bureaucrats to fix a property claim into the record. If in the previous case the state bureaucrats derived their authority from knowing when to ignore gaps between the record and the ground, in cases like this one, backed by powerful developers, it was incumbent on Suresh to fix the image, utilising the digital survey to conjure property into the record. Importantly, it is precisely the inability of territorial instruments to reckon with the area's complex landscape alongside the developers' ability to manipulate bureaucratic actors and materials that structure the form of private property's realisation.

DIGITAL FUTURES

Uncertainty structures property-making spaces and strategies across Gurgaon. Not only is uncertainty coded into the structure of property records and cadastral maps, organising the duplicitous spatiality of the bureaucratic office, but also the standards of calculation that substantiate property titles on the ground have uncertainty and improvisation hardwired into them. This uncertainty provides space for *patwari*s to fix property to the needs of corporate capital, for liaisoners to conjure up enclosures through the office and for competing actors to stretch, contort and duplicate property on the ground. Of course, uncertainty is no stranger to the frontier. Territorial frontiers – themselves produced spaces of opacity, signifying the limits of official recognition – are interstitial sites of sedimentation and improvisation that proliferate new political, economic and sovereign spaces. As 'elastic territories', frontiers are deployed to conjure up the governable, and in this case commodifiable, from the agrarian world. On the agrarian frontier, uncertainty produces certain kinds of state space and practice, and facilitates certain forms of territorial accumulation.

This of course runs counter to narratives of technologies of property-making and property-enforcing espoused by the central government. Over the past fifteen years, the Government of Haryana has sought to introduce a series of reforms designed to end the scourge of uncertainty in land records. These include the digitisation of land records, property registrations, cadastral maps and plot partitions. Premised on the settler colonial *Torrens System*, the project seeks to introduce a system of 'conclusive titling' through which property is fixed, automatically updated and insured by state instruments. Forming a part of national-level reforms to land governance,[29] the reforms shift power away from spaces like Patwar Ghar and Gwal Pahari, and towards computer operators and algorithmic technologies in faraway command centres. The Haryana reform programme has won various national awards and been celebrated in the media by politicians and the World Bank for its ambitious aims to digitise and automate property records. The reforms are not simply about tightening the integration of rural land with global real estate investment but conjuring up new state spaces, more akin to the hegemonic command and control centres of the global smart city that displace dusty courtyards and are legible to new kinds of citizen and investor. And yet, beneath the celebratory glare of the reforms, these digital technologies remain dutifully bound both to their analogue predecessors and vulnerable to social and material quandaries of calculation. The rush to digitise primarily represents a war on modes of enclosure – these are tussles to capture and control uncertainty. It is these bureaucratic tussles for uncertainty that are shaping real-estate-led urban development in Gurgaon.

In not too distinct terms, progressive scholarship typically views titles registries and cadastral maps as exacting technologies that coherently impose conditions of land enclosure and dispossession to the coherent resistance of rural communities 'on the other side'. By emphasising property's uncertainty, I want to gesture toward a refocus on the politics of property socio-material realisation. Private property dominates our understandings of contemporary urban processes the world over – such is the centrality of enclosure, land commodification, private property to the global narrative of urbanisation; critical scholarship and activism can at times affirm private property's realisation merely by writ of state legislation, decree or desire – all too often we echo a narrative that capital tells us about itself – as a coherent and totalising social force, always already actualised in practice. The attendant narrative that runs through much critical geographical scholarship is to position those barriers to private property – usually the rural world, the peasant, village and the urban poor as always-already subjects of dispossession and land conversion.

Examining the ways bureaucratic uncertainty structures, and sometimes undermines, processes of digitised land calculation attends to the vernacular ways capital seeks to capture land, and the ongoing ways land outside the metropole remains otherwise to narratives of global land enclosure and urbanisation. Bureaucratic spaces and materials remain key frontiers at which (non-)commodified futures are worked out, improvised and stalled.

Notes

1. Hull, *Government of Paper*.
2. Scott, *Seeing Like a State*, 82.
3. Roy, *City Requiem, Calcutta*; Ghertner, *Rule by Aesthetics*; Pati, 'The Productive Fuzziness of Land Documents'.
4. Roy, *City Requiem, Calcutta*.
5. Li, 'What Is Land?'; Harvey, *The Limits to Capital*; Blomley, 'Law, Property, and the Geography of Violence'; Bhandar, *Colonial Lives of Property*.
6. Verdery, *The Vanishing Hectare*.
7. Narsinghpur, Khandsa, Begumpur Kataula, Fazilpur Jharsa.
8. The slow digitisation of the land revenue bureaucracy had encompassed many of these more routine work requests, transferring them to the jurisdiction of computer operators in the Mini Secretariat and leaving Manoj to focus on other kinds of work.
9. *Patwari*s may be appointed to oversee more than one room, and thereby take hold of the revenues flowing through each room.
10. The record books, *jamabandi*, are prepared.
11. A land claim may, for example, be affected by pro-tenancy reforms passed in the 1950s that gave certain tenant-cultivators ownership rights. These rights have however been diluted by the *patwari*'s office who hold the power to assign a tenant's tenure and eligibility under the legislation and have tended to side with landowners in recent disputes.
12. Sub-district revenue official.

13. Of course, it may be no surprise that those who draw their livelihoods from navigating paper record books would be opposed to a system that transfers jurisdiction (and revenues) to a separate set of actors and operates through a distinct set of social and cultural logics.
14. I became increasingly aware throughout my time in Patwar Ghar, and other *patwari* offices across Gurgaon, that my access to the office while originally enabled by the fact that I am a white man, of similar age to most *patwari*s, was increasingly being facilitated by my enveloping in similar kinds of *bhaibandi*. Having spent time with *patwari*s at cricket games, religious festivals, weddings and birth celebrations, I was – partially – enveloped into the social energies of the office. I moved between Gurgaon's *patwari* offices referencing friendships I had with *kanungo*s and *patwari*s at Patwari Ghar; at these offices, I would often meet *kanungo*s and *patwari*s from Patwar Ghar who would substantiate my standing, relaying that I was a researcher from the UK, researching the workings of the revenue office.
15. Scott, *Seeing Like a State*, 11.
16. Ibid.
17. This was work Parveen claimed that he would not perform. Nevertheless in 2020 the Haryana government suspended all property transactions in Gurgaon in response to the growing number of property transactions in the city's unauthorised colonies registered through the *patwari* office without NOCs.
18. Harriss-White, *India Working*, 80.
19. Kaviraj, 'On the Crisis of Political Institutions in India'.
20. Benjamin, 'Urban Land Transformation'; Chatterjee, *The Politics of the Governed*.
21. Banerji, 'Field of Fixing'.
22. HUDA, rebranded as the Haryana Shahari Vikas Pradhikaran (HSVP) in 2017, bought out land and developed residential sectors of Gurgaon in the 1980s before the city's rocketing land market relegated their activity to urban infrastructural provision. There is as such a patchwork of territorial jurisdictions across the city with HUDA – a state coloniser – the private developers and the HSIIDC, each responsible for their separate territories within the city. Each run their own 'revenue offices' parallel to the District Revenue Department, employing 'revenue' officials and conducting cadastral mapping in parallel to the district state. The liaisoner, then, is an actor of the private sector's revenue office.
23. I would very frequently encounter liaisoners from Patwar Ghar during fieldwork in Gurgaon's subdivisional *patwari* offices.

24. Roy, *City Requiem, Calcutta*.
25. Hull, *Government of Paper*.
26. Mandelbrot, 'How Long Is the Coast of Britain?'.
27. Verdery, *The Vanishing Hectare*.
28. Roy, *City Requiem, Calcutta*.
29. Today organised under the Digital India Land Records Modernisation Programme (DILRMP).

BIBLIOGRAPHY

Banerji, Sangeeta. 'Field of Fixing: Negotiating with the Urban Bureaucracy in Mumbai.' Unpublished manuscript, 2021.

Benjamin, Solomon. 'Urban Land Transformation for Pro-Poor Economies'. *Geoforum* 35, no. 2 (2004): 177–87.

Bhandar, Brenna. *Colonial Lives of Property: Law, Land, and Racial Regimes of Ownership*. Durham; London: Duke University Press, 2018.

Blomley, Nicholas. 'Law, Property, and the Geography of Violence: The Frontier, the Survey, and the Grid'. *Annals of the Association of American Geographers* 93, no. 1 (2003): 121–41.

Chatterjee, Partha. *The Politics of the Governed: Reflections on Popular Politics in Most of the World*. New York: Columbia University Press, 2004.

Ghertner, D. Asher. *Rule by Aesthetics: World-Class City Making in Delhi*. New York: Oxford University Press, 2015.

Harriss-White, Barbara. *India Working: Essays on Society and Economy*. Cambridge; New York: Cambridge University Press, 2003. http://dx.doi.org/10.1017/CBO9780511754319.

Harvey, David. *The Limits to Capital*. Oxford: Basil Blackwell, 1982.

Hull, Matthew S. *Government of Paper: The Materiality of Bureaucracy in Urban Pakistan*. Berkeley; Los Angeles: University of California Press, 2012.

Kaviraj, Sudipta. 'On the Crisis of Political Institutions in India'. *Contributions to Indian Sociology* 18, no. 2 (1984): 223–43.

Li, Tania Murray. 'What Is Land? Assembling a Resource for Global Investment'. *Transactions of the Institute of British Geographers* 39, no. 4 (2014): 589–602.

Mandelbrot, Benoit. 'How Long Is the Coast of Britain? Statistical Self-Similarity and Fractional Dimension'. *Science* 156, no. 3775 (1967): 636–38.

Pati, Sushmita. 'The Productive Fuzziness of Land Documents: The State and Processes of Accumulation in Urban Villages of Delhi'. *Contributions to Indian Sociology* 53, no. 2 (2019): 249–71.

Roy, Ananya. *City Requiem, Calcutta: Gender and the Politics of Poverty.* Minneapolis: University of Minnesota Press, 2003.

Scott, James C. *Seeing Like a State: How Certain Schemes to Improve the Human Condition Have Failed.* New Haven; London: Yale University Press, 1998.

Verdery, Katherine. *The Vanishing Hectare: Property and Value in Postsocialist Transylvania.* Ithaca; London: Cornell University Press, 2003.

5 | The Tenement*

> Thousands of us form a daily mass demonstration of sleepy bodies, of multiplied insomnia, of dreams against the day, marching towards the machines. Having left the rural, being reluctant to arrive. At some point in time Kapashera – its thousands of backyards and rooms and roofs – might become a social borderline in struggle; a borderline between the certainties of a forlorn present and the collective desire to go beyond rural return or urban arrival, beyond push and pull.
> – *Gurgaon Workers News*, 2010

I moved into a tenement room on Kapashera in late 2014. My building formed part of a dense gridded matrix of four-storey tenement blocks that houses thousands of migrant workers – predominately migrants from Uttar Pradesh and Bihar – who come to work on the garment export lines in Gurgaon's Udyog Vihar industrial estate on temporary contracts. My tenement awakes at 6 a.m., as Ashmita, the building *pradhan*, unlocks the front gates and switches on the whirring water pump, and a chorus of hissing pressure cookers and tinny radios call in the new day. At around 7:30 a.m. dreary, red-eyed young men amble through the front gate, exhausted from a long night shift in the industrial estate and collapse into their rooms, swapping out bed-space with roommates already taking their morning bucket shower at the rear side of the building. Soon the alleyways of Kapashera become choked with an army of workers, lunch boxes in hand, making the march toward the industrial estate.

---

*A part of this chapter was originally published as 'The Village as Urban Infrastructure: Social Reproduction, Agrarian Repair and Uneven Urbanisation' in *Environment and Planning E: Nature and Space* 4, no. 3 (2019): 736–55. Reprinted with permission from SAGE Publications. A passage of this chapter was originally published in 'Rooted Flexibility: Social Reproduction, Violence and Gendered Work in the Indian City' in *Gender, Place and Culture* 28, no. 1 (2018): 66–87.

Labour contractors flank the main arteries flowing out of the tenements negotiating day rates and hours with workers before shoving them onto auto-rickshaws and into the sea of marching workers. This wave of workers that completely consumes the main road from Kapashera marches past the swanky farmhouses that occupy the Delhi–Gurgaon border, past the whisky shops where exhausted elderly workers lay drunk like roadside premonitions of industrial decay, and all the way up Peer Baba Road to the towering export houses in Gurgaon's Udyog Vihar (Figure 5.1).

Mornings in Kapashera are buzzing with activity. Freshly arrived workers – bundles of blankets and clothing in hand – alight at Kapashera bus stand and wander the alleyways in search of tenement rooms made available by workers who circulated away in the dead of the night. While my neighbours take a moment's stretch and breath of fresh air on the tenement rooftops, some stand in line waiting to collect freshly washed and ironed clothes from rooms repurposed as laundry units, others line up for tiffin boxes from window kitchens and young children weighed down by giant backpacks hurry to the private nurseries and schools set up on the tenement alleyways by enterprising landlords. By 8 a.m. the roadside 'master shops' managed by workers chewed up and expelled from export lines fill up with fresh arrivals skilling up on sewing and cutting machines for the industrial estate, and the basement workshops that feed the production of batch-garments into the formal export lines, begin whirring away.

Not long after, emptied of the lion's share of its residents, an eery quiet falls over the tenements, leaving only the dull stuttering hammer of the basement sewing machines. Night-workers are already fast asleep, resting before the next shift, tenement landlords arise for morning roadside card games and the tenement awaits the return of its residents.

*

Thus far the chapters have been concerned with land – how it is captured, made sensible to developers and investors, and transformed into real estate through a series of creative practices, compromises and alliances with agrarian institutions, tenurial regimes and class compositions. In this chapter I turn to explore questions of labour in Gurgaon. First, I explore how flexibilised industrialisation enjoined with neoliberal urbanisation in 1990s Gurgaon to produce the need for low-cost tenement housing in the urban villages. In tying together politically embedded industrial and rentier economies, the tenement plays an active role in producing forms of labour

Figure 5.1 Early morning walk from Kapashera to Udyog Vihar
Source: Photo by author.

mobility that harmonise production in the city. The fortunes of Gurgaon's largest economies – real estate and manufacturing – are pinned to the villages, that provide the fixing points for the circulation of industrial and real estate capital. Rental economies that flow through village tenements pin the 'labour question' (how to capture and transform people for productive uses for capital) to the 'land question' (how to capture and transform land for productive uses for capital); the tenement gives spatial and political expression to what Marx called the 'trinity formula': land (rent), labour (wages) and capital (profit) that when in harmony underpins conditions of capitalist expansion.[1]

Second, the chapter explores how governance regimes in the village tenements structure a hypermobile worker-tenant who rhythmically moves to the whims of localised rentier and globalised commodity economies. We see in tenement villages how forms of tenant regulation and control perform the work of producing 'migrant' workers held on the edges of both formalised employment and the city itself. The capacity for village landlords to wield mass rental revenues sufficient to draw themselves into urban land markets requires the tight disciplining of tenants' out-of-placeness, of their permanent marginality within the villages tentatively held by a minority class of landlords. Finally, the chapter examines the kinds of cultural production and working-class agency that are expressed within tenement-labour regimes, pointing to the ways in which the tenement system inculcates spaces of 'minor liberation' often bound to feelings of freedom among male working-class residents.

Urban Nomads

In modernist and some Marxist accounts of Indian industrialisation, land and labour as commodities occupy distinct moments. Under India's Second Five-Year Plan (1951–56), the 'Feldman–Mahalanobis model' advocated heavy state investment in public works and industrialisation in order to inculcate distributed labour-intensive growth and strong domestic goods consumption. From Nehru's 1950s government, right up to the 1980s, labour-intensive industrialisation was a key focal point of capitalist development. And while the ambitions of the Second Five Year Plan were only partly realised, the New Economic Policy that began in the 1980s, and went full speed after the balance of payment crisis in the early 1990s, not only stripped back and privatised public sector industries relocating the manufacturing industry to concentrated export zones but also as we have seen inaugurated a reorientation of the Indian economy toward financialised urban and industrial development.[2] The traditional industrial cities were hollowed out and repurposed for real estate, finance and service-based accumulation as industries set up shop in new export-oriented production units, with hyper-flexibilised workforces on cheap land in the urban periphery. These new spaces for flexibilised production are an important, if often elided, component of the new urban India that form vital components of contemporary cities like Gurgaon, where manufacturing houses rub shoulder to shoulder with financial and IT parks and high-end real estate. While it is undeniable that the Nehruvian vision of distributed labour-intensive industrialisation and state-facilitated agrarian transition floundered, industrial production did not go away, nor was it cleanly parted from the ascent of finance, real estate and services. Spaces of export-oriented commodity production in places like Gurgaon are instead animated by and deeply entangled with the same territorial politics that underpins real estate speculation and extraction in the city. Not only do we see the agrarian elite–state–corporate capital alliance discussed in previous chapters mirrored in partnerships between industrialists and villagers, who share and distribute wages and rents, but also the material base of the agrarian classes' incorporation into land markets rests on the viability of the worker's tenement housing.

The tenement villages in and around Gurgaon that sit directly adjacent to upper-class and corporate commercial and residential enclaves seemingly fulfil a much-repeated trope of India's spatially bifurcated urban economy. One characterised by increasingly privatised spaces of corporate capital and metropolitan elites, and another non-capitalist 'need' economy where 'surplus populations' eke out a meagre, 'improvised' existence cut off from waged labour and serviced by a developmental state apparatus. India's new cities are often characterised within scholarship as a schizophrenic enclaved landscape of capitalist wealth and informal poverty.

In work that draws on J. K. Gibson Graham's exposition of capitalist 'outsides' and Antonio Negri's work on the immaterial,[3] Kalyan Sanyal argues that contemporary post-colonial capital secures conditions for its reproduction by drawing on resources outside of its own (informalised commodity production) while excluding the rural poor from modern capitalist sectors.[4] The rise of financial and real estate capital in the post-liberalisation period, for Sanyal, extenuates the superfluity of low-waged labour, giving rise to new hyper-exclusive urban settlements. Cities, Sanyal writes in a later essay with Rajesh Bhattacharya, 'have been transformed from sites for production of surplus to sites for management of surplus, dominated by finance, banking, retail and insurance ... where production in the city is involved, immaterial labour replaces material labour as the hegemonic form'.[5] For Sanyal and Bhattacharya, cities like Gurgaon are enclave developments, where capital investment is concentrated and hermetically sealed within the boundary walls of cyber parks, gated communities and shopping malls.

Sanyal's work has influenced contemporary approaches to the politics of the urban poor in contemporary India, and chimes with accounts that view labour outside the North Atlantic as differently surplus and externalised to mainstream capitalist economies. This account is most clearly crystallised in Mike Davies' *Planet of Slums*. Here Davies, following a line of argument incredibly popular across distinct political spectrums, argues that workers in the Global South, unable to fully proletarianize nor access 'culture[s] of collective labour' turn against their workplace as a site of social struggle and towards 'episodic' and 'discontinuous' social and cultural struggles in the 'slum, street [and] marketplace'.⁶ An analysis of agrarian city-making in the contemporary conjuncture, by contrast, draws upon heterodox Marxist accounts of labour's partial subsumptions and multiple forms.⁷

The separation of questions of production from that of 'the social' in contemporary analyses of post-industrial cities mirrors the longer occlusion of relations of social reproduction from those of immediate surplus value production. In part a critique of the concrete spatial form of Fordist industrialisation in Europe and North America that cleanly divided the space of the household from that of the workplace, feminist scholars from the 1970s sought to draw attention to the relations of reproduction of capitalist accumulation that took place outside the wage-form.⁸ In doing so, feminist scholars draw attention to how capital relied upon 'hidden abodes' produced by bordering practices that made spaces and labours outside formal waged employment appear superfluous to production. The importance of feminist social reproduction scholarship has been to show the line being drawn (and thus the potential for it to be redrawn or erased), how the crafting of 'waged' and 'wageless' realms together constitute value production.⁹

Outside the Global North however these boundaries have always been quite differently pitched, and as we saw in Chapter 1 colonial capital relied upon codifications of caste to differently compose class hierarchies and shape combinations of waged and unwaged, free and unfree modes of labour. Agrarian scholarship in India has long interrogated these boundary drawing practices that compose forms of labour that are differently subsumed into the capitalist production. Indian capitalism, this body of work argues, is composed of varying degrees of 'free' and 'unfree', really subsumed and formally subsumed labour, anchored to cultural deployments of caste, ethnicity, religion and gender.¹⁰

Producing configurations of labour amenable to conjunctures of capitalist production requires significant cultural and social work on the part of capitalists and the state, work that subtends class struggles that push against such configurations. In contemporary urban India, this work is geared toward the production of insecure, mobile and so-called 'surplus' workforce held in perpetuity on the boundaries of subsumption to capital, between distressed agricultural villages and precarious work in the city. This tenuousness is upheld as Jan Breman's work in Gujarat has shown, through systems of labour contracting and brokerage, credit and tied labour, caste and kinship networks, the inputs of unwaged household members and the putting-out of production to devalued, often gendered, informal sites.[11]

Rather than demonstrative of a failure of Indian society to fully inaugurate conditions of modern capitalist development, as Jairus Banaji's work argues, actually existing capitalist formations are composed in hierarchised and uneven spatial configurations of exploitation not exclusive to the waged form commonly presumed in Europe and North America.[12] The boundary lines that produce the 'unwaged', the 'home', the 'neighbourhood' and the 'workplace' refer to configurations of value that subjugate and externalise the costs of certain labours, carried out by the most marginalised groups, to outside actors.

An examination of tenement-labour regimes in and around Gurgaon refute commonly held scholarly narratives that appear content to reaffirm the redundancy and superfluity prescribed by capital to racialised and gendered labours. Here we are asked to simply take capitalists at their word; superfluity becomes a social fact untethered from its historical production and internal contradictions. Labour's superfluity, I argue, is merely a symptom of capitalist attempts to segment, unevenly valorise, and pitch working classes to the rhythms of flexibilised capital accumulation.[13]

In the villages in and around Gurgaon's industrial estates, flexibilised labour and tenement systems operate together to produce an idealised worker-tenant subject that sustains both rentier and industrial capital. Migrant workers in Gurgaon are neither fully proletarian nor nomadic peasants, neither formally employed nor permanently excluded, they are the operative subjects of flexibilised tenement regimes, tenuously knitting together the frictions between industrial and rentier capital. Their political agencies are thus reflective of these conditions – daily struggles persist at the workplace and living space. Gurgaon's tenements stitch these fluctuating modes of employment together. A central way in which production lines remain competitive in Gurgaon is by outsourcing the costs of making workers, making mobile workers, and indeed the costs of making a host of commodities – to the tenement, the family and private rentier actors. This outsourcing creates possibilities for other actors and logics taking charge of the labour process, while animating labour's mobility and exploitation, to equally lead to the production of less-than-mobile, permanently temporary workers in the city.

A MOBILE CITY

Gurgaon's industrial sectors produce two-thirds of India's cars and motorcycles and approximately a quarter of India's total garment exports and 5 per cent of the global BPO workforce out of over 55 square kilometres of industrial space and countless informal workshops hidden within the villages. Fitting capital's decidedly uneven development in post-liberalisation India, while industrial development elsewhere in the country has stagnated, Gurgaon has been at the epicentre of Haryana's steadying industrial growth since the late 1990s; by 2008 industrial growth in Gurgaon was twice the national average, with an annual turnover of 73,500 crore rupees (11 billion US dollars). Haryana as a whole has the highest net domestic product and highest per capita industrial investment in the country. The concentration of Haryana's labour-intensive industrialisation in Gurgaon, a city with one of the most expensive land prices in the country, has been secured through a series of new production technologies, labour regimes and territorial settlements that secure flexibilised, hypermobile labour amenable to both globalised industrial production and localised rentier extraction.

Labour flexibilisation involves the breakdown of Fordist ideals of employment and production, and shifts towards 'flexible specialisation', where firms hire less-skilled, 'temporary' and sub-contracted workers across partly automated production lines on non-standardised working hours and rates. The aim of flexibility, particularly in labour-intensive industries, is to flatten barriers and position workers on the boundaries of employment, tied to systems of subcontracting and putting-out that avoid protections, regulations and skills training that would increase labour costs. This produces a hypermobile worker, constantly on the move between different industrial centres, work contracts, departments, shop floors and skills.

In Haryana, successive state industrial policies from the late 1990s sought to institute labour's flexibility and create a deregulatory environment for industrial manufacturing. These included introducing measures to cede authority within industrial zones to private actors, introducing practices of 'self-compliance' that exempt employers from a raft of labour protections and regulations; extending maximum working hours for both male and female workers; restricting collective bargaining rights to an increasingly minority permanent workforce; and notifying certain industries as exempted from labour regulations under the Factories Act, 1948. Successive state governments in Haryana, for example, were keen to exempt industrial estates from various protections and regulations. Not only was Haryana the first state to introduce the central government's SEZ policy in the mid-2000s, but also the state government's 2011 Industrial and Investment Policy, states that the 'government ... promote[s] an environment of industrial harmony and peace by adopting measures that motivate the employer for *voluntary compliance* of labour laws relating to working conditions and wage levels of the workers' (emphasis mine). Meanwhile, the 2015 industrial policy proudly promotes the state's policy of industrial noncompliance for industrial capital under the tagline 'minimum inspection and maximum facilitation'. While much attention has been given to the SEZ model of the mid-2000s, through which the central government sought to produce exempt deregulatory islands for global investors, very few notified SEZs were ever operational across the state. Instead, regular industrial policy, augmented by the Gurgaon model (and its agrarian affixtures) neatly avoided the politically toxic SEZ model by legislating deregulation by other means. It was under this deregulatory environment that Gurgaon's garment-export and automotive industries grew across the 2000s. Between 2004 and 2010, for example, the number of garment-export factories in Gurgaon rose by 180 per cent with steep increases (160 per cent) in the development of large industrial units employing over 250 employees.[14]

Gurgaon has a long history of industrialisation, dating back to the opening of Sanjay Gandhi's Maruti automobile plant on 450 acres of state-acquired land on the Delhi–Gurgaon road in the 1970s.[15] The Maruti plant had an enormous impact on the economic landscape of the future city. The opening of the factory spurred both the early development of tenement housing and an auto-parts supply chain in villages surrounding the plant – Mullahera, Sarhaul, Dundahera and Kapashera – themselves dispossessed to make way for the plant and its adjoining industrial estate, Udyog Vihar. Union organising at the Maruti plant in the 1980s took housing as a key priority and demanded the construction of rental housing for the Maruti workforce. Through a succession of strikes and tool-downs, the union forced the company to invest and develop two worker neighbourhoods in the city, Maruti Vihar and Maruti Kunj.[16] While the development of Maruti Kunj and Vihar ultimately represented a compromise between the management and union – the housing was financed through a mortgage model and largely benefitted the company's floor management – they nevertheless provide an early indication of the politically charged character of workers' reproduction in the city. In the early 2000s, it was in these neighbourhoods that workers at the plant – now owned by Japan's Suzuki – organised uprisings against policies of workforce retrenchment and flexibilisation that ultimately led the company to shift production to IMT Manesar. The succession of class struggles at Maruti Suzuki reflect a dramatic transformation in industrial production through the 1990s that saw Indian industrialists shed their previous Fordist organisation and shift towards lean, just-in-time production systems and hyper-flexibilised labour arrangements.

The garment-export industry has a more recent but no less significant history in the city. Following a political crackdown on industrial units in central Delhi led by a Congress-led government sensitive to an emerging upper-class civic politics,[17] garment-export firms began to shift production to the large units of Gurgaon's Udyog Vihar. Coinciding with the phasing out of the multi-fibre agreement – that limited the export capacity of 'developing' nations – industrialists sought to take advantage of Haryana's low tax and deregulatory policy environment, existing industrial infrastructure and subsidised plots to set up large export units adjacent to the Delhi International Airport. In contrast to other parts of Delhi-NCR, Gurgaon's garment industry is nearly entirely export led (88 per cent) and chiefly consists of large, consolidated units.[18] As of 2009, there were 675 ready-made garment units in Gurgaon, employing around 100,000 workers including 15,000 women. The cluster specialises in woven, outerwear and fashion products, and is worth 10.64 billion US dollars with a projected year on year growth of 15 per cent.[19]

Labour regimes in Gurgaon's garment-exports and automobile industry today largely run on speed, heavily reliant upon a hypermobile workforce. Around 90 per cent of workers in Gurgaon's garment-export sector are hired on a mixture of 'contract labour' hired through a network of subcontracting agencies on a series of temporary contracts – fixed term, piece rate and day rate. The city's auto-assembly and component production plants have a slightly higher number of permanent employees, although they still hire approximately 75 per cent of their workforces on an assortment of temporary contracts. Workers in the auto-sector work twelve-to-sixteen-hour shifts, typically on ten-month contracts. Work in the garment-export sector is closer harmonised to the rhythms of export demand, with ten-hour standard shifts, followed by four hours overtime in low seasons and up to eight hours in high seasons. Workers across sectors are typically working inside the workplace for fifteen to nineteen hours a day.

Of course, this construal of labour's mobility is entirely confected. The political economy of Gurgaon – controlled by labour-hungry industrialists and land-hungry farmers and developers – is dependent on labour that moves on the production of a 'migrant' labour force, albeit one that is decidedly made up nominally by Indian citizens. The desire to concoct a hidden, hypermobile and easily disposable workforce by local industrialists and tenement landlords is realised unevenly across spaces of production and social reproduction.

Sushil Singh, is the co-owner of one of Gurgaon's largest garment firms, exporting around 200,000 pieces a year to retailers in Europe and North America with an annual turnover of 60 million US dollars. The company operates across six units in Gurgaon, employing 6,000 workers hired on three-to-ten-month contracts through a variety of internal subcontractors.

Sushil explained the companies approach to labour: 'Our industry is still very labour-intensive, ideally we should go wherever labour prices are low [but] on the other hand convincing the entire industry, our entire supply chain to shift from Delhi to the labour source is a big challenge.' He explained that despite the high labour prices in the region, the company keeps costs low by automating parts of production and utilising networks of sub-contracting:

> When we first shifted to Gurgaon from Delhi [in the late 1990s] we stumbled around for the first few years not making much profit ... but we did our research, we looked into education rates, labour costs, and [even] the dexterity of our employees' fingers ... our employees are uneducated people from rural areas, we had to make the system as easy as possible to find the right kind of employee ... here we keep a handful of permanent employees, they are our *pillars*, and around them, we hire labour as and when needed.

The chain-production systems introduced across the garment-export system in the 2000s, in which each workers' job-task is reduced to its most basic form – the stitching of a collar or sleeve, for example – enabled companies to reduce training costs and homogenise production. Sushil explained:

> [Moving] to the chain enabled us to shift away from high-skilled labour, we were able to take decisions away from the worker, we can change how he would want to work and take his choice away ... this way, we do not have to worry about training, about this worker or that worker, the machine does the work, we just need operators ... this was vital.

Both the chain and the machine dramatically de-skill and disembody the worker and empty out the meaning of the labour, enabling quick training: a worker only needs to learn to perform one simplified task on a machine that 'does the work' and each task is meticulously overseen by a hierarchical structure of 'thinking' senior positions.[20] The capacity to reduce workers' job-tasks to the minutiae of repetitive actions provides firms broad scope of control over both labour and the production process. As Harry Braverman explains in his landmark study *Labor and Monopoly Capital*, following the 'separation between hand and brain', production processes can be carried out 'more or less blindly'.[21] In Gurgaon and Delhi-NCR more broadly processes of labour de-skilling facilitate the rapid circulation of workers with little capital input through the city.

De-skilling forms part of a broad skimming down and outsourcing of the immediate costs of social reproduction to external actors. Indeed, unlike industrial clusters in South India, the flexibilisation of Gurgaon's industrial workforce has been achieved without significant processes of feminisation, over 80 per cent of employees in the organised garment-export sector are young men between twenty and forty years of age. In lieu of feminisation where gender is deployed as the principal arbiter of labour devaluation, in Gurgaon workers are kept cheap and mobile through processes of automation and de-skilling in the factory and complex networks of labour training, subcontracting,[22] credit and discipline within the city's worker tenements.

TENEMENT CITY

Indeed, the mobility of workers, as Pun and Smith note in work on southern China,[23] is not simply a temporal question but is equally spatial; it requires fixing and embedding global production processes into local institutional and political settings that can organise the churning of people into productive uses for capital and their timely disposal to make way for further market expansion.

For ten months in 2015 I lived in a tenement block on Kapashera Extension's eleventh *gali* (lane). Kapashera houses the bulk of Gurgaon's migrant garment-export workforce. Administratively located in New Delhi, the village straddles the Gurgaon–Delhi border – a fifteen-minute walk to the industrial estate. In 1990 the village had around 7,000 residents mostly employed as agricultural labourers or within the informal service economy; by 2014 the village population reached approximately 200,000.

The layout of the village is ordered along class and caste lines, each neighbourhood corresponding to a particular kind of resident and source of rentier accumulation. Yadav landowners reside in the original settlement on the far north of the village in large brightly painted houses serviced by a subterranean sewerage system. This neighbourhood has a flurry of textile shops, social centres, small office rooms, temples and the Yadav *chaupal* where landlords meet to socialise and discuss village business. To the immediate south is the mass tenement housing in Kapashera Extension, iteratively plotted and constructed on land brought into the *abadi* in the 1990s along a gridded matrix of alleyways that are superimposed on *kila* lines of the village's consolidated fields. This central neighbourhood is where the majority of labour tenements are located (Figure 5.2).

The tenements that entirely occupy Kapashera Extension and numerous villages across Gurgaon are multi-storey buildings composed of six windowless rooms on each side of a central, communal corridor, each housing between 200 and 300 workers at a time. At the rear of the floor are twelve locked taps, one for each room, a communal toilet and a small space to wash and clean clothes and cooking equipment. The uniform design and aesthetic of the tenement blocks across all tenement villages is partly attributable to the small number of contractors employed to build them, as well their quick, cheap construction and efficient use of space. Every complex of buildings owned by a landlord will have at least one street-facing room leased out as the landlord's grocery shop.

The basements of the tenements in Kapashera Extension are usually leased out for informal garment workshop production. These workshops predominately hire women on piece-rate pay and feed batch work into large garment-export units in the industrial estates. The prevalence of workshops waxes and wanes in response to the demands of the industrial estate:

228 | Subaltern Frontiers

Figure 5.2 Tenement lanes and blocks in Kapashera Extension, Delhi–Gurgaon border
Source: Photo by author.

during my first stay in Kapashera in 2013, workshops predominated only certain sections of the village; by 2018, in response to significant challenges in Gurgaon's garment-sector, nearly all available space in the village was occupied by one or another workshop.

To the adjacent south of Kapashera Central, across the *ganda nala* (dirty river) that serves as the village waste depository, is the informal Kapashera Border neighbourhood. The neighbourhood's dirt lanes are occupied by butchers, large workshop units, storage warehouses and waste recycling centres which process the household and industrial waste of the nearby city. At the backside of the neighbourhood right on the Gurgaon border is one of the only bars for migrant workers in Kapashera. The bar, a makeshift set of tables pitched on a sandy patch of land, serves fried fish, whisky and local spirits to exhausted and alienated young men throughout the evening. Accommodation in Kapashera Border predominately consists of lane tenements, single-storey concrete rooms with corrugated iron roofs, constructed in parallel lines off the main path. Here, the poorest class of

Figure 5.3   Tenement floor, Kapashera Extension
Source: Photo by author.

workers – single women with children, rickshaw pullers, young scheduled-caste migrants without the familial connections to access the block tenements and local scheduled-caste service and cleaning workers – reside in a much more exposed and impoverished environment.

Rooms in the Kapashera tenement blocks were around 3,000–5,000 rupees per month depending on their condition and the number of residents (Figure 5.3). Water, electricity, groceries are extra, and the increasing living costs in the tenements have opened up landlord credit streams that add to workers' monthly payments. Owing to strict punctuality discipline in most of the factories, the closer the tenement to the main road and industrial estate, the more expensive the room. Workers sharing rooms pay extra, while those wishing to bring children pay an extra thousand per child. Alongside poor living conditions, the rent levied on children is frequently cited as a reason many workers' keep their school-age children in their villages and contributes to numerous factors pushing worker's in circulation between the tenement and the village.

The village's gridded complex of lanes, flanked by towering tenement buildings that allow only streaks of sunlight past, are entirely occupied by spaces functional to workers' daily reproduction. Aside from a series of small businesses owned by landlords that service the migrant community – informal clinics, private nurseries and schools, chemists, gyms, butchers and fabric shops – the village is otherwise entirely consumed by tenements. There are few working-class organisations, social clubs, party offices or cultural spaces found in the tenements in and around Gurgaon like Kapashera; the entire space is meticulously designed and controlled for minimal daily replenishment of labour.

Characteristic of the capital-agrarian pacts at the heart of Gurgaon's real estate settlement in Gurgaon, the cost of workers' everyday reproduction alongside ancillary supply-chain production is offloaded to proximate tenement villages organised under the logics of rentier extraction. The entangling of industrial production with tenement villages stands opposed to the kinds of 'enclave' industrialisation typically attributed to neoliberalism.[24] The productive linkages that spill out between the tenement and industrial estate are unevenly distributed and highly circumscribed to landowning classes in the villages with the capital to invest in tenement construction, and as discussed in Chapter 2 village rentiers were well aware of the economic and social limits of their inclusion into the millennium city. Nevertheless, it is striking that in Gurgaon, a city so dominated by private capital and neoliberal modes of governance, there remains dizzying relational networks of rent, commodities and wages that flow in and out of the tenement villages, loosely weaving together the social and material conditions for industrial capital accumulation. Just as the non-privatised, customary land of the village provides the conditions of possibility for real estate markets in the city, they equally underwrite and form an intimate part of industrial production.

Gurgaon's tenement system in this way resembles East Delhi's Viswas Nagar, once India's largest producer of electronic components where, as Solomon Benjamin writes, local landlords and ex-workers exploited customary land tenures and porous bureaucratic channels to develop an entirely non-legal industrial cluster in a working-class neighbourhood.[25] Similarly, as Sharad Chari shows, Tirrupur's globally integrated knitwear cluster grew as peasants transformed themselves into 'worker-capitalists', drawing on agrarian capital to develop a 'decentralised factory' across the village.[26] Industrial production in Gurgaon – and the social reproduction of the conditions for capital accumulation – are not hermetically sealed into the industrial estate but are rather composed as an uneven geography of tenement villages responsible for churning through workers and small-scale production and so-called organised production within the industrial estate. In Gurgaon, the tenement factory system is an outcome of the kinds of territorial class alliances described in previous chapters and relies upon the enjoining of industry's desire for a 'footloose' capital and labour and tenement landlords' desire to maximise rental revenues while suppressing their tenant's residency rights in the city.

Geographies of industry in Gurgaon are strung out across sites of formal and informal, urban and rural commodity production, sandwiched in sites of massive real-estate-led urbanisation, and laboured on by a tenuously hired, hypermobile workforce. This socio-economic landscape rebukes theories of modernisation that trace a linear movement of economic development from small-scale agrarian production with non-proletarianised, migrant workers to large-scale organised industrial production, improved standards of living and standardised employment. It also stands against urban modernisation theories that assert a linear 'capital switch' from commodity-producing industrial production to extractive circuits of rentier and finance capital laced through the built environment. In Gurgaon the rebuke is founded in the tenements. The 're-bundling' of spaces of daily reproduction and commodity production itself into village territories, governed under distinct rentier logics, hides a dizzying reciprocity between the spaces of 'formal' commodity production and those charged with readying commodities and labour from unregulated spaces.

Uneasy Alliances

Cognisant of high land prices and living costs in Gurgaon vis-à-vis neighbouring states, industrialists are quick to praise the system of tenement villages that supply workers and commodities to their factories. Sushil Singh, introduced previously, explained:

> There is no formal relationship [with the villages] nothing like that, it just fell into place naturally, it's a natural ecosystem here from the time of Maruti.... Really, it's a win-win situation, we benefit from the housing, the local villagers benefit from our business ... the government cannot compete with developers [for land] in Gurgaon so this way the local people can benefit.

This 'win-win' situation is however the outcome of a concerted effort to paper over an extractive relationship between industry and the villages, and cement alliances between industrial firms and tenement landlords. Alliances of village councils and industrialists are frequently formed in response to industrial disputes within Gurgaon's industrial estates. In 2012 as the strikes and protests ripped through IMT Manesar and Udyog Vihar in response to the Maruti Suzuki factory occupation, village *panchayats* were called to denounce the strikes. During the strikes and uprisings across the city between 2014 and 2015 discussed in the following chapter, it was principally pressure placed on workers within the tenements by landlords and contractors that matters to an end.

This ought not be surprising given the extant material dependencies between the tenement villages and industrial capital. Gurgaon's tenements host entire production supply chains – including over 5,000 informal industrial workshops – that feed components and workers into the industrial estate. The village boundary once again allows for processes of devaluation that industrialists are heavily reliant upon. While many of the industrial plots in Udyog Vihar and IMT Manesar are owned and leased out by aspiring tenement landlords. There is no easy cleaving of the corporate industry from village rentierism in the city. Writing on the automobile sector in IMT Manesar, Nitin Bathla's recent work explores how Maruti Suzuki invested significant sums in local community development plans in villages adjacent to its IMT Manesar plant.[27] These investments seek to paper over tensions between industrialists and landowners who were dispossessed to make way for the IMT Manesar in the 1990s. Such corporate social responsibility programmes are largely proscribed to the corporate automobile firms and are frequently distributed to powerful actors within their adjacent villages, itself contributing to patterns of uneven development within and between tenement villages.[28] Nevertheless, the impact of these financial connections between the largest industrial force in the region and its proximate villages, as Bathla notes, is indicative of ongoing attempts to inculcate alliances between corporate capital and local landowners that have the potential to quell potential working-class uprisings.

TENEMENT CIRCULATION

For industrial firms this uneasy alliance principally serves to facilitate the control and quick churn of cheap workers through the city. The principal function of the tenement villages is to provide a constant supply and circulation of cheap workers at the factory unable to root down nor engage in sustained collective organisation. The tenement-labour regime, to borrow from Pun and Smith, chiefly operates to control the temporalities of labour in the city and facilitate its constant churn through ten-month contracts. For industrial firms the tenement firms form part of an extended industrial infrastructure that ensures the seamless circulation of labour, commodities and rent through the city. Yet an infrastructure that – like all infrastructures – can leak, be subverted and rewired for quite distinct means. Raja explains:

> I've been here twelve years now, so much has changed you wouldn't believe. I came to [North Delhi] first to live with my uncle, we were living in a *jhuggi* [slum] then, it was horrible there was sewerage on the street and all kinds of people, then after six months we shifted to Kapashera....

Raja and two roommates were playing a weary game of evening cards in a tenement room in Kapashera while another roommate readied himself for the evening shift. Raja explained how when his uncle's workplace shifted from North Delhi to Gurgaon in the 1990s, an entire workforce shifted to Kapashera to take up work in Udyog Vihar. 'None of this was here then, it was quieter, locals spoke softly with us, now look around – the entire world lives in Kapashera now ... the work was more manageable then too, now the companies want more and more work for the same pay!'

When Raja's uncle brought his wife and young children to live with in a room in Dundahera, Raja returned to his village and on his return brought a cousin and two neighbours whom he has shared tenement rooms with ever since. They pay 4,500 rupees for their room and earn around 6,000 each working in tailoring positions in workshops and export firms.

Raja was in his early thirties, originally from Bihar; his family owned a small piece of land that he explained was barely enough to make ends meet. He had worked on garment-export shop floors and lived in tenement rooms in Kapashera and Dundahera villages since the mid-2000s. As he moved across ten-month contracts, Raja had shifted positions within the factory but had for the most part worked as a tailor, stitching single pieces on a chain production system alongside fifty or so others, earning between 5,000 and 8,000 rupees a month.

> First I was stayed with my uncle and cousin here, I worked in a workshop on piece-rate ... then there was a *thekedar* [contractor] in my building, a friend of my uncle, he got me a job as a cutter in a company [in Udyog Vihar]. I worked there for three months or so but the pay was so low I had to leave; after some time he gave me some work at the same company as a tailor, the pay was better but I didn't like the people there so I left ... after returning to the village I got a job as a tailor in my uncle's company ... it works like this here, there is always work somewhere....

Raja's staccato circulation across job contracts is characteristic of work in Gurgaon's garment-export sector. Such was the dizzying movement of workers across work positions that many would refer to their workplaces not by name but by their plot number in the industrial estate. This movement, as is the case for Raja, is chiefly facilitated by labour contractors. For the thousands of workers, the tenement operates as a terrain of knowledge, connections and social networks often established through familial or regional affiliation that can help stitch together longer periods in the city. The contractor will keep a record of attendance and hold basic identity proof of workers but there are no formal contracts signed between contractors and workers.

Labour contractors residing in the tenements are by and large 'field contractors' who supply day rate or payroll workers to registered contracting firms tied to firms in the industrial estate. These field contractors are drawn from the reserve of exhausted former workers still present in the city. Zakir, for example, was a middle-aged contractor who lived in a tenement room that doubled as a hiring office on my lane. He had worked as a garment labour contractor in Delhi-NCR for a number of years, having previously worked as a quality checker in one of the garment-export companies. As a checker in the factory, Zakir informally supplied labour to in-house contractors in his department. It is incredibly common for senior members of the shop floor (line managers, HR employees) to informally supply friends and relatives to the factories. Using connections to the industry, Zakir began supplying what he called 'extra workers' cutters, helpers, finishers to the companies be employed with in-house subcontractors for a small (2 per cent) commission. He provided around 100 workers during the peak seasons of production (over the winter) both on piece-rates and monthly contracts, although he maligned the unpredictability of demand from the firms: 'One day they ask for fifty, the next they don't want any, it's difficult to say these days.' Contractors lodged into the tenements are crucial features in workers' capacity to exit jobs, switch sectors, and move in and between employments in order to stitch together a livelihood. Zakir explained how he 'looked after everything' for the workers, providing advances on the first month's wage, sourcing rooms on rent and putting workers' into 'good jobs'.

Credit

Credit – provided by landlords, grocery shops and contractors – forms another key circulatory and disciplinary technology. As rent and living expenses have increased in the city and salaries flatlined, debt has become increasingly central to lubricating the circulation of workers through the city. Raja explains:

> When I first came here, we were paying 1,500 a month for a room, a little extra for electricity and water, and we earned 4,000–5,000 in the company, but the landlords here put the rent up 200–300 rupees each year, electricity and water too, now we pay 4,000 or 5,000 for a room but the pay is more or less the same in the companies, I used to go back [to the village] for two months each year but now it's too expensive but it's also expensive to stay here.

A 2014 report by the Delhi-based Society for Labour and Development found that migrant workers in Gurgaon and Delhi-NCR pay on average 1,000 rupees a month in loan repayments, with rising debt and shrinking incomes a common feature in many tenement households. Debt is taken on to pay for rising expenses, medical bills or to send back to the village. As we shall discuss, without access to local residency most workers are compelled to use expensive social services and groceries supplied in the tenements. Debt however is perhaps most commonly used to stitch together periods of unemployment. As Raja explains:

> This is the problem we face, if we stay here [over the summer low-season] there is not much work, but to travel back is also expensive, so

we build up bills [debt] with the landlord which can take three or four months to pay off ... most people are paying off debts for this reason.

Krishan, a young man who lived with his wife and two young children on the third floor of my tenement, added that building up debts with the landlord often caused trouble. In a previous tenement, he borrowed money from a landlord to send back to a sick family member in the village. The landlord barely gave him six weeks to repay the loan, took his gas cylinder, ceiling fan and evicted him from the room. Financial duress pushes workers into more strenuous living and working conditions – taking on more overtime work, moonlighting as security guards and enlisting family members into the workplace. Indeed, household debts related to unemployment and illness were the two biggest explanations provided by women who had taken up work in the workshops and factories. Just as credit is an important tool for correcting the frictions between the rhythms of production in the industrial estate and rentier economies in the tenements, they can also trap workers in the tenement, putting a stop to circuits of mobility and cause the enlistment of women onto the highly masculinised shop floors of Gurgaon's garment industry.

Workshops and Training Shops

Workshops and tenement training centres are two other key infrastructures of labour's mobility lodged into the tenement space. Hussein's training shop that sits just off the banks of the *gande nali* in Kapashera consists of two rows of six sewing machines and promises to train up newly arrived workers on the basics of stitching on a chain system for 800 rupees in two weeks, offering a course in (higher paid) quality checking for 1,000 rupees. 'I used to be able to charge 1,000 rupees for fifteen days [stitching],' he explains while idly checking a young trainee's work.

> These days it's totally different, back then we were training them to make whole pieces, to become artisans, you know? These days it's the piece-system it's all done by machine so there is less skill involved ... the labourers coming here are much poorer – and some of the companies only want helpers, cleaners, washers – they don't really need training....
> But we can get them in [to the factories] that's all they want.

We discuss changes in company demands over the previous eighteen years:

These days the workers are not skilled people, everything is done on the chain system, piece by piece. This is what has changed. Before we artisans [*karigars*] were making whole pieces for the markets in Delhi, but then the companies came, from America, Dubai, Chennai. I worked here in the companies but there is no respect for *karigars* [so] I set up this training centre…. These days everything is done on the machine, the companies simply want people who can work fast, meet the quotas and so on.

Hussein previously had his training centre on a central lane of Kapashera and benefitted from the high footfall of passing traffic but rent increases and a dispute with his landlord forced a shift across the river into the Kapashera border. As well as training up workers, Hussein doubles up as a labour contractor supplying freshly skilled workers on commission on both day and contracts, drawing on connections built up with contractors during his time working in the industrial estate.

Figure 5.4   Workshop, Kapashera
Source: Photo by author.

After I sat watching Hussein deliver instructions to five women working away on sewing machines, he took me round the back of the building to a large room – with forty sewing tables organised in single lines. It turned out that the bulk of Hussein's income came not from the training shop or labour contracting but from a garment 'fabricator' workshop – here workers earn 25–40 rupees making an entire piece. The measurements for the piece are written on a whiteboard and workers work their way through a pile of materials (Figure 5.4).

Tenement workshops form part of the extended regional supply chains that compose commodity production across unevenly valued waged and unwaged spaces, made possible by the village boundaries. According to reports there are currently 5,000 informal workshop units like Hussein's located in Gurgaon alone, not including those in Kapashera that feed into Gurgaon's export sector. Kapashera workshops and the auto-component units that occupy villages around the Hero Honda plant in central Gurgaon are characteristic of what Benjamin calls 'the neighbourhood as factory'. Benjamin notes that while this kind of formally unregulated, small-scale production is typically parted off to the 'informal sector' and relegated to the foot-end of developmental linearity within modernist narratives, these territorial configurations of small-scale workshops and 'formalised' production units – embedded in local tenurial regimes – constitute the bulk of surplus accumulation in southern cities.

Tenement workshops also play a particularly important role in absorbing wasted, indebted workers that fall out of circulation in the industrial estate. Numerous contractors I interviewed alluded to a preference for 'fresh' (*taazaa*) workers: young men and women untied to family commitments that might provide some semblance of stability and rootedness in the city. Younger workers, Hussein explained, 'work quicker with less trouble, they are here for money only nothing else'. Hiring practices that demand a constant supply of 'fresh' and mobile workers equally require disposing workers once past a certain age. This preference for youth divides labour across distinct spaces of production. Export factories in Gurgaon engage in the time-sensitive churning of 'fresh workers' through their 'productive years' and out again by their mid-thirties to make way for new rounds of labour. It is at this point that tenement workshops provide spaces of absorption for wasted labour. The youth of workers, a disguise for an absence of social and community commitment, is a source of great value in the workplace, but too long in the workplace – even across multiple temporary contractors – and exhausted workers become less and less attractive.

This appears to be far more exaggerated for women. Women form the minority of the workforce in Udyog Vihar but dominate employment in the tenement workshops. This can partly be explained by the historic masculinisation of garment manufacturing and historic feminisation of household and informal-based production in Delhi-NCR. Women's labour is directly devalued by gender and their double work responsibilities in the unwaged household. Describing why she left her previous employer, a large garments-exporter in Udyog Vihar, Puja explained, 'I went back to my husband's village for the festival, when I returned they wouldn't hire me, they won't hire any woman over thirty, they took one look at my face and decided.' While there certainly are women over the age of thirty employed in the garment factories, there is a noticeable movement of woman workers through spaces of declining job security as they age; from the factory to day-hires and finally informal workshop employment.

As a broad range of scholars have argued, waste and the wasting of commodities is a crucial component of capitalist value. 'Waste,' Gidwani and Reddy argue, 'is the political other of capitalist "value", repeated with difference as part of capital's spatial histories of surplus accumulation.' As we walk across the floor of his windowless workshop in Kapashera, Hussein retorts, 'You can see the entire life of a *mazdoor* [worker] here. First I see them young [in the shop] and five, six, seven years later they are back here with me!' The compact life cycle of a labourer begins and ends in the tenement villages.

Tenement Discipline

'Our biggest problem here is labour,' Sushil explains. The company has a 40 per cent attrition rate and struggled to hold onto the workforce they choose to hire on temporary contracts. 'Our labour class have no loyalty, they will shift for a little extra money, one day he will show up to work, the next he will leave for a little extra money elsewhere, we have no control over this.'

In response, a series of firms with the support of state governments have attempted to set up dormitory-factory complexes at the 'labour source' in Jharkhand, Bihar and Rajasthan. Sushil directly referenced the dormitory complexes and urban villages of south China that allow for the continuous access and control over cheapened reserves of migrant labour bound to the workplace through residency permits.[29] 'Dormitory complexes,' Smith and Pun argue, 'in concentrating and yet circulating labour between capitals ... represents a powerful labour management regime, which China is currently using to fuel its integration with the world economy.' Firms such as Orient Craft, one of the largest garment-exporters in the NCR, have sought to follow this model investing 16 crore rupees in a dormitory complex adjacent to a new plant in Rajasthan. Sushil's firm has also invested in dormitory facilities in a new plant in Jharkhand, explaining, 'We are beginning to experiment with the dormitory format, this way we have more control of labour and they will be always available to the factory.' Thus far these attempts, Sushil admits, have not led to a significant shift in investment away from Gurgaon and Delhi-NCR, but nevertheless signal concerns within the industry over the fragility of the tenement-labour system.

Control is a key issue particularly for a garments industry moving away from seasonal production; the tenement system provided a successive supply of cheap labour tied to distant village homes onto the factory shop floor but the outsourcing of workers' living conditions also meant relinquishing control over workers time to tenement landlords, contractors, *pradhans* and workers themselves. This tenement labour system relies upon the interests of landlords and systems of tenement management that actively produce workers temporariness in the city.

The landlord (*makaan malik*) is the tenement's principal disciplinary actor. Landlords in villages like Kapashera and Khoh are organised through their respective village councils (and the RWA in the case of Kapashera). These groups not only allow tenement landlords to plan tenement development and tenement infrastructure but also resolve landlord–tenant issues. Residents in Kapashera commonly explained that landlord councils made it difficult for workers to voice grievances with their living conditions. Pushpa lived in a room in the scalding heat of a tenement rooftop in Dundahera. Her landlord raised the rent by 200 rupees each year and had limited the amount of water available for cooking, washing, cleaning to just thirty minutes a day. She explained how she felt anxious leaving her room and spent the few hours she had between shifts 'just lying here, thinking of our village, keeping out of sight'. After a dispute over unpaid debts left by her husband who had since left the city, Pushpa explained how the landlord had begun to harass her:

I pay the rent early each month to the pradhan, I don't like [the landlord] coming up here.... Our home here is a birdcage, we are captive.... No one stands up to the landlords and the *pradhans* ... it's their rules or find somewhere else to live ... they fix rents, discuss tenants, put pressure on us – it's difficult to shift rooms in the neighbourhood, they all know each other and won't take someone in who has disputed with another landlord.

In each tenement, the landlord keeps a ledger book containing the details of each tenant, their parents' names, home village, community and workplace. In many tenements the rules of stay are painted on the side of the walls: 'Tenants must keep clean at all times', 'No guests', 'Tenants will be fined 200 rupees for wasting water', 'The late payment of rent will be penalised', 'Groceries must be purchased from the [tenement] shop'. Security deposits are taken up front alongside copies of identity proofs that are registered with the local police station.

The primary concern of landlords is, as a landlord of two tenements in Dundahera village remarked to me, 'to make a business and protect our village'. The mass construction of tenement buildings in the villages, while profitable, has, many tenement landlords argue, transformed once 'tranquil' villages into densely packed working-class 'slums'. The same landlord remarked, 'You see across the border [Kapashera], it is like Dharavi, very dirty and all sorts of outsiders living there, labourers, *goondas*, sex workers, criminals also – just ten years ago our villages were very peaceful and quiet, now look. We make some money, but these people are destroying our home.'

The landlord's comments speak to how village landlords look to govern their ancestral homes. Eager to 'make a business' and extract the highest amounts of rent possible, they must do so while ensuring they retain social and political dominance over what is numerically a superior class of 'outsiders'. The primary way in which this is achieved is by denying migrant workers' access to local residency paperwork. Local residency would allow workers to access social security, subsidised healthcare and rations, employment guarantee subsidies and housing in Gurgaon. It would also, tellingly, allow workers to vote in local elections. Just as control over Hukou residency permits mediate the permanent temporariness of workers in Chinese cities, the denial of residency documents in and around Gurgaon conducts the same work.

Nearly every landlord I spoke with in tenement villages all across Gurgaon refused to provide residency paperwork. In a survey of workers across Delhi-NCR conducted by Mezzadri and Srivastava, only 4.4 per cent held paperwork for their place of residence. For landlords, not only was the paperwork bureaucratically onerous and expensive, requiring trips to the village councillor, *patwari* and municipal office, it was decidedly not in their interests. Were their tenants to have residency paperwork, landlords would claim, locals would lose control of their villages. The Kapashera municipal councillor who holds court in a small fabric shop in the heart of the landowner's neighbourhood of the village was steadfast in his support for the practice:

> This will always be a Yadav village. If we give papers, we will become the outsiders here in our own homes! We will be ruled by Biharis!... These are not local people, they will stay today, tomorrow they will be somewhere else, why should we pain ourselves to register outsiders?

As the municipal councillor, all residency paperwork would require his signature, his refusal to do so in effect assures that residents, even those with sympathetic landlords, are unlikely to access residency in the city. The denumeration of the tenement villages is such that the vast majority of village residents are rendered opaque to the local state. This opacity does not immediately signal an absence of state control but rather expresses a form of bureaucratic labour discipline that meets the rentier interests of landowners while absolving the state of responsibilities to invest in swelling village infrastructure. Indeed, migrant residents are not entirely hidden from state view. All tenement residents are registered with the local police station, which routinely works with landlords during periods of industrial dispute to search out and identify troublesome tenants. Workers in the city are to be hidden from certain views of the state while centred in others.

The denial of paperwork occludes migrant residents from the official census. According to the 2011 census, for example, Kapashera's population grew from around 20,000 in 2001 to 74,000, of which 80 per cent were migrants; yet the 2011 electoral role for Kapashera has only 1,300 (1.7 per cent of the official population) registered to vote. Most third-party sources put Kapashera's population at between 200 and 500,000 residents. The same can be said for the other large tenement villages in Gurgaon such as Dundahera, Nathupur, Cartepuri, Sikanderpur and Kasan. This under-resourcing can be profitable for landlords. In the place of state-provided infrastructure, landlords benefit from controlling the price and delivery of private rations, water, electricity and waste services for their worker-tenants, stimulating an entire tenement economy based upon the resident's confected non-residence. Workers without paperwork are obliged to access expensive, informal services (informal clinics, childcare facilities, rations) within the urban village or else return to their home villages.

Paperwork operates as an important bureaucratic technology that reproduces particular kinds of worker-tenants desirable to landlords and industrialists, temporary and tentatively held in the city. As Veena Das notes, in Indian cities residency documents are 'material embodiments of the right to dwelling'. The denial of a right to dwelling for workers in Gurgaon, or rather their displacement of that right to faraway sites, operates to order workers as temporary and mobile, their futures as uncertain, ensuring their constant, fretful circulation out of the city.

Violence

The threat of violence was one of the most regular concerns voiced by my neighbours, and particularly by women in the tenements. Everyday discussions and storytelling among neighbours were littered with tales of beatings, murder and sexual violence directed toward workers. The absence of any localised cultural or social institutions makes migrants – especially those indebted or deemed transgressive (either due to lower-caste or gendered class positions) – particularly vulnerable.

One Saturday I sat in the doorway of a room of a newly constructed lane in Kapashera border with Rohit. Rohit had successfully secured a room in the lane for a meagre 800 rupees per month, following his eviction from a block the week before. The lane rooms in Kapashera Border are, aside from the slum, the most precarious form of housing. The box rooms are smaller than in the block and with corrugated iron roofs the rooms get intensely hot in the summer months, while the dirt floors, shared water taps and open sewers make for common bouts of sickness.

Rohit was from a scheduled-caste community originally from Bihar and had come to Kapashera in 2010 with his brother to work in the garment-export companies. The work, Rohit explained, was 'exhausting … the shifts are all day long, sometimes fourteen-fifteen hour everyday and the supervisors give a lot of abuse, if we make the quota they want more, if we don't they use all kinds of abuse.' Through a contact with the lane *chowkidar* (maintenance contractor), Rohit secured a job as a driver. When his landlord found out, he demanded he quit and work for him instead. While landlords would often be at pains to deny any tensions in the tenements, caste-based discrimination and violence were rife in the villages with particular scorn reserved for those in debt and scheduled-caste workers who were deemed successful.

Rohit, facing a lower wage with the landlord and decidedly longer hours, refused. Soon after, Rohit was violently attacked, his room looted, and he and his partner were evicted for causing trouble. At the factory Rohit had met and fallen in love with Rupa, who had moved to Kapashera with her husband but since been abandoned as he circulated on to work elsewhere in Delhi taking on a new family. Unmarried and with Rupa from a higher-caste community, Rupa explained that their 'love relationship' had made finding a room in the tenement blocks difficult. As such, Rohit and Rupa moved across the river and into the less-desired tenement lanes, 100 meters deeper into the Kapashera border. 'We are not used to living out [in the open] like this, this area is for little people, rickshaw pullers, sweepers and so on, they are living from one day to the next, the landlord is a nice man but the water is too dirty here we cannot drink it, when we have some money we will try to leave.'

Women were more exposed to outbursts of violence from landlords, *thekedars*, line managers and family members. Sexual violence and extortion were commonly directed toward women in debt or those accused of 'dishonouring' their families by working outside the home in workshops and industrial estates. Of course, it is frequently mechanisms of debt, exhaustion and mobility that push migrant women into waged work in the factory and workshops, holding them in a double bind between masculinised, often violent workplaces and impoverished, surveilled tenement rooms.

One Sunday afternoon I sat with Rohit and we discussed a recent incident at the factory that his partner worked at where 200 workers were dismissed for attempting to form a union. The factory worked closely with contractors to harass the leaders of the action in their rooms, breaking the arm of one of the leading figures and forcing their eviction from the blocks. In another instance in 2014, during my time in the tenements, there were riots in the industrial estate after contractors at Gaurav International, a large garment export firm in Udyog Vihar, beat and hospitalised a worker for arriving late to work. The workers of the plant stopped production, walked out, smashed the factory windows and set cars alight across the industrial estate. That evening, the police swept through the tenement lanes in search of rioters who had long packed up and moved on. Rumours spread across my floor that it was all a ploy, the company had hired goons to riot in order to justify cutting the workforce.

It had long occurred to me that while structurally weak and invisible to the state in both the factory and the neighbourhood, workers' collective political practice came through much more explicitly on the factory shopfloors and workplaces than it did in the tenements where there was seldom collective protest against exploitative living conditions. The consensus within scholarship on urban India is that surplus workers like Rohit, in the absence of the collective cultures of the workplace, ought to be turning their political claims and agencies towards sites of the social – of the street, slum and square. I asked Rohit why there was such an absence of collective and political resistance to exploitative social conditions in tenement villages. Rohit remarked:

> The landlords are dominant [*majboot*] here, we're outsiders, this is not our land, not our culture, truly we are in a foreign land ... in Kapashera it's much more dangerous [than the factories] the locals here kill people. In our village there is a panchayat system which provides support, in Kapashera there is nothing. In the factory you may lose your job, but I can find another job, but here, we have no one to turn to, there is no police, no union, no *panchayat*, no family.... If I raise my hand I need someone reaching down to help me, and then I can grab onto it – we don't have this.

*Pradhan*s

In many cases however landlords are seldom present in the day-to-day life of the tenement. Indeed, the spatial segregation of landlord and worker neighbourhoods in Kapashera is such that the everyday atmosphere is one of creeping surveillance and quiet anonymity. Most landlords make sparing visits to the tenement neighbourhoods, to collect rents at the start of each month, provide credit and recall debts, oversee work on tenement extensions and sometimes oversee religious festivals.

The heavy work of disciplining workers' is subcontracted to a series of tenement-based actors: the building *pradhan* (boss); the *chowkidar* (caretaker) and the *dukandar*s (grocery-store owners). While smaller subsistence landlords may be able to manage a single tenement on their own, within the larger tenement complexes in Kapashera, located far from landowners' residences, the everyday management of tenement life in delegated to building *pradhans*.

During my stay in a tenement in Kapashera, I lived opposite my building's *Pradhan*, a woman in her late forties called Ashmitaji. Indeed, it was only with the landlord and Ashmitaji's permission that I was able to take the room. *Pradhans* are usually either former workers exhausted by the fast production regimes of the factory or a longer-term resident in the building, stuck living permanently out of place in the city. Pradhan's oversee tenants, collect rents, organise cleaning workers, enforce curfews, discipline unruly behaviours and carry out evictions. Owing to enduring patriarchal relations in north India (and indeed much of the world) that feminise household labour, this role is commonly (not exclusively) carried out by migrant women in the blocks.

Ashmitaji, originally from Uttar Pradesh, moved to Kapashera twelve years ago and lived with her husband who worked a twelve-hour night-shift as a security guard, and her eighteen-year-old daughter who worked in both a tenement blood clinic and tailoring workshop in Kapashera. Ashmitaji was commonly referred to as both *pradhan* (boss) and sometimes durwan (gatekeeper). The use of both words is telling of the kind of work Ashmitaji did for the tenement-labour regime. *Pradhans* are traditionally understood as senior figures in rural and urban poor neighbourhoods that control and mediate the community's relationship with the state and outside world. As Sanjay Srivastava notes, 'The urban pradhan is a master of the hybrid cultural and social economies of the city that relate to the poor ... on behalf of whom he negotiates with the world beyond the basti.'[30] *Pradhans* and durwans, by contrast, have a longer history as company hands employed to discipline and manage colonial plantation and industrial worker lines. Arup Kumar Sen describes how from the late nineteenth century, company-hired durwans controlled the Bengali jute mills and worker lines; 'The subordinate staff of the mills', Sen writes, 'in addition to their official functions, tied the workers in multiple ways in their everyday life.' The *pradhans* in and around Gurgaon's industries play a similar function. They are the vanguard of the tenement disciplinary regime that seeks to extend the reach and control of the landlord into the minutiae of daily life, tentatively tying workers into the tenements while allowing for their immediate disposal at any point.

Each morning Ashmitaji opens the gates to the building and each evening she locks them again, enforcing a curfew on the movements and freedoms of the residents and regulating movement from the building in line with work times of nearby factories. Ashmitaji manned and rationed the tenement water supply, limited to two hours in the morning and two hours in the evening, a constant source of conflict within the building. She collects, negotiates and delays rents with all tenants in the block; she holds keys to all the rooms, has the power to evict tenants, manages the payment of sanitation workers.

One of the *pradhan*'s key tasks is to screen potential tenants and fill rooms. Sitting outside her room at the front of the building, Ashmitaji would watch passers-by on the outside lane and take enquiries about available rooms. Typically, enquirers looking for a room got a swift reply: 'Where are you from? Who brought you here? What is your name? Bachelor or married? Where are you working? Who are you with?' Wiser travellers would bring labour contractors, relatives or friends with them or the recommendation of former landlords. Accessing a room is often helped by knowing a relative, neighbour or caste-community member in a tenement or with connections to the landlord or *pradhan*. Around half of the neighbours in my block came from the same village in Bihar. On their yearly return to the village workers frequently arrive with cousins, nephews and neighbours, arriving to try out work in the city. These familial and community-based links – cultivated by workers themselves – are the initial source of information concerning jobs, tenements, contracts, training centres and workplaces that pattern forms of labour migration and operate to mitigate the fast churn of workers through temporary positions in the workplace. Alongside access to landlord and contractor credit, they also help workers' stay during periods of unemployment and stabilise workers' movement across tenements and workplaces without returning home.

While always adamant that she did not discriminate nor segregate the tenement, Ashmitaji's screenings were clearly intended to exclude undesirable tenants, those without familial connections to the building, 'troublemakers' from other buildings, lower-caste enquirers. There were many Muslim residents in my tenement block but being outwardly Muslim was clearly a disadvantage. Many workers take on non-Muslim names and adorn their rooms with Hindu decorations in order to assuage exposure to discrimination.[31] Quite often single women – deemed transgressive and troublesome – would be told to come back with their husbands or fathers, while I encountered many in inter-faith and non-normative relationships who were cast out to the more precarious tenement lanes.[32]

The disciplining of intimacy and maintenance of normative patriarchal household and family – in my block at least – was an implicit priority of the *pradhan*. 'We don't take troublemakers,' she explained. 'We prefer families, good people that is all.' Ashmitaji would scold women for socialising outside, not controlling their children or preparing food for their husbands, domestic disputes and violence directed towards women were often settled by threats of eviction. As a young *pradhan* in a tenement in Khoh village, adjacent to IMT Manesar, explained:

> We have no troublemakers in our building, the bachelors are just fine, they stay for eight, ten months then go back to the village … but sometimes with ladies [*sic*] they come to the city looking for fun, they step out of their homes for work outside thinking they will have fun in the companies.

Figures like Ashmitaji who reside in nearly all tenement buildings across the city, hold significant influence within day-to-day life in the blocks, holding the power to place and evict tenants, provide credit, and liaise with police and labour contractors in periods of industrial unrest.

Nevertheless, such is the high turnover of workers through the tenements, the significant demand for rooms, and eagerness of landlords to keep the tenements full at all times, these kinds of screening practices only partially shape the make-up of the block. The point of tenement discipline, much like that inside the factories, is not simply to subjugate migrant workers, but importantly – just like the commodities that circulate between the factories and the workshops in the urban village – to keep workers in motion by ensuring that residents are held tenuously to the tenement villages with little access to resources that might upend the hegemony of landlords.

A LIFE'S WORK

'We have no time for ourselves here, we don't have time for television, we don't even have time for cards, here we are always working,' Jitender, Raja's roommate explained. 'I go to bed at 9:30 p.m., then I have some time to think but my life is not here … twelve, thirteen, fourteen hours we are working – we socialise at work, we eat at work and shit at work, we are only here to sleep.' Jitender and so many of those 'living' in the tenements are what Marx refers to in the *Grundrisse* as capital's 'pure labouring machines'. In this context, the spatio-temporalities of Jitender's *reproduction* as a 'labouring machine' were fragmented across tea-breaks, affinities on the shop floor, dreary walks to work and brief moments in the dormitory room. If I had mistaken the tenement as a clear-cut realm of 'the social', Jitender was keen to impress that conditions in the tenement previously described merely served to squeeze the entirety of his domestic life onto disparate shop floors. A person's value for capital is intimately bound to the time it is commanded by capitalist production; as Marx writes, labour 'becomes exchange value in labour time'.[33] And within the current conjuncture, workers' need to be commanded, they need to work, in order to live. The time outside of labour time is not only hazardous for workers fearful they may be flung out onto floating surplus army waiting to be commanded but is carefully controlled by capital. Outside of labour-time, workers are alive, subject of their own creative desires and unregulated affinities. Capital is thus forced to carefully regulate the social conditions under which workers are reproduced, forever compelled to be commanded and held tenuously into capital's embrace. The churn and squeeze of tenements 'life' – where workers like Jitender sleep but do not 'live' – is an expression of this regulation.

The temporariness of stays in the tenement is such that workers' keep sparse possessions. Rooms occupied by groups of men tend to contain a mat for sleeping, with bags of possessions and cooking equipment, hanging on hooks on the walls – away from the reach of pesky tenement rats. The longer the time spent in the tenement or across different tenement rooms in the village, the greater expenditure can be justified: family rooms might have a tall double bed, relatives arriving in the city for work bring electrical goods – fans, coolers, small televisions. When a tenant is abruptly evicted or quietly escapes on the cycle for work elsewhere, these goods are claimed by the landlord and sold on. The uncertainty built into employment is such that tenement rooms are set up to precipitate the swift movement demanded and confected by the tenement labour system.

The lack of space nevertheless makes the tenements space intensely communalised with collective associations built along lines of family, regional or linguistic belonging. People share bed space, rooms, meals and information on employment opportunities. The dearth of space in the tenement ensures that life spills out of the rooms and into the communal corridors and stairways. Where possible this reproductive labour is conducted by women, who share water, cleaning and childcare responsibilities. Indeed, despite the heavy domination of men in the tenements, there remains where possible a gendered division of labour in the tenements. Small groups of women embark on 'second shifts' after long twelve-hour shifts in the factory – preparing rice, doing laundry while chatting in small groups, while men play cards and drink whisky in their rooms. Groups of lone men, of course, do not have this luxury.

Between the cramped rooms, communal corridors and the heavily surveilled lanes there is very little private space and the density of the tenements along the lanes bring a permanent darkness to the buildings. To escape, workers assemble on the flat-top roofs of the tenement into the late evenings, idly chatting, playing cards and sleeping. Long arduous shifts and near-constant circulation between tenement rooms and workplaces have the effect of transposing much of daily life – of friendship, courtship, leisure, daydreaming into the cramped walls of the factory. These conditions leave workers both mentally and physically exhausted. In the evenings, the tenements blocks are strewn with wasted-out workers, red eyed, laid out on the concrete floors and the stairs, drinking whisky, or sleepily eating dinner. This exhaustion in effect caps the time workers are willing to labour in the city and also leads many to bring household members to the city and into waged employment, and opt for the far more precarious conditions of piece-rate labour in the workshops.

Workers experiences of exploitation and mobility in the city were not restricted to one workplace, the 'factory'; their interests often exceeded the limits of this particular contract or tenement, and rather stretched across multiple, fractured workplaces, tenements and skills. The amorphous and blurred geographies of work and life for workers in contemporary Indian cities is reflective of the spatial composition of industrial accumulation under neoliberal auspices. Distant from the planned integrated townships and industrial training centres developed sparingly during the post-colonial period, of which Maruti Suzuki is a good example, industrial capitalism on the urban frontier draws in the post-agrarian class structure and tenurial regimes, and as much as possible relies upon offloading social reproductive costs and breaking through barriers on the near-total subsumption of working-class lives to the spatiotemporal rhythms of industrial production.[34] These are localised settlements of exploitation that while blurring boundaries between life and work, equally erect boundaries bound to workers' embodied difference, of 'migrant', gendered and racialised subjects that neither belong in the city (or nation) nor in waged employment. In Gurgaon, the tenement and hierarchised social relations within it do this bordering work.

Freedom

Despite these relations of domination, circulation and surveillance, the tenements are also infrastructures for workers' own resistances and disorderly mobility. Strikes, tool-downs and walkouts are sporadic features of industrial life in Gurgaon. The city's auto sector, with its high capital intensity and embedded history of unionisation, is discussed in the following chapter. The garments-export sector focused on here has no such tradition of organised unionisation and high levels of labour turnover, and entrenched systems of labour law evasion have made it difficult for workers to collectively bargain. Yet, while formal union-based activity may be less common, workers – across sectors – frequently engage in wildcat strikes, riots and quieter tactics of confrontation in the workplace to achieve increments in pay, re-appropriate stolen wages or lower production quotas. In 2014, for example, the contracts of twenty-five workers at the Modelama garment-export unit were not renewed by the contractor who also withheld their last month's wage. The workers forced their way into the factory, beat the contractors and occupied the HR office until their due was paid. That year 700 workers at a garment-exporter stopped production on the line for an entire day after not receiving their nominal Holi bonus. The company refused to provide such a bonus but announced a wage rate increase that same day. News of these confrontations rarely leave the walls of the factory and do not make the pages of local media in the way that an organised strike of unionised workers might, but they are nevertheless a regular feature of working life for the army of casualised workers in the city.

The most widespread form of dissent however – engaged in by the workers across all industrial sectors – is to enact distaste for working conditions by leaving, exiting one workplace for slightly better opportunities, more control over one's time or less abuse elsewhere. This kind of exit-politics is an extremely common way to express one's distaste for work and ranges from individuals quietly leaving to small workplace disputes, to hundreds of workers walking out en masse. Exiting is a subversive expression of mobility that redeploys conditions of transience for disruptive means. Workers' mobility in the garments industry is supposed to – according to employers – take place at the end of the ten-month shift, carefully timed for low seasons in global garment production. Workers' mobility is mobility for capital, not something to be autonomously enacted. Exiting then is ostensibly an act of dissent, of disturbing the tenement-labour system's disciplinary gaze that routinely orders workers to the rhythms of the rentier and industrial capital.

Exit politics is also, then, a feature of tenement life. In response to debt, violence and extortion, workers abandon rooms without notice, leaving possessions and debts behind in the middle of the night. Those caught leaving face beatings, heavy fines, while others are reported to the police. As Geeta, a young export-worker from Bihar who lived in Dunderha tenement block, recounted:

> You cannot unite because there are so many kinds of landlords you cannot fathom ... the other day they were beating a man in the neighbourhood. He was a hefty fellow, seemed from Haryana but was from Bihar. He had gone home for two months without informing the landlord of his absence. They had made him strip naked in the bitter cold and were whipping him with a jagged stick ... blood running down his fair skin.... I could not eat for two days after that. My husband says this is why we must always pay our rent early, one must never get too familiar with the Landlord.

These forms of violence are in part prosaic features of everyday urban life, described previously by Rohit, but they are also keenly deployed at points of a potential breakdown in the spatio-temporal control of sovereign landlords. And yet, while landlord actors work to enforce the temporalities of life in the tenement, the tenements in other ways facilitate disruptive forms of mobility. Workers build relationships with labour contractors, neighbours, relatives and clandestine lovers with the intention of holding themselves on the boundaries between one job and the next. The collective infrastructures inculcated in the tenements allow workers to move on their own terms; share knowledge and anticipate change within contexts of deep uncertainty. In gossip in the slithers of time between shifts, on the walk to and from work, laid out on tenement roofs in the evenings, workers share information about contractors, wages and working conditions in different workplaces. These disturbing movements are materially expressed in the textures of daily life in the tenements: the training shops that can re-skill a worker in a matter of days; the printed *avashyakta* (wanted) signs which cover the tenement walls advertising temporary factory jobs; the emptied-out rooms quietly departed in the middle of the night; and the early morning state buses bringing in young men with bags of possessions and taking others out to venture elsewhere. The tenement, while not a desired space to root down in place, is nevertheless a vital launching pad from which workers are able to mobilise scant resources and piece together lives of mobile flexible work. This involves tricky, collective practices of anticipation, what Abdou Maliq Simone, in 'Relational Infrastructures in Postcolonial Urban Worlds', describes as 'knowing when to make a "next move", of the incremental accretion of capacity and possibility'. These clandestine spatial practices – navigating tenement surveillance, collecting information, enlisting support, rotating to work elsewhere – each express the germs of subaltern resistance lying dormant within technologies of domination and exploitation.

And yet workers' mobility – no matter how disorderly or untimely – equally reflects the absence of local working-class institutions through which workers might sustain collective solidarity and improved conditions. Indeed, these exit practices are commonly expressed by workers through a language of 'freedom'.

Sat in a recently abandoned workers' room in Rampura, whose previous occupiers had clearly departed in a hurry – leaving blankets, floor cushions and cutlery – I was in conversation with Sachin, a thirty-year-old originally from Kanpur in Uttar Pradesh who had recently returned to a Rampura tenement room to take up work in a nearby auto-component plant. I asked Sachin where he worked. 'Work? I work everywhere,' he replied, laughing. Noting my confusion, he straightened up and added, 'See, right now, I work at 277 [an auto-components supplier], but in two weeks I will be going back to my village.'

Sachin worked as a 'helper' operating a machine at a moulding plant that made pieces for Maruti Suzuki. I was particularly interested in speaking with Sachin because there had been a spate of tool-downs and strikes at another factory owned by his employer. Naively I thought perhaps Sachin would regale stories of righteous resistance and solidarity among the otherwise fragmented and mobile workforce. But Sachin took little interest in discussing the workers' struggle. The strikes were, he said, not his concern; he foresaw no positive outcomes to their strike. 'Perhaps,' he said, 'some will be taken permanent, but the company will make the rest suffer.'

Sachin had moved in and out of Gurgaon's factories over the course of ten years, working across different sectors, skill sets and production lines. He explains:

I have worked here for ten years now – in garments, pharmaceuticals, auto-parts, electronics. I was a security guard for a company for two months too ... but I didn't like standing around all day.... I've had rooms in Kapashera, for some time in Raj Nagar and in Rampura [tenement villages], I work anywhere I want. This is our freedom [*humare azadi*].... I have worked on piece-rate, day-rate, I have worked with many contractors. Here nothing is permanent, we go back to the village, change jobs – we work, change rooms as we like, we're outsiders here! I have been here many years, I have connections in many villages here, with contractors and [workshop] masters, it's not difficult to find work here.

Sachin was in many ways the quintessential hyper-flexibilised subject of contemporary capitalist production; like so many male workers I spent time with in Gurgaon, Sachin's work was characterised by a constant flux between sectors, contracts and tenement rooms in the city. The bewildering number of low-paid, partly-automated jobs on offer across Gurgaon merely serves to flatten potential barriers to labour supply, facilitating a swifter movement of workers in and between adjacent sectors. And yet not only do conditions of work and life in the city push workers in cycles of mobility, but also this mobility is internalised and valorised in working-class culture as personal freedom.

Manu, a neighbour in my tenement, was originally from Bihar and had come to Gurgaon in 2012. Manu had worked as a tailor in a garment-exports unit in Udyog Vihar but recently, through a contact in his village, gained employment at a non-governmental organisation (NGO) that provided legal support for migrant workers in Gurgaon. He worked in the field, collecting information on workers' working conditions for the NGO, distributing information on workers' rights and supporting the organisation to set up informal unions in the industrial estate. His wife had just given birth and he was supplementing his NGO salary with working night-shifts on piece-rate in a Kapashera workshop. Just like everyone else, Manu's relationship with waged work entangled with other forms of income. Nevertheless, his experiences with the NGO had left him rather despondent over the potential for change in the lives of workers:

> [Garment workers] have no education, they work November to June and most are very young, like you. Some of them, young ones, they come and go as they may have a little land, perhaps they have a quota in the village, the youth they come and hope to save for studying, others move around from one place to another they will work just to survive,

but most, around 75 per cent, they demand this life. The problem is, they demand their freedom, freedom to come and go, freedom from their wives, their family, the line manager, the landlord, you can't really blame the companies for this … in my opinion, it's the workers who are careless, they demand their freedom, they don't want to stay here in the city and improve [the situation], they want to shift jobs, shift rooms, and so on.

Manu's diagnosis of labour mobility and organising in Gurgaon speaks to the complexities of tenement freedom. For many the promise of so-called 'standard employment' under unscrupulous employers and exploitative landlords is simply not desirable. Between the certainties of exhausting work in the factory and permanent exclusion in the tenements, it is perhaps no surprise that workers bind their collective identities to the one condition under their control, their freedom to move. This 'freedom' is of course short-lived and chimes with the industrialist's and landlord's desires for a mobile, temporary workforce. But, nevertheless, it is a mobility taken on the workers' own terms, a mobility that moves out of rhythm with global production lines and localised rentier economies. For many male migrant workers, the ability, or compulsion, to withdraw from a particular workforce provides a semblance of social value in atmospheres otherwise characterised by smothering discipline and exploitation.

Freedom is of course the paradigmatic feature of waged labour. The freedom to sell one's labour, and to only sell one's labour is the founding principle of a Marxist understanding of the 'so-called primitive accumulation' of capital. In the accounts of Sachin and Manu, we see how hegemonic conditions of labour mobility and flexibility – produced materially through the tenement system – equally rely upon the enlistment of discourses and cultures of individual freedom. This identification with 'freedom' is, to borrow from Paul Willis, central to the 'lived cultural production of the working-class' that shape the reproduction of the social relations of capitalism in the tenements in and around Gurgaon. Sachin and Manu's 'freedom' may structure their permanently temporary status in the city, and subject them to exhausting, often abusive, low-paid work across numerous workplaces, but it also affords them collective resources to intermittently disrupt and disturb these conditions, however fleeting or meagre these disruptions.

Rather than reifying classical modes of labour agency based around the formal–informal employment divide – freedom discourses and practices shine light on how the actually existing sites and practices of workers' common sense might provide an immanent terrain for insurrection and 'minor liberation' against the tenement-labour regime.

This freedom is of course bound to gendered social orders in north India (and elsewhere) that not only limit the free movement of female workers outside the household but also equally tie women's labour to more sticky sites of unwaged work in the home. The frequent utterance of 'freedom' among my male neighbours in Kapashera glossed over the hidden systems of unfree gendered labour holding that 'freedom' in place.

Rooted Flexibility

While male workers who make up the vast majority of Gurgaon's waged industrial workforce are able to circulate in and out tenement rooms, workplaces and employment, this circulation is frequently dependent upon both the unwaged labours of female household members and their capacity to take up waged employment to reproduce the household during periods of male circulation and unemployment.[35] The tenements facilitate the movement of a less-than-mobile female workforce in and out of industrial employment in low-paid positions in workshops and the industrial estate. Any time spent in village tenements in and around Udyog Vihar, one will find large numbers of migrant women working in informal workshops, clinics, cleaning tenements and carrying out daily reproductive work. As Alessandra Mezzadri's work has highlighted,[36] despite low levels of formal employment in organised industry in Delhi-NCR, migrant women dominate informal workshop employment within the tenement neighbourhoods that are gendered as 'feminine' owing to the more precarious, 'unskilled' character of production and location in proximity to the feminised space of the home.

If flexible labour in the factories is ostensibly masculinised by male workers' greater access to mobility and circulation, migrant working-class women's spatially rooted and inflexible position within the labour tenements is buttressed by discourses and practices that stigmatise and discipline their free movement outside the feminised space of the tenement home. Take, for example, Anita, a member of a migrant worker support group run by an NGO in Kapashera.

Anita worked as a 'helper' in a garment-export factory in Udyog Vihar. Anita is hired as a piece-rate worker through a contractor, earning approximately 5,600 rupees a month. Anita was in her mid-twenties and had lived in various tenement rooms in Kapashera and Dundahera, spending the previous eight years moving between various positions – thread-cutting, stitching, finishing – in a number of workshops and factories. She had never worked beyond a ten-month contract and unlike many of the workers discussed in this chapter, was yet to return home to her village.

Anita's move to Gurgaon and decision to take up waged employment in the factories was precipitated by her husband's withdrawal from waged labour. After failing to secure a government job in the village, Anita's husband withdrew from all economic activity, fell out with his family, began drinking and eventually poisoned himself. To cover the costs of his medications, Anita's family sold their small parcel of land and migrated to Gurgaon. Ever since Anita has moved between precarious work in factories and workshops in order to piece together a wage to pay off the family's debts and reproduce her household. Her experiences working on export lines and tenement workshops were marked by everyday abuse and sexual extortion. When we first met at a meeting of an NGO that provided legal support to female workers in Kapashera, she had been recently fired for resisting the sexual abuse from a line manager. The manager later sent contractors to her tenement room who beat her and broke her arm. Sighing forlornly, Anita noted that she was unlikely to ever return to her home village. 'I came here to make a living only.... I can't stay here [but] I don't know how I'll manage to go back.'

As we discuss in the following chapter, the gendered conditions of female workers' (im)mobility through the tenements and workshops produce quite distinct political agencies and struggles, anchored to certain futures captured within tenement systems designed for mobility.

The Tenement Fix

In Gurgaon the tenements that cluster in villages surrounding the city's industrial estates stage key processes in the making, remaking and wasting of the city's working classes. These processes are vital for producing a cheap, mobile labour power in the waged and unwaged workplaces and form the basis of land-based capital's rentier expansion. The tenement is an integral space in which labour power, commodity production and social reproduction are trained and disciplined to produce tenuously employed, permanently temporary working subjects. Here we see how complex, non-privatised land tenures play an essential role in industrial urbanisation. In Chapter 2, we found customary, non-privatised land tenures at the centre of a hegemonic territorial alliance between agrarian elites, the state and real estate capital; here we see another alliance at play between those same agrarian actors, the state and this time, industrial capital. The tenement both comes to express the configuration of labour's exploitation in the city, representative of the boundary-drawing practices – the uneven geographies of labour subsumption that underwrite commodity production. Importantly, we can trace the role of the tenement for industrial capital to the role of the village for real estate capital. The tenement village as a particular territorial and social fix for industrial flexibilisation enables circulations of land and labour commodities through the city, dictating their particular forms and rhythms in ways that enable Gurgaon to take its particular brash and hubristic neoliberal form.

By 'territorial fix' I do not wish to imply that the tenement villages are 'fixed' within a hierarchy of scalar geographies of production,[37] but rather I use the term to express real estate and industrial capital's reliance upon complex, non-privatised land tenures to craft suitable land and labour markets and mediate tensions between real estate value extraction and industrial capitalist accumulation. In the work of the tenement, we see the interests of local industrialists, construction firms and service industries enjoin with that of real estate firms, brokers and rentiers. Like all fixes, the tenement's function for local capitalist accumulation provides the germs of its dysfunction and reconfiguration. As David Harvey writes in *The Limits to Capital*, spatial fixes describe capital's attempts to resolve its crises through geographical restructuring. Harvey, for the most part, is writing in the context of capital's need for territorial expansion and the rewiring of over-accumulated capital into non- or under-commodified resources. Here, however, the fix is more to do with pinning down a political-spatial settlement that can produce disposable labourers and open up land for commodification, all while neutralising the contradictions between the two forces.

Importantly, this 'fix' emerges not singularly from the commodity moment but rather relationally as the commodity logic is grafted onto landowners' territorial monopoly over customary lands to produce a social order adequate for conditions of surplus accumulation.

As we have seen, the tenements are essential for regulating the timely mobility of Gurgaon's flexibilised labouring subjects. Mobility, the enduring idiom that characterises the conditions under which the vast majority of people live and work in India, expresses the complex recycling of labour power through different spatio-temporal modes of exploitation: from fixed term contracts in the factory to unemployment or precarious work in home villages to informal workshop labour to unpaid household labour. Labour's mobility does not express the permanent exclusion of workers from capitalist exploitation and their segregation into non-capitalist realms of labour – often described as spaces of 'need', endurance, resilience and hustle – all characteristics no doubt of capitalist subsumption of labour. Workers move in a dizzying fashion between differently regulated and waged employment all the time. As Gidwani and Maringanti argue, 'The modal condition of work within capitalism (postcolonial or otherwise) is neither full inclusion nor absolute expulsion of laboring populations from capital's reserve army, but rather the spatiotemporal flux in and tenuousness of capital's embrace.'[38]

The tenement system operates to harmonise this spatio-temporal flux to the demands of local industry. It is ultimately the search for a hypermobile labour-tenant that the tenement operationalises, and yet, by fixing people into a space-time, the troubles of illiquidity emerge. Both the remodulated practices of 'freedom' that the tenement affords, and the tentative social collectivities developed across tenement rooms, can disrupt the seamless movement of workers through the city and frequently provide the stage for the kinds of solidarity, mutuality and fleeting permanence that can be seldom forged in contexts of deeply segmented, disciplined and mobile labour regimes. The tenement is not simply a space at which workers return wasted after the ten-to-twelve-hour shifts; it provides the structures of material and social disciplining that shape labour's cyclical movement in and out of the city, of rooms and workplaces, lovers and friends and in so doing, concurrently inhibit and spark social collectivities that shape a politics of mobility across the city.

Yet it is clear that the ability and capacity to simply 'move' when one feels aggrieved or bored is not open to simply anyone. If mobility comes to define hegemonic class struggles across the tenements and workplaces, what kinds of cultural resources do these struggles depend upon? And who do they exclude? In the following chapter I explore how gender and patriarchal restraints on women's work and mobility come to shape an altogether different working-class experience and mode of politics in the tenement city.

NOTES

1. Coronil, *The Magical State*.
2. Numerous accounts detail this process. See, for example, Khanna, 'The Transformation of India's Public Sector'; Agarwala, *Informal Labor*; Maurya and Vaishampayan, 'Growth and Structural Changes in India's Industrial Sector'.
3. Gibson-Graham, 'The End of Capitalism'; Negri, *Marx and Foucault*.
4. Sanyal, *Rethinking Capitalist Development*.
5. Sanyal and Bhattacharyya, 'Beyond the Factory'.
6. Davis, 'Planet of Slums'. This analytical outcome can also be found in Dipesh Chakrabarty's *Rethinking Working-Class History*, where in a study of working-class culture in Kolkata in the 1930s he argues that proletarianisation has been blocked by workers enduring dependency on agrarian peasant economies.
7. Banaji, *Theory as History*.
8. Fortunati, *The Arcane of Reproduction*; Federici, *Revolution at Point Zero*; Dalla Costa and James, *Women and the Subversion of the Community*.
9. See Mies, *The Lace Makers of Narsarpur;* Mitchell, Marston and Katz, *Life's Work*.
10. Banaji, *Theory as History*; Chari, *Fraternal Capital*; Harriss-White, *India Working*; Breman, *Footloose Labour*.
11. Breman, *Footloose Labour*.
12. Banaji's *Theory as History* argues that even in the so-called metropole networks of 'unfree' labour precipitate and underpin the wage relation.
13. Kalb, 'Class'; Kalb, 'Regimes of Value and Worthlessness'.
14. Mezzadri and Srivastava, *Labour Regimes in the Indian Garment Sector*.
15. The acquisition of land in the villages of Dundahera, Mullahera, Inayatpur, Sarhaul, Shahpur and Mullahera villages was subsequently subject to a judicial inquiry that was highly critical of the process.
16. Bhargava, *The Maruti Story*.
17. Sharan, 'Claims on Cleanliness'; Ghertner, *Rule by Aesthetics*.
18. Mezzadri and Srivastava, 'Labour Regimes'.
19. Ibid.
20. Braverman, *Labor and Monopoly Capital*.
21. Ibid., 112–13.
22. Mezzadri and Srivastava, 'Labour Regimes'.
23. Ngai and Smith, 'Putting Transnational Labour Process in Its Place'.
24. Ong, *Neoliberalism as Exception*.
25. Benjamin, 'Neighbourhood as Factory'.

26. Chari, *Fraternal Capital*.
27. Bathla, 'Planned Illegality'.
28. Take, for example, the village of Prem Nagar on the western flank of IMT Manesar, the village *abadi* cut off from its land by the Maruti Suzuki plant and the Kundli–Manesar Expressway, where landowners I spent time with complained that while some village benefitted, their corporate social responsibility payments from Maruti Suzuki were mostly embezzled by local bureaucrats.
29. Hsing, *The Great Urban Transformation*; Ngai and Smith, 'Putting Transnational Labour Process in Its Place'.
30. Srivastava, *Entangled Urbanism*, 7.
31. Cowan, 'Rooted Flexibility'.
32. Ibid.
33. Marx, *Grundrisse*, 266.
34. Mitchell, Marston, and Katz, 'Life's Work'.
35. Cowan, 'Rooted Flexibility'.
36. Mezzadri, *The Sweatshop Regime*.
37. Allen and Cochrane, 'Assemblages of State Power'; Bok, '"By Our Metaphors You Shall Know Us"'.
38. Gidwani and Maringanti, 'The Waste-Value Dialectic'.

Bibliography

Agarwala, Rina. *Informal Labor, Formal Politics, and Dignified Discontent in India*. New York: Cambridge University Press, 2013.

Allen, John, and Allan Cochrane. 'Assemblages of State Power: Topological Shifts in the Organization of Government and Politics'. *Antipode* 42, no. 5 (2010): 1071–89.

Banaji, Jairus. *Theory as History: Essays on Modes of Production and Exploitation*. Leiden: Brill, 2010.

Benjamin, Solomon. 'Neighbourhood as Factory'. PhD diss., Massachusetts Institute of Technology, US, 1991.

Bhargava, R. C. *The Maruti Story: How A Public Sector Company Put India on Wheels*. Noida: HarperCollins Publishers India, 2013.

Bathla, Nitin. 'Planned Illegality, Permanent Temporariness, and Strategic Philanthropy: Tenement Towns under Extended Urbanisation of Postmetropolitan Delhi'. *Housing Studies* (2021): 1–21.

Bok, Rachel. '"By Our Metaphors You Shall Know Us": The "Fix" of Geographical Political Economy'. *Progress in Human Geography* 43, no. 6 (2019): 1087–108.

Braverman, Harry. *Labor and Monopoly Capital: The Degradation of Work in the Twentieth Century*. New York: NYU Press, 1998.

Breman, Jan. *Footloose Labour: Working in India's Informal Economy*. Vol. 2. New York: Cambridge University Press, 1996.

Chakrabarty, Dipesh. *Rethinking Working-Class History: Bengal, 1890–1940*. New Jersey: Princeton University Press, 1989.

Chari, Sharad. *Fraternal Capital: Peasant-Workers, Self-Made Men, and Globalization in Provincial India*. Stanford: Stanford University Press, 2004.

Coronil, F. *The Magical State: Nature, Money, and Modernity in Venezuela*. Chicago: University of Chicago Press, 1997.

Cowan, Thomas. 'Rooted Flexibility: Social Reproduction, Violence and Gendered Work in the Indian City'. *Gender, Place and Culture* 28, no. 1 (2021): 66–87.

Dalla Costa, Mariarosa, and Selma James. *Women and the Subversion of the Community*. Bristol, UK: Falling Wall Press, 1972.

Davis, Mike. 'Planet of Slums'. *New Left Review*, no. 26 (April 2004): 5–34.

Federici, Silvia. *Revolution at Point Zero: Housework, Reproduction, and Feminist Struggle*. Oakland, California: PM Press, 2012.

Fortunati, Leopoldina. *The Arcane of Reproduction: Housework, Prostitution, Labor and Capital*. N.p.: Autonomedia, 1995.

Ghertner, D. Asher. *Rule by Aesthetics: World-Class City Making in Delhi*. New York: Oxford University Press, 2015.

Gibson-Graham, Julie Katherine. 'The End of Capitalism (as We Knew It): A Feminist Critique of Political Economy'. *Capital and Class* 21, no. 2 (1997): 186–88.

Gidwani, V., and A. Maringanti. 'The Waste-Value Dialectic: Lumpen Urbanization in Contemporary India'. *Comparative Studies of South Asia, Africa and the Middle East* 36, no. 1 (2016): 112–33.

Harriss-White, Barbara. *India Working: Essays on Society and Economy*. Cambridge; New York: Cambridge University Press, 2003. http://dx.doi.org/10.1017/CBO9780511754319.

Harvey, David. *The Limits to Capital*. Oxford: Basil Blackwell, 1982.

Hsing, You-tien. *The Great Urban Transformation: Politics of Land and Property in China*. Oxford: Oxford University Press, 2010.

Kalb, Don. 'Class: The "Empty Sign" of the Middle Class; Class and the Urban Commons in the 21st Century'. In *The Blackwell Companion in Urban Anthropology*, edited by Don Nonini, 157–77. Oxford: Blackwell, 2014.

Kalb, Don. 'Regimes of Value and Worthlessness: How Two Subaltern Stories Speak'. In *Work and Livelihoods*, edited by Victoria Goddard and Susana Narotzky, 123–36. London: Routledge, 2016.

Khanna, Sushil. 'The Transformation of India's Public Sector: Political Economy of Growth and Change'. *Economic and Political Weekly* 50, no. 5 (2015): 47–60.
Marx, Karl. *Grundrisse*. UK: Penguin, 1993.
Maurya, Nagendra Kumar, and Jayant Vinayak Vaishampayan. 'Growth and Structural Changes in India's Industrial Sector'. *International Journal of Economics* 6, no. 2 (2012): 321–31.
Mezzadri, Alessandra. *The Sweatshop Regime: Labouring Bodies, Exploitation, and Garments Made in India*. Delhi: Cambridge University Press, 2016.
Mezzadri, Alessandra, and Ravi Srivastava. *Labour Regimes in the Indian Garment Sector: Capital–Labour Relations, Social Reproduction and Labour Standards in the National Capital Region*. Centre for Development Policy and Research, 2015. http://eprints.soas.ac.uk/21328/1/Mezzadr_file106927.pdf. Accessed 1 January 2020.
Mies, Maria. *The Lace Makers of Narsapur: Indian Housewives Produce for the World Market*. London: Zed, 1982.
Mitchell, Katharyne, Sallie A. Marston and Cindi Katz. 'Life's Work: An Introduction, Review and Critique'. In *Life's Work: Geographies of Social Reproduction*, 1–26. Oxford: Antipode, 2004.
Negri, Antonio. *Marx and Foucault: Essays*. Cambridge: Polity Press, 2017.
Ngai, Pun, and Chris Smith. 'Putting Transnational Labour Process in Its Place: The Dormitory Labour Regime in Post-Socialist China'. *Work, Employment and Society* 21, no. 1 (2007): 27–45.
Ong, Aihwa. *Neoliberalism as Exception: Mutations in Citizenship and Sovereignty*. Durham; London: Duke University Press, 2006.
Sanyal, Kalyan. *Rethinking Capitalist Development: Primitive Accumulation, Governmentality and Post-Colonial Capitalism*. London: Routledge, 2007.
Sanyal, Kalyan, and Rajesh Bhattacharyya. 'Beyond the Factory: Globalisation, Informalisation of Production and the New Locations of Labour'. *Economic and Political Weekly* 44, no. 22 (2009): 35–44.
Sharan, Awadhendra. 'Claims on Cleanliness: Environment and Justice in Contemporary Delhi'. *Sarai Reader: The Cities of Everyday Life* 2, no. 1 (2002) : 31–37.
Simone, Abdou Maliq. 'Relational Infrastructures in Postcolonial Urban Worlds'. In *Infrastructural Lives*, edited by Stephen Graham and Colin McFarlane. New York: Routledge, 2014.
Srivastava, Sanjay. *Entangled Urbanism: Slum, Gated Community and Shopping Mall in Delhi and Gurgaon*. New Delhi: OUP Catalogue, 2014, 7.

6 | The Camp*

WORKER STRUGGLES IN THE AGRARIAN CITY

The chapters thus far have examined the deep entanglements of the agrarian world and global capital that have shaped Gurgaon's spectacular development from agricultural hinterland to global city. In this chapter I want to think with and from the everyday struggles of migrant workers in Gurgaon, questioning what kinds of solidarities and struggles emerge from conditions of marginality and flexibility described in previous chapters, and what these solidarities reveal about subaltern urban politics in the contemporary moment. Where the previous chapter examined tenement-labour regimes, how everyday relations of the worker tenement patterned the mobility and working conditions of Gurgaon's migrant working classes, this chapter is interested in how these conditions shape attendant demands and claims for a place in the city. As I will show, the everyday struggles traced across this chapter are not made to housing, belonging or urban services – the typical registers of subaltern urban politics detailed in urban scholarship – but rather reflective of lives dominated by flux, mobility and precarity, the struggles coalesce around tentative demands for a dignified life. If contemporary scholarship on subaltern urban politics has centred on the territorial warfare waged between global capital and subaltern actors over access and use of urban land, the political struggles traced in the chapter align with the more expansive urban political agenda set out by Henri Lefebvre, as faltering calls for a *transformed and renewed right to urban life*. Borrowing from work elsewhere on *subaltern cosmopolitanism*,[1] the chapter understands these disparate political struggles as informed by conditions of labour exploitation both in the home and

---

*A part of this chapter was originally published as 'Subaltern Counter-Urbanism: Work, Dispossession and Emplacement in Gurgaon, India' in *Geoforum* 92, no. 1 (2018): 152–60. Reprinted with permission from Elsevier.

workplace, migrations between the city and countryside, and ad hoc support networks that characterise the everyday lives of migrant workers in urban India. Attention to the workers' subaltern cosmopolitanisms provides a way of getting at not only the gendered conditions that inform the workers' willingness to engage in political action but also the strikingly tentative and speculative character of the demands being made.[2] How have conditions in Gurgaon's tenements and workplaces, described in the previous chapter, shaped particular kinds of politics and agency among migrant workers that exceed claims to freedom? As I will discuss, here demands for *urban life*, while embedded in everyday conditions within the tenements, are temporally and territorially unbundled from the city. By exploring worker struggles in the city, I hope to push back against analyses that view migrant labour as a silent object pushed and pulled between the city and the village to the whims of globalised capital and shed light on the non-territorial urban struggles being waged against oppressive conditions of everyday working life in India's fledgling post-liberalisation cities.

THE HOMEMAKER'S BATTLEFIELD

I met with Sonu in late 2014 in a municipal park in Old Gurgaon. The park sits underneath the crowded streets of the old city, and as one of the only green spaces in the neighbourhood, it has been used by residents and migrant workers for public rallies and meetings for a number of years. The morning I met Sonu, hundreds of women, former employees of an auto-component factory that I will call Azadiplex, sat in the shade under the park's pagoda, while Sonu and two other women took turns to lead discussions on the previous six months of industrial dispute and struggle at their workplace. Rallying calls of 'mazdoor ekta zindabad!' (long live worker unity!), common in workers rallies in Hindi-speaking India, were peppered with evocations of female dignity (*izzat*), unity (*ekta*), power (*shakti*) and diligence (*mehanati*). The women's park rally was unlike political rallies I had previously attended in the city where elderly activists would deliver sermons on capitalist greed from a stage, and the NGO meetings where middle-class women with international visitors in tow (often me) would facilitate orderly discussions with observant 'beneficiaries' while junior colleagues scribbled answers into feedback forms. The park meeting was a far livelier affair. The women sat in a large circle, in deep discussion on a range of topics from sympathetic supervisors to violent landlords and absent colleagues. Those present disagreed furiously, interrupted each other relentlessly and frequently broke off into smaller discussions while their children ran around, in and out of the pagoda. This was a quintessentially anarchic political assembly. Groups of men, not accustomed to seeing such large groups of working-class migrant women out in such a public space raising slogans and discussing political strategy, clustered at the edges of the pagoda curiously looking in. A male representative of a prominent Communist Party union invited to speak at the rally, stood awkwardly at a distance, notes in hand waiting to be called upon to speak. Sonu sat on her haunches in the middle of the pagoda eyeing up the male onlookers, and quietly noted to the group that they ought to be wary of speaking too openly, the company may have sent spies and 'local boys' may recognise them from their tenements.

As the meeting wound to an end, the union official got his two minutes to make a solidarity speech to a largely disinterested audience before the women picked up their children and made for the exits, quickly departing on shared auto-rickshaws back to the urban villages.

And so as quickly as the meeting had assembled, the park was deserted again; a fleeting assembly of anti-systemic strategy squeezed into a busy Sunday's housework. Sitting with Sonu in the park, watching her co-workers quickly disperse, she highlighted the fault lines on which their six months of struggle at the factory and in the tenements had hinged. 'Earlier women were not given any position in society. Now to get our position, we have to get down on the battlefield. Whether at home or outside, *homemakers* now want to be valued as they should be!'

Indeed, for Sonu and many other women, engagement in the wave of workplace struggles in Gurgaon across 2014 provided a basis to begin to challenge the situated gendered hierarchies, restrictions on behaviours and mobilities and subjection to precarious everyday lives that are central to returning the women as cheap labour power and precarious urban residents.

SUBALTERN URBANISM

As discussed previously, the advent of contemporary urban India brought with it an unfolding of forces that shifted state policy away from supporting labour-intensive industry and agriculture and towards enticing finance, real estate and service-led development. The subsequent agricultural decline in rural areas has pushed millions of people to urban areas in search of work and yet the informalisation of the urban industrial sector has left these people neither able to find work in the village nor in the city. Left bereft of the material capacity to support themselves in the city, those termed 'surplus populations' by certain scholarships, enter informal sector employment, occupy and construct their homes on public lands and gain access to urban services by embedding themselves in localised patronage networks.

One consequence of this conjuncture is a shift in the way in which urban politics is located and discussed. If Subaltern Studies scholars located subalternity in the peasant uprising and prosaic revolts against colonial rule, and the post-colonial subaltern subject was marked as the industrial and agricultural worker, the builders of a modern independent nation,[3] then the twenty-first-century subaltern subject is markedly urban, decidedly marginal and makes claims not to work nor the nation, but to the city.[4]

'Subaltern urbanism', a term coined by Ananya Roy, describes a whole host of often discrete political negotiations and relationships urban surplus populations engage in with different entities of the state in order to survive in the contemporary city.[5] Roy defines 'subaltern urbanism' as a body of scholarly work that 'undertakes the theorization of the megacity and its subaltern spaces and subaltern classes' and 'seeks to confer recognition on spaces of poverty and forms of popular agency that often remain invisible and neglected in the archives and annals of urban theory'.[6] Subaltern urbanism takes the subalternist method of the 1980s and thrusts it into an analysis of the marginalised geographies and actors latent within contemporary global urban landscapes. Much of this work is concerned with a particular territorial war running through the Indian city, between the state and global capital's quest for land and ordinary residents' quest for survival. In such narratives, each actor in the story of India's spectacular urbanisation takes part in a pitched battle over the purpose, use and meaning of urban territory. Global capital seeks it out, the entrepreneurial state facilitates access to it, an emergent urban elite demands its attention and urban poor actors are defined through their strategies to hold onto it. This prosaic war over access to territory, housing, water, electricity and sanitation have come to define the way we understand contemporary urban politics, state authority and the fault lines of capitalist urbanisation in India. These are no doubt essential components of post-liberalisation urbanisation, and the past chapters are key to understanding the Gurgaon story. Nevertheless, there is a broader tendency within urban studies to identify authentic urban struggles in the spatial politics of encroachment, occupancy, squatting and autogestion.[7] In this vision of contemporary urban struggles, precariously employed migrant workers like Sonu, their provisional living and working conditions, everyday negotiations with contractors, brokers, supervisors and landlords, and their near-constant movement across the breadth of the country, fall by the wayside. The transition of the Indian economy towards urban-led growth has, in other words, produced a decidedly territorial ontology of politics in India. One consequence of this shift of attention, among scholars, toward the territorialised struggles of global capital and subaltern actors is an elision of the struggles and subjectivities of actors decidedly unvested in the here and now of the city. It is my contention that understanding contemporary urban politics in India must include an analysis of the waves of subaltern struggle evoked by those 'floating populations' discussed in the previous chapter whose cheap labour and foundational alienation from the city are vital for the construction, commodity production and servicing of the agragrian city.

DOMESTIC COSMOPOLITANS

In 2017 in neighbouring Noida, over a hundred domestic workers burst their way into the Mahagun Moderne luxury high-rise apartment complex to protest against the forced capture and enslavement of a fellow domestic maid who had been missing for days. The workers smashed windows and blocked the entrance into the elite enclave before being pushed out by armed police. Images of the abused maid being carried out of the high-rise, vomiting and limp by her fellow domestic workers were pasted across national media outlets that evening. Like most domestic workers in Delhi-NCR, the maid lived in a rented tin shack in a slum adjacent to the high-rise apartment. In line with the political atmosphere among urban upper classes that has positioned domestic workers as dangerous migrants intruding on elite urban space,[8] in the aftermath of the riot the maid was labelled a thief and 'illegal immigrant' by some of the residents of the complex. As they are compelled to move in and through elite territories of the city, territories premised on the exclusion of lower-caste, working-class people, domestic workers mark out the 'disjunctive inclusions'[9] that characterise the contemporary Indian city.

The events in Noida were not a surprise to me. As I followed news of the riot on social media in the summer of 2017, I was immediately reminded of similar struggles latent in the urban villages of Gurgaon. Across the city from Sonu's park rally, surrounded by the new city's plush residential condominiums, gated parks and upscale shopping complexes, lies Sikanderpur village. Sikanderpur is one of a series of urban villages that predominately house the city's low-wage service sector workforce: security guards, waiters, shop assistants, call-centre operators, auto-rickshaw drivers and domestic maids. Subia resides in a small tenement building adjacent to the village dump with her two daughters and unemployed husband and works as a domestic maid in four households seven days a week earning 8,000 rupees per month. Subia's work, like all domestic workers in Gurgaon, is not regulated by labour protections – there is no formal trade union operating in the sector, conditions of work are negotiated on an individual and ad hoc basis between urban middle-class 'masters' and predominately female, migrant and lower-caste 'help'. This system is commonplace but nevertheless enables widespread exploitation of domestic maids.

I first met with Subia at a meeting of the Gharelu Kamgar Sangathan (GKS), an informal trade union group set up by a local NGO that provides legal and institutional support to migrant workers in Delhi-NCR. That day I found myself again in a park, albeit one nestled in the centre of one of Gurgaon's elite residential colonies, where elderly residents do their morning exercises and dogs are taken for their daily walks. Subia was busy handing out pamphlets to a group of fifteen or so women all of whom worked as domestic maids in the neighbourhood. The pamphlet, produced by the NGO, detailed various laws that should safeguard domestic workers from exploitation and provided a step-by-step protocol for addressing sexual harassment and extortion within their workplaces. Sat in a circle the women interjected to provide personal stories of exploitation and abuse while residents of the nearby condominiums, with their overweight dogs in tow, stood around listening in with seeming disapproval. The NGO worker explained to me that many women are not able to discern between appropriate and inappropriate behaviours of their employers, to which Subia took particular issue. Summing up the structurally weak position of so many domestic workers across the country: 'It is not an issue of knowledge, these are poor women, they need the work!'

Subia works in four households in neighbouring Silver Oaks Avenue each day earning 2,700 rupees in the first household, 2,000 rupees in the second, 1,000 rupees in the third and 3,000 rupees in the fourth. Her working conditions, fraught with violence and extortion, are common to many domestic workers across the country:

> They don't give us leave if we are ill and they've never paid for our medicines ... and start picking up a huge fight if you ask for sick leave ... recently a friend's master slapped her when she'd made a mistake with the food ... he literally hit her.... She told him that she would clear out of there as soon as he tells her – but not to hit her.

The union had been set up to organise women working in Gurgaon's elite condominiums against everyday abuse and harassment, and to organise standardised pay conditions across different work tasks. As an entirely unregulated and dispersed form of work, domestic workers' wages are in constant flux, dependent upon the capacity for workers to bargain with their *masters* and fend off other workers more willing or able to work for less.

> It's no good if I demand more money, some other woman will come and do that task for less, we must all agree to a rate first. Suppose that we could fix the wages for doing their laundry or a certain amount for doing the dishes. We must also get the wages for doing extra work: in case guests arrive and we have to cook for more people, we must get the payment accordingly.... All the [GKS] women with us are relentlessly demanding for four days leave a month and fixed wages so can make us work according to the money they pay us. Anyways, they always take a lot of work from us! The problem is the mistresses will fight with us. Whether it's the question of taking leave or fixing proper wages they're up in arms against us every time we raise it.

Subia was originally from Kolkata in West Bengal and migrated to Gurgaon in 2010 after debts accumulated from illness pushed her and her husband out onto the circuits of job hunters moving through the city. Subia's experience migrating to the city to find work is not uncommon. Millions of people across India are forced to abscond from villages run down by agricultural decline and rising private debt in search of work in nearby and far-flung cities. Subia forms part of India's so-called 'floating population' expelled from land to make way for the monuments of new urban India and set adrift into an unassailable current that drags millions of people from one space of precarious employment to the next; a current, as discussed in the previous chapter, orchestrated between the tenement and the workplace.

Subia's 1,000-mile migration from West Bengal to Gurgaon was not her first. Like most women, after her marriage at the age of sixteen, she moved from her small slum-shack in central Kolkata to her in-laws' village in rural Bihar. Subia's shift from the city to the village counteracts common narratives of rural-to-urban migration, one only discernible when we begin to consider the ways gender unevenly structures people's mobilities, constraints and possibilities. In the village, Subia encountered a life entirely different to the one she had known in the city.

> I had no idea what poverty was. Everyone lived in one piece of clothing! I used to think that there is so much freedom in our Kolkata, if they're living like this here why can't they send their husbands to the city to work? How could they all live in a single piece of cloth, and use the earth to clean their teeth?

As a self-proclaimed 'daughter of Kolkata', Subia decided early on to put her 'city knowledge' to use in the village. She began by learning book-keeping with the aid of an uncle and began training other women in basic arithmetic, reading and writing. 'The problem is,' she remarked, 'the women had never stepped out of the four walls of their house. They don't know what freedom is.' Subia participated in a women's self-help savings group in the village (the kind celebrated by international financial institutions and neoliberal policymakers) and spoke fondly of the freedom afforded by the weekly discussions at the group. Just as Subia transported skills from Kolkata to survive and develop networks of solidarity in the village, these skills would soon be transported to Gurgaon and put to work in union organising in the city.

After six years in the village, Subia fell ill.

> Up until then my husband pulled a rickshaw and we made a living by selling fish. There were not many expenses in the village. And my father chipped in money for us too ... sometimes. He was our only support. After he passed away, it was all over for us.

Racking up significant medical debts, Subia and her husband sent their son to live with an uncle in Kolkata and secretly migrated to Gurgaon in search of work.

Subia's narration of her passage from Kolkata to Gurgaon, mediated by mobility and shaped by the gendered expectations of the household, elucidates a quite distinct story of migration then usually attributed to India's 'floating populations'. While academic work has been keen to bear witness to migrant labour's unrelenting structural weakness in the face of increasing hostility to rural migrants in the big cities and unrelenting precarity of working conditions, narratives like Subia's point us to quite other geographies of mobility, transfer and negotiation that help explain the emergence of collective political activity. Subia's movement across the fragmented geographies of post-liberalisation India, from post-Imperial Kolkata to Bengal's devastated countryside and onto the neoliberal city, is a story of a subaltern cosmopolitanism: the 'worldliness, mobility, and geographies of connection crafted by marginal groups'[10] that come to inform subaltern politics in the present. As Gidwani and Sivaramakrishnan note, when stripped of its liberal and Eurocentric baggage, cosmopolitanism is fundamentally about a 'general and historically deep experience of living in a state of flux, uncertainty and encounter with difference' that can be mobilised to generate new solidarities, possibilities and claims to place. For so many migrant workers toiling across Gurgaon, their migration to the city was not merely a physical movement, one easily represented in tables and charts, nor one solely characterised by the hunt for a wage, but equally forged through the movement and development of new subjectivities.

And yet, as discussed in the previous chapter, gender interrupts labour mobility in unpredictable ways. Like many migrant women, Subia's journey has been fixed in one direction, structured by a 'rooted flexibility' that simultaneously expects labouring mobility and feminised emplacement. In our long conversations on Subia's monthly day off, Subia was quick to restate that while she yearned to return home, she was bound to her small tenement room.

> There's a small mud house of ours [in the village] there's no place for me.... I am the only one in my extended family who works. Apart from my mother and sisters, no one at my in-laws' knows that I work here in Gurgaon and earn money. That is why I've come so far so that no one gets to know about this and I can solve my problems as well. When the entire family comes together, I can't even mention that I earn my bread ... the other sisters have been married into big families in Bombay and elsewhere ... I feel bad that I'm not up to their level, that I earn and live, if they find out they'll say 'she is so dirty'.

Domestic Struggles

Subia initially heard of the union through a neighbour soon after arriving in Gurgaon and quickly became a leading figure in the group. While the primary activity of GKS was directed by the NGO that provided rights training, chaired weekly meetings and published educational materials, the daily work of the union was conducted by women like Subia. The union members made daily clandestine trips across the city to elite residential colonies in the city, handing out pamphlets, holding brief roadside discussions and setting up social media groups to stay connected. During the anti-corruption movement that swept India in 2011, Subia organised for thirty-five union members to travel up to central Delhi to attend the now-famous Ramlila rally addressed by the Gandhian elder Anna Hazare. 'There were so many people there. I really loved it. They discussed labour and the amount that we must be paid. They discussed our rights. It was fun.'

In an interesting class encounter, characteristic of the populist zeal of the anti-corruption movement, upon arriving at the rally Subia was confronted by one of her employers who was also attending the demonstration.

> She'd caught me red-handed. I said lightly that I'd not committed any crime.... I told her that I'm now part of the Domestic Workers' Union. She told me not to go around engaging in such groups and making a mess ... she said, there's no one here for you. What if something happens to you? So I assured her that nothing would happen and that it was only for bringing together the domestic workers.... I told her that we discuss about how to work, how to receive our payment, how to take leave, and so on. Well, my mistress visibly stiffened. I read her body language and had to tell her that I'd not go against the hand that feeds me.

Laughing, Subia adds, 'Sometimes my mistresses say – when we speak to you it seems you are educated – but I tell them no auntie don't worry I am not, I never went to school.'

Subia's friend and co-conspirator Nadiya arrived in Gurgaon aged nine from West Bengal, and lived in a slum neighbourhood at the backside of Sikanderpur village.

> Earlier there was nothing here, we had *jhuggis* made out of cardboard. We had to go and relieve ourselves in the forests around.... There was nothing ... the Gurgaon that I'm seeing now and the one that I had seen before – there is a huge difference.... We paid 300 rupees then, and we had electricity and water included, what do I pay now? In this very same room, my rent was 800 ... and now 3,200 [and] the landlords here, are absolutely horrible, they enter our rooms drunk unannounced, demanding all sorts, I spoke sharply to him so he doesn't peek in my room.

At the age of nine Nadiya began work as a maid in an upper-class home in DLF City.

> The man promised my sister he would educate me, teach me to read and write and so on.... He used to wake me up at 5:30 in the morning after I had finished all the chores in his house – he'd drop me at his in-laws' place. There would be three–four iron pails full of dirty laundry there – that I had to do. I had never even washed my own clothes till that point.

Nadiya has worked as a domestic maid ever since; having never returned to her village in West Bengal, she was permanently a 'migrant' worker, out of place and static in a sea of mobility. The feeling of de facto entrapment for workers like Nadiya and Subia was expressed in the following interaction:

> TC: What do you feel you have gained since organising with the union?
> Subia: I figured that I could get leave.
> TC: Leave?
> Subia: Yes...
> Nadiya: [Shrugging] Earlier, they did not allow us to use the washroom, now we can...
> Subia: Sometimes, if a good mistress understands that we are outsiders and very poor, then we have even managed to get a raise – if the mistress is stubborn, it is not possible.

Subia and a smaller group of women involved in the union had begun utilising their newfound networks to mobilise in direct opposition to intense exploitative conditions of domestic work in the city. Indeed, while some of the women had been able to negotiate with their employers for standardised pay and working conditions, most recognised the partiality and individual nature of these demands; one woman had managed to negotiate one day off per week, while another was struggling to earn enough to feed her children. Both Subia and others accepted that these were conditions of work and life not unique to domestic work, the problem was one facing most migrants in the city. When I asked Nadiya if they had considered working in a different sector, she remarked, 'Well, they have fixed government holidays, proper timetables, their [pension] is subtracted from their salary and at least fixed standards for salary – other benefits too, I believe,' while Subia interjected to note that the union had made connections with other worker groups across the city and were aware of the difficulties elsewhere.

If we get a factory job ... well and good ... in a factory that is good and pays well – we are ready to work hard. But there is that garment factory we met with where they are also clamouring for a proper salary – we just had a meeting regarding that ... for us women no matter where we work, it will be a struggle.

It was clear that the domestic workers' union was shifting beyond the narrow education-based remit that was intended by the NGO, forging links and unruly connections with other social forces in the city and building oppositional movement in the centre of elite Gurgaon. One afternoon I was called urgently by Subia to come to Nadiya's small windowless home in Sikanderpur village. On arrival I was told that the previous week the women had been arrested for lying down on the road and obstructing the entry of a local police station. That day they had received notice on the union social media channel that a domestic worker had gone missing in a nearby condominium.

Nadiya explained:

We found her hanging from the fan in her room. The police said it was suicide, if it was a suicide ... why were her feet still on the chair below?... She was hanging there from her own scarf.... The knot was so loose she could have easily come undone ... the landlord had raped and killed her.

Both Nadiya and Subia knew this scene disturbingly well; it fell neatly into everyday lives saturated by prosaic acts of sexualised harassment and violence cautiously implied in so many of our conversations. Nadiya and Subia attempted to block the police from leaving the scene and subsequently organised a rally at the police gates where they were later beaten and arrested. Nadiya said, 'It is because of the union that we come to know these things.'

Subia had recently physically confronted her neighbour who had been violently beating his wife for months. She had been reluctant to intervene in the private matters of her neighbours for months but after speaking with neighbours was convinced to intervene. Subia organised for the woman to stay elsewhere and blocked the man in his room while she convinced the police to come to the house. Subia noted, '[The policeman] told him that he had no right to get drunk with the money that his wife had brought home through hard labour, while he sat there doing nothing.' With evident delight she remarked that the policeman ridiculed the violent man. 'He doesn't dare meet my eyes these days.... My husband [tells] me don't go looking for trouble, but I tell him, it's all right good will come out of it.... I always consult my sisters from the union before I take any step.'

Subia and Nadiya's interventions into the everyday subjugations of migrant domestic workers in the city, their willingness to fight back against gender-based violence in the neighbourhood, formed part of a diversity of tactics – from physical confrontations to mutual support – engaged in by the union that frequently exceeded the remit of the NGO. The union was fundamentally a social space, providing the women with a fixed terrain upon which they could mobilise skills and knowledge developed in 'different worlds', build connections with other marginalised groups and make claims to a different kind of life incarnated by stretched lives of migration, exploitation and empowerment across fragmented geographies. Crucially, like the subaltern cosmopolitanisms described elsewhere, the activities of the GKS members are not solely attributable to the bounded and territorialised particularities of Gurgaon per se, but rather speak to a politics ignited through movement and marginality across rural–urban landscapes, now settled within the precarious conditions of Gurgaon's worker neighbourhoods.

In my final visit to Subia's small one-room home in Sikanderpur, I asked her what it was that motivated her to take collective action with the GKS women despite her family's frequent pleas for her to avoid the group and the significant stress it appeared to place on her time; she was resolute in her participation:

> I work here only. One day I will leave this place, I want to create a better atmosphere for those who are going to come after me. If we could fix proper wages for them, then they will work well and we can achieve a sense of unity in all of us. This will be important for when we are in trouble. If the help is being beaten up by the master, or if she is falsely accused of theft by her mistress then people can stand together against them. We don't have any of our own people here. We need a support system to live here. I think then that I should stay associated with this – so that when trouble comes, I have this group standing up for me.... I've worked hard to come here and I want to go to better places.

The political demands of migrant domestic workers in Gurgaon are not demands particularly upon the state for citizenship rights, as discussed in Rina Agarwala's fantastic study of construction and *bidi* worker movements elsewhere in India.[11] Indeed, the idea of 'citizenship' for many of my interlocutors was strained by a structural out-of-placeness – engineered through the tenement system – that placed those kinds of rights somewhere and sometime else. Rather, the demands of the workers – particularly as they articulated through GKS – were directed against employers for workers' rights and landlords for basic rights to daily reproduction. And yet, the workers were not primarily motivated to the here-and-now of the city, nor bound to the territorial spatialities prominently discussed at length within subaltern urbanist literature. Subia is well aware that her union's collective organising is partial, a small win may involve forcing an employer to pay back stolen wages or file a police report against exploitation. Some of this was counteracted by a deeply precarious and often violent vulnerability in the city. It is important to appreciate the extent to which Gurgaon offers merely one stop in a lifetime of uncertainty, flux and movement for many labour migrants. Groups like GKS are expressions of cumulative experiences in labour, neighbourhood and household organising across multiple dislocated spaces.

Indeed, migrant working-class women's politics can be thought of as informed by translocal movements and connections momentarily fixed in the everyday relations of the city.[12] Here I am borrowing from David Featherstone's discussion on the translocal circuits of black activism and thought, forged through encounters that 'can exceed and refuse the obviousness of national spaces'.[13] Subia's movements are not transnational; nevertheless, her political thought and activity refuses the bounded and contested territorialities of the city. Subia narrates her political demands through appeal to a future-oriented imaginary of place in the city, her remarks are temporally disjunctive, skipping from the present to the future and back to the present tense, they imagine a sense of unity for all domestic workers but not necessarily for her and not necessarily today. When Subia makes a demand for 'a sense of unity in all of us', she is conjuring up what Doreen Massey termed an 'extroverted' sense of place,[14] speculative and tentative, structured across multiple times, bodies and spaces.

AZADIPLEX

On 10 February 2014, 2,000 workers at auto-parts factory Azadiplex, in Gurgaon's IMT Manesar industrial estate, arrived for work and refused to enter the factory. The workers demanded permanent contracts and wage increases from 5,800 rupees to the state minimum wage of 8,100 rupees.

The following day the company attempted to prevent a repeat of the strike by ordering the bus drivers – who ferry workers from the city's tenements to the industrial estate – to drive directly into the factory premises. The Azadiplex workers refused to stay on the bus and marched from the highway two and a half miles across the industrial estate's wide avenues to the factory gates. Seventy per cent of workers at Azadiplex – that build speedometers and wire harnessing for the city's automobile industry – are women, 80 per cent are hired on casual contracts through a network of subcontracting agencies. The Azadiplex strike was entirely illegal, there was neither a union registered to the factory nor an organisation representing the workers; this was an entirely wildcat action. After three days on strike, the company relented and agreed to increase all wages by 1,000 rupees and institute double pay for all overtime.

Sonu, introduced at the outset of the chapter, was a prominent figure in the Azadiplex strikes. In her late twenties, Sonu is originally from the neighbouring state of Rajasthan and moved to Gurgaon in her late teens along with her parents and older sister Varsha who also worked at the plant. Sonu explains:

> The reason was that if you complete three months in the company, you're supposed to be through the company ... become permanent that is. That's how it works in other companies ... within three or six months you get to be permanent. In [Azadiplex] there was nothing like that you could neither get to be permanent, nor get a bonus or even a raise ... this is why we had to go on a strike.

Sonu's sister Varsha, who also worked at the plant, explained the gender division of labour on the shop-floor: 'Men are nearly all in lockset and quality checking – women do most of the actual work.' Feminised assembly-line roles are waged at 5,800 rupees per month, masculinised checking roles are waged at 7,000 rupees per month. Not only are all Azadiplex workers precariously employed with low, unstable wages, but the women workers, who carry out the lion's share of the productive labour, also earn significantly less than their male colleagues. This division of value was not one reluctantly accepted by the workforce, as Varsha was keen to highlight: 'Women [not only] do much more work than men, [but] women [also] do better quality work than men, are more sincere with their work.... Men just have fun.' Nodding, Sonu remarked that 'girls ought to get [paid] as much as boys do! When boys work, they make a mess of it – one of the parts falls here, another there, one of the parts left-out ... they work carelessly. Women actually work hard and sincerely!'

The resolution between Azadiplex management and the workers was short-lived. After six months without implementation of the promised wage increase, the women embarked on a second strike. On 12 September 2014, 200 women workers stood at the assembly line and refused to start production until the pay increase was implemented. The following day the women obstructed the factory gates blocking materials from entering the factory. The police responded by beating the workers away from the gates. After being forced out of the factory by the police, the workers constructed a protest camp at the factory gates, refusing to enter the factory or return home.

As detailed in Chapter 5, dominant narratives of migrant labourers in the contemporary Indian city have emphasised the deep precarity of working conditions, hostility of urban living conditions and constancy of migration and flux. This series of vulnerabilities, we are told, informs a weakening of the collective and associational bonds required for the leverage of workers' power. Women workers are viewed as doubly vulnerable, placed in the most precarious forms of labour and structurally subjugated by patriarchal codes that impute moral worth to women who refuse 'outside' work and remain in the home. Together capitalist and patriarchal exploitation conjoin to produce the seemingly unmovable weight of exploitation placed on the migrant woman worker.

With this in mind, while the Azadiplex workers' actions are somewhat characteristic of industrial struggles the world over, that they were taking place in the post-industrial moment, in Gurgaon India's showcase neoliberal city, and led by migrant women is significant. I enquired with Sonu how she felt about staying at the camp all night and day. This after all was the first time in IMT Manesar's history that women workers had engaged in such a public political struggle. She remarked:

> For those twelve days, we had been right in front of the company gates.... The company had set goons on us to get us out of the way [but] even throughout the night, the women stayed. [Locals] got drunk and wandered around us [but] we created this entire ruckus for them and they disappeared. [The company] had tightened the security a lot – the police were around twenty-four hours ... [but] in the hot sun, at nights we stuck together.

Throughout the strike, the company's contractors had made extensive appeals to the families of the workers to, as one contractor put it to me, 'get their daughters home and off the streets'. The camp was the subject of violent attacks from both police, security guards and local 'drunks' wandering around at night. Sonu was undeterred.

> Honestly, fear had long gone, almost completely gone by the fifth day. We did not care for our jobs. I really did not care if I was fired, but I did think that those of my friends who remain after me must get their rightful due [and] I still think this way.... All of our families had said that there's no need for a strike. Either you work or you return home. I had 300 girls watching my back and at least 100 guys too. Seeing all that, who wants to give up such a long battle and return home?

The Azadiplex women articulated their struggles as a demand to stay put, and like Subia previously, to control the conditions of futures of work. Mobilising a language of unity (*ekta*) the Azadiplex women's discourses evoke a sense of potential place within lifetimes of certain work. In conversation with Sonu and Varsha, I asked why workers at other surrounding plants had not been willing or capable to participate in wildcat strikes like those in Azadiplex. What was special about Azadiplex? Sonu was quick to respond. 'Azadiplex is very different. It's all women here. There are no men. This company is running thanks to its women.' Thinking that perhaps I had not expressed myself properly, I suggested that even if there were a lot of women employed at the plant, what was it about Azadiplex that led the women to strike? Sonu remarked: 'Well ... the girls are different here. If any trouble happens, they are the first to step forward. This is special at Azadiplex, we have unity.'

After twelve days on strike, the company agreed to allow all workers back into the factory, promising another wage increase, festival holidays while fifteen women were promised permanent contracts. The two-week strike cost the company 60 million rupees in revenue and, disrupting IMT Manesar's just-in-time auto-supply chain, prompted key vendors to switch their supply to other plants. Remarkably, against a backdrop of highly precarious, structurally weak labour relations, non-unionised temporary female workers managed to secure concessions on nearly all demands made on the factory management.

> When we jammed the road, the police had attacked one or two girls with lathis. But we remained sitting on the road, jamming the way. [Then] at last, there was a hearing ... the head of HR said that I will take the women back, but ten of them I won't.... Gradually, it became nine days on strike – more and more women came forward.... On the

ninth day, men and women workers from [the other two factories in the complex] also came forward.

As the Azadiplex factory sits at the corner of one of IMT Manesar's main arterial avenues that lead executives and buyers up to the Maruti Suzuki plant, the public character of the Azadiplex camp was particularly provocative. News of the camp spread to activists and students in Delhi (including me) who made daily visits to the camp, while workers from neighbouring villages offered facilities for the women to take a rest and wash. At the camp the female workforce freely mixed with each other along with male workers, visitors and passers-by, breaking with hegemonic disciplining of the spatio-temporality of the factory, where women were segregated not only from male workers on the shopfloor, canteen and company buses but also from each other. In this regard, the Azadiplex workers broke from the moral code of the factory and urban village that bind women to the private and domestic realms; here, at the heart of Gurgaon's premier industrial estate, migrant women asserted their oppositional politics in full view.

Dipu, a twenty-year-old worker at Azadiplex, explained that she was soon to be married back in West Bengal so was trying to experience 'as much freedom as possible' before her return. I asked Dipu about the protest camp, of her experience sleeping out on the side of the road throughout the night. She remarked:

> The strike was not uncomfortable – the problem was the company. They cut off our water supply so we had to bring in provisions from elsewhere, and the police, they harassed us – they took the side of the management and when we blocked the road they beat us.... This was a fight, these things happen. My salary was not going to be increased and conditions [at the factory] were very bad so I thought we should strike. We knew about other factories ... we speak to sisters, mothers, friends, neighbours, so we knew our conditions were bad.

Much to the seeming annoyance of her elderly auntie who sat with us, there was a sense in the joyful way in which she recounted the camp, that Dipu revelled in the relative freedoms waged factory work had allowed. Sonu and Dipu's repeated assertion that the strike was about entering the workplace on one's 'own terms' speaks to the will of many women at the plant to control the terms of their labour, a control which, like the previous chapter outlined, stands in contrast to the conditions under which many women enter into waged and formal work.

Sonu too felt vindicated: 'They gave in. We got our solution!' The women re-entered the factory with a renewed sense of solidarity. When later that year the Diwali bonus was not paid, Sonu locked the HR manager in his office and organised a walk-out of a hundred Azadiplex workers. In contrast with discourses that characterise female workers as docile and deferent and prefigure subaltern women as passive victims of exploitative practices, the workers at Azadiplex appropriated the fixed space of the tenements, factory shopfloor and industrial estate to build nascent horizontal gender- and class-based political praxis against the precarious conditions of work and life in Gurgaon.

Returning Home

Six months after our last meeting, Sonu invited me to visit her tenement home in an informally plotted neighbourhood in Khandsa, central Gurgaon. It had been one year since the Azadiplex strike and upon arriving at Sonu's room, she revealed that she no longer worked at the plant: 'I was sacked. My mother was very sick in September, I told them I had to take care of my mother for one week, when I returned they refused to take me back. My husband told me I should just accept it.' To Sonu's evident discomfort, her husband interjected to explain that Sonu, now pregnant, would have had to leave the plant sooner or later anyway.

The Sonu I met that day was altogether different to the one rallying women in Kamla Nehru park or from our previous meetings in Gurgaon. Her dismissal from the factory had withdrawn her from the collective social realm iteratively developed at work.

> I miss the work, I miss my sisters – I worked there for six years, and to be honest, it's boring here. I miss the tea breaks, the lunch breaks and chatting with friends – these days after my husband leaves in the morning I stay here in my room, I'm so bored.

The contested social space of the Azadiplex shopfloor, and the avenues of IMT Manesar that Sonu and her co-workers had successfully shaped to their advantage, seemed a distant world to daily life here in the neighbourhood. 'Staying here you get involved in all this neighbourhood gossip, which I don't like. I go over to my mother's room to hide from it all.' Sonu was clearly nostalgic for her time in the factory and resented her movement from being a housewife-worker to a housewife spatially bound to the neighbourhood. Here the workplace, and not the much-celebrated neighbourhood, attained a certain social importance. It is within the workplace that practices of social reproduction, care, conviviality, encounter and transformation took place. For the Azadiplex women, ties to responsibilities and labours of social reproduction and the home, their inability to engage in the hypermobility that characterises men's labour conditions imbued the workplace with a heightened significance that informed strategies of unity and staying put.

Sonu's return to life as a housewife reminds us of the precarious and uncertain character of migrant women's politics in the contemporary city. A sudden illness, a household emergency and unemployed relative, and gendered social reproductive demands pull migrant women back to the household.

Rokaplex

Two months after the Azadiplex workers dismantled their protest camp and returned to work, another wildcat action led by a predominately female workforce of an auto-components plant began on the other side of IMT Manesar. On 1 November 2014, 350 contract workers were immediately dismissed from work at the Rokaplex plant. Rokaplex is a subsidiary of a Japanese conglomerate that manufactures wiring harnesses, switches and printed circuit boards for Gurgaon's auto industries. The plant employs 500 employees on its assembly line, 350 employed through subcontracting firms. Like Azadiplex, Rokaplex's assembly line was predominately occupied by migrant women earning significantly less than the male checkers and supervisors. Like Azadiplex, at Rokaplex working-class labour is divided along gendered lines. On the morning of the 1 November, a notice was pinned to the canteen noticeboard:

> Due to lack of work in the company … it is necessary that all contract employees be removed, this is agreed with the union representatives … all contract workers will receive paid holiday between 3rd and 8th of November. Permanent employees will continue to be present on their respective tasks.

Two hundred and fifty workers immediately stopped production and sat at the production line effecting a factory occupation. By the evening the police violently cleared the factory of the workers.

Six months earlier, 350 contract workers and 125 permanent workers underwent a series of internal tool-downs and go-slows in order to force through the registration of a factory union. Collectively, the Rokaplex workforce funded a bribe for the labour department in order to push their registration through a highly bureaucratic union registration process. Throughout May, with the support of the contract workers, the newly formed union campaigned for the company to bring contract workers in-house, initiating a month-long slowdown in production at the plant. By August the management came to an agreement with the union to institute a wage increase of 10,000 rupees for permanent workers and 3,000 rupees over three years for contract workers. The coalescence of the Rokaplex workers' political demands around the formation of a union marks a significant distinction between the Rokaplex and Azadiplex struggles. The Azadiplex workers, who operated completely independent of any external institutional or legally bound body, were able to both maintain a level of unity across shopfloor workers and flexibly manoeuvre their practices and demands independent of sluggish and bureaucratic processes. The intervention of the union in the Rokaplex dispute came to – unexpectantly – divide the workforce, between a unionised male minority and a non-unionised female majority.

Two days after their dismissal from the factory, 350 workers set up a protest camp at the factory gates demanding their immediate reinstatement; the workers were not calling for money, better conditions or permanent contracts, they were demanding that the company give their jobs back. I visited the camp regularly throughout its duration. Unlike Azadiplex, the Rokaplex camp was tucked away in the far northern corner of the estate, far away from the arterial avenues and swathes of workers walking to work in the mornings. Around 300 women sat under the marquee in their Rokaplex uniforms; each day they would assembly outside the tent and ceremonially march 100 yards toward the factory gates where the police would arm up ready for battle. This routine was repeated daily. Union leaders and workers from neighbouring factories would visit the camp to give stirring speeches of solidarity much to the ire and exhaustion of those at the camp. While the camp operated to break down the spatio-temporal grip of life's work, fashioning out a space on the side of the road for women's collective participation, conditions at the camp were not comfortable, the camp was surveyed at all times by contractors standing on the opposite side of the road, while the company had paid a cameraman to film the workers. At the protest camp, Shilpa, a middle-aged assembly-line worker from Uttarakhand, remarked:

> At first it was not great, we were outside and it was winter so it was very cold. But we came to know each other, other workers, night-shift workers that we'd never met before, we began listening to each other, and helping each other, we had so much time to sit ... this was important.

Like the Azadiplex strike, the Rokaplex protest camp was at times jovial – the evenings were full of conversation and laughter, young students made the journey from Delhi to sit and listen to the speeches, political groups of different persuasions hung out having discussions on strategy, workers' children ran around the tent, food was shared and despite the conditions, spirits were high. The camp fundamentally expressed a spatial and temporal provocation. Sat square in front of the factory gates, the Rokaplex camp was a demand to be recognised. The camp was equally a reclamation of the deeply masculinised public space of the city and a refusal of the gendered labours of the household. After all, the protest was not only confronting the company, but it also withdrew labour from the tenement households. The camp represented an opportunity to retake control of the social space of the industrial estate and reclaim time from the household. In this way the camp formed part of an alternative cartographic repertoire of a subaltern politics that marks a presence of migrants in the city within a material and discursive milieu that renders them, and particularly women, indiscernible.

On 26 December 2014, the Rokaplex protest camp was violently torn down by boys from local landowning families in nearby Aliyar village. That it was boys from the local village that tore down the camp was perhaps no surprise. For weeks they had been harassing the workers during the evening, while the *gram panchayat* had directly appealed to the management and local police to remove the camp from the streets, declaring the presence of women sitting all night on the open roads as distasteful and immoral. In the aftermath of the camp's destruction, the protest moved off the streets of IMT Manesar, the workers returned home. Soon after, in order to stave off legal action taken by the workers, Rokaplex offered the 350 contract workers 25,000 rupees each in compensation. Most of the workers took the compensation. Shilpa was one of the thirty workers who refused the compensation and continued with legal action.

LIFETIMES OF WORK

'I hate weddings, I don't go to them,' Shilpa remarked as two young men struggled to erect a wedding gazebo at the entrance to her village on the side of the NH8 highway. I had come to meet Shilpa in her small tenement room in a workers' village on the outskirts of the city. Shilpa had been working through a contractor at Rokaplex since 2011. She had originally moved to Gurgaon alone with her brother-in-law and sister and was keen to distinguish herself from those women whose labour market decisions were mediated by alcoholic husbands or abject poverty. For Shilpa it was ostensibly the unjust conditions of her unwaged household labour within the home that compelled her to migrate from the village to the city. Importantly, it was these experiences that shaped her willingness to engage in the political action at the plant.

> I come from a family that is open-minded but after marriage I had to live with my in-laws, and it was very, very controlling, I had to get out of there, I could not stay in the home all the time.... I couldn't bear it.... I felt strongly that I had to leave.... These days women are getting out of the home because the husband ... wastes all their money on alcohol, so they have to go out and get a job to support their families ... for me, I was financially stable, but I was not psychologically stable, I could not live there....

Echoing sentiments made by Subia, Nadiya and Sonu previously, Shilpa's remarks acutely highlight the terms through which household labour conditions the willingness of migrant women to, against great odds, engage politically in the city. Migrant working-class women's subaltern cosmopolitanism, their geographies of connection, mobility and transfer are deeply affected by gendered demands on their labour within the home. What is more, Shilpa expresses her experiences of social reproductive work in the home as *work* yet work that can neither provide the meritocratic promise of the factory, nor the platform to 'speak up' and remedy the conditions of her subordination.

> Inside [at home], you come into a new family and there is only so much you can do. There's no training, you cannot progress, you just have to accept it. But in the company, you get training and then at some point you understand and you become the equal of that person that taught you. At home, your mother-in-law is always your boss, you can't

change anything, you have to put up with things that you can't do much about, no chances or choices ... when you're inside you behave like this [gesturing to the room around her], but outside you have eight hours, and you can behave differently....

Shilpa's attitude towards 'outside' work in part explains why it was so important to her, and her co-workers, that she retained employment at Rokaplex. For Shilpa, and indeed many workers at the plant, the workplace and the collective sociality developed within it was a far cry from the isolation and certainty of household work both in the tenement and home village. During our many conversations over the course of my field research, Shilpa was always keen to explain her transition from a quiet, compliant housewife to Shilpa *didi*, the 'Rokaplex lady':

> When I first joined the factory, at first I worked on my own ... most people work in a group, but I worked alone. I had a reputation for being nice and submissive, but then the strike began ... there was a time, at the beginning ... one of the company drivers [assaulted] a woman, I told him you can't do this to us, look how many of us there are. That's when the men started to take me seriously.

In part this, according to Shilpa, is what made the Rokaplex strike so notorious, garnering attention from activists and students in Delhi and the local and national press. Shilpa noted that the assumption of women's docility was both 'condescending' and what spurred women workers on to take struggles forward: 'No one thought we could come together like this.'

During my afternoon at Shilpa's home, her brother-in-law who had a permanent contract and as such remained working at the plant, intermittently came to sit with us. It seemed jarring to me at first to listen to Shilpa's righteous anger at the Azadiplex management in conjunction with the ambivalent and matter-of-fact tones of her brother-in-law. I was interested in what was motivating Shilpa's engagement in what would certainly be a long, arduous litigation.

> I don't want to have to start from scratch, there is a lot of pressure on the factory, [so] I think it is worth fighting for. All the companies here have a policy of only hiring women under the age of 25 ... they just look at your face and decide.... My family are putting a lot of pressure on me ... my mother-in-law doesn't know what lies outside the door.... But there is no guarantee that if I go to the next work I won't be treated exactly the same, I could have a lifetime like this.

Shilpa's continued participation in the legal action was in short not a demand to Rokaplex in particular. Like the struggles previously mentioned, Shilpa participated in the legal case ostensibly to disrupt a 'lifetime' of certain drudgery whether at the workplace or the household.

Conclusion

The struggles detailed in this chapter may seem fairly prosaic events, the kind that take place every day in cities the world over. Nevertheless, the presence of migrant women engaging in neighbourhood organising, workplace occupations, roadside protest camps in India's showpiece neoliberal city, the vanguard of a new post-industrial urbanism is significant. The women worker's struggle, not least a publicly discernible strike, has no place in the material and discursive repertoire that has come to define 'world-class', 'neoliberal' or even the 'subaltern' city. The struggles detailed here draw attention to the manner in which gendered demands, labours and translocal connections shape attendant forms of urban politics.

Subia, Nadiya, Sonu and Shilpa each invoked a set of political demands and practices that were informed by translocal geographies of migration and gendered work and transcend the immediate spatiality and temporality of their everyday lives. In order to uncover the geographies of those locked into structural conditions that always already render them placeless and exploited requires attention to quite different imaginaries and epistemologies of the city. Borrowing from Katherine McKittrick's work, I view these as 'heterogeneous, alterable political sites'[15] that challenge the methodological city-ism of territorial warfare, slum politics, land-based dispossessions and reclamations. And yet, as discussed in the previous chapter, have their roots in a relational politics with rents-wages-capital turned through the tenements.

The camp, tenement, bus, roadside and assembly line come to form these material sites in Gurgaon, but there are also quite evidently intangible sites at play too. When Subia makes a demand for 'a sense of unity in all of us', when Nadiya discusses her newly recognised freedoms to 'leave', when Sonu yearns for the class collectivities of the workplace, and when Shilpa expresses her struggles via the tortures of household labour, they are each drawing out the deeply relational, shifting geographies of work in the contemporary city that belie grounding to one particular site or space. Tentative class consciousness forms through a shared understanding of collective interests, the 'unity' generated at both sites of production and reproduction, and through the gendered unevenness of labour's geographies.

Crucially each of these struggles makes demands for emplacement that recognises the partiality of their position within broader structures of violence and abstraction. This place, while transtemporal, is equally uncertain and contingent. The struggles narrated here denote a mode of contingent political practice that seeks to appropriate and reclaim stretched and fragmented spaces of everyday exploitation and immiseration, enacting forms of radical gendered class-based difference against the prosaic violence of the city. These are indiscernible and aporetic practices, demands for a kind of urban life that is temporally delayed, speculatively placed in the future. This subaltern place is unspeakable and certainly unheard of because it bears no reference to the immediate aesthetics or materialities of the urban that binds political demands of the subaltern to territorially defined spaces.

In the previous chapters I have explored the frontiering work of planners, developers, agrarian peasants and bureaucrats to transform the hinterlands of New Delhi into a new vanguard of neoliberal urbanisation. These frontiers are the internal foundations of the city, and as we have seen, these foundations are deeply troubled. By placing the fortunes of the city's social and economic reproduction in the hands of land brokers, bureaucrats and villagers, the state's attempts to build and maintain a global city are frequently disrupted and upended. In this chapter I have considered the political practices and imaginaries of Gurgaon's migrant working classes. As permanent visitors to the city, the politics of female labour migrants emerges from fraught conditions of marginality in the city discussed in Chapter 5 but is equally informed by stretched lives, untethered to the specificities and fixities of place.

Transporting knowledge, experiences, strategies and vocabularies across the length and breadth of the country, I have sought to highlight the *subaltern cosmopolitanism* of these struggles, one that gives voice to peculiar, *extroverted* claims to a dignified life across times and spaces. Crucially, the stories told in this chapter are not incidental to the city. No doubt the collective organising and direct actions detailed here are disruptive to business as usual in Gurgaon. Industrialists, real estate developers and upper-class residents have all decried the incidence of working-class revolt that have sporadically swept across the country since the Maruti Suzuki strikes in 2011. With each turn, corporate and political elites have sought to clamp down on the freedoms and conditions of Gurgaon's migrant working-class residents, spatially reorienting the geographies of production and social reproduction in the city – the tenements, workplaces, highways and transit corridors – in response to the geographies of migrant revolt. As Andy Herod has argued, workers produce geographies too.[16] In Gurgaon, the very spaces of working-class exploitation and control – the industrial estate, tenement, masters' home – have been turned on their heads and strike fear into the heart of the agrarian city.

NOTES

1. Gidwani, 'Subaltern Cosmopolitanism'; Featherstone, 'Black Internationalism'.
2. See also Agarwala, *Informal Labour*; Hill, 'India: The Self Employed Women's Association'; Ray, *Fields of Protest*.
3. Roy, *Beyond Belief*.
4. Chatterjee, *Are India's Cities Bourgeois*.
5. Roy, 'Slumdog Cities'.
6. Ibid., 224.
7. Benjamin, 'Occupancy Urbanism'; Bayat, 'From "Dangerous Classes" to "Quiet Rebels"'; Holston, 'Insurgent Citizenship'; Ghertner, *Rule by Aesthetics*; Chatterjee, *The Politics of the Governed*.
8. Srivastava, *Entangled Urbanism*.
9. Mbembé, 'Aesthetics of Superfluity'.
10. Featherstone, 'Black Internationalism', 1408.
11. Agarwala, *Informal Labor*.
12. See also Hill, 'India: The Self Employed Women's Association'.
13. Featherstone, 'Black Internationalism'.
14. Massey, *Space, Place, and Gender*.
15. McKittrick, *Demonic Grounds*, 59.
16. Herod, *Labor Geographies*.

BIBLIOGRAPHY

Agarwala, Rina. *Informal Labor, Formal Politics, and Dignified Discontent in India*. New York: Cambridge University Press, 2013.

Bayat, Asef. 'From "Dangerous Classes" to "Quiet Rebels": Politics of the Urban Subaltern in the Global South'. *International Sociology* 15, no. 3 (2000): 533–57.

Benjamin, Solomon. 'Occupancy Urbanism: Radicalizing Politics and Economy beyond Policy and Programs'. *International Journal of Urban and Regional Research* 32, no. 3 (2008): 719–29.

Chatterjee, Partha. *Are Indian Cities Becoming Bourgeois At Last? Body City-Sitting Contemporary Culture in India.* Delhi: Tulika Books, 2003.

———. *The Politics of the Governed: Reflections on Popular Politics in Most of the World.* New York: Columbia University Press, 2004.

Featherstone, David. 'Black Internationalism, Subaltern Cosmopolitanism, and the Spatial Politics of Antifascism'. *Annals of the Association of American Geographers* 103, no. 6 (2013): 1406–20.

Ghertner, D. Asher. *Rule by Aesthetics: World-Class City Making in Delhi.* New York: Oxford University Press, 2015.

Gidwani, Vinay K. 'Subaltern Cosmopolitanism as Politics'. *Antipode* 38, no. 1 (2006): 7–21.

Herod, Andrew. *Labor Geographies: Workers and the Landscapes of Capitalism.* New York: Guilford Press, 2001.

Hill, E. 'India: The Self Employed Women's Association and Autonomous Organizing'. In *Women and Labour Organizing in Asia*, edited by Kaye Broadbent and Michele Ford, 133–53. London: Routledge, 2007.

Holston, James. 'Insurgent Citizenship in an Era of Global Urban Peripheries'. *City and Society* 21, no. 2 (2009): 245–67.

Massey, Doreen B. *Space, Place, and Gender.* Minneapolis: University of Minnesota Press, 1994.

Mbembé, J.-A. 'Aesthetics of Superfluity'. *Public Culture* 16, no. 3 (2004): 373–405.

McKittrick, K. *Demonic Grounds: Black Women and the Cartographies of Struggle.* Minneapolis: University of Minnesota Press, 2006.

Ray, R. *Fields of Protest: Women's Movements in India.* Minneapolis: University of Minnesota Press, 2000.

Roy, Ananya. 'Dis/Possessive Collectivism: Property and Personhood at City's End'. *Geoforum* 80, no. 1 (2017): A1–11.

———. 'Slumdog Cities: Rethinking Subaltern Urbanism'. *International Journal of Urban and Regional Research* 35, no. 2 (2011): 223–38.

Roy, Srirupa. *Beyond Belief: India and the Politics of Postcolonial Nationalism.* Durham; London: Duke University Press, 2007.

Srivastava, S. *Entangled Urbanism: Slum, Gated Community and Shopping Mall in Delhi and Gurgaon.* OUP Catalogue, 2014.

Conclusion
Urban Limits

This book has sought to explore processes of agrarian city-making on India's urban frontier. Gurgaon, like many peri-urban developments that have sprung up since the end of the twentieth century, has been developed through imaginative, calculative and political technologies that have been deployed to reorganise the countryside for real estate and industrial accumulation. As the narrative goes, Gurgaon's rapid ascendance as the figurehead for a 'new urban India', where private urban development and governance models cleanly capture mobile capital, has produced space for a hegemonic urban upper and middle class, signalling India's arrival at a global (capitalist) stage. This book has sought to complicate this well-run narrative. Since the early 1980s, Gurgaon's urbanisation has relied upon a terse remediation of agrarian spaces, institutions, actors and histories. As I have argued across this book, this project has depended upon the reproduction of a territorialised class alliance between capitalists, state institutions and so-called 'dominant' agrarian caste communities. It is this alliance that not only willingly opens and converts rural land into urban real estate but also manages the distribution and circulation of rents, wages and capital that underpin industrial accumulation.

This class composition was irrevocably shaped by uneven agrarian development in the colonial and post-colonial periods and are a result of hegemonic struggles engaged in by capital to forge the social and political conditions for its expansion into the countryside. This of course comes at a cost. Across this book I have sought to explore the subalternity of the frontier: the repurposing of state development agendas, the blockages in the 'open field' of capital circulation, the quiet delay and subversion of bureaucratic property-making and the disorderly class politics threatening the stability of the city's agrarian–urban alliances. Subalternity here describes unstable hegemonic alliances, not sociological or spatial identities. In this sense, many enrolled at the frontier are not 'the subaltern' classically defined. The first half of this book traces attempts led by landowner-cum-landlords and speculators to form part of a neo-middle class embedded in the urban economy, attempts not only marked by a structural subordination to global capitalist actors but also ones which are terse, incomplete and for some will inevitably fail. The final half of the book explores the geographies of actors more proximate to the identity-position and spatialities of 'the subaltern' but whom I think more productively as simply the working class. And yet here too, as I discussed, it is within the differentiated gender migration conditions of working-class exploitation that alternative worlds are attempted and forged. The subalternity I have explored in this book is primarily a troubling relation of difference that coheres within the centres of power. The subaltern is relational, always defined in relation to the conjunctural forces of domination that seek to master, dominate and subsume it. Analysing subalternity requires attention to both practices that seek to fashion dominated groups, places, subjects into a desired object, and the profoundly conjunctural practices of those groups seeking to subvert domination, rationalisation and mastery. Above all it requires attention to an uncertain dialectical relation that internally coheres within hegemonic social relations, the 'subaltern' and 'elite' are not stable, foundational forms but relations wrought through conjunctural historical material relations.

This hegemonic re-composition from the 1980s compelled agrarian cultivating castes, predominately the Jats and Ahirs, to implicate themselves, their lands and institutions into state projects of land speculation, territorial calculation and mapping, housing development and industrial labour management. In doing so, of course, it set the terms of industrial and urban development within the vernacular of agrarian class and caste politics, allowing for the disturbance and alteration of abstract plans and desires of the state. Amid this hegemonic settlement quite other logics of capitalist totalisation have been deployed, characterised by compromise, uncertainty and opacity. By hitching urban development to agrarian vernacular, agrarian city-making equally produced spaces within which working-class struggles could spill out and disrupt complicated networks of rent, wages and agrarian territorial power that sustain circulations of capital through the city.

Throughout this period, as I hope the book has been able to demonstrate, this hegemonic class compositions has enlisted the agrarian world into city-making; writing urban accumulation in the grammar of the village in ways that are provisional and fraught with fractures. The promise of ascending real estate value and incorporation into a formal urban economy – a promise that has been the bedrock of not only Gurgaon's story but of the Indian state's 'India Shining' post-liberalisation campaign – one that compels agrarian society to throw themselves into city-making projects, was beginning to falter during the middle of initial fieldwork in the city. The real estate frenzy of the 2000s that supercharged land markets in Gurgaon slumped after the 2008 financial crisis and began to create significant trouble in the city by the mid-2010s. Real estate shares dropped concurrent to a global credit crunch and property prices across the country began falling by up to 20–30 per cent, precipitating as Llerena Searle's work has shown a dramatic rush by international corporate investors to 'exit' as quickly as possible.[1] In Gurgaon, the real estate downturn was subtended by a series of more local crises. Real estate firms, enthused by Haryana's unending potential to produce land value, had used pre-sale investments to jump-start new projects which, when corporate investment dried up, left middle-class buyers with disconnected and half-built residential developments. Completed projects suffered from an absence of demand, and land acquired for large-scale urban developments lay empty, frustrating those who were dispossessed or had negotiated equity partnerships premised upon future rental incomes. This slump in supply and demand, of course, fractured the speculative promise of real estate development which had, as Chapters 2 and 3 argued, implicated landowners into tentative projects of property-making on the frontier.

This real estate slump was appended by a series of land scandals, including a high-profile cash-for-land use change scandal implicating Congress Party officials and large development firms including DLF.[2] This political-economic conjuncture is subtended to by broader economic stagnation in both agricultural and urban sectors that in Gurgaon was gradually eating away at the legitimacy of the city's promise to agrarian classes and eroding the legitimacy of liberal politics more broadly. To compound these structural issues by the mid-2010s, Gurgaon was growing a reputation as a dysfunctional city and 'failed' urban experiment. Traffic jams, failed infrastructure, real estate scams and crime were fast outpacing narratives of urban modernity. A 2012 *Forbes India* article titled 'Gurgaon: How Not to Build a City' summed up the mood, decrying Gurgaon as 'a disaster, a horror story' symptomatic of a hapless state and greedy local builders.[3]

At this very conjuncture we see the rise of majoritarian politics and the electoral successes of Narendra Modi's right-wing Bharatiya Janata Party (BJP) at both the national level and in Haryana in 2014 built upon a coalition of urban middle classes and lower- and middle-caste peasants cultivated since the late 1990s.[4] The election of the BJP and their selection of Manohar Lal Khattar, a member of the far-right paramilitary Rashtriya Swayamsevak Sangh (RSS) group, as Haryana's first non-Jat chief minister since 1996 exploited a popular anti-corruption mood in Haryana, attributing economic stagnation to the Jat-led Congress Party officials, and in its place offering 'clean' economic development wedded to Hindu majoritarianism. The BJP's neoliberal developmental agenda, as numerous scholars have shown,[5] is hitched to a fascist identity politics that, amongst other things, asks 'dominant' agricultural caste communities in Haryana to think of themselves neither as *kisan*s (farmers), nor in caste terms as Jats or Ahirs, or in class terms, but as Hindus, bringing together the urban middle classes, bourgeoisie and the 'angry young men' excluded from urban formal economy.[6]

The BJP's promise of rapid economic developmentalism – characterised by untrammelled capital access to land and labour and mass infrastructure development programmes was short-lived. The government was unable to restructure the previous government's Right to Fair Compensation and Transparency in Land Acquisition, Rehabilitation and Resettlement Act, 2013, that is broadly viewed as a check on the power of the state to access cheap land by eminent domain, while Modi's 'Make In India' campaign, which aimed to produce 20 million jobs a year by deregulating scant labour protections, has been accompanied by a significant drop in manufacturing's share of national GDP, declining private investment and rising unemployment.

And so, my fieldwork in Gurgaon was marked by economic uncertainty, the declining reputation of the Gurgaon model, cracks in the hegemonic pacts built over the previous two decades and an emboldened Hindutva politics that latched onto the unfulfilled hopes of young men in particular. In 2016 Gurgaon was formally renamed Gurugram, a reference to upper-caste Hindu figure Guru Dronacharya who features in the Mahabharata and is said to have originated from the city. The renaming of Gurgaon is part of a broader cultural politics of 'Hinduisation', which the government and its supporters in the media have been all too keen to focus on amidst economic disarray. Stories of Haryana's notorious far-right Gau Raksha Dal (Cow Protector) groups that parole the highways inflicting brutal violence on Muslims and Dalits that they claim are transporting cow meat for sale became more common. This kind of far-right vigilantism is certainly not new to Haryana: in 2002 five Dalit men were lynched by a mob in a village near Jhajjar for allegedly skinning a cow. And yet, since the election of the BJP in the state, Haryana has emerged at the forefront of a Hindutva cover-up of economic disarray. In 2015 Khattar's government passed the Gauvansh Sanrakshan and Gaushamvardhan bill that bans the slaughter, sale, consumption and storage of cows, with up to a ten-year prison sentence, and established divisions of the police dedicated to 'cow protection'. And these kinds of far-right vigilantism are not the preserve of the countryside; in 2018 various Hindutva vigilante groups violently attacked the Muslim *namaaz* in a number of public places across Gurgaon. This forms part of a broader upsurge in the street politics of Hindutva outfits, what Christophe Jaffrelot has referred to as the 'saffronisation of the public sphere' where more spectacular programmes to ban beef, imprison dissenters and rewrite textbooks coincide with the more 'banal' exclusion of Muslims and minorities from jobs, housing and public spaces. This programme is directly pitched to the erstwhile dominant agrarian communities whose promised inclusion into urban modernity is rapidly fading.[7]

The surfacing of a far-right vigilante Hindutva politics in Gurgaon, while never a dominating factor in my fieldwork nevertheless quietly saturated my encounters and engagements. Time spent in the bureaucratic offices I explore in Chapter 4 was perhaps my most acute confrontation with Hindutva and everyday Islamophobic beliefs held by some of the actors in the office.[8] Ironically, given the levels of Islamophobia and casteist language within everyday discussions in the office, the work of the *patwari* is acutely dependent upon Muslim bureaucrats. The pre-Independence *jamabandi*s frequently required to substantiate ancestral property claims are written in Urdu. Every now and again, where a client or villager would need to provide evidence of an ancestral claim, we would make our way to the land record archives in an office sectioned off from Patwar Ghar. Here *patwari*s would make requests for translations, substituting their Islamophobia for quiet pleasantries. 'We have no issue with them,' a particularly Islamophobic bureaucrat remarked to me on one visit to the archives. 'These are not Mewatis, these are the good Muslims.' Elsewhere, as I discuss in chapter 3, Islamophobic discourse is routinely deployed by the local state to delegitimise property claims and enforce the state's territorial agenda. Indeed, conversely it is often the class and caste status of landowning Jats and Ahirs that substantiate ambiguous territorial claims. Finally, casteism and Islamophobia shape job access in the tenements and factories discussed in Chapter 5, leading many to adopt Hindu-sounding names as a measure of protection from the precarity of everyday life.[9] And yet, levels of voiced and actioned support for Hindutva politics across my fieldwork always appeared provisional, set at an awkward position against the cross-caste and even sometimes cross-religion kisan *bhaichara* (farmer brotherhood) that lubricated the work of producing property in the city.

For the migrant working classes of Gurgaon, the city's 'Hinduisation' has worsened an already hostile urban environment. Modi's flagship 'Make in India' campaign and catastrophic demonetisation policies have deepened the precarity of informalised industrial working classes, and when joined to the Hindutva programme, have extended the terms of marginalisation for Muslims and Dalits. Industrialists, factory management and tenement landlords were precisely the urban demographic spurred to mobilise quietly held Hindutva beliefs and support the transport of Modi's 'Gujarat model' to the centre.

The rise of Hindutva fascism in and around Gurgaon is specific to the socio-economic and spatial geographies of agrarian city-making on the urban frontier. That is, it can be viewed in part as a response to faltering material and ideological conditions that have enrolled landowners into arms with global capital and underwritten the procession of real estate and industrial capital into the countryside. To borrow from Don Kalb, this moment can be thought of as a countermovement against the integration of the agrarian world into highly uneven, precarious and speculative urban economies. If previously this land–rent–capital coalition was held together by caste-based politics, there has been an attempt to supplant the *kisan* with the Hindu, and the village with the nation. As I have sought to emphasise across this book capitalist projects on the urban frontier are fragile and tentative. They rely upon the mobilisation of uncertainty, the repurposing of agrarian institutions and property regimes and the rhythmic discipline of working-class disenfranchisement. The conjunctural arrangement of histories, property technologies, territories and labour is a conceit that always holds the possibility of breaking down. As I discussed in the Introduction, capitalist urbanisation at the frontier is constantly under threat from the subsumptions that simultaneously give it life.

SHIFTING COALITIONS

In 2018 Patwar Ghar was abuzz with news that Prime Minister Modi would be holding an official public rally in Gurgaon. The rally came in advance of the 2019 state and national elections, and under particularly challenging circumstances. Even as the BJP's cultural politics appeared unthreatened and catastrophic headline economic policies had yet to dent Modi's personal popularity, at a local level many of the government's big economic commitments – the promise to fast-track infrastructure development and jobs for local communities – had yet to materialise.[10] The continued mass rallies, protests and strikes led by Haryanvis calling for inclusion into OBC reservations, an inclusion that would provide greater access to public jobs – had been often violently rejected by Khattar's government. What is more, Gurgaon's ongoing real estate slump had been popularly attributed to the BJP's anti-corruption and implicit anti-landowner stance. I attended the rally that day with others from Patwar Ghar, eager to catch a glimpse of the prime minister in action. The rally was held in Sultanpur, a small village containing a large national park and bird sanctuary on the north side of the city. Sultanpur was chosen due to its proximity to the Kundli–Manesar–Palwal (KMP) Expressway that churns its way through the middle of the village. The 136-km so-called 'smart' highway that runs along the western periphery of Delhi-NCR had been held up for over a decade, and the BJP were keen to use highway trouble to put forward a strong developmental message. So, when Modi alighted from a helicopter at the back of the sparsely attended rally and took to the stage, he opted not perhaps surprisingly for Hindutva bravado but spoke rather of his developmental promise, to complete the highway, override delays attributed to the previous Congress government and bring economic prosperity to local people of the region. This was perhaps a quiet acknowledgement of the limits of the Hindutva programme amidst rising economic disarray, Modi's rally was an attempt to reform the older hegemonic coalition of *kisan*-powered development to get the old gang back together – an attempt that would soon be firmly rebutted.

Almost exactly two years later the KMP Expressway would become ground zero for perhaps the largest organised protests in India's history. In 2020 hundreds of thousands of farmers and agrarian workers from across India occupied and blocked points on the KMP Expressway in protest against three farm bills passed into law by the government in September of that year. The bills ostensibly seek to open up Indian agriculture to global agribusiness.

The three bills strip back minimum support prices (MSP) put in place in the 1960s to protect farmers from market fluctuations, remove regulations that had restricted contract farming and allow agribusiness to stockpile agricultural commodities. The bills were a full-frontal attack on the agrarian sector – a sector that while slowly declining economically retained significant social reproductive and cultural value among a broad section of north Indian society. The protestors for months had brought tractors onto the highways, establishing encampments along the road, in petrol stations and on railways lines on the route to Delhi, in an attempt to place a strategic stranglehold on the capital and force a full repeal of the bills.

The protests, which were originally led by farmers and farmer unions in Punjab, quickly spread across the country elsewhere and by 26 November 2020 over 250 million farmers and workers took part in one of the largest popular strikes in world history. Two months later, on 26 January, India's Republic Day, with a series of failed talks ongoing between farmer unions and the government and months of brutal violence and arbitrary detention inflicted upon farmers by the police, tens of thousands of protestors marched into Delhi with their tractors and, deviating from a route approved by the government, entered the Lal Qila (Red Fort), the symbolic monument to India's independence from colonial rule. Subsequent attacks from police to evict the protestors from Delhi saw thousands of farmers injured.

Despite historic tensions between Punjabi and Haryanvi farmers, between Jat landowners and Dalit farmworkers, and those keenly cultivated between Hindus and Muslims, the protests were notable for bringing together a wide subsection of an agrarian society.[11] The roadside protestors broached previous divisions through the establishment of 24/7 kitchens, free accommodation, cultural programmes, libraries and legal advice centres.[12] Indeed, while commonly conceived as a successor movement to the Jat reservation politics a few years previous support for the protests in Gurgaon and southern Haryana, areas with a higher proportion of Ahirs (in Gurgaon) and Muslim Meos (in Mewat) point to a broad-based support among agrarian communities in Haryana.[13] As Singh, Singh and Dhanda note, these 'vital infrastructures of mutual aid, care and collectivity are – in an otherwise highly stratified casteist patriarchal society – potentially transformational'.[14] While it is unlikely that these solidarities will entirely transform class positions and privileges structured between workers and farmers, dominant caste and Dalit communities, the camps provide a space where such transformation might begin.

In an essay in *Spectre*, Aditya Bahl notes that the roadside encampments that are stationed at border points along the infrastructural 'lifelines' connecting the capital to the countryside are commonly referred to by popular media and farmers as cthe borderc. For Bahl, this 'border' is not simply an expression of violent state exclusion of farmers from the capital – a border imposed – but more productively a border against, one produced through ongoing militant agrarian struggles towards making new worlds.[15] This border against is precisely what I witnessed some miles south in Rokaplex, and in tenements across the city. Both were ultimately shut down by the unrelenting violence of the state and pressure from local landowners, both struck at the heart of the hegemonic coalitions that upheld capitalist urbanisation in the region and both were brought together and sustained by elements of solidarity across the otherwise fortified social division. Both, finally, point to shifts and fractures in the bucolic alliance between corporate capital and agrarian propertied elites praised in K. P. Singh's origin story.

As recent scholarship has argued, the farmer protests in Punjab and Haryana must be understood not solely as a response to an agrarian crisis, characterised by sectoral decline and the threat of mass dispossession, but also of an urban crisis characterised by faltering promises of inclusion into urban formal economies and real-estate-led growth. This also, perhaps for the first time at this scale, demonstrates the provisional character of Hindutva class coalitions in north India. As Satendra Kumar argues, not only has the BJP been unable to deliver on their promise of urban employment – with highly precarious urban employment leading many to retain one foot in the village for their social reproduction – but majoritarian-fascist policies had a negative impact on the agrarian economy, driving Muslim and Dalit labourers out of the villages. In response, not only has there been a resurgence in cross-faith farmer coalitions, but as Kumar writes in 'Jats into Kisans', Jat men have begun to de-Hinduise, 'reclaim the kisan identity and identify with the farmland' once again.

While watching the protestors occupy key frontier infrastructures of contemporary accumulation that feature across this book, and which Narendra Modi chose to pitch his political offer to rural Haryana on, I was reminded of the subaltern frontiers that structure my understanding of agrarian city-making across this book. Of the dialectical compositions of agrarian and urban development, the entanglement of agrarian institutions, actors and politics in urban infrastructural development, the occupation and rewiring of key frontier devices – highways – in an uprising wrought through fracturing hegemonic coalitions. Uprisings that express a subaltern territorialisation of space – the projection and experimentation of new geographical worlds taking place on the roadside just as I witnessed at Rokaplex and elsewhere. The strategic occupation of the urban infrastructure that has both churned through rural communities and stood as the material promise of their transformation, igniting speculative land markets and irregular property claims, is symbolic of the complex articulation of the agrarian with the urban that I have explored in this book. Reminding us of the utterly contingent politics that might emerge from capital's messy attempts to capture and command land and labour on the frontier. Frontiers, as I have argued, are contingent; they are, Weizman notes, 'deep, shifting, fragmented and elastic territories'[16] shot through with compromise and uncertainty. It is precisely this provisional character that gives expression to the re-composition of hegemonic class coalitions. Whether the emerging fractures in the Hindutva project will reorient an urban development highly dependent upon the conscription of the agrarian world, led by a promise of inclusive growth, is yet to be seen. What is clear is that what I have variously called the 'agrarian–urban' frontier across this book is a site not of predestined capitalist urbanisation, where fated real estate and industrial markets are realised through the force of history, but rather disturbing points of possibility, spaces of experimentation where the future is being worked through.

Mobility Suspended

The COVID-19 crisis brought Gurgaon and the world to a standstill from March 2020. A series of national lockdowns across the country not only prevented social gathering and commercial operations but importantly shut down vital supply chains – of both commodities and people – that sustain urban life on the frontier. The pandemic in other words stilled industrial–urban projects premised upon hypermobility that I discuss in Chapters 5 and 6. This particularly impacted the export-oriented garments industry that alongside auto manufacturing predominates in Gurgaon's industrial estates. The last minute twenty-one-day lockdown announced by the central government in March 2020 shut down all sectors and sparked scenes of thousands of workers, repelled from their workplaces and urban residences, walking hundreds of miles along the highways toward their rural homes.

For many of my research interlocutors who chose to stay in the tenements, whether due to an erosion of rural familial relations or to a belief that work would soon pick up, were subject to intensified surveillance and restrictions in an already heavily uncertain and precarious urban environment.

Villages I had spent time living and working in between 2012 and 2018 became sites of an altogether different set of bordering practices to those seen later that year at the farmer protests. As the COVID lockdowns hit state practices emerged that established territorialised borders on movement and bureaucratic borders on access to services that have exacerbated the precarity of working-class migrants in the city.[17] The key pandemic response enacted by the central government, the Haryana government and the Gurgaon district government was to restrict movement, fixing in 'containment zones' and border points between neighbourhoods, districts and regional states. While the elite gated communities evicted their working-class maids and shut themselves off from the outside world, working-class villages and districts were cordoned off and bounded.[18] The informal infrastructures of tenement surveillance and control that I discuss in Chapter 5 were keenly utilised by the state to enforce lockdown measures upon populations that were, as I argued, previously induced to move.

Communication with friends and research respondents in Kapashera, Dundahera and other villages relayed a story of growing indebtedness and precarity for people in the tenements. Landlords had lost crores in rental incomes and some of that economic anxiety came to be expressed in heightened intimidation, extortion and violence. The hyper-segregated spatial pattern of Gurgaon's urbanisation no doubt served as a handy instrument in imposing the differentiated lockdown upon the city's residents.[19] Without record of urban residence nor access to housing, localised rations, healthcare and social reproduction, Gurgaon's migrant working classes were further entrenched under the exploitation of the tenement system. The pandemic response, in other words, brought the informal infrastructures of labour mobility into stark light, revealing the dependency of the city on migrant working classes.[20] While the glimmers of charity and support that I witnessed from tenement landlords to their tenants during my time in the villages would have no doubt ameliorated the destitution for some workers, stories of growing indebtedness and violently enforced repayments remind us of the central role that tenement rents play in balancing agrarian city-making in Gurgaon and elsewhere on the urban frontier.

Perhaps, the most relevant to the arguments of this book, are the ways the pandemic, and government response to the pandemic, intervened in systems of labour mobility carefully cultivated by factory management, landlords and contractors. As I discuss in Chapter 5, the coalition between agriculturalists, the state and industrial capitalists hang in the balance of a hypermobile, flexibilised workforce. Workers' mobility, I argued, is fine-tuned to fitful and rhythmic demands of these class compositions. To this mobility, a broader politics of gender instils a degree of disruption or what I call 'rooted flexibility'. The mass intervention into the temporalities and mobilities of Gurgaon's working-classes, what Mukta Naik has termed the state's 'bordering practices', places these coalitions under significant strain.[21] Upon watching the pandemic unfold from afar, I was drawn to my research interlocutors in Kapashera and other tenement villages. To those young men for whom mobility was the last preserve of autonomy afforded to them in highly exploitative and precarious urban and agrarian economies. And to the young women like Subia and Sonu for whom a unidirectional emplacement in the city tenements – that produced both a restricted movement and collective social milieu – was the foundation of solidarities and collective class consciousness driving their workplace and tenement struggles. The suspension of these (im)mobilities no doubt will reshape these emerging geographies of working-class organisations and struggle in ways not yet known.

Trouble

Subaltern Frontiers has sought to contribute to lively contemporary debates on both post-colonial and peripheral urbanisation by focusing on the frictions through which agrarian city-making on the urban frontier is made and unmade, placing difference, practice, slippage and disruption at the heart of analyses of seemingly totalising urban social formations. My intention in exploring Gurgaon's urbanisation has not been to provide another case study in difference from a North Atlantic or even post-colonial urban standard, but rather to unpack the Faustian bargains at the heart of urban capitalists' attempts to expand into the countryside.

In doing so, throughout this book I have drawn on a broad range of analytical traditions and approaches, most prominently feminist geographies, cultural studies, subaltern studies and agrarian studies that in different ways, at different times, have contributed to the development of a heterodox Marxism; one that traces the undetermined, relational dialectical processes at the heart of capitalist value. In a paper titled 'Relational Comparison Revisited' Gillian Hart returns to earlier work where the author seeks to develop an open, non-totalising dialectical analytical tool for understanding 'how key processes are constituted in relation to one another through power-laden practices in the multiple, interconnected arenas of everyday life'.[22] For Hart 'relational comparison' allows a way of thinking about the thick constituents of ideology, culture, political economy and materialism in their processual movement between situated and abstract contexts. Importantly for Hart, an examination of these 'connections and mutual processes of constitution – as well as slippages, openings, and contradictions – helps to generate new understandings of the possibilities for social change'.[23] The dialectic that Hart, and Bertell Ollman whom she draws on,[24] elaborates is neither 'teleological nor totalizing' but rather a series of internal relations which proceed from the 'concrete' world toward a series of conjunctural and troublesome concepts, determinations, values, class compositions through processes of abstraction. Crucial here are these messy, conjunctural parts and mediations that sit at the core of seemingly inexorable social abstractions. By tracing these mediations first, in this book I have sought to satirise the pomp of capitalist urban expansion and draw out the points of political weakness, compromise and alliance.

A focus on the spatial and historical mediations of abstract 'urban' codes and norms, this book has sought to reveal the nervous core of abstraction. For Lefebvre abstraction refers to a historical process wherein capitalist logics confront and attempt to integrate space, combined with a discursive and symbolic order which materialises in the technocratic rationality of the state. Together these material and discursive modes of abstraction, upheld by political power, seek to represent a homogenous urban space that is emptied out of actually existing social conditions. This book has centred on the troubled and compromised trajectory of this project, as it is confronted with socio-territorial blockages and layered with class compositions. In doing so, I have sought to take seriously the active agency of difference and speculative material practice in carving out capitalist landscapes. As Lefebvre remarks, 'Abstract space is not homogenous; it simply has homogeneity as its goal, its orientation, its lens'.[25] I have sought to show how projects of real estate and industrial accumulation that seek to present land and labour as abstract commodities are animated and troubled by sedimented class projects, bureaucratic uncertainty, territorial compromise and subaltern rejection. I conceptualise these as the trouble on the capitalist frontier, what Vinay Gidwani[26] has referred to as 'contaminations' which provide the sustenance for conditions of accumulation and yet pollute potential conditions for a fully captured use value for capital.[27] At times these contaminations aid and abet conditions of accumulation, at other times these contaminations develop into full-blown subversion. It is only by tracing the trouble that we are able to pull out the potential for agrarian city-making to be quite otherwise to dominant scripts – drawn from the North Atlantic – for landowning farmers to subtly redraw property boundaries or for migrant workers to repurpose alienating tenements and workplaces.

As critical scholars entertained to try to understand and change the world for the better, there is much to gain from holding on to the trouble that maintain before, alongside and after capitalist totalisation. *Subaltern Frontiers* attempts to get to grips with this relational dialectic not by reifying a binary between consent and resistance, or urban and agrarian, capitalist and non-capitalist, but rather by drawing into the constant, internal tussles of difference that forge the frontier. As Gidwani argues, the 'electric buzz' of difference is always present as a subaltern feature of capital, unintelligible, uncaptured, which remains a constant source of trouble for the state and capitalist actors.[28]

The two (ongoing) political moments, the farmers' movement and the COVID-19 response, draw out this residual trouble at the heart of agrarian city-making discussed in this book. Both interventions emphasise the negotiated and temporary geographies of property and labour, agrarian and urban accumulation, introduced at the outset of this book. The stagnation of industrial capital; the flexibilisation of working classes; the faltering ascent of Hindutva politics; and re-emergence of cross-class agrarian struggle, all point to key fractures in the class composition that uphold Gurgaon's urbanisation as described in this book. As Modi's stump speech in Sultanpur attests, the question of enabling capital's access to 'undercapitalised' resources, while posing such a strategy in populist, increasingly fascist terms, is one of the most pressing issues for the Indian state. Can the alliance of farmers, industrialists and bureaucrats be pulled back together and 'inclusive' real estate accumulation resecured? Or will Haryana's resurgent *kisan* politics re-emerge perhaps this time with a more egalitarian core? And how might this cloud the promise of real estate development that drives agrarian city-making? How might such a hegemonic breakdown be captured and reshaped by tenement working classes to forge alternative agrarian–urban worlds?

Notes

1. Searle, 'The Contradictions of Mediation', 323.
2. See, for example, Pandey, 'CBI Files Charge Sheet against Hooda in Manesar Land Scam Case'.
3. The exclusion of the city from the government's smart cities urban renewal programme in 2015, after failing to meet requirements for public infrastructure and good governance, was no doubt a kick in the teeth. After all, Gurgaon trailblazed the public–private partnership model so favoured by the smart city programme.
4. Jaffrelot, 'The Rise of the Other Backward Classes in the Hindi Belt'.
5. In the 2014 Lok Sabha and Vidhan elections, the BJP won all of the seats in the Gurgaon district, both those dominated by the upper-class gated enclaves and those of the villages.
6. Poonam, *Dreamers*.
7. Anti-BJP sentiment among Jats is particularly stoked by their exclusion from OBC categorisation in the implementation of the Mandal Commission from 1990. This excludes Jats from access to reservations for public sector jobs, see Jaffrelot, 'The Rise of the Other Backward Classes in the Hindi Belt'.
8. While a sizeable number of my interlocutors were avid supporters of the government, and put their support in quite explicit terms, others voiced opposition to the Hindutva agenda and a small number had political ambitions and connections with opposition parties currently opposed to the government's agenda.
9. Cowan, 'Rooted Flexibility'.
10. Over the previous five years, for example, there had been a string of mass protests led by Jat political organisations calling for Jat's inclusion into the OBC category, which would provide access to affirmative action reservations in public sector jobs.
11. Sandhu, 'Left, Khaps, Gender, Caste'.
12. Ibid.
13. In December 2020, a *mahapanchayat* (large meeting) organised in central Gurgaon by local *panchayat*s publicly backed the farmers' movement and proposed blockading the National Highway 48 in support of the protests.
14. Singh, Singh and Dhanda, 'Resisting a "Digital Green Revolution"'.

15. Bahl, 'The Postcolonial Autumn'.
16. Weizman, *Hollow Land*.
17. Naik, 'State–Society Interactions and Bordering Practices in Gurugram's Pandemic Response'.
18. As Naik and Bathla note, the bordering of movement across regional districts meant that workers in the Kapashera tenement village were unable to access their jobs across the border in Gurgaon when the economy opened up again, and had become stuck without jobs, with increasing pressure to pay rents. Naik and Bathla, 'Sealing Delhi's Borders'.
19. There was, as Mukta Naik's work argues, also a push among upper- and middle-class residents to respond to a growing crisis of impoverishment and hunger among the city's working classes, and organise support for affected communities, echoing the mutual aid infrastructures that emerged globally during the pandemic. See Naik, 'State–Society Interactions and Bordering Practices in Gurugram's Pandemic Response'.
20. Ibid.
21. Naik, 'State–Society Interactions'.
22. Hart, 'Relational Comparison Revisited', 6.
23. Hart, 'Denaturalizing Dispossession', 996.
24. Hart returns to Bertell Ollman's *Dance of the Dialectic*, and Harvey's *Justice Nature and the Geography of Difference*.
25. Lefebvre, *The Production of Space*, 142, 287.
26. Gidwani, *Capital, Interrupted*.
27. Ibid.
28. Ibid., 197.

Bibliography

Bahl, Aditya. 'The Postcolonial Autumn'. *Spectre*, 29 January 2021. https://spectrejournal.com/the-postcolonial-autumn/. Accessed 1 January 2021.

Cowan, Thomas. 'Rooted Flexibility: Social Reproduction, Violence and Gendered Work in the Indian City'. *Gender, Place and Culture* 28, no. 1 (2021): 66–87.

Gidwani, Vinay K. *Capital, Interrupted: Agrarian Development and the Politics of Work in India*. Minneapolis: University of Minnesota Press, 2008.

Hart, Gillian. 'Denaturalizing Dispossession: Critical Ethnography in the Age of Resurgent Imperialism'. *Antipode* 38, no. 5 (2006): 977–1004.

———. 'Relational Comparison Revisited: Marxist Postcolonial Geographies in Practice'. *Progress in Human Geography* 42, no. 3 (2016): 371–394.

Jaffrelot, Christophe. 'The Rise of the Other Backward Classes in the Hindi Belt'. *Journal of Asian Studies* 59, no. 1 (2000): 86–108.

Kumar, Satendra. 'Jats into Kisans: The Unmaking and Remaking of the Farmer Identity in Western UP'. *India Forum*, 2 April 2021. https://www.theindiaforum.in/article/jats-peasants. Accessed 21 August 2021.

Lefebvre, Henri. *The Production of Space*. Vol. 142. Oxford: Blackwell, 1991.

Naik, Mukta. 'State–Society Interactions and Bordering Practices in Gurugram's Pandemic Response'. *Urbanisation* 5, no. 2 (2020): 181–90.

Naik, Mukta, and Nitin Bathla. 'By Sealing Delhi NCR Borders, Covid Has Ended Fluidity between Where Labourers Live and Work'. *The Print*, 25 May 2020. https://theprint.in/opinion/by-sealing-delhi-ncr-borders-covid-has-ended-fluidity-for-labourers/428151/. Accessed 1 January 2021.

Pandey, Devesh K. 'CBI Files Charge Sheet against Hooda in Manesar Land Scam Case'. *The Hindu*, 2 February 2018, section 'Other States'. https://www.thehindu.com/news/national/other-states/cbi-files-charge-sheet-against-hooda-in-manesar-land-scam-case/article22633413.ece. Accessed 1 January 2021.

Poonam, Snigdha. *Dreamers: How Young Indians Are Changing Their World*. London: Hurst, 2018.

Sandhu, Amandeep. 'Left, Khaps, Gender, Caste: The Solidarities Propping up the Farmers' Protest'. *The Caravan*, 13 January 2021. https://caravanmagazine.in/agriculture/left-punjab-haryana-caste-gender-solidarities-farmers-protest. Accessed 31 August 2021.

Searle, Llerena Guiu. 'The Contradictions of Mediation: Intermediaries and the Financialization of Urban Production'. *Economy and Society* 47, no. 4 (2018): 524–46.

Singh, Tanya, Pritam Singh and Meena Dhanda. 'Resisting a "Digital Green Revolution": Agri-Logistics, India's New Farm Laws and the Regional Politics of Protest'. *Capitalism Nature Socialism* 32, no. 2 (April 2021): 1–21.

Weizman, Eyal. *Hollow Land: Israel's Architecture of Occupation*. London: Verso Books, 2012.

Glossary

abadi deh	village residential area
avashyakta	wanted
banjar qadim	long fallow land
barani	rain-irrigated land
benami	a property transaction made using a fictitious name or a third-party actor
bhaibandi	brotherhood
bhumidar	landowner
chahi	well-irrigated land
chakbandi	process of field rectangularisation
chaloo	cunning
chowkidar	maintenance contractor
dukandar	grocery-store owners
ekta	unity
gadbad	jumble
gair mumkin	uncultivatable, waste land
gali	lane
gora deh	open space surrounding village periphery used to store cattle
intkal	mutation register
izzat	female dignity
jajmani	feudal system of labour exploitation wherein lower-caste village residents undertook agricultural work for dominant and upper-caste residents in exchange for food or goods
jamabandi	record of rights

jumla mushtarkan malkan	form of common-use land vested with *panchayat*s in which proprietors own an undivided share and are entitled to compensation according to their share
kanungo	senior *patwari* supervisor
khap panchayat	caste-based community or social organisation
khasra	a village field list each given a number
khet	agricultural land
khewat	record of shares in land
khud khast	self-cultivated land
kila	a field registration of 1-acre measurement
kisan	farmer
lal dora	red thread boundary
lambardar	village headman
makaan malik	landlord
malikan deh	village proprietary body
marusi	tenant possession
mazdoor	worker
mehanati	diligence
mustil	a rectangle composed of 25 acres
namaaz	prayer
naukarshah	bureaucrat
panchayat	elected village council
Patwar Ghar	*patwari* office
patwari	field bureaucrat in the Haryana Revenue Department
phirni deh	see *gora deh*
pradhan	boss
roznaamcha	a diary of daily work kept by the *patwari*
sanrakshat	guardians
shajra	a cloth map of a village estate
shakti	power
shamilat deh	village common land
taazaa	fresh
tehsildar	senior revenue official responsible for a revenue area, *tehsil*
thekedar	contractor
thola/patti	commonly held part of a village

Index

74th amendment to the Indian Constitution, 46

abadi deh, 55, 88, 106–07, 129*n*
abstract labour, 24
accumulation by dispossession, 28, 53, 89, 92
actually existing neoliberalism, 43–44
Agarwala, Rina, 260*n*, 276, 290*n*
agrarian bypass, 98
agrarian city-making, 6, 14–19, 43, 52, 60, 135, 220
agrarian studies, 96, 303
agrarian transition, 7, 51, 96, 107, 121, 126
Ahirs (Yadav), 26, 51, 58, 65–67, 71, 74, 76–77, 97–98, 105, 111, 118, 135, 139, 293, 295, 297, 299
Amoore, Louise, 142, 173
Anna Hazare, 273
auto-parts manufacturing, 301
Azadiplex, 265, 277–85, 287

Balagopal, Kandall, 51, 80*n*
Balakrishnan, Sai, 35*n*, 78, 80*n*
Banaji, Jairus, 17, 35*n*, 82*n*, 221
Banerjee-Guha, Swapna, 79*n*, 92, 128*n*
banjar qadim (fallow land), 164, 191
Bear, Laura, 140, 152, 196

Benjamin, Solomon, 30, 36*n*–37*n*, 129*n*, 143, 160, 174*n*–75*n*, 198, 212*n*, 230, 238, 260*n*, 290*n*
Bernstein, Henry, 97, 128*n*
bhaibandi, 119, 187–88, 191, 201, 212*n*
bhaichara, 58, 297
Bharatiya Janata Party (BJP), 295
Bharatiya Kisan Union (BKU), 51
Bhattacharya, Neeladri, 55–56, 58
Braverman, Harry, 226, 260*n*
Brayne, Francis, 66–70
Breman, Jan, 12, 32, 35*n*, 38*n*, 221, 260*n*
bureaucracy, 30, 183, 197–98
bureaucratic materials (paperwork), 30, 181–82, 189, 193, 195–96, 202, 207
Byres, Terence, 35*n*, 95

cadastral maps, 28, 73, 141, 157, 178–79, 181, 185–86, 189–91, 194–95, 203–05, 209–10
cartographic improvisation, 181
chakbandi. See land consolidation
Chakrabarty, Dipesh, 23, 36*n*, 260*n*
Chakravarty-Kaul, Minoti, 56, 64, 80*n*–81*n*, 175*n*
chaloo, 195–97, 205
Chari, Sharad, 38*n*, 99, 128*n*, 231

Chatterjee, Partha, 37*n*, 80*n*, 198, 290*n*
commodity frontiers, 19
common lands. See *shamilat deh*
controlled areas, 48, 52, 147–48, 161
Cross, Jamie, 143

Darling, Malcolm, 59, 70, 72, 81*n*–82*n*
Davies, Mike, 62, 220
debt, 235–36, 252
Delhi Development Authority, 49, 107
Delhi, Land and Finance, 8, 53
development plan, 47, 53, 89, 103–05, 109, 111, 129*n*, 133–34, 136, 138, 141, 147–48, 161–62, 169
dialectics, 16, 304
digitized land records, 192
dispossession, 15, 28–29, 31, 91–94, 96–97, 99, 102
DLF Cyber Hub, 153
domestic workers, 268–70, 275–77
Dundahera village, 37*n*, 116–17, 121–24, 128*n*–29*n*, 153–54, 223, 233–34, 240–42, 257, 302
Dwarka Expressway, 155, 158, 185

East India Company, 54, 61
elastic planning, 146–50
eminent domain, 5, 52, 92, 94, 100, 295
exit politics, 251–52
expressways, 155–56, 185, 298
Factories Act, 223
Famine Commission, 56, 65
Fanon, Franz, 27
farmer protests, 2020, 156, 300
Featherstone, David, 23, 36*n*, 277, 290*n*
Feldman–Mahalanobis model, 218
flexibilisation, 222, 224, 226, 258, 305
freedom, 251–56
frontiers, 27–34

gair mumkin land, 157, 164, 191
Gandhi, Sanjay, 223

garment manufacturing (GKS), 239, 272, 276–77
Gau Raksha Dal, 296
Gharelu Kamgar Sangathan (GKS), 269, 272, 276–77
Ghertner, Asher, 79*n*, 129*n*, 175*n*, 211*n*, 260*n*
Gibson Graham, J. K., 219, 260*n*
Gidwani, Vinay, 26–27, 36*n*, 37*n*, 64, 81*n*–82*n*, 130*n*, 239, 259, 261*n*, 272, 290*n*, 305, 307*n*
Goswami, Manu, 61, 81*n*
Gramsci, Antonio, 21–22, 26
Green Revolution, 71, 76–77, 94, 107, 134
Grundrisse, 15, 24, 248
Guha, Ranajit, 22, 36*n*
Gupta, Akhil, 186
Gurgaon experiment, 67–70
Gurgaon–Manesar Urban Development Plan, 133–34, 196
Gurgaon model, 4–5, 8, 12, 29, 34, 43–45, 48–49, 52–53, 67, 78–79, 143, 199, 223, 227, 295
Gurugram, 34*n*, 295
Gururani, Shubhra, 35*n*, 80*n*, 147, 164, 174*n*
Gwal Pahari village, 160–63, 165–69, 171, 207, 210

Hall, Stuart, 17
Harriss-White, Barbara, 198, 212*n*
Hart, Gillian, 99, 304
Harvey, David, 28, 125, 258
Haryana Development and Regulation of Urban Areas (HDRUA), 48
Haryana Housing Board, 148
Haryana State Industrial and Infrastructural Development Corporation (HSIIDC), 100, 123

Haryana Town and Country Planning Department, 3
Haryana Urban Development Authority (HUDA), 48
Haryana Urban Development Authority Act (HUDA Act), 48
hegemony, 21–22, 25–26, 37, 50, 77, 108, 167, 172, 248
Hindutva, 34, 170, 295–98, 300–01, 305
Hooda, Bhuphinder Singh, 147

India Shining, 294
Indian National Congress, 79n
Indian National Lok Dal, 51
Indian uprising of 1857, 58, 61
Industrial Model Town Manesar (IMT), 1–3, 100, 115, 123–24, 224, 232, 248, 277, 279–83, 285
International Monetary Fund, 45
intkal register. See property mutation

jamabandi, 158, 179, 185, 189–92, 195, 211n, 296
Jats, 26, 51, 58, 65–67, 71, 74, 76–77, 80n, 97–98, 105, 111, 118, 135, 139, 293, 295, 297, 306n
Jawaharlal Nehru Urban Renewal Mission (JNNURM), 47
joint holdings, 182, 194
jumla land, 165–67
kanungo, 178, 180, 185, 193, 199, 201–02, 207, 212n
Kapashera village, 112–14, 116–17, 121, 124, 234, 240
khap panchayat, 51, 77, 80n
kisan politics, 52, 305
Kundli–Manesar Expressway, 155–56, 261n, 298

labour contractors, 216, 234, 237, 247, 252
Lal, Bansi, 48
Lal, Bhajan, 48, 79n, 82n, 144–45
lal dora, 55, 88, 109, 111, 114, 129n
land agglomeration, 15, 148, 179
land aggregators, 121, 151, 188–89
land boundary demarcations. See land survey
land clearing, 157–60
land consolidation, 30, 61, 72, 75, 107, 165, 194, 204, 206
land (plotting), 138, 168
land record books. See *jamabandi*
land scandals, 12, 294
land settlement, 56–58, 60–61, 68, 111, 164
land survey, 180, 203, 208
land tenure, 15, 21, 28–29, 58, 69, 125–26, 140, 143, 156, 160, 163, 188, 231, 258
Lefebvre, Henri, 15, 24, 36n, 127, 264, 304, 307n
Levien, Mike, 5, 34n, 37n, 52–53, 79n, 80n
Li, Tania Murray, 152
liaisoners, 151, 185, 189, 199–203
living labour, 24

M3M, 201
Mahalwari, 55–56, 64, 111
Make in India, 295, 297
malikan deh, 55
Manohar Lal Khattar, 295
Maruti Kunj, 223
Maruti Suzuki, 1–3, 6–7, 10–11, 13, 100, 224, 232, 250, 253, 281, 289
Maruti Vihar, 223
Marx, Karl, 15–16, 23–24, 26, 28, 35n, 36n, 91–94, 127n, 217, 248–49, 261n
McNeilly, Katherine, 135, 173n

Meos, 58–59, 98, 299
migrant labour, 125, 225, 240, 265, 279
Mill, John Stuart, 55
Mitchell, Timothy, 193
Modi, Narendra, 295, 300
Moore, Jason, 19, 35n, 130n

naukarshah, 187. *See also* bureaucracy
Negri, Antonio, 219
New Economic Policy, 45–46, 218
Ngai, Pun, and Chris Smith, 261n
no objection certificate, 197
non-resident Indian, 45, 144
Noterman, Elsa, 35n, 142, 174n

panapalat, 57
panchayat, 74, 80n, 95, 107–08, 110, 113, 118, 122, 129n, 163–65, 232
paperwork, 154, 158–59, 166, 168, 172, 180, 186, 188–89, 192, 196, 199–201, 241–43. *See also* bureaucratic materials
pattidari, 58
Patwar Ghar, 184–89
patwari, 30, 180–86, 188–93, 196–99, 201, 203–04, 207, 209, 211n–13n, 242, 296
perception, 152, 156, 160, 166, 172–73
Permanent Settlement, 54
planetary urbanisation, 15–16
planning, 52–54
*pradhan*s, 215, 240–41, 245–48
Prakash, Gyan, 12, 35n, 59, 81n
presumptive titling system, 190
primitive accumulation, 28, 89, 92–93, 96–97, 255
property-making, 138, 140–41, 148, 152, 159, 173, 182, 190, 209, 292
property mutation, 185, 188, 192, 197
property shares, 179
protest camps, 279, 281, 283–85, 288

Punjab Alienation Act, 65
Punjab Land Revenue Act, 55
Punjab Scheduled Roads and Controlled Areas Act, 48

Rajiv Gandhi, 9, 48
Rashtriya Swayamsevak Sangh, 295
record digging, 189–93
rectangularisation. *See* land consolidation
relational comparison, 304
Reliance SEZ, 103, 105, 109
rent, 117
rentier capital, 116, 120, 125, 143, 221
resident welfare association, 113
revenue bureaucracy, 110, 211n
Ricardo, David, 55, 57–58, 64–65
Rokaplex, 283–85
rooted flexibility, 256–57, 272, 303
Roy, Ananya, 18, 24, 36n, 47, 53, 148, 183, 207, 267

Sanyal, Kalyan, 35n, 93, 128n, 219, 260n
Scott, James, 36n, 57, 183, 194
Searle, Llerena, 146, 174n, 294, 306n
Second Five-Year Plan, 218
shamilat deh (village commons), 56, 164–65, 191
Sikanderpur village, 242, 269, 273, 275
Singh, K. P., 6, 9–11, 13, 18n, 67, 146, 300
Smith, Neil, 9
social reproduction, 32–34, 75, 118, 220, 231, 257, 283
Society for Labour and Development, 235
special economic zone, 12, 46, 103, 105
speculation, 135, 139–44, 149, 173
Spivak, Gayatri, 22–23, 36n
strikes, 2, 223, 232, 251, 253, 278–82, 285, 288–89, 298–99

subaltern cosmopolitanism, 264–65, 272, 276, 286, 289
subaltern frontier, 19–27, 127, 303, 305
Subaltern Studies Collective, 21–24, 27
subaltern urbanism, 24–27, 267
subalternity, 19, 21–22, 25–27, 135, 267, 292–93
Sultanpur village, 298
surplus populations, 11, 219, 267
survey stones, 203–06, 208

tehsildar, 192
tenement fix, 257–60
tenement-labour regime, 218, 221, 233, 246, 256, 264
tenement landlords, 216, 225, 231–32, 240–41, 297, 302
tenements, 215–60
thekedar. *See* labour contractors
Torrens System, 210
trinity formula, 92, 217

Udyog Vihar, 112, 122–23, 153, 215–17, 223–24, 232–34, 239, 244, 254, 256
uncertainty (politics of), 182–84
uneven development, 15, 17, 19, 21, 29, 43, 47, 51, 68, 71, 77–78, 134, 157, 222, 233
unmapping, 111, 202, 207
Urban Land Ceiling Acts, 46
urban villages, 12, 29, 33, 109, 113–14, 116, 120, 124, 169, 216, 239, 243, 248, 266, 268–69, 281
Verdery, Katherine, 183, 211n, 213n
village workshops. *See* workshop production
violence, 243–45

waste (wasting; wastelands), 60–64, 76, 96, 239
Weizman, Eyal, 155–56, 301, 307n
West Yamuna Canal, 62
workshop production, 216, 227–28, 238